Unraveling on the Old Silk Road
Hitchhiking China and Beyond

Antonio Cammarata

© Copyright 1998 Antonio Cammarata
ISBN #1-889534-24-2
Published by
Jay Street Publishers
New York, NY 10023
212-580-9700

Manufactured in the United States

Cover designs and photograph by Mona Cammarata
Inside photographs by Antonio Cammarata

For Mona
who shared my romance
with the road —

and those fellow travelers
who helped make my journey possible,
and, consequently,
my journal.

PROLOGUE

You emperors, kings, dukes, marquises, earls and knights, and all other people desirous of knowing the diversity of the races of mankind, as well as of kingdoms, provences and regions of all parts of the East, read through this book and you will find in it the greatest and most marvelous characteristics of the peoples, especially of Armenia, Persia, India and Tartary (China), as they are severally described in the present work by Marco Polo, a wise and learned citizen of Venice, who clearly states what things he saw and what things he heard from others. For this book will be a truthful one.

Travels of Marco Polo
(Descriptions of the World)

TABLE OF CONTENTS

	Overview	13
1	Under Way – Under the Weather	19
2	Swan Song/Canton (Guangzhou)	25
3	Guilin	32
4	Yang Shuo or Down the River Without a Paddle	38
5	Guiyang & Huangguosha Waterfalls or Yining of the Yang	45
6	Kunming and Going	50
7	Dali High	60
8	On to Lijiang and The Long March	67
9	Tracking Marco Polo: The Night Train to Emei/Leshan	76
10	Emei	82
11	Leshan In the Shadow of the Grand Buddha	87
12	Chengdu	93
13	Last Train to the Coast	97
14	Yangtze Love Boat	101
15	Hankou	108
16	Palace of Heaven	113
17	Interrupted Journey	118
18	Departures	125
19	Xian	130
20	Journey to Hua Shan and Back	135
21	Journey to Lanzhou	141
22	The Golden City	148
23	Arrival in Xiahe	155
24	Of Monks and Marx and Mona Lisa	162
25	Yak to Yak, Belly to Belly	169
26	Hello, Dalai	182
27	Strawberry Fields Forever	190
28	Foreign Devil on the Silk Road	197
29	Journeys to Jiayuaguan	205
30	Beyond the Pale	209
31	Off the Wall	219
32	The Adventures of Dunhuang	222
33	View from the Top	228
34	Revenge of the Monkey King	233
35	Through the Land of the Salamander	236

36	The Rules of the Road	240
37	Turpan	244
38	The Northwest Passage	252
39	Between a Rock and a Hot Place	258
40	The Return of the Conquered Anti-Hero	270
41	Pushing On	272
42	A True Believer	276
43	The Road to Kucha	280
44	The Road to Kashgar	286
45	Star Struck	289
46	A Knotty Situation	293
47	Home of Melons and Fruits	296
48	The Road to Kara Kuli	303
49	Muztagata's Revenge	309
50	The Party is Over, The Jig is Up	318
51	The Great Escape	329
52	A Path to Shangri-La	338
53	In a Secret Land	345
54	Gilgit	352
55	Undertow	358
56	The Road to Kalam	363
57	The Sultan of Swat	366
58	Riding that Tide to Ararat	370
59	Alexander's Ragtime Band	376
60	A Kafir in Nuristan	381
61	A Long Walk in the Hindu Kush	387
62	No Room in the Ark	393
63	Peshawar to the Khyber Pass	399
64	A Short Walk in Afghanistan	408
65	A Sinking Ship	414
66	Rolling Down to Rawalpindi – for Eid Milad	418
67	Islamabad – Vis-Vis a Visa	422
68	Check Mate	426
69	Karachi Choo Choo	430
70	In the Wake of the Indus Flood	437
71	Arrival in Karachi	442
72	American Express	445
73	Departure	450
74	Serendip	455
75	Sunset	460

A boat of sandalwood and oars of magnolia. . . .
Pretty singing girls, countless flagons of sweet wine.
O let me follow the waves, wherever they take me.
                    Li Po, *Tang Dynasty*

He rocked his only world, and everyone's.
Forgive the hero, you who would have died
Gladly with all you knew; he rode that tide
To Ararat; all men are Noah's sons.
                    Richard Purdy Wilbur

OVERVIEW

*Said Jesus, on whom be peace, the world is
a bridge, build no house on it.*
     Inscription on Akbar's Arch at Fatehpur

  And there you have my reason for travel – risking being buried in Central Asia, when I already had one foot in the grave. But I'll go a step further than Jesus and say, "Cross that bridge!"
  Of course, the accepted wisdom among armchair travelers is that the truly footloose, screw-loose are really searching for a home. Yet what Jesus, Lao Tzu and countless fellow travelers down the ages were saying is that home is where you find God. . . .
  I didn't want to be any more analytical than the nonlyrical Marco Polo, whose path I was forever crossing. Give the publisher what he wants. But what about Lady Justice and all the women enamored of the romantic? For the true traveler is a troubadour and Marco Polo remains a merchant til the end. The seeker returns home a pilgrim. With empty pockets. And a song in his heart. (It is not always a love song.)
  Still, I had an affinity for the intrepid Italian who put the Silk Road on European maps, and whose experiences went unbelieved. Oh, he told a fish story or two, but now an English publisher, inspired by my tongue-in-cheek doubts, has come out with a book that purports that Marco never went to China. In the end Italians will only get credit for the Mafia.
  If I have a rule of thumb, it is to stick it out and up. My nose will know the way as surely as Don Quixote's horse. It is the way of Lao Tzu's poetry in motion, the Tao. The eternal now.
  Don't doubt that travel is work, or as one routard put it,

"voyageur, c'est travailler" *(travel is travail)*. Hence, *Travel & Leisure* is an oxymoron, the traveler a moron. But I take solace in Bion's admonition that "the road to Hades is easy to travel," because it sure as hell hasn't been easy.

Chesterfield said those who travel "heedlessly from place to place...set out fools and will certainly return so." Yet, as the great South American liberator, Simon Bolivar, said, "The three greatest dolts in the world: Jesus Christ, Don Quixote and I." Good company to be in. You may say there are fools and there are fools, but I happen to be an idiot savant; eminently qualified to interpret the contradictions of Asia.

But truth is forbidden fruit, cumbersome baggage on the modern journey to "virtual reality," special interests and a world safe for Disneyland. It is just as well that my book was typed on a ribbon so faded that my manuscript was virtually invisible. A metaphor for a sometimes impassable Silk Road that took me to the ends of the earth and my own fading personality. Bold type would be less acceptable. I needn't have gone to Afghanistan to be investigated. Or wander into Tibet's restricted areas....

Let me explain. Briefly. I am America's most censored and, perhaps, harassed writer. You can be sure that the blacklist is more seminal than the bestseller list. Nor have I fared well in Europe, where my *Tramping to Jerusalem*, a book about the Middle East, was suppressed. It was supposed to appear at the 1990 Frankfurt Book Fair.

By 1992 I had thrown in the towel and traveled to China with Mona, dreaming of recapturing our adventures of a more innocent time, in one of the few countries I had never visited. I wanted to get lost in the beauty of ancient China – and bit off more than I could chew. China had just opened its doors to Israel.

I had no intention of going near the Silk Road, but following the sun with my thumb seemed like the only way to break loose of China's red tape – even if I were going in the opposite direction of the East and the easy way out of China. With barely a plan to go by, Mona and I had begun our journey in Massachusetts, our home at that time, heading for Seattle and the cheapest way to China. Essentially, we were retracing our trip of a quarter of a century earlier, albeit thousands of feet above Route 66, or whatever numbers were involved in a cross country trip that became our journey to the East.

Yes, it was in 1967 that we embarked from San Francisco on the Brazil Maru, not flower children, but those perennial innocents abroad. Most of the passengers were returning Japanese farmers who had settled in Brazil a half-century earlier, and still worshipping the sun aboard the ship, would be back in Japan in time for the cherry blossoms. We later sailed on to Taiwan (Formosa), that still Fascist island that is a hundred miles or so from what was then the forbidden mainland – as mysterious in those days as Mars (and the gods of war) and as difficult to reach.

And now we were finally crossing the Straits of Formosa, a far cry from a slow boat to China or Japan – and high above ships that mostly transported oil. Passenger ships had gone the way of flower children. Much of the flight traffic from Hong Kong, our destination, would be fleeing residents setting up shop in Canada. (My own flight from New York would be one-way, thanks to a crush in the Canton airport a few days hence. I could have lost my pants along with my Seattle/New York ticket, when a professional pickpocket artist working in collusion with the officials got the jump on my jet lag. Silver fingers also picked up a pretty penny.)

We had followed an almost stationary sun, until our changing course allowed the reddening orb to sink out of sight – the longest day into night. Traveling in the opposite direction, we had pretty much taken the route of those earlier emigrants to the Americas many millennia ago. (Not all the tribes were east Asian in origin, borne out by the scientific discovery of ancient white bones in 1996 in the American West. The ancient presence of a fair-skinned race in the Americas would explain why the Aztecs awaited the return of the white man.) But then the Indians may have discovered China.

My own parents crossed a different ocean to get here. And you should really know where I'm coming from if you are to accompany me, for you are about to enter terra incognita and are not prepared for the journey ahead. The journey to my head. It may be bumpy at times but then that's travel, and if you want to understand the free spirit, you are getting it from the horse's mouth.

And so this is neither fish nor fowl. Travel produces sui generis and I am that porpoise who likes to cavort, yet dives deep. I am an explorer first, and if I am to record my observations, I want the journal to be as surprising as the journey. I was a serendipiter crossing Asia, and the pages that follow.

The Silk Road, the first real information highway, connected China with the shores of the Mediterranean. But my own thread out of the labyrinth took me to a more exotic shore, Sri Lanka, the Serendip of old, coincidentally Marco Polo's last port of call on his homeward bound voyage. Mona had abandoned ship thousands of miles before, after our disastrous Yangtze "cruise." Our continental drift amounts to a shakedown cruise for my solo sequel.

Look at my travels as the white thread that runs through a Navajo rug, crossing all its borders. It is the "spirit line" and leaves at the end of the weaving – for every creation has a life, and its spirit must not be contained. Like the wind and the true traveler, this spirit must be able to come and go.

Bottom line.

Part 1

YEAR OF THE MONKEY

1

Under Way – Under the Weather

Hong Kong. Saturday, June 20. Just arrived. The sun has finally set on us. Bus through crowd and noisy streets to the Golden Horn. The next day the heat was oppressive. Tony saved the day when he bought soybean drinks. I never realized how much I would come to depend on that bean throughout our journey. Macao. A short ferry ride. Got excited when I saw for the first time someone painting in the traditional Chinese style. . . .

Mona

Dusk. Junks gently bobbing in the harbor and our rust wagon chugging into the South China sea. The sparkling lights of old Macao give way to the eternity of the stars – and the woman I love awaits me in the cabin. The stuff of romance, even for an old salt.

But I strain to hear the lyrics of that forties and fifties ditty, "I'd love to get you on a slow boat to China, all to myself alone," for it is my wife who is below and she has become an instant albatross around my neck. I can't hear the tune for the tinnitus. This was supposed to be a kind of second honeymoon, and there were two strangers in a cabin that fell far short of the love boat standards that the hysterical Mona had envisioned. Fortunately, it was only an overnight voyage to Canton, but this was another sleepless night since leaving Seattle, a long stopover after New York.

The couple we shared the cabin with were strangers to each other. The woman was returning from a hospital. He, silent, lurked in the shadows. I slept with my clothes on, under a blanket; in my demi-sleep imagining probing fingers trying to strike it rich. Surely there was a pocket of gold somewhere on my person. Several. But I was almost pick-proof. Almost.

Before leaving Macau, Patrick, the manager of the Peninsular Hotel, warned us about China, but I thought his rap was mostly capitalistic pap. Macau, actually, was in a twilight zone. A Portuguese outpost, a lighthouse on China that had lost its shine – and nearly all the Europeans. It was a colony in name only, at least from what I could see. The signs, the menus remained in Portuguese, but I can't say I ever saw a Portuguese, even at that paragon of Portuguese culture, the Pousada de Sao Tiago. The hotel is an endearing shell of Portugal, the cavernous entrance way was dripping with antiquity, but nary a fado was to be heard. And this was something to lament, indeed.

The churches remained, but Macau's faithful had returned to Ma, the ancient God of the fishermen, encountered by the Portuguese in the sixteenth century. Carved out of a hill, the temple is a series of ascending sanctum sanctorum. The sacrificial bowls in the Chinese temples often tempted me. But the new British Governor of Hong Kong, I was told, actually went for an apple under the roof of the Queen of Heaven. (An aide prevented a faux pas.) The British had yet to get the boot.

With little more than Mona's bare-bone diary to go by, I don't have many pictures of Hong Kong or Macao. (Mona often lets her diary go for a week, so I guess technically she kept a weekly.) I was too shot to take any photos, only interested in big game anyway. I had my sights on China.

I must wait awhile until my mental snapshots have been developed in the darkroom of my mind. Only when I'm off the road, after a little background reading, can I bring my trip into focus and get beneath the surface of those highways and byways.

The defining word is freedom, and traveling with a guidebook is like taking your coals to Newcastle. Reading when I return to wherever I have hung my hat is not so much a matter of putting my horse in back of my cart, as it is a question of being in the saddle (one foot in the stirrup) when I set out on a journey. Mona is Sancho, but God is my co-pilot. And if the reader doesn't always follow the rider and my tenses sometimes leave you hanging, consider that life itself is but the past and future intertwining in the perennial present of the double helix – and the double cross. Avanti!

The clearest image I have of Macau is the one I imagined before making landfall. Unlike the imperial British, the Portuguese had the laid-back style of the Ottomans and Macau was slow in entering the twentieth century (and perhaps in a hurry to leave it). I had pictured the Casablanca of the Far East, a backdrop for a Humphrey Bogart movie. But it seems that the spies weren't hanging around for what could have looked like World War III. And yet there was at least one sign that Portugal hadn't completely relinquished the reins. That sign was in the boat terminal for China, conveniently located between the floating gambling casino and Peninsular Hotel. Dominating the waiting room, the lighted sign showed a Marlboro man inviting us to join him in a smoke, but with the un-Chinese proviso that smoking was a danger to your health.

The Chinese government is not in the business of warning people about the hazards of cigarette smoking. Like the Japanese, they are in the business of the manufacture and sales of cigarettes. Mao may have been disgraced, but the Chairman's tobacco patch was an outgrowth of the almost mythical civil war, practically rendering the cigarette sacrosanct. The spirit of the Long March lives on in the coughing, hacking lungs of the Chinese. Wedding capitalism to cancer in Wuhun, is China's largest television tower. Towering over the Yangtze River, the letters **K E N T** can be seen from miles around. But it's doubtful that Kent will cut into the sale of the Chinese weed in the lifetime of the average smoker. It is likely the American company was suckered into buying expensive advertising space.

In Hong Kong I saw signs of neither Kent nor Kung Fu, but there was no escaping the elemental force and spirit of tai chi and the eternal China. Tai chi can read Big Energy. The Big T, as Tai is big or even great, much as in "all the tea in China." Chi can also be read as tea, and nothing is as eternally Chinese – China comes from chi, the people who drink tea – than the perennial cup or portable jar of tea, which is more a part of Chinese dress than a pack of cigarettes. (Actually, China derives from Qin or Chin dynasty.) But the Chinese were best known as the "silk-people."

Tai chi grew out of Tao or the Way — of nature – its own origins lost in the mists of time. Like autumn, all color and change, civilization is really degeneration, a glorious looking but short-lived spectacle. Something in my bones, like the reading of an oracle, tells me that it is in the springtime of history, in the nomadic cultures that hope sprang eternal and man knew the wisdom of the way of nature.

In the tropical oasis that is Kowloon Park in Hong Kong, against the grating backdrop of concrete and steel, there is an ancient China with all the grace of a palm tree on a balmy day that belies its strength in a storm. Tai chi is the face and the mask of China, the face of the sea itself, the liquid movement of arms, waves in slow motion, pushing and merging into one another, creating, they say, a continuous flow of energy. A weathered woman brandishing a sword in the bright sunlight reflected the raison d'etre of all this poetry. If Tao had an unconscious or natural evolution, tai chi was created in the more troubled sixteenth century as a martial art.

> *From one end of the Great Wall to the other*
> *from the foothills of the Himalayas*
> *to the edge of the great Gobi*
> *and beyond the pale*
> *emerging from the mountain mist*
> *and the pollution of the sprawling cities*
> *or stark against the desert sky*
> *in the early darkness calling forth the day*
> *cobras uncoiling swaying to and fro*
> *to the tune of the Maestro*
> *measured movements*
> *a contained force*
> *that are the swirling swords*
> *sinking fangs*
> *when the music stops.*
>
> A Double Edged Sword
> Tony Cammarata

Under Way - Under the Weather

With all the Arabists coming out of the British occupation of the Middle East, it seems strange that the colonizing of even a sliver of the Orient did not produce a Lawrence of China. With no commercial sphere of influence to speak of, the Germans went to the Far East as scholars and culled its esoterica. And when the Long March got underway it was a German who was at the side of Chairman Mao and company. Was there something about China that made Britain uncomfortable? It was one thing to carry the white man's burden in India – and nobody gave a fig about Africa – but that kind of superciliousness or super silliness didn't wash in China, especially after you tried to drug a superior culture into submission. And then make war because this ancient civilization won't buy your opium. Barbarity is more difficult to justify if your scholars study and perhaps even understand the people you are trying to destroy. The Chinese were invisible, and don't the native Americans and Palestinians understand all too well what it is to be beyond the pale.

Hong Kong, King Kong, high-rises with higher prices gleaming in the sweltering heat formed cacophonous canyons that led to the seas, but we took the escalator from the lobby of the Royal Pacific down to the China Ferry Terminal. We didn't stay at the Royal Pacific, instead, following the advice of some huckster at the airport, took the A1 bus to the "Fun in Hong Kong Golden Crown Guest House," the stop for Citibank. Golden Crown may sound like Royal Pacific, but it was a crown of thorns and one reason we were determined not to spend another night in the crown colony. In fact, we had wanted to sail to Shanghai from anywhere in the Americas, and failing that, to fly there or Beijing and we had something in the works, but....

And so we spent the night in a cardboard box, too beat to move on. The sun hadn't set until we circled the airport after flying halfway round the world. The guest house was basically a dormitory with a few double rooms – ours was one — thrown in for class (at mainland prices in a luxury hotel). This was not the Hong Kong that William Holden looked out on from his "high and windy hill."

Like a temple gong, Hong Kong still has a magic ring to it – it more than Taiwan became "China," when the cold war

Unraveling on the Old Silk Road

froze Mao out of the picture. More alluring than Acapulco, Monaco and Macau combined, Hong Kong was probably the most photographed tourist attraction after Rome. However, the Crown Colony was also high adventure, a cable car to the stars. It was not the Orient we were looking for; the China we had conjured up was somewhere over the rainbow.

Despite my own travels through the Chinese communities of Asia, including Borneo, my picture of China was a scroll, Hsu Wei's "Bamboo" or Hsia Kuei's "Pure and Remote View of Rivers and Mountains," a little soiled, perhaps, by the facts. Contradictions abounded.

David Chin was my friend in high school, but I grew up reading the Daily News's "Confucius Say" strip, had seen all the Charlie Chan movies long before he was camp, and knew "no tickie, no laundry" from experience. Confused say.

The China Ferry Terminal was pretty much closed down on Sunday. Had we reservations we would have waited for any ship going anywhere near the mouth of the Yangtze River, but without that incentive the last minute knowledge that there was a "boat" departing for Macau immediately, prompted us to make a run for it. So, instead of sailing up the Yangtze on one of those much advertised love boats, we would go with the flow on anything that floated because once we were in Macau, Canton would be our point of entry into China, and fate dictated that we go overland to the source for that pure and remote view of rivers and mountains.

Update: As Hong Kong became Chinese and Macau's gambling and what goes with it became big business, the Chinese Triad (Mafia) turned this charming backwater into a bloody battleground.

2

Swan Song/Canton (Guangzhou)

It was a sticky gray morning when we tied up in the Pearl River, uninteresting as Chinese rivers go. In Canton junks as well as junkies were considered an impediment to progress, as the old name, Canton, itself. Our own ship was without a name. At least it drew a blank on my ticket from HK/Macau Navigation Company, one of those scraps I take back with me from wherever I go to remind me that it all hasn't been a dream. Not that reality has been anymore real back in the USA.

Breakfast aboard this tub was in a lounge in dirty disarray. We were late in getting up there, where we had our first real taste of Chinese surliness and little else, beyond a bowl of rice. In this man-eat-dog-world the waitress couldn't resist mocking my hangdog face. I often feel that the Cultural Revolution never ended. You recall the Revolution was about Mao trying to clean house and throwing out the baby with the bath water. In some corners the end result has been a lingering contempt for foreigners. We appeared to be the only devils aboard, the only remaining people in the lounge aside from a cluster of custom and immigration officials who were in no hurry to pull themselves away from the heaping table.

Officials finally gave us forms to fill out attesting to our sanity and give assurance that we were not lepers. I could not be certain on either account, but we managed to pass muster. Surely these are questions that should be asked of passengers at the point of embarkation – when they leave China.

Disembarking was a breeze, but we saw no taxies. I

didn't look very hard, anticipating a runaround, so we simply hoofed it out of the port. It's something I've been doing since my Navy days, gravy days – what we've done since we disembarked in Casablanca thirty years ago at the opposite end of the Orient, but whereas life just outside the Moroccan port, the little we saw of it, was in slow motion, our introduction to Canton was a disorienting swirl of bicycles, hundreds of buzzing bees with some distant destination, almost inhuman sense of purpose and precision that made the commuters half-man and half-machine, or a school of fish in unison, without collision unflappable contestants in a Grand Prix. Ah, but this was a huge flock of "Flying Pigeons" (bicycles) homing in on the future.

After another sleepless night this rush hour river of riders was simply overwhelming. Let me rip-off a page from the diary of a mad housewife and you'll have Canton in a nutshell:

Canton. June 23. A dizzy feeling seeing hundreds and hundreds of people on bicycles. We walked and walked through the streets, through parks of tai chi exercisers and mah-jongg players.

I think Mona would have cracked had she not become transfixed by a game of mah-jongg – and maybe that was a sign that she had already gone around the bend. In this flurry of activity, in this most foreign of countries (after India, actually), the mah-jongg effected Mona the way the vacuum cleaner moved Paul Theroux in his Old Patagonian Express, for this was a touch of home, something familiar on which to get your bearings, though in Theroux's case he simply missed his armchair.

Having a Jewish mother, Mona related to mah-jongg, so that this most Chinese of games transported her to Florida and a clutch of very senior women.

But the tranquility of the players in this waterfront park did little to stay Mona's growing panic at being set adrift in China. In fact, it was unnerving that everyone was doing his/her disparate thing in very close proximity – oblivious in the mounting heat to the workaday rush that steamed by, streamed by, that only gave the packed park the fishy air of a vast outdoor insane asylum run by the patients, with the frenzied attendant

Swan Song/Canton (Guangzhou)

looking on. We had spent too much time away from New York.

We found our own asylum in a run-of-the-mill hotel across the way from the waterfront, but it was not up to par and it was impossible to communicate with anyone anyway, so we returned to a cacophony that creates madmen and women of people with hyperacusis, walking as close to the river as possible and away from the noise until we found a ferry to take us across the river. We had only Hong Kong dollars, unacceptable to the ticket seller, but as the growing line behind us grew impatient with my bickering, somebody plopped down a couple of coins on the counter and motioned for us to board the boat. An old man with a stringed instrument serenaded the passengers.

The White Swan Hotel towered above the river, a seductive beacon, but once we were on the other side of the Pearl, there was no sheltering riverside park affording us a view, and lost in a maze of streets, found our Virgil in a travel agent. Travel agents boasted the only signs in English, but they were really marks of status and we were probably the first English-speaking people to walk in off the street.

We found an agent who actually spoke English and pointed the way. The new brochure/map we had picked up at the port listed every rattrap and tourist attraction in English as well as Chinese, but our goal shown with no identifying number was described in barely legible Chinese characters. The White Swan is truly one of the "Leading Hotels of the World," but that probably meant the government got a small piece of the action, so it wasn't listed as an attraction. It surely drew more Chinese visitors – even if they couldn't check in – than number 49, the Peasant Movement Institute "run by Comrade Mao Zedong to train the peasant cadres in 1926."

The Peasant Movement was a more likely bet than the White Swan, but by the time our ferry had crossed the Styx, I realized that our staying at "an authorized five-star hotel" was more a necessity than a luxury, as Mona was ready to flee the coup.

It was as if we had arrived in heaven, a dream sitting in the cocktail lounge later in the day drinking English beer. President Nixon said it was the finest hotel in the world. Tony had to

Unraveling on the Old Silk Road

leave the hotel for boat tickets. How awful for him not to be able to escape that madness for a while. Mona.

A future subway towards which we paid a "tube construction surcharge," tacked onto our hotel bill, might go a short way towards alleviating congestion and indigestion, but I contented myself with taking a bus to the shipping line. One of the Swan's managers wrote down the address in Chinese, marking the pier on a map of the city. I noticed that we had bypassed a bridge when we left the port that would have taken us directly to Shamian Island, had that been our destination in the first place.

A ship was leaving for Shanghai within a couple of days, but I couldn't be sure that we would have the cabin for ourselves, and returned to the Swan empty-handed.

In the lobby of the hotel a statue of a white swan greets the visitor. A live swan could have been shanghaied from this oasis, even if a more exotic cuisine hung from hooks further up the road. I don't recall the symbolism behind a swan. It's not the city's mascot. Five rams represent Canton. In Yuexiu Park a statue of five goats holds the high ground. According to legend, five Daoist Deities descending from heaven astride the animals, brought with them the promise of plenty, in the form of sheaves of rice.

The problem with staying at a place like the White Swan, in a country like China, is that it is harder to plunge back into the chaos beyond this order, the waterfall and pond, that sense of space you get looking out over your beer to the river below and the sky above. From where we were sitting for a good part of the day, we had left Hades behind us. And if this is the view from your window, then the railway terminal couldn't be much different than Penn Station. Casablanca and even Bombay was a piece of cake. And the customer-is-always-right manager wasn't about to be the fly in the ointment. He suggested we get a ride to the railway station on the airlines bus that shuttled between the White Swan and the CAAC ticket office. The station was a few blocks away.

A ramp, an elevated highway provided a comfortable non-stop ride. Little traffic of any kind added to the surreal quality of this long ride above the Dickensonian sprawl. For a guy usually in the thick of it, this was a distant scene in black and gray. But the luxury of distance came to a screeching halt when we pulled up to China Airlines. We hadn't walked – ran is more like it – a block when a man with a club caught my eye. Casually approaching several men loitering around a buttressed pole, he let a seated idler have it on the side of his head a couple of times, as if he were kicking garbage out of his way, hardly breaking his stride. Was this one of the notorious street wardens at work? Aside from his club there was nothing about his dress that indicated he was a cop.

The thing that strikes me most about Chinese rail terminals is the parking lot-like space that fronts the stations, great expanses of concrete, large enough to serve the needs of any American shopping mall.

Pushed back by the flood tide – people from the hinterland seeking to strike it rich, to get some of that economic miracle to rub off on them – we retreated to the tourist office, and were informed where foreigners buy their tickets. Evidently, we didn't look hard enough. Returning to the railway station, checking out the lines, in and outdoors, I spotted a sign in English, but no sign of anyone who could speak English, much less sell us a ticket. Failing to make a policeman understand our problem, we went into the travel agency above the station. The staff was sacked out all over the office, on desks, benches, in what appeared to be an extended siesta.

"Por favor," I pleaded, "how the hell do we get on the train for Guilin?" This two thousand-year old city with the nickname "Best Sight Under Heaven" (an expression freely used throughout China) would make a great stopover on the high road to Dali.

No dice, an invention of the Chinese. These young men and women were out to lunch. Mao used to say, "Better a Chinese train that ran late than a capitalist train that runs on time" – and we don't want capitalists to ride them, seemed to be the motto of these slackers.

We returned to the tourist office. After the usual double-talk, I was convinced that tourists were not being encouraged to travel by rail, for several reasons, after my pocket was picked in the airport where the action is. Like smuggling, pickpocketing seemed to be a government run enterprise.

I bought our tickets at CAAC while Mona sat out this dance at China International Travel (which practically has a monopoly on foreign travel within China). An upstairs ticket office is similar to the railway, with that sense of urgency that is catching, like so much in China. Was I getting the last plane to the coast, or rather, away from it? Boarding the airport bus outside the ticket office was worse, and boarding the airplane itself had the air of an airlift. These people were more evacuees or refugees than passengers, although Guilin was a short inland hop leading nowhere. The explanation seemed to lie in the fact that in China, as in much of Asia, there has always been the fear that this may indeed be the last plane, cart or boat. Travel has always been associated with calamity or necessity. Of course, it is so much easier to get your pocket picked in a mad scramble and I came to think that even this was orchestrated.

Far fetched? It is better to go overboard (if that is possible in Asia) than to pretend to be above it all, when there's no limit to Murphy's Law. A true adventurer doesn't enjoy washing his dirty clothes in public (or anywhere else for that matter) and would really like to get on with the show, but there is no understanding Asia or the visitors vanquished by it if the writer is going to cast himself as Mr. Clean or as some invincible invisible man. Doesn't the reader want to know where the reporter is coming from, as much as where he is? Obviously not.

We cursed our luck in ending up in Canton and an extra day at that, but then regretted not taking in some of the major sights. Much of old Cathay was here, but aside from being under the weather, we had to be urban archeologists to dig up a past buried under the future. We spent one night at the Xiang Jiang Hotel – advertising itself with a photo of a fleet of buses parked in front of the entrance.

A saving grace was a window overlooking Yuexiu Park, with many of the interesting sights within walking distance of the hotel. But first you had to cross a hellish highway where you were as likely to get hit by a dodger as something on wheels. Canton, like Istanbul, had solved its traffic problem by eliminating traffic lights. In Canton's case a post-Mao aversion to the color red. Better dead than red!

Modern China is also enshrined in Canton, in vestiges of the 1911 revolution led by Sun Yat-sen and the many martyrs' mausoleums to commemorate soldiers killed in the wars against the Nationalists and the Japanese. Sun Yuan Li Old Temple stands as the monument of China's opposition to free trade, or rather, the open or opium market, for it was here that the Chinese took on the armies of the drug-pushing foreign merchants who lived on Shaiman Island, still home to the largest Catholic Church in China.

We saw the rams, dragons, the ancient tomb of the Muslim missionary, Abbey Wangus, but the sight, the feeling that will always stay with me was our exit from that warren of hovels in the port, and aside the ramp, standing mesmerized before the silent spectacle of a Gulf Stream of bicycles. Everybody spinning their wheels, the background din of the city, the thunder coming out of China. Didn't Napoleon say that should the Chinese dragon awake it would make the whole world tremble?

Addendum. After the Cultural Revolution, Canton was officially known as Guangzhou, but most maps will show Canton and I like its sound. Whim has also determined my spelling of ancient names, though I generally conform to the more common pinyin spellings as in the case of Beijing – so long known as Peking.

3

Guilin

Guilin is the quintessential China. The geography from which ancient cultures sprang. The springtime of history, a source where water is never found wanting and the caramel-colored Li Jiang carved out caves where poets left behind stone inscriptions. Many of the serrated peaks resemble Rio's Sugar Loaf, and the litchi is as sweet as any candy. It is not the land of the lotus-eater, but eating the mouth-watering "nuts" on a floating restaurant, watching the swaying sampans be swallowed up in the engulfing dusk, this Ulysses could forget for at least a few moments, that his pocket had been picked.

    I can only speculate about the arrangement Chinese officials had with silver fingers, but with all the screening at the airports, it would seem that a favored few non-passengers have access to the free market zone that is the Canton air terminal and that the proceeds from a picked pocket is shared in the manner of the deal that has been struck by the money changers and the law. Anyway, somebody got himself a one-way ticket Seattle/New York (half my cash was in the envelope) shoved into a very deep pocket, for paying an unexpected (legal, I assume) departure tax, I gave myself away and may just as well have given my money away, because when push came to shove the thief had gotten the upper hand.

    At any rate we avoided an air crash. In this respect Chinese airlines are above average, offering a fan as a sort of consolation prize. The landing strip had been home to the Flying Tigers in World War II, but one sorry paper tiger, descended the ramp. CIT or the tourist mafia was on hand to greet the incoming passengers, but my tale of woe rolled over them like water over ducks. Either a picked pocket was par for the course or they had not been programmed for any situation that could not be translated into bucks. We weren't even advised to report the theft to the police or anyone else.

But I had a taste of things to come at the Chinese Consulate in New York where I paid triple to have our visas processed within the day.

Israelis were getting ready to leave Guilin. My China Southern Airlines ticket had me flying from Canton to Kowloon or Hong Kong. It is likely our destination was marked Hong Kong because my Hong Kong dollars – preferable to Chinese yuan – was acceptable only if I was flying to Hong Kong. But how did they get us aboard the plane bound for Guilin if my ticket read Kowloon? Simple. The Chinese characters or ideogram next to the destination in English read Guilin. So this is one case where a ticket stub did not remind me of where I had been but where I was coming from, where the wildest flight of the imagination is firmly rooted in the reality of official double-dealing.

Still, Mona's cup runneth over. It was this living and breathing scroll that rolled before us that had inspired her to learn how to pen Chinese ideographs, but the picture scrolls themselves that we saw lacked the magic of the paintings we had seen in books and museums before we came to China. The contemporary landscape artist, if in fact he had the ancient flame, kowtowed to the real or imagined tastes of tourists, and Mona was not buying.

It was a sacrilegious corruption of the spirit that reflected the government's whitewashing of history and art writ large in this headline in the China Daily, *Ideology Not Art's Only Role*. A Standing Committee Member of the Political Bureau of the Central Committee of the Chinese Communist Party is quoted as saying, "We have had high hopes and tried hard to give full play to the ideological function of literature and art, to its role in political education, but it is impossible to instill in every work of literature and art the function of political education." But not to worry. "China's literature and art circles should take advantage of an extremely favorable situation to firmly serve economic development – the country's focus – and to create more and better works for the people."

And so one can only wonder who or what is behind this earlier headline in the China Daily: *"Bandits Rob Guilin of Its Natural Treasures."* "Bang! Boom! Bang! Boom! Thunderous explosions are destroying the world-famous karst caves in Guilin, Guangxi Autonomous Region, as stalactite bandits rip-off one of China's greatest tourism resources. . .Japan is reported building a stone forest with the Guilin stalactites."

In a separate article, on the same day, about "Ideological Work" in China's leading English-language paper, the writer struggles "with the introduction of a socialist market economy, strong ideological guide and a multi-level morality system. . . ."

What's happening in this fascist country, this budding capitalist state, is that at bottom, bottom-line baby boomers with the late Deng's O.K. have put a new face on the cultural revolution. Cult of Mao is gone but the revulsion remains. 1994 was more advanced than Orwell's 1984 (the late sixties and early seventies). The Red Guard has been replaced by a Right Guard designed to neutralize the stench of repression. At least Mao made no bones about his crimes, but today appearances are uppermost in the minds of an upper echelon trying to win American approval – along with the hearts and minds of the Chinese. It remains so in 1998.

Trying to reconcile the sight of the tai chi practitioners outside my window (in the Yu Gui Hotel), the poetic grace of the past with the doggerel of the present, I could ask with Lord Macaulay before the British Parliament, "What does anybody here know of China?"

The worldly Lord summed up the predicament of today's Westerner when he stated, "Even those Europeans who have been in the Empire are almost as ignorant of it as the rest of us. Everything is covered by a veil, through which a glimpse of what is within may occasionally be caught. . . sufficient to set the imagination at work and more likely to mislead than to inform."

While the Chinese are still reluctant to show their hand,

Guilin

they are playing with a different deck, more than a century later practically playing the same game. Part of what made China inscrutable was the fact that it had a more sophisticated set of values, generally, and we truly were "the barbarians of the Western Ocean." The unkempt West, "a class of brutes," did not wash well with one Celestial court or another. The Emperor of the World could dismiss the British as beneath contempt. And yet, not long after a Russian delegation, representatives of a "daft race," got the boot, Mao was embracing Stalin. That the stock market has become the ultimate temple, that the Chinese could go from Mao to Mammon in so short a time, indicates that the way has long been littered with idols.

Given the situation in China at the time – and for some time before that – Mao was the Man or God for the job. He just should have retired a lot earlier. But in the Longer March ahead, only a Lao Tzu or Hsia Kuei will lead the way back to that "Pure and Remote View of Rivers and Mountains."

But what does anybody here know about China? Of course, America is an open book – written by a Hollywood screenwriter. With a lot of bad actors in leading roles. At least, the Chinese ruling classes, for centuries, have been there; they've been to the mountain, but Americans haven't the foggiest notion that we can not even begin our journey until we allow nature to reduce us to the size of that lone monk at the bottom of the mist-shrouded landscape scroll.

Mao's poetry shows that he was open to the spirit of the "landscape:"

I care not that the wind blows and the waves beat, it is better than idly strolling in a courtyard, today I am free!

Not bad for a sixty-four-year-old man who just completed a swim across the Yangtze River. Mao allowed the current to carry him a good part of the time, but, then, going with the flow is the only way to get there. Yes, Mao was a sixties man, a hippies' man.

Where have all the (wild) flowers gone, indeed! Americans must become what they all but destroyed in the Indian. But we will need a young Mao – when he was a walker rather than a floater– before we can begin to fathom Lao Tzu, whose spirit spoke to the jointed stems of the ancient bamboo beyond my window. Some of the elderly on Elephant Hill could have been Lao Tzu himself or adepts of the historically younger Ch'an, the Buddhist sect that the Japanese call Zen.

Graduating from the school of hard knocks, myself, I have experienced the kind of temporary Satori that a good whack across the shoulders has brought to the Zen Buddhist. Closer to the Tao source, Ch'an's creative calm, reflected in the landscape painting, was apparently free of the often prerequisite knock on the head of the enlightened Zen Buddhist.

Though not many people under fifty were into tai chi, it seemed that most of Guilin's senior citizens were devotees and that they were engaged in their mystical calisthenics (esthetics) opposite our hotel on Elephant Hill. Every landing, any place they could get a toehold, was alive with their early morning dance. I will never forget the sight of these conjurers summoning the sun. They are the dawning of creation, like the Tao Indians in the American West creating the dawn, for the sun never failed to burn away the mist when their ablution was done.

Rising out of the Li River and the tributary that helped shape the bathing elephant, I couldn't imagine how the hill got its name. Not until I learned that the complete name of the park is Elephant Trunk and the quasi-aquatic tunnel that ran through the jumbo hill is the space between his trunk and the rest of his submerged body, and there was no mistaking this when viewed from the proper angle. Aye, there's the rub, and yet the limestone colossus is a classic example of the Chinese imagination wedded to an eye for the actual. Actually, beauty.

I failed to find the grandfather in Grandfather Mountain outside the Smokey Mountains, and even Europeans generally give empty names to their natural monuments. You can't top Mount Blanc for drawing a blank in inspiration and imagination when many of Switzerland's mountains are blanketed in eternal snow. On the other hand, I feel that a person inclined to anthropomorphize nature – especially the ephemeral cloud – usually lacks the capacity to see nature for what it is: The abstract art of God, to add one to Dante: a means to meditation, the way beyond idly imagining animals and the road to idolatry.

For we bring the mountain to ourselves through transcendence as the whole show is a Divine Comedy, and the unutterable Producer/Director has left his/her/its impression on the entire production.

What separated the Taoist from Mohammed and Confucius and many saints across the map and over the centuries is that ultimately he saw ritual and dogma as a harmful spectacle and prop that defeated the purpose. Lao Tzu, like Christ, was pre-empted by priests who gave their worshippers their money's worth, in what was to become a less than divine comedy.

Lao Tzu embodied the spirit of the classic Chinese scroll. In the words of a passing poet, that passing speck in the lasting landscape.

Scale the mountain without moving, or as Confucius is said to have remarked about Lao Tzu, after meeting him, "Of birds I know they have wings to fly with, of fish that they have fins to swim with. . .but who knows how dragons surmount wind and cloud into heaven? This day I have seen Lao Tzu and he is a dragon."

4

Yang Shuo
or
Down the River Without a Paddle

If Yang Shuo isn't in the "Lonely Planet," this sugar loaf of loafing tourists seemed to be in everyone else's book. It is a big Guilin drawing card, the idea being to go on a river cruise that usually deposits passengers in Yang Shuo. Downriver from Guilin, it is already an in-spot and one reason I could do without the boat ride, which promised to be a kind of high priced, half-Circle Line cruise where sugar loaves were the skyscrapers of Guangxi's East River. No, saccharine skyscrapers is too prosaic a description for that indescribable blue-green ribbon wending its way around the exotic, if not erotic, lushscape.

Well, I tried. I could have done better had I actually gone on the cruise, but we took the bus instead, thinking (Mona was disappointed) we could still see a good part of the Li without the distraction of the leering tourists oohing and aahing all the way to Yang Shuo (or is it Tandi and a tour bus the rest of the way), snapping and yapping away. Nothing is more irritating to me than having a reverent trance rudely interrupted by photographers who would be equally delirious over Disneyland or a delicious piece of cake.

Israelis were returning from Guilin, where they had made train reservations for Dali. Guilin was the beginning of a latter-day hippy highway for points west, southwest, but every self-respecting wanna-be or have-not stayed sixty miles down the road in the Yang Shuo Youth Hostel. Youth as in young-at-

Yang Shuo or Down the River Without a Paddle

heart or cool. As in Kathmandu.

Regressing a bit, I considered the Katy accommodations, but just the thought of sleeping in one of the cubicles was enough to drive Mona up the walls. The girl Friday in the "lobby" attempted to calm Mona with an unwelcome massage while she sized up a seal on display. Mona bought one of the "chops" but she was about to give the aggressive chick a chop herself when she persisted in kneading the unyielding dough that was my wife.

The seal was on the bottom of a statue of a Lao Tzu look-alike, a wizened ancient in flowing whiskers leaning on a staff. Underfoot was Mona in Chinese characters, but it would be a long time before she was inclined to press that chop against her painting even if she was guarding it like money, hiding the seal wherever we stayed, for China was fast taking the wind out of her sails.

And a most disorienting scene this youth hostel, done in tacky American, posters, a cooler filled with beer and soda, with Western kids indulging their nostalgia for the States or where lingua franca is spoken, while the Chinese owner is openly hustling every foreigner in sight to illegally change money – and not a mile beyond this mock grunge, the unrivalled scroll unraveled, the bend in the Li River that is the bottom of that landscape painting stretching from Guilin.

The nether world did not end at the door of the hostel, but affected the very young of Yang Shuo. Like the hippy haunts of old in Nepal where little children go in for mooning. In "uncool" Guilin a larger, more stable community is a counterforce against a counterculture lost in the crowd. And when the hip make the trip to a more expensive "tourist trap," they don't hang around very long. It's a question of familiarity breeding contempt, among other things.

But all this was so much water under the bridge when we stumbled upon the River Restaurant – written in English. Spelled Rive, it could be French. One of those refuges that makes it all worth it – those necessary valleys that allow you to appreciate the mountains. As Mona said in her diary:

I could have stayed forever. So peaceful, so relaxing, like stolen moments – a little romance.

Under the upturned roof, over the cascading tributary that fed my own stream-of-consciousness, Mona looked out upon the Li and beyond to Yearning-for-Husband's-Return Rock (really!) for truly I was out to lunch.

Sitting smack on the river with a cool beer was better than going with the flow, we were in the flow. And there were Chinese ideographs and enough bamboo for ambience – although, despite fish and fowl, the classic yin/yang representation of a balanced landscape, the sensuous scenery leans towards the yin, lacking the contrast of the more temperate Alpine scene. The Li is the Tahiti the Chinese dub "fairyland."

What need was there of violins, when we were being carried away by Water Music more moving than Handel. One of the many things that mystified me about China was the absence of musical substance. A Brandenberg Concerto, some Bach to Bach fugue that swept me away. So much of Chinese music, to my ear, is a sing-song that is more yin than anything. Was the absence of great range in the music, that made so few ripples, rooted in the philosophy of keeping an even keel in a landscape often knee-deep in water? Mountains abounded, but nowhere in the music was that climactic climb to an orgasmic finale, for the essence of China was in the river, in controlling the yin, eater of men, and leaving the mountains to the gods. Chinese music reflects their tendecy not to make a spectacle of themselves.

I think you would have to be a very dull man not to be seduced by Chinese scenery, reduced to poetry. In this I see my own reflection, for I am what I see – even if I don't always see what I am. Are we to conclude then that Chinese otherworldliness is merely a reflection of the fairyland that they imbibed for countless generations? Look what Disneyland did to the Americans in one generation.

Oh, how we dreaded leaving the Rive Gauche and that murmuring, mothering womb beneath Snow-Lion Hill. Or was that the faceless Page-Boy Hill, where beyond summoning, summiting, I could climb no higher than the first pavilion. The Mona of old was ready to chance the youth hostel, down the

Yang Shuo or Down the River Without a Paddle

river without a tooth brush, but we thought better of leaving our things overnight in our hotel and took the last rattling bus back to Guilin.

Our return to Guilin wasn't exactly anticlimactic. The city may have an even more traditional rive side than Yang Shuo, beyond the shaded esplanade and floral waterfront, sometimes wildly so, taking me back to old Mexico. "Cassia is the city flower which blooms and fills the city with vagrants in autumn and is sweetly appealing." Sampan and cormorant, part of the river magic, go together like a horse and carriage – on the surface a very happy marriage.

I had associated the cormorant fisherman with the ocean, but there they were on the Li River, using what is truly a sea bird to catch fish. Released to dive under the water, this large collared bird is unable to swallow his catch. Caught in the cormorant's throat, the fish are retrieved when the frustrated diver surfaces. The bird is "reeled" in and the fish shaken into a basket. And this Sisyphus of the sea forever conquered by his collar dives the whole day long, to get his comeuppance when the fisherman has had his fill. The birds were brought here from the coast.

Mounting Elephant Hill, we were struck by the absence of foreigners, and how friendly the Chinese climbers were – only to realize soon enough that in this Year of the Monkey, we were regarded with more interest than would have been the case. Like us, they were tourists, fellow travelers, and while stone forests and zoomorphic hills were in abundance in the nearby boondocks from whence they came, they had little opportunity to see anything like bigfoot and his mate climbing about. Cameras clicked away, anticipated proof of their trip to the big city. With their cameras they brought him and her back alive.

But we were more than exotic trophies or butterflies to be pressed in an album. To many Chinese we were feathers in their hopefully modern caps, and it was de rigeur to be photographed with a light-skinned if hairy "friend" who represented much of what they coveted. Hence we were constantly importuned to pose with strangers who took our pictures with cheap cameras that were in themselves symbols of status. Carrying this friendship theme to an extreme I placed my arm around a comely but grateful beauty. Older people were camera shy – but that's on the receiving end. Tribes descended from the "minority people" are still afraid you will capture or take their soul when you take their picture. The young feel they have nothing to lose. Often.

Under the Elephant's tail is a kind of fun house or Asian Coney Island in miniature. It was and still is, partly, a temple. You could generously call this place a museum, but the main attraction in this grab-bag of attractions is the Chinese tourist – dressed to kill. One room had tourists, photos of tourists decked out in Mandarin costumes, exquisite gowns and regal hats that appealed to their un-Communistic sense of making an appearance. We peered into the room, marvelling at this Mandarin mania, and the barker/photographer beckoned to us. Step right up, folks, and see the greatest show on earth – yourself!

How could we resist. We were invited to try on the costumes and be photographed. Was it worth getting into these cumbersome robes in the stifling heat? Mona wouldn't take "no" for an answer. It was one thing to be a princess, but to be a Dowager Queen was the ultimate in royal lineage and she delighted in dressing to the nines. What a get-up, with the regal but ridiculous hats looking even more bizarre atop our Caucasian heads. The barker readied us and there we sat waiting for a camera to snap. Nothing happened.

The barker/photographer pointed to my camera. Was this a question of why waste film when the Westerner has his own camera? A good camera. No camera other than my own was in sight. Was this entrepreneur simply renting the costumes to the tune of a dollar a minute? Few Chinese were walking about with cameras capable of taking or making a picture in this dark room. The barker would photograph you, but if you didn't have a camera up to the job, you didn't have the price of the picture, so why bother investing in equipment necessary to produce a picture.

And yet, roadside photographers who will dress you up in costumes did have their own cameras and seemed to be running a brisk business. But they couldn't dress you as lavishly and the low overhead of the often open sky didn't require a flashbulb. These photographers gave me a picture of Chinese character I little expected. Opening the shutters on an overweening pride buried under the Confucian ethic of the collective consciousness, the seemingly unassuming stoic became a showoff. All it took was the spark of a camera to inflame a low-key ego.

Were these mostly dirt poor poseurs merely emulating the egomaniacal Mao, still revered off the beaten path, who dressed like a peasant but ruled like an emperor? Conversely, they couldn't rule like royalty, but could look like the mad-hatter if they so desired and have the image recorded for posterity for only a second's worth of unbecoming behavior, or public display. And that picture retains the soul of the imposter in that magic moment of the lives of the primitives who go in for this kind of theater. What these theatrics or pictorial boasting boils down to is the proud peasant (or the city slicker without a pot to piss in) putting on airs, overcompensating for the austerity that Mao preached and dressed up for, but that they lived. Posing with a Westerner was part of this need to impress, which has been customarily exhibited in eating extravaganzas that most Chinese can ill-afford.

An ancient Chinese ruler once said that for the king to be surrounded by people is heaven – but the Chinese people are in heaven when they are surrounded by food, and people spending a lot of money on many courses. If one is to ponder over the Chinese puzzle, what better laboratory than the restaurant. And the lavatory (I use the word loosely) if the stinking truth be told. And how revealing that in this squalid but constant corner of Chinese life, there is no attempt to save face, for at the bottom (and all the babies and small children go bottomless) the Chinese are an earthy people.

Adding to the paradox of the bottomless box is the fact that the Chinese are so far down the road from Lao Tzu and nowhere was there a greater distance – before the advent of Mao – between the teeming salt of the earth have-nots and the cultured but decadent despot who could look upon these green hills and see "emerald hairpins" where the peasant saw a heaping bowl of rice. Sugar loaves? He was lucky if he had tea, and to this day he drinks his tea plain, if he has the leaves to put in his hot water.

By 1997 hundreds of desperate Chinese were paying $40,000 a head to be smuggled to New York, usually by air, with forged visas. They try to pay off their endless debt in the Chinatown sweatshops or prostituting themselves for the "snakeheads" who arrange their passage here. Illegal immigrants in virtual bondage, and their relatives in China are under constant threat of extorsion and bodily harm from a Chinese Mafia that could not operate without collusion in high places.

5

Guiyang & Huangguoshu Waterfalls or Yining of the Yang

Capital of Guizhou province and 1,071 meters above sea level, Guiyang is an ancient alpine city. Its residents include both Han and minority nationalities such as Miaos and Bouyeis. Famous spots include Jiaxiu Pavilion, built in 1587 on a huge rock in Kunming River. Huangguoshu Waterfalls are 150 kilometers from Guiyang. Its drop is 67 meters. Largest in China.

National Tourism Administration

June 29. Wanted to go directly to Kunming, but Tony thought it best to break the journey, and kept saying, the journey broke us. The train ride was two nights from Guilin, so we decided to stop over in Guiyang. We met a couple from Hong Kong, otherwise it may have been a real hassle looking for a hotel at 11 PM. (Nightmare city.) Even they had a problem trying to communicate with managers who wouldn't let us have a room. They had been on the train with us; met getting off. They were going soft bed – four to a cabin. We went hard bed – which reminded me of pictures I had seen of army barracks, rows of racks, one on top of the other. Older Chinese on train sharing berths above and next to us (I don't know if I could have climbed to top) never offering us anything to eat – they ate continually. Using tin cups (as did all Chinese on long journeys) to make their instant noodles, just adding boiling water supplied on train. Everyone had jars of tea (always tea leaves in jars). Thermos for everyone, biggest I have ever seen. I will never forget them, so much a part of our lives, boiled water in a thermos.

Mona

Unraveling on the Old Silk Road

It was near midnight by the time we checked into what may have been the best hotel in Guiyang. The city, famous for its strong-arm methods of birth control, is about as "alpine" as Acapulco. The carpeted corridors looked like they were regularly flooded – for starters. Dulled by heat and lack of sleep, we were conned into going on a tour to the waterfall, when it was almost halfway to Kunming and required we be up at the crack of dawn. It was well into morning when we took our showers and tried to dry off on the dish rags that were passed off as towels. But there are always sheets (if you pay enough) and one doesn't want to be a carpinger. The bathroom was a little cramped, but you could shower and fill the sink at the same time – or sit on the toilet and wash your face. Ah, the innovative Chinese – it's all a question of the bottle being half-empty or half-full. Actually, our cups runneth over and we could have skipped the waterfall and settled for a shower, one of the tributaries that fed the hall. Mona wanted the red carpet treatment. And in fact the carpeted corridor was indeed red, if a little discolored, by frequent flooding.

Instead of breakfast aboard the bus, we had televised Kung Fu. Speeding down an empty highway on an empty stomach with the television blasting away, I could see where the information highway was taking us. The start of the tour was promising enough. A uniformed hostess, who turned out to be little more than a barker, a well-turned advertisement that misinformed the tourist that they would be traveling in the lap of luxury. After two or three stops in the downtown area, our presumed guide disappeared, abandoned ship and we found ourselves in the capable hands of a Bruce Lee look-alike – one of the more popular Hong Kong exports. Hong Kongese were the only foreigners other than ourselves being taken for a ride, though paying less for the tour.

With the end of the century approaching, it appears that China is once again the great innovator. Chile (perhaps inspired by China) was the first country where I saw television on the boondock buses, but only in China have I seen a row of television sets placed above the ticket booths in the railway stations. A lure, a taste of the new life to be found at the end of the line.

Guiyang & Huangguoshu Waterfalls or Yining of the Yang

This tranquilizer for the restless masses was having the opposite effect on me and I made a mad dash for the "Yellow Fruit Tree," the waterfall, when we arrived at our destination. I nearly plunged into the gorge below when we took a little-used path fallen into disrepair as almost all the tourists used the elevator to get to the falls.

I appeared to be the only Taoist (as opposed to Daoist) willing to soak up the scene for any length of time, while others simply got soaked as the Niagara thundered a Way. I was as mesmerized by the Yellow Fruit Tree as that lone monk at the bottom of many a Chinese scroll – but only at the risk of falling into the river. Where a monk once stood in deepest meditation, was an inscribed poem on a stone tablet, and chattering Chinese centuries removed from the spirit nourished by the Yellow Fruit Tree. Named for the oranges grown in the area.

We took the elevator up to the restaurant area with our friends from Hong Kong. The memory that stays with me is the label I peeled from my bottle of pijiu – Shancheng beer written over an abstract picture of a waterfall. Interesting, that the word for "waterfall" – where yin/yang finds its ultimate, om, expression – is "pupu."

Yunnan Province, a few miles down the road, is more famous for its Stone Forests, Bouncing Dragons and Leaping Tigers, Mother and Son Traveling Together, etc., but in South China it is very easy to find yourself between a rock and a hard place. If there is no karst formation suggesting Lot's Wife Turned to a Pillar of Stone, one brochure I picked up shows a busty broad – a Caucasian, of course – posing before an imposing phallus.

We didn't have nearly enough time to see everything and I was fuming we did not have our backpacks with us, though it is unlikely hotels in the area catered to foreigners. We would be passing this way on a train, and maybe could have taken a bus to within a mile of the falls, enroute to Kunming. The ride back to our hotel featured warmed-over Kung Fu for an early supper, and I was dragging my ass more than any dragon and was as mean by the time we returned to Guiyang. I best remember this soggy city for the open manhole that our tour bus driver narrowly missed. Yet, standing, talking to the driver, I barely blinked an eye, for I was back in India where buses are swallowed up by wells. What was more surprising to me was the driver's surprise at the sight of the yawning gap before him. Surely this was par for the course and the unnerved navigator was very tired.

Guiyang is, after all, that neck of the woods where surreality and cruelty are bedfellows. Learning a lesson from India, where transistor radios weren't enticement enough to encourage birth control, China, Guiyang in particular, discourages second births with fines and beatings and taking the family cow, even demolishing the home of the fornicators or procreators in question.

And yet, Draconian methods of birth control, including the forced sterilization of women whisked away to clinics by local cadres, seems necessary if China doesn't drown in her sea of humanity, unsettled by the many men who feel they have dishonored their ancestors if they are the end of the male line.

The deputy manager of the hotel swindled us out of our hard beds and had us sitting up the whole night for the same price on the Iron Cockroach. Evidently, the young punk had bought our tickets from CIT, sold them at a profit and stuck us with the hard seats that he bought for next to nothing.

I could never sleep with one eye open, much less two – but that's what it took if we weren't going to be robbed blind. Oh, that long night into day, the endless hacking and spitting – I never thought I'd see the light at the end of the tubercular tunnel. Yet the government makes a big show at the tourist sites – in English – that spitting is forbidden. I wonder if their generally obedient people are confronted – confounded – with such signs in Chinese. The signs are an obvious deceit designed to contradict this spitting image of China, that any tourist with open eyes cannot miss, because certainly the government isn't worrying about English-speaking people – or anybody else, apparently – spitting. If the government didn't want people to cough up their lungs, it would divert some of that economic miracle into less toxic fuel.

A rising tide of garbage left those standing in ankle-

Guiyang & Huangguoshu Waterfalls or Yining of the Yang

deep debris. The morning light revealed tracks littered with styrofoam containers and biodegradables, which with all my love for trains, had gone out the window. With Mona barely hanging on.

6

Kunming and Going

July 1. At 10:00 in the morning we arrived in Kunming – very distraught – actually I was half-crazy – feeling so dirty, vomit all over the train didn't help and I needed all the luxury I could get. So we walked into the King World Hotel. If it weren't for these hotels, I could not go on. I'm sure all the pickpockets were watching from across the street and wondering when they could make their move...First time I realized I might have difficulty getting a ticket for Hong Kong for return trip. Tony doesn't know how getting home...We finally found a decent dictionary – learned a few basic words – please – thank you – how much? – no spice – toilet...could not really get into learning the characters because of the many distractions – trying to protect yourself from pickpockets, making sure you have boiling water....
                                                                Mona

Capital of Yunnan Province and a historical and cultural city, Kunming is 1,895 meters above sea level on the Yunnan-Guizhou Plateau. Its residents include over 20 nationalities. Its climate is mild and spring-like...and is often called "Spring City" or the "Capital of Flowers."
                                                            China Tours

Mona's "diary" after the fact – she couldn't bring it up to date until her return to the States – will indicate that Kunming is also the capital of pickpockets. Guilin is supposed to be the place of exiles and bandits – the last pocket of Ming loyalists held out here until three years after the establishment of the Republic of China in 1911 – because of its remoteness,

Kunming and Going

but Kunming was even more remote, and Mona would have paid a king's ransom if that's what it took to transcend the nitty-gritty of the city of flowers and the train that took us here.

Kunming may be best known as the beginning or end of the Burma Road and the main base for the Flying Tigers during World War II, and, of late, its Stone Forest (almost a hundred miles out of town), but in my book it will always be remembered for the chutzpah of its pickpockets. In the evening we checked out a nearby bookstore, empty but for the fugitives from the Iron Cockroach, whose shabby entrance into elegance did not go unnoticed by a well-dressed man who had awaited (perhaps he had been hanging around the lobby) our return to the street and tailed us to the bookshop. Wasted as I was, my nocturnal vigil had alerted me to every move of anyone within arm's length of my person, and yet my shadow wasting little time browsing, gentle as a tropical breeze, with as much effort as a magnet had managed to draw a ten from deep within my back pocket. I caught him in the act just as the bill was ready to fly the coop. But not believing my bloodshot eyes, the sight of the ten dangling from my pocket, I allowed the young gentleman to take his leave with barely a murmur – until the incomplete transaction had registered.

"Geezus Christ! Did you see that?"

"What?"

"That guy tried to pick my pocket – in an empty bookstore!"

Mona, tiring of my "paranoia" and unable to absorb any more surreality, implied the ten wiggled out of my pocket. But she got a knowing glance from the clerk – not a bat of a pretty eyelash, but a sort of but-of-course, motioning to Mona's purse, clutching an imaginary handbag. You're next, kiddo. I don't think Mao's little Red Book was for sale.

I don't know if it was ten yuan or ten dollars that I had back there, but it was basically a decoy, as the big bucks, mostly checks, were in other less accessible places. No, I didn't go that far. Though I could understand why merchants were doing a brisk business in quasi-flak or flap jackets that were all zippered up and buttoned down outside, inside, wearable, walking safe deposit boxes lacking only combination locks – the only (perhaps) fail-safe security measure.

Going out to Yuantong Hill on a soupy day, we encountered a thief or would-be thief, less fortunate than our sleight of hand bibliophile. The Hill is a unique park that climbs above a zoo overlooking the Yuantong Temple. Once, the park was accessible through the temple at the foot of the hill, but this made easy pickings for the likes of the poor soul we saw handcuffed to a pole just off the closed-off through-path.

We were a couple of dripping noodles seeking to freshen up, when we came upon a cottage, a two-room building, that faced a courtyard. It appeared to be the annex of a complex that may have been a farm turned restaurant, now closed. The upper part of the park, with pavilions and gardens gone to seed, was a far cry from the pandemonium below. We only knew that the place was occupied and where there are people there is something to drink. After huffing it most of the day in "spring-like" weather, pushing 90°, we gave little thought to what we were getting into, or going into. We had had our surfeit of surreality for the day and if a man was chained to a pole, we were sure he had a good reason for being so encumbered. Maybe he was holding the thing up, was afraid of falling asleep and sliding to the ground. My first reaction was that he was a kind of Houdini who bit off more than he could chew and his audience left him to his own devices. Or vices.

Anyway, we were graciously received in the small building above the temple, little suspecting that the gentleman who prepared tea for us was tending to China's booming cottage industry. In welcoming gestures another man bid us to make ourselves comfortable. I sat between Mona and a woman who sat opposite a large desk, focused on the progress of the boiling water. The woman paid us no mind and simply went on chatting. She seemed a mite uncomfortable, but then Mona had also lost her bearing and it was logical to attribute her manner to the weather. (We were always thirsty, but don't ever recall seeing bottled water.)

After a cup or two of tea we took our unguided tour of the courtyard. Putting one and one together, my initial sur-

Kunming and Going

prise at seeing a man casually leaning against a post – with some support – in the beating sun, turned to recognition and I surmised that I was in the rear of the police station and that the man's better half was being interrogated by the gentlemen gendarmes.

Our winding ascent from the temple, through the zoo or animal farm, up to the police station, was a metaphor for the progress of China. But the Kunming and environs of today is small town America compared to the Southeast Asia known to Theodore White, a Time correspondent in China at the outbreak of World War II. Writing about the China-Burma-India theater of operations in the spring of 1942 in his *Thunder Out of China,* White quotes Americans as saying that you needed a copy of Alice in Wonderland to understand it.

"It had everything – maharajas, dancing girls, warlords, headhunters, jungles, deserts, racketeers, secret agents. American pilots strafed enemy elephants from P-40's. The Chinese gestapo ferret out beautiful enemy spies in our own headquarters....Chinese warlords introduced American army officers to the delights of the opium pipe; American engineers doctored sick work elephants with opium and paid native laborers with opium, too. Leopards and tigers killed American soldiers, and GI's hunted them down with Garlands....American agents climbed through Himalayan passes to negotiate with the Dalai Lama for the friendship of Tibet. The U.S. Navy....also trained the dread State Police of China. American experts taught Chinese everything from potato-growing to the newest methods of artificial insemination."

Following the logic of American foreign policy to this day, one must wonder if White is writing about people or potatoes. The reason for this theater of the absurd was to bring the curtain down on Japan in China – and to stay put when the play was done. We lost China, but very much have our eye on Tibet, as the Dalai Lama becomes a cult figure.

Our Flying Tigers stopped the Japanese advance up through Burma, only thirty miles south of Kunming. A volunteer force of maverick Americans, including their commander, Claire Chennault, the courageous Tigers knocked out of the sky a good portion of the Japanese Air force committed to the conquest of China, and put an end to the bombing of the city – in what was known as "Stilwell's War;" General Joseph Stilwell, another hero in this incredible cast of characters, including the less heroic Generalissimo. Perhaps this very important phase of China/American relations is downplayed by us because our disastrous support of Chiang K'ai-shek – the virulent protests of Vinegar Joe Stilwell not withstanding – presaged our propping up of that other puppet in Vietnam, General Diem (or whatever the hell his name was, there certainly was more than one), who had a wife to match Madame Chiang.

The Generalissimos, really, were pulling the strings – they got the arms they asked for, even if things turned out terribly for all concerned. After nearly two decades of brainwashing about a "Communist takeover" anywhere signifying the end of the world, you can understand why many Americans in government preferred the corrupt general in Vietnam to the people's choice, Ho Chi Minh, but with the winding down of World War II, the Communists were our allies and yet we went along with the running dog or warlord, Chiang (and the darling of sophisticates, his bitchy wife), when the reformer, Mao, had literally won the support of the Chinese in many campaigns and was the only man capable of pulling them out of the age-old morass of poverty, superstition and corruption. If he failed in his noble endeavor, it is because we pushed him overboard – and the Chinese are only human, after all.

Gunboat diplomacy had been ruling the waves since America wrung its first trade concessions from the Manchu Empire in the treaty of 1844, and our one concern has been – is – the protection of the expanding market, and obviously, we thought that the fascist Chiang was the man to oversee that New World order that was just around the corner. Ironically, the Communists had a better feel for capitalism than the Kuomintang, if Theodore White read the cards correctly (in what was considered a classic before the embarrassed powers-to-be stole his Thunder....):

"The Communists wish to leave light industries in the hands of free enterprise, because they distrust the abilities of the Kuomintang bureaucrats. They feel that free businessmen, out of the time-honored profit motive, can create more quickly than anyone else the goods for which the peasants are crying."

And ultimately the Chinese Communists came around to that, but as President Clinton does an about-face on the bottom line, turning his back on human rights, we again help create the conditions that bring a Mao to the fore.

Mao, in his westward trek, passed to the north of Kunming in 1934. This has always been the China of the "minorities," who lived in mortal fear of the exploitative Han, none more hated than Chiang K'ai-shek, and his "White Chinese." Encountering these tribal peoples, Mao won them over in a common fight against the Kuomintang – changing the status quo for awhile – but the Red Army proved to be no more a friend to the Lolo or the Yi than the Nationalists. The eventual Cultural Revolution had no place for nonconformity, though some people were more equal than others. Wandering about the Yuantong Temple, I was happy to see to what extent the ancient customs and dress of the Yi and Miao had survived Mao. Coming from the hinterland, the colorfully outfitted indigenous people were experiencing the big city and once again, apparently, enjoying religious freedom.

When Marco Polo came this way on his own long march, having already journeyed the length of the Silk Road, he found in Kunming (then known as "Yachi") a mixed population "consisting of idolaters, Nestorian Christians, and Saracens or Mahometans...." and natives who "do not consider it an injury when others have relations with their wives, provided the women be willing." Wife sharing was fairly common throughout Asia, and this custom, making its way across the Bering land bridge, survived amongst those Eskimos who eluded the missionaries' grasp, until the turn of the last century. I don't think this degree of generosity – really a wide range of reasons for the practice – held on that long in China, but General Stilwell and other reliable sources hint at more sanguine habits in the hinterland surviving or maybe being revived. There have been recent reports of cannibalism in China. You can't be sure who Marco Polo was having sex with.

All but Christians and Muslims were considered idolaters. The bastardized Buddhism, common through much of China by the thirteenth century, was, in Marco Polo's eyes, idolatry. Although the merchant of Venice heard of Buddha, and even relates the story of his life, he sees the many statues of Buddha and the holy men who served him as idols, just as someone from another planet could logically assume that the statues of Christ, Mary and the saints in incense-filled cathedrals were just so many idols, with as much to do with spirituality as wife-swapping. And it may be you don't have to travel that far to see that any religion gets in the way of a religious experience, though a church's stained glass can be a window on eternity.

The Yuantong Temple has changed little since the young Roman Catholic sailed out of Europe's Middle Ages, and its trappings were more bizarre than Buddhist. Commissioned by the Great Khan, Marco Polo was in Kunming on business and in the style of the time never gets personal, but as a good Christian and looking for an easy mark, we must assume he was obligated to dismiss Buddhists with an insult. Then, as now, if you hang around long enough, the Temple is a riot of ritual and mostly traditionally dressed worshippers easily passing for "pagans" or American Indians. But today there are more idlers than "idolaters" and though the drab work uniforms of the Maoists have mostly disappeared, the white shirts of the Hans contrasting bleakly with colorful embroidery, can bleach the spirit out of a scene the dollar-conscious government has come to regard as a goose that lays a golden egg. It makes more economic sense to allow an inconsequential minority to do its own thing, and if in some cases a tourist attraction is quite literally the opium of a potentially troublesome people, so be it. (The Temple could be Daoist.)

The French, looking for a grand market for their colonies, built a railway from Hanoi to Kunming, but losing their pants in Southeast Asia, also lost their toehold on China. Down the road it was my displeasure to meet a Frenchman who entered China via Vietnam, longing for what might have been. And the British, also, presented a picture of Janus. They may have been fighting for democracy in Europe, but to the Ameri-

Kunming and Going

cans the British appeared more interested in maintaining the status quo in India than in the defeat of Japan.

We crossed the Beijing Road and moved into the less expensive Golden Dragon Hotel. The smart, nay, chic, brochure shows it to be in Kunming, Chine. An 'e' rather than an 'a' at the end of China is less a misspelling than a concession to French influence. With its sweeping, flowing, lobby-length mural or mosaic, a barely abstracted primitive-proletariat á la African-American Indian, I had returned to the Halls of Montezuma. But the Golden Dragon was built on a grander scale than any hotel I knew of in Mexico City.

An American in this lavish belly of a beast had been stationed here during the war and couldn't recognize a thing, except for the Flying Tigers barracks out on Shilin Highway. And maybe the Western Hills overlooking Dianchi Lake. (Pilots homed in on this mountain when they returned from their missions or brought in supplies.) He and his wife raved about the American breakfast they just had in the Dragon's restaurant, *La Brasserie*. Mais oui. The old soldier didn't fare so well when he last dined in Kunming, though the Chinese in charge of mess served American food.

Theodore White, thundering on about China in general and Kunming in particular, gives us some idea of what life was like for our new friend. "He lived on bad food, in stinking, rat-infested Chinese hostels; he had to fight off the heat, mud and disease. No one bothered to explain to him what the war was about...The U.S. government was Uncle Chump from over the hump; Chiang K'ai-shek was Chancre Jack; Sun Yat-sen was Sunset Sam; all Chinese were 'slope-headed bastards.' "

It was enough to give a Vietnam vet a very bad case of déjà vu. Similarities between the Vietnam War and the China war went beyond the estrangement that came from going through hell to help a little understood, less respected ally, indistinguishable from the hated minority enemy. Just as the "slope-head Chinks" may well have been the "slant-eyed Japs" in the earlier war up the river, eventually all the Vietnamese became "gooks."

Yet, if the GI in Kunming and Guilin, with the memory

Unraveling on the Old Silk Road

of Pearl Harbor forever in his heart, and an almost universal support of the war effort back home and more understandable reasons for fighting could gripe as he did, how much harder was it for the savvy guys in Saigon and Mekong Delta who had their R & R and deadening drugs, yet often understood, as well as those who chanted "hell no, we won't go" or got deferments, that it was an unjust, unpopular war against a people oppressed by the very politicians and warlords we supported, and who in no way threatened them until they went to Vietnam, not knowing "Charlie" from Tom, Dick or Harry; it was "kill or be killed" and being driven to the point where it did not matter. The major difference for the Americans in the respective wars was that the World War II GI knew who the designated enemy was, even if he could put the Japanese and Chinese in the same boat and like to see it sunk.

    I suspect that that strange nostalgia that brought the younger Americans to the scene of their war, making a kind of peace, is what inspired the return of the old soldier who was so happy to have a decent American breakfast. The Kunming he had first tasted was far worse than the "splendid city" Marco Polo had known. Prostitution had supplanted the easy women and until the arrival of the Americans, the prostitutes were penned in like wild animals. In the name of the war effort, Kunming was given a face-lift and young GIs learned if there was any truth to the racist salmagundi about Chinese women having a "sideways pussy" ' a side of China that encouraged pilots bringing in supplies to get over the Hump. As an ex-airborne sailor who flew aboard World War II seaplanes and wanted to home in on the red light, this is a subject I can warm up to, but we must move on.

    In a mad dash to catch the bus for Dali, we spent little time at the receptionist desk checking out of the hotel, but we didn't get too far down Beijing Road before two panting clerks from the Dragon were badgering us for our receipts to see if we drank anything from the fridge in our room. We had no idea what they wanted and Mona was wondering what crime we had committed before they had found what they wanted. A minor misunderstanding and the bus was late, but the ticket seller who had sold us the tickets the day before ticked her off.

She looked around the dingy bus station, the lobby of a Chinese hotel. Welcome back to reality. After the golden heights, she had crashed. "They're so different," she said. "I often feel that we're the enemies and we're just tourists." Dawn was breaking and Dali was at the end of a long day.

Today, in this neck of the woods, it is the independent traveler who is on the front lines (and, oddly enough, just beyond Dali, American soldiers recuperated in the hospital in Myitkyina in World War II).

7

Dali High

The way to do is to be.

Lao Tzu

    Leaving the city of Yachi (Kunming) and traveling ten days in a westerly direction, you reach the chief city of the province of Karajan, which is also called Karajan (the city of Ta-Li, located on a great lake). The country is in the dominion of the Great Khan....gold is found in the rivers....they likewise use cowrie shells in currency, although these are not found in this part of the world, but brought in from India.
    As I have said before, these people never take virgins for their wives....I was assured as a certain fact that many persons, and especially those who harbor evil designs, always carry poison with the intention of swallowing it in case they are captured and face torture.... Before they came under the rule of the Great Khan, these people were addicted to the following brutal custom: when any stranger of fine quality and personal appearance happened to lodge at the house of any one of them, he was murdered during the night – not for the sake of his money but in order that the spirit of the dead person, endowed with this talents and intelligence, might remain with the family, and all their affairs might thus prosper.

Marco Polo

    Boarding the bus for the long trip to Dali (Ta-Li) were about six other tourists. An American girl from Michigan had a jar of peanut butter, crackers and bananas. What seemed odd was that she never went to the toilet. We did make several stops for this. I pray that I won't have to pee. On one occasion two large pigs (the largest pigs I ever saw) were in a pen in the toilet. After eleven hours, we arrived. On market day we took a bus up to Xizhou... One bus appeared to be reserved for the Israelis...our friend with the dreadlocks...The 'Italian lady' was to make her first appearance. Mona

Dali was the cradle of civilization in southwestern China, but neolithic sites were overrun with the neo-Neanderthals and there was nary a toilet to be had outside our hotel. Nouveau hippies staying at the dorm across the way didn't fare as well, but it was recommended in the Lonely Planet and has something going for it beyond lower prices. In my book they were dilly Daling; and the dormitory was Dali High.

The town was a magnet for anybody with an ounce of adventure in his or her soul, but that ain't exactly heavy stuff. It was nearer to Kathmandu physically and in every other respect, than I imagined. Dali is nearer to Indo-China in spirit and miles than it is to Cathay. For centuries the people of the Mekong went against the current, following the river to its headwaters in China, but as history winds down – speeds up – the culture goes with the flow. And didn't the Vietnam War, like the flooding of the Mekong Delta, really have its source in China?

The Lazy Cat said where the young tourists were at – or wannabe. In the Hungry Eye or Running Nose I came across jazzy graffiti. If I have forgotten the name of the eatery, I can't forget the poetry:

> *To be is to do* – Kant.
> *To do is to be* – Sartre.
> *Do be do be do* – Sinatra.

Kant has done well by me, and *"to be is to do"* sounds like something out of his Metaphysics of Morality, but how can you be in China and into this do do and omit the father of being, Lao Tzu, who said, "The way to do is to be," which predates, more succinctly, that scribbled bit of enlightenment attributed to the German by almost two and a half millennia. But it's really cool and I've never seen Western philosophy summed up more playfully or profoundly. While I can only attest to the veracity of the

Unraveling on the Old Silk Road

Sinatra quote, the author has encapsuled in a nutshell the evolution of Western thought. Sinatra's sentiments, of course, are more musical and he did do it his way – which puts him on the right track and closer to Lao Tzu, although some may say: to do or to be, that is the question.

On a more serious note, it's poetic that late twentieth century art is little more than popcorn and baby talk. I resisted, adding: you're damned if you do and you're damned if you don't.

Sadly, this off-the-wall-wit did not reflect the spirit of the characters I encountered in their home away from home. An Australian girl teased the diners about the possible source of the food they were eating, regaling us with some of the meals she had on her bicycle trip across China. I took what she said with a cup of salt, although bicycling about China was becoming as popular as dog meat. Granted there are a few sour grapes in my own rendition, regret at the flight of my sweet bird of youth, a wife going bananas because she was looking forward to a love boat and ending up doing China on cattle cars and buses – the acid test for any marriage.

It's bad enough for a middle-aged man having to take a leak or whatever comes naturally in the boondocks. I knew the word for toilet, but I often had as much luck with it as I had on my first trip to Mexico, where I excitedly cornered several Mexicans and attempted to ask them where the men's room was. Asking "Donde quatro hombres?" instead of "cuarto de hombres," I had demanded to know where were the four men. The startled men assured me it was not they I was looking for. The Chinese word for toilet, conveniently, is *cesuo*, which sounds much like the Spanish pronunciation of Jesus, but I was directed to neither a restroom or a church, which didn't much matter because I was coming to do what did matter al fresco. You have more success asking for an outhouse – which I invariably avoided anyway. Not that I was put off by pigs or other creatures of the night (as in night soil), but for a guy enamored of horse manure, I would seek out the side of a barn before I would squat – or stand like a man – in a Chinese abomination. Wherever I went, I would sooner be caught without my passport than toilet paper.

Dali High

The driver of the Dali-bound bus did not appreciate unscheduled stops and he was surly to begin with. My agitated request for a toilet must have sounded like swearing to the South American on board, but when the driver was equally baffled or pretended to be, I performed a pantomime. At one stop a young woman speaking a little English stopped Mona on her way to the lu – skip to the lu, ma darlin' – and invited us to be her guests. Not now, Mona pleaded to the insistent woman, and they quickly exchanged addresses.

On the other side of the walled city is a many tiered wedding cake built in the ninth century. One of the whitewashed pagodas of Cangsheng Temple rises sixteen stories above a stream and the squat dwellings of Dali. With a top like the bottom of a top or the tips of the stupas of Nepal, Cangsheng is more like the candles than the cake. The temple supposedly houses the remains of Buddha, just as the Temple of the Tooth does in Sri Lanka. I imagine that Burma with its million temples has the lion's share of his teeth, and God knows what relics.

The stone lions standing guard at the gates of Dali are more in keeping with the spirit of Cathay.

Dali, once again, has become a confluence of cultures. Historically the shores of Erhai Lake, a basin for many streams – flash in the pans – was where the north met the south. An exotic mix of tribes and customs and costumes. We took a picture of some men in turbans outside the Cangsheng Temple. A carryover from Burma – or the Muslim past? Today East meets West and the Middle East is in the middle of it all.

We will always associate Dali with Israel, not only because of all the Israelis there, but because Dali and Israel boast of a locale that is likened to Switzerland. I don't know which reveals the most chutzpah, the hill opposite Kibbutz Megiddo, the Armageddon of old with its planted evergreens being compared to Switzerland, or the folder for my Dali postcards. "The flowers of Shangguan, the wind of Xiaguan, the snow of Cangshan and the moonlight of Erhai Lake was acclaimed by foreign travelers as the Switzerland of the East."

There are two distinct worlds here, the gayly costumed Bai and other nationalities or "minorities" coming to sell their wares and maybe barter, and the local fishermen sitting or resting on the shaded shore below the colorful tumult. They fished in the marshy area, setting up nets or casting them from dugout boats that seemed never to venture far from the protected area.

The heat drove us to the water's edge, undisturbed by the whims of the marketplace (or tourists). It was one thing to sell a purse or bag, very common in and around Dali, or the crafts and trinkets of bells, bangles and beads, but a fisherman had little trouble disposing of his catch. Fulfillment rested in its size. The fishermen were a barrel of laughs. Not a sight of the murderous hospitality Marco alluded to – civilized behavior compared to our own reasons for killing.

The fishermen looked more Sino than Mongol, but the hill people came from over the mountains and the mouth of that great river that may be the source of the Mongol peoples. The Mekong River is an international highway, a bridge and a border for the Burmese, Laotians, Thais, Cambodians and the Vietnamese, not to mention Chinese. Outfitted as they were, the hill people could pass for Navajos – had that faraway look of nomads whose emigrating ancestors went to the ends of the earth. Like a rising tide, so many tribes flooded the vast China shore, ever so slowly fanning out and spilling over into the Americas and the southern seas, finding a home, however temporary, in the most remote and least hospitable corners (to our thinking), like the sea itself finding its own level and exploring every shore.

But whenever possible, the primitives gravitated to akin places that best suited their skills and temperaments and created a kind of continuum. After adapting to the Asian arizona, some subtropical tribes of the subcontinent would be at home in the American southwest. So much so, that when the Indians of the Rockies and the open range were exiled to Florida, they, like so many of the snowbirds of today, perished. Those Asians who did gravitate to the Americas' jungles or dense woodlands, had never outgrown their deepest roots. Those wandering Asians who traveled the furthest, whether in time, space, changed topography or culture, like the topmost branches of a tree, little resembled the trunk. The connections of East and West indicate the emigrants were as much settlers as they were nomads and that they were really returning home, as those parts of the Americas where they planted their deepest roots were really chips off the old block, those continental plates that were broken when the planet itself became a traveler.

And while our forebears may have been on all fours or more when God turned up the heat in the kitchen, man is but the stuff of magma that came and went before him. The early searchers were drawn to these haunts like magnets – destiny (and like everyone else, wanted to come to America). Maybe the Indians liked Central America so much because it had once been connected to Southeast Asia. Were the Middle Americans, who set the deepest roots here, actually trying to put the plates back together again? But it's a Humpty Dumpty, dumped upon world and all the king's horses and all the king's men. . . .

And so the Asians didn't so much leave home as home left them. That eerie lake could have been Lake Chapala in Mexico, Siamese twins that went their separate ways. And in newer Mexico, is there no connection between Tahoe and Tao? But looks and not language say more about people, and the same customs on opposite sides of the world speak louder than words. In fact, neighboring Indians can speak totally different languages, but the Yi or Lolo people of the Dali region used to plant grain as the Navaho did. Poking a sharp stick into the earth, they dropped a grain of corn into the hole and prayed for good weather. Tapping an inner spirit, the Navahos sand paint, engage in a mystical communion with the planet that is identical to the Tibetan's: "Land so high, made so pure, without equal, without peer, land indeed! Best of all! Religion, too, surpassing all."

The Bai people, closely related to Tibetans, most resemble the Navaho. Dressed in long pink shirts, given shape with striking sashes, fringed with stripes and a floral weave, wearing feathery bonnets similar to the American Indians, they lend themselves to our own southwest. But Dali was an important post on the Burma road, intersecting with the Yunnan-Tibet Highway – which ultimately led to the Americas.

Not only do these people share common ground, but they

Unraveling on the Old Silk Road

worshipped it in the same way. The Tibetan took on the trappings of the Buddhist, but the Dalai Lama's mother could be the mama of any Navaho. A famous photo shows her against the background of the Potala, that monastic palace in the magic kingdom. A "Small Potalaka" is on Lake Erhai's opposite shore. Small world. Joseph Campbell could attribute similar customs to the collective consciousness, but the Indian mother's papoose could well be a carryover from the Old World, the father's sand painting the finger of Tibet in America.

8

On to Lijiang and The Long March

Cold is the west wind.
And the cry of the wild geese is heard in the
    frost air of the morning moonlight.
This very day with one great leap we shall pass
    its sea blue peaks.

Narrow pathways, silent forests, delicate moses,
Where will our footsteps lead us today?
The red flag unfolds like a sun in the wind. . . .
Day will be dawning in the east.
Let no one say we have begun to march too soon.
Man does not grow old walking through greening hills.
                                                    Mao

Bus from Dali to Lijiang. Friend saw us off. . .Waiting for the same bus were several tourists. I think they were all Israelis, including the South American couple. When we arrived in Lijiang somehow we began talking and walking with an older Israeli couple – first noticed them in cafe at the market town near Dali. It was incredible to hear Tony speaking with this Israeli, who had been setting up the new embassy in Beijing for the past two years – Tony talking about his book, Tramping to Jerusalem, etc. and then ending up next door to them in the same hotel. Cold and damp, but the ancient town worth the long and agonizing journey and the long walk from the station. At one stop we bought little roasted birds with their heads still attached. Never thought I could eat it, but nothing else I would consider. I was sitting next to an American-

Unraveling on the Old Silk Road

Israeli girl reading 'Lonely Planet.' *"How can you travel in China without it."*
Mona

May you live in the most interesting of times.
Ancient Chinese curse

We woke up to an overcast day. The only bright spot was the tai chi conjurers in the temple courtyard below our window. Try as they may there was no Kiplingesque dawn that comes up like thunder across the China Bay – though it sure as hell looked like rain. As we were drifting into the monsoon season or whatever it is called at that latitude. Anyway, we were on our way, starting our day with the Bai guy who owned the Lazy Cat Cafe. Cat as in Kat man do be do be do. He said he would open early for our benefit and have soft-boiled eggs ready for us. They were not ready, but not to worry, the bus for Lijiang was always late in leaving. Why did he name his cafe the Lazy Cat? I asked.

"You know how cat like to lay around, same with tourists. They know they can be comfortable in my cafe." Lazy, man, lazy.

The night before he told us he liked Mark Twain. Our new friend had studied to be an engineer, spoke English better than any of the Chinese we had met, but he had no connections or money to, as Mona said, "grease the chopsticks." That sounds a lot better in Chinese, as that fantastic invention is known as "nimble fingers." Not to be had in the Lazy Cat. But the main reason for his failure to get the job for which he was qualified was that he was a "minority." Of course, speaking English as he did, the government felt he was eminently suited for his present position. And may have had a push.

Our crazy cat and his wife couldn't move or relocate and were evidently checkmated by population as well as birth control. Bai people who went over the quota managed to elude the head counters if they lived in the hinterland and left their children with relatives and could manage to move; the government net wasn't so fine that minor folks could not slip through it. There was not the spy network that was at play outside the

On to Lijiang and The Long March

tribal regions. Here, the large family was its own lifeblood.

The young restaurateur had about as much freedom as a military man, allowed to go where he was needed and fill the job of the moment. His business was slow in getting started, too much competition and not grungy enough. The kid was not hip. He accompanied us to the ticket office, a short way from where the bus would be able to park. As Mona wrote in her diary: *a moving farewell – so good to be more than just another tourist.*

At this juncture, we part company with Marco and take up with Mao, actually continue to outflank him in his feat of outflanking the ensconced Chiang K'ai-shek in Chongquing – our own destination in a most roundabout way, which entails crossing the path of the saunterer extraordinaire himself:

> *The Red Army fears not the rigors of a forced march;*
> *to them a thousand mountains, ten thousand rivers,*
> *are but a gentle walk.*
> *The Five Ridges ripples by like little waves,*
> *And the mountain peaks of Wumeng are but mounds.*
> *Warm are the cloud-topped cliffs above the River of*
> *Golden Sand,*
> *Soft are the iron chains that span the Tatu River.*
> *Soldiers delight in the ageless snows of Minshan,*
> *And they smile proudly as the Army crosses.*

About two or three hours up the road, we began our delectable climb into the rain-soaked heights. Lijiang, less than 150 miles away as the vulture flies, is circled by mountains that dwarf the Alps. But we never got above the clouds.

Local passengers did not know what to make of us. Perched in almost inaccessible places, their crude houses were extensions of that broad sweeping Himalayan underbelly that stretches from here to that eternity of K, the King of Mountains topping Everest itself, in the far northwest of China. An endless range of peaks and valleys that has sustained and inspired those many tribes that eventually got the drift of things, ending up in Borneo and beyond.

The bus station, with a dorm above it, was at the edge

of town, with the only other hotel, a guest house, at the opposite end of Lijiang. The older Israeli couple tagged along with us, but upon learning about my book, the diplomat husband had some questions to ask.

"Why were you interested in Israeli politics?"

"What's so political about disliking the oppression of the Palestinians?" I responded.

After dealing with the Chinese for two years, he could twist me around his chopsticks. "It's political when you criticize the government in Israel."

Israelis who have been around, an advance man and woman to boot, could never be too careful. Our new neighbors were on a mission for their government, which made them feel more vulnerable than the average Israeli. Yet, they were all faced with the quandary of having this instinctive need to band together against a "hostile" world, while very aware of the danger of a group sticking out.

The embassy people were friendly as you might expect diplomats to be, but to have them on our tail when we wanted so much to be beyond the pale, did not sit well with us and we were off and running without showering.

Like many Old World cities, Lijiang has its old and new side. Actually, the complete name of the city is Lijiang Nazizu Zizhixian. The administrative, newer Chinese part, is mostly symmetry and cement, gritty grids we had to suffer through before we crossed the river and were into the trees. Not many of these, but crossing a miniature bridge of moss-covered stones we found ourselves on the back lanes of town where aproned women wore blue bodices. Nazizu has nearly as many bridges as nature-embellished houses, running water, streams, channels winding in and out of it. I drank of this wine, improved with time, as if time itself was running out.

I am forever struck by the people, that pure, timeless visage, sage look, that only "progress" erases. This basically matriarchal society never had much room for Mao, but lurking in a doorway had been a man dressed in a suit, now waving a piece of paper, materializing before us like an apparition or apparatachek. Probably Han, he had seen us wandering this

On to Lijiang and The Long March

way and that and perhaps dressing for the occasion, waylaid us:
"I'm a poet!" he exclaimed. "Read this!"

I don't recall any introductory foreplay such as, "Are you an American? How do you like China?" No, this man wasn't wasting any time. He was in his sixties, at least, and the chemistry of poets was at work here. Instant recognition and the need to communicate with a soul brother. He held up his poem for me to read:

"There is no greater honor than working in the factory, people working together building a new China."

Vintage Cultural Revultion. He had done Mao proud, but before I could respond to this assault on my sensibilities, he had crawled back into his hole. This encounter was indeed odd since the resident Nakhi people were imprisoned by the Chinese.

Perhaps something was lost in the translation. I wonder if he wasn't a messenger sent to tell us that this is the China that will endure and you had better back off with your sedition and perdition about individual freedom. Even the big city yuppies who own the factories eat a pseudo simulated fare in the Cultural Revolution restaurants that are sprouting up in the east like corn. Camp? But we also have the power of nostalgia at work here.

In and out of the rain, following winding lanes and the free-flowing water, was enough to work up an appetite in a blackened building. It seemed we were in Lijiang a couple of days because a darkening downpour would deceptively signal day's end, only to be followed by yet another sunburst.

Returning to our guest house, we ran into the Planeteers. The Survival Kit lists the address of a gathering place for local musicians. I caught a few refrains but pooped from pijiu could not remember the memorable. I can say the music wasn't Chinese. I joke about the spacey music of the Chinese reflecting extraterrestial origins, yet if the sound is out of this world, it is because their music was as fixed as the stars, as ordered as everything else in the celestial society of old, since each note had the emperor's imprimatur and to deviate from the prescribed sound would result in the malefactor facing the music.

We were sorry to leave our ramshackle refuge, so reminiscent of the colonial bungalows in India's hill country – the respite from the heat as attractive as the break from the concrete jungle below. All the more sorry to be leaving at four in the morning. With all the doors bolted shut, we were lucky to get out of the place. Luckier to find our way to the bus station. Again, I was flying blind in the pitch of night and I wasn't sure we were heading for the station until cooking fires lit up the road like a World War II runway, and then like the control tower that it is, the Lijiang Dorm lent its own light to the dark site.

Who were all these people making breakfast at this ungodly hour? Were these the woks of workers, food vendors, travelers who brought their own cooking utensils with them? Shadowy figures gave the street a spooky air. About this time I developed my hacking cough, common to cigarette smokers in the west and Chinese who may or may not smoke, but must breathe the sulphur laden air. The charcoal in China is fortified with a toxic material that will take your breath away.

We boarded the bus in darkness, but gracious hostesses sporting sashes, festooned as if on a maiden voyage, and armed with flashlights showed us to our seats. In my sleep-starved state I was seated aboard a luxury airliner, until the light of day, when absconded stewardesses and a bumpy flight, put me in the cockpit of a Flying Tiger. We were going over the "hump" in yet another South American reject. Missing were those crosses at especially precarious bends in the road that mark the spot where Peruvian buses go over the side. A break in the clouds revealed the upper Yangtze or Golden Sand in all her glory wending her way around Mian Mian Shan. Mao could wax poetic but he lost hundreds of men to exposure in the Mian Mian mountains. His closest comrades were literally carried away by the scenery.

A narrow range of peaks separated the Yangtze from the Mekong or Lancang River (to the Chinese). Something in my solar plexus, tells me that this was the nexus of the planet. Many rarely seen, almost unknown mountains of "sea-blue" majesty rippling away like so many muscles from the upper belly

On to Lijiang and The Long March

of the Himalaya Shan, between their Switzerland-sized folds some of the world's greatest rivers flowing to the sea. Coming out of the north the Mekong and the Yangtze run a parallel course for hundreds of miles before going their separate ways. Improbably originating on almost the same Tibetan Shan, the Yangtze, Yellow and Mekong Rivers finally define the whole of China and beyond.

But nearer to the source the people were wild and wooly – silk a long way downriver. In 1935 Mao and his ragtag army encountered a naked people living in temporary shelters and unlike the Lolo, few of the natives were friendly. It staggers the imagination to think of the struggles of these stragglers entering Sichuan, with yet another 2,000 or 3,000 miles to go to the Great Wall and journey's end in Shaanxi. Aside from hostile tribes and extremes of nature, Mao and company had to contend with the Nationalists brave enough to venture into the "countryside" and engage them. But the natives were less receptive to Chiang's fascist troops who had turned some against all outsiders despite Mao's evenhandedness. The democratic queen of one tribe would boil alive anyone talking to Red or "White" Chinese. Compared to Mao's exploits in this bristling neck of the woods, most of the explorers of "Darkest Africa" were on a Sunday picnic. Dr. Livingstone, I presume? A church picnic, no less.

But Mao won the friendship of most minorities and peasants by disciplining his army – as opposed to the brutal exploitation of the Nationalists. Mao's eight rules, a kind of Eightfold Path of Buddhism, stressed that his "fighters" (not to be confused with hated soldiers associated with the Nationalists) speak politically, pay fairly, return what you borrow, don't strike or swear at people, don't take liberties with women. . . which did not prevent Mao from being a womanizer.

I can not be certain where on my map we crossed the Upper Yangtze, much less where Marco Polo, and centuries later Mao and his merry band of "bandits" (in American eyes) did. But there have not been many places that the gorges permitted a crossing by boat or bridges, which puts us near the doorstep of Dukou and Sichuan province – home of the world-

Unraveling on the Old Silk Road

famous Szechuan cuisine, where in Mao's time anybody could turn up in the pot. Sichuan (the new spelling) is also home of the mandarin orange, bamboo, and the pandas that find food and shelter in these sacred succulent plants that nourished Chinese culture, as well. Tobacco, grown here, served the needs of the chain-smoking Chairman.

But as Mao trekked northward he entered the nether land known as the "grasslands." Eventually, I came upon the grasslands myself, but the high plains and alpine pastures I experienced is paradise compared to the mosquito infested miasma that Mao and his men endured, traversing swamp and quicksand before emerging on the higher and drier ground that leads to the "ageless snows" of his beloved Min Shan. Having taken the high road out of the east myself – a detour from the Silk Road — and entering the Tibetan enclave of Xiahe, I came to know the adobe huts that sheltered the Red Army and the mostly barley mix that would sustain them in their flight up Min Shan. Above the grasslands, aside a fluttering prayer flag, I could see the north side of Mao's last great natural hurdle.

Running into an enemy blockade, the Red Robin Hood veered to the northeast where the "Tartars," Chiang's Mongol allies, swept down the steppes to stop the Communists. Red machine gunfire served as Mao's elephants as the frightened ponies of the "Moslems" threw their riders. The victorious Chairman and his men, mounted on the captured Mongol ponies, arrived at the Great Wall on October 20, 1935. Completing his crossing of the Chinese Alps, the Asian Hannibal ended his 6,000 mile march with only 7,000 of his 100,000 man army. In retreat for more than a year, winning the hearts and minds of many along the way, Mao stands firm in Shaanxi province, ultimately driving the Generalissimo into the sea.

In 1967, a couple of decades after the fleeing Chiang and the KMT, taking with them much of China's treasure, set up shop in Formosa (the Portuguese name of his beautiful island retreat), Mona and I, like most Americans not permitted to visit the mainland, ended up in Taiwan, sleeping in the Generalissimo's bunker. An earthquake shook me out of my bed that night. Really! Apologists for the glorified warlord and his so-called Nationalists should consider that he likened the Japanese to a "skin disease." His real enemy, the much greater threat to his body politic, were the cancerous Reds. It is easy to forget that while China was at war with Japan, it was Mao who marched all over the Japanese.

It should come as no surprise that when the Chinese tire of today's robber barons, also collaborating with the Japanese and Americans, they will resurrect their Mao, Moses – their Bolivar – tramping to Jerusalem.

9

Tracking Marco Polo: The Night Train to Emei/Leshan

Kaindu is a western province which was formerly subject to princes; but has been brought under the dominion of the Great Khan....It contains many cities and castles, and the capital city....is likewise named Kaindu. Near to it is a large salt lake that abounds in pearls....a mountain in the neighborhood yields the turquoise stone. The inhabitants....have the shameful and odious habit of considering it no mark of disgrace that those who travel through the country should have relations with their wives, daughters or sisters.... When strangers arrive, each householder endeavors to bring one of them home with him....leaves him in the position of master of the house, and goes off....Here also the animals that yield musk are taken in great numbers....In the country are found tigers, bears....The wine is not made from grapes, but from wheat and rice with a mixture of spices....Ginger grows there....besides many other drugs, of which very little is ever brought to Europe....Upon leaving the city of Kaindu, the journey is ten days to the opposite boundary of the province....you reach the great River Brius or River of Golden Sands, which bounds the province and in which are found large quantities of gold dust.
Marco Polo

Left Lijiang very early. . . .hostesses collecting tickets on bus. 'Italian lady' on board and Israeli guy. Also Frenchman coming from Vietnam and English girl who thinks she is speaking with an Italian woman. Bus arrived in Dukou late. . . no chance to change money for train. Frenchy short-changes Tony – he's yelling at him – dollar bills all over, holding up people waiting to get ticket. Group going to Chengdu, but of course shared our compartment with the 'Italian lady.' Never saw Tony so paranoid. Had 'soft beds' but I wished I had sat up in the train. The lady is

Tracking Marco Polo: The Night Train to Emei/Leshan

working in China – showed work permit at ticket counter for discount. She has a jar of instant coffee – offered us some. She was surprised when we got off at Emei. More surprised when Tony said "Shalom." Said goodbye, and never saw her again.

Mona

It is as difficult to keep track of the roving ambassador (Marco) as it is avoiding his tracks. Ancient names have disappeared or changed, misspellings abound and the translator, editor and Marco himself do not always know the east from the west or if in fact the Khan's emissary has been where he was sent. And doesn't the galloping Italian ever board a boat? Further complicating things for the reader, coming from the opposite direction, I am on his toes rather than his heels. An ancient map shows his return journey from Burma on much the same route, but there are no known sites that remotely resemble the line of march of which he relates. Marco seems to be hopping around like today's travel writers. If thirteenth century China had a flying machine, the airlines would have been more efficient then than they are now.

As Marco did not write his own tale, there was much lost in the telling. It's hard enough for me to piece together a trip a couple of years down the road; how much more of a task was it for the jailed Venetian to retrieve memories sometimes a quarter of a century old. And then, like some of my own manuscripts, the damn thing kicked around for one hundred and eighty years before getting into print – and as different manuscripts were in circulation, we have another deciding factor in differing renditions.

Kaindu may have been the ancient capital of Chamdo, in the Tibetan province of Kham. With a large salt lake brimming with pearls? "Standing at the entrance of the province" hundreds of miles to the north, how can it only be a ten days ride from the Golden Sands? Which is really in Las Vegas anyway. And then only a "five days journey" *(next chapter)* from the river to Kunming, in a "westerly direction" no less. Of course, Americans don't know when, where or even care if Washington crossed the Delaware, and I'm sharing this very

Unraveling on the Old Silk Road

foreign fixation with you. It matters diddely. On the other hand, Marco Polo is becoming popular as pizza pie, (to the extent that a British librarian could write a well-received book purporting that Marco didn't go to China) even if the Chinese invented that, too. And if Marco Polo did not go to China, Americo Vespucci did not go to America.

If Marco did come this way, it is a gross oversight that he failed to mention a monument or figure which sits two hundred and fifty feet in height, gargantuan hands resting on knees, easily visible from the opposite shore of Leshan, or from the river, the more popular approach to the Grand Buddha and the fantastic complex of Tang dynasty temples and pagodas. I don't know what the professional speculation is on the matter, but it is possible that, like many a traveler to this land of navigable rivers, Marco simply went with the flow, continuing, at least, to Yibin, long a major port. His account of bamboos, fifty feet high and two-and-half-feet in girth, is accurate since this region is known as the South Sichuan Bamboo Sea and is famous for some of its more spectacular specimens. At the time, actually, Grand Buddhas were less remarkable. Even if completed in 803, it is the largest stone Buddha in the world.

And if Marco doesn't mention tea, that is because tea, usually herbal, is drunk all over Asia. Chopsticks? "Tartars" used their fingers.

If an editor or scholar considers the Yangtze upstream of Yibin to be the Golden Sand, Marco could have crossed the river near Yibin, traveling in an easterly direction before going west to Kunming, really not knowing if he was coming or going – a very familiar traveler's tale.

Yes, this is much ado about nothing and even nuttier when any hack playing with his computer, but not knowing Sichuan from Saskatchewan, can come up with the answer in minutes (even if non-existent), but ready answers are like fast-food compared to the hunt, the preparation of the meal and a drink to go along with it. Damn the explanations, the joy of explorations lies in stumbling upon your discoveries, for then they are yours. Lacking foresight, it's love at first sight. Lacking foreskin the love is less intense.

Tracking Marco Polo: The Night Train to Emei/Leshan

Forgive me if I've taken you down this road before, but my fascination with maps begins when the trip is done.

When I'm on the road, on the scent of something good, I'm too caught up in the chase to focus on the future. Is it a wonder then that when my brains are being scrambled by the heat, I tend to jump out of the frying pan and into... the other side of serendipity. My interest in maps paralleled a developing taste for those "French postcards" of old. Maps may whet my appetite for what lies ahead, but mostly they enable me to digest the moveable feast. Avanti!

The Polos' own compulsive globe-trotting, centered on the Mongols, may lie in their Venetian roots (which could not have run very deep), for the oddest thing about the Polo odyssey is that in ending up in the court of the Khan, they are going home again. The fact is that Venice was settled by retreating Mongols, Attila's Huns, about eight hundred years before Marco was caught up in the power struggles of Attila's descendents. Aptly referring to this Asian beachhead in Europe, Venezia means "One who has come so far," but the returning Marco can not be blamed if he thought Venice was speaking to him. Spaghetti, Venice – next they will tell us that Marco Polo, himself, was Mongol – which could, at least, explain his extraordinary relationship with Kublai Khan.

If the map produced for a former New York Times columnist trying to trace Mao's trail is correct, I did not cross the Golden Sands where the Red leader made his crossing, which may very well have been in the wake of Marco Polo's traverse, north of Kunming. It is entirely possible that not only were we on Mao's tail, but Marco's tracks as well, when our Emei-bound train was chugging towards Xichang, which could also be Kaindu. But then, it is understood that Marco's Desciption of the World is not limited to places he personally visited.

We made our first crossing below Lijiang, upriver from Mao's row across the Yangtze. My greatest challenge, when our bus made it to the other side, was adding my own golden stream to the Golden Sand. It was not easy to get the driver to make this unscheduled stop. The "Italian lady," never imagining I was paying homage to Mao, seriously thought I was ab-

Unraveling on the Old Silk Road

sconding when bounding from the bus, I ran a good hundred feet to do it my way. She was more relieved than I was when I returned to the bus. The much younger Mao did not have this problem, but it did take the harried helmsman nine days to get his troops to the other side of the churning river.

By late afternoon we were skirting a much darker Yangtze in our approach to Dukou and another river crossing at the city itself. With our descent into the lowlands, I got correspondingly lower and ever hotter as we bypassed giant smokestacks and power plants that marked our return to pollution and a bustling abundance of people. I didn't realize just how remarkable the upriver metropolis is until I returned home and saw a recent Hammond area map that omitted it. And so has a Chinese map placing Panzhihua where Dukou should be, but not bothering about this important railway stop, unless they are one and the same. Or Panzhihua is the name of the station town, some distance from Dukou. Odd, I care more about where I've been than where I'm going.

In Dukou, like everywhere else in China, the past is cheek and jowl with the present. Below the city a rapidly rising river was threatening the freshly planted crops on the muddy banks. I was struck by the absence of boats on such a wide river, and wondered if this was because of the risks of navigating so swift a current, or because Dukou was in the middle of nowhere – though surely as a powerhouse on the Yangtze at the gateway to Tibet and Southeast Asia or Indo-China where there is unrest, it is strategically located, if you can find it. One hundred or so miles downriver Mao managed to get thirty thousand troops and civilians across a more dangerous spot. Using scores of boats in this operation or evacuation under the "cloud-topped cliffs," it is one of the more celebrated accomplishments of the Long March.

As our destination was the railroad station, I was surprised when our bus pulled into an open area that could have nothing to do with the railway. This was an open-air carwash where the bus got a good scrubbing down before completing its last lap of the day. After buying our train tickets, I tried desperately to break our journey here (where there was no problem

Tracking Marco Polo: The Night Train to Emei/Leshan

getting reservations) and make our break with the group, but the one hotel opposite the station was to Mona a worse alternative to going on and we simply waited out the arrival of the train in a nearby restaurant. Bonding like glue after such a hair-raising ride, the seemingly orphaned group sat out the remaining time till the arrival of the train on the station step. Of the step-children, we knew Frenchy had enough for the price of a beer, a cup of tea. . . .Were they so afraid of being stranded in darkest Dukou, or wherever the dunce or duce we were, that they couldn't risk grabbing a bite to eat or simply moving.

The English woman advised that if I wanted to leave China on the cheap as easily as possible, Monkey Business was the best way to get around Chinese hijinks. In the Year of the Monkey how could I resist such a travel agency. She gave me the address of the Beijing office. Or was it Hong Kong? Monkey Business was her ticket to ride on the Trans-Siberian Railway, the way she entered China, and I thought a good way to leave the country, when I still thought we were going to sail all the way down the Yangtze and catch up with Marco, who had spent three years near the mouth of the great river but had little to say about it.

10

Emei

> *Something hidden. Go and find it.*
> *Go and look behind the Ranges –*
>
> — Kipling

Emei. July 8. The heat hit us in the face – bus from station – looked for hotel. . .villa style near entrance to Mt. Emei. Tony says passageway thru gardens like giant keyholes. No money. . .left backpacks in lobby. . . .never bothered with black market but now we need it. In big cities pestered to death. Enough to eat. . . .outdoor kitchens all over mountain sanctuary. Tony's cough worse than two packs a day – wants only to "get above the weather and storm-trooping pilgrims." I'm exhausted. . .want only to return to hotel, but we're going higher and higher. Changed money with help of two Chinese students – seemed genuinely nice. . .good to meet people who didn't want anything from you. Got yuan instead of funny money tourists must use. Returned to hotel. Tony continuing on with students.

Mona

I climbed about a half-mile with my new-found friends before we stopped at a teahouse squat on a limestone saddle. When I tried to dodge the smoke of a neighbor, they helped me move our table. Launching into a tirade against tobacco, I asked if the "people's" government was trying to discourage the Chinese from smoking.

My more fluent, taller friend said, "No. The government owns the cigarette companies."

Beyond the inhumanity of this indifference, I mentioned the uneconomical side of smoking, the health care costs.

"But the government owns the hospitals. We pay."

Not a raised eyebrow. Not many lines to read between, but I think he was saying, government sucks but I'm not about to say as much, not if I hope to be in a position where I might be able to change it some day. Pointing out the little changed conditions of the peasants, their paltry income, he was indirectly denouncing Beijing, where he had a government address, the advanced academy he was attending.

When I remarked how well he spoke English, he told me about his American teacher – and their differing approaches to playing basketball. Their respective philosophies were reflected in the larger game of life. If his teacher lost a game, he was immediately clamoring for a rematch – revenge – while the Chinese accepted the loss as a part of life. There was no hurry to even the score. Where the Chinese cut their losses, the Americans upped the ante; nowhere more disastrously than in Vietnam. This was a classic case of a now or never culture (I use the word loosely) clashing with a mañana one, which understood that staying-power is the only kind that counts. We were already a Pepsi generation going flat when the fizz is gone. And now that I think about it, that "do be do be" cafe in Dali was actually named "Coca Cola" (also unregenerate), owned by an American and his Chinese wife.

I guess it boils down to the difference between ping-pong and basketball diplomacy. Clumsy giants charging down the court, dribbling, drooling all the way, only to dunk their doughnut through the net. And when push comes to shove there is a fist fight.

With Kipling and many another who have bit the dust, I have said, "You'll never plumb the Oriental mind, and if you did, it isn't worth the toil," but we usually come around to, "Though I've belted you and flayed you, by the living God that made you, you're a better man than I am, Gunga Din!" But the Chinese leadership is like flotsam rising to the top. A law of physics, leadership floats along with its consort censorship until a voyager rocks the boat. It's been so since the Chin dynasty. Everywhere.

I was amazed by the stream of devotees ascending the holy mountain, but lest anyone get carried away by this religious craze, the government was keeping things in perspective with a conspicuous monastery that showed where the true path lie. Bypassing the lower mountain we had just hiked and much of the carnival atmosphere below, a winding road allows for bus service to within a short walk of Loyalty-to-the-Country Monastery. Clearly, the Chinese "Communists" were saying: Big Buddha is on the river, but Big Brother holds the high ground. You can have your opium, your incense, but we want your sense. Render unto Caesar what is Caesar's, you owe your soul to the Company Store.

Climbing on we came to the Crouching Tiger Temple, immediately above that grounding-in-reality and seemingly a metaphor for the perils of any real spiritual ascent. Above that, perched over a waterfall is the Thundering Monastery. The cascade was my escape from a crowd. Making reservations with a monk, my friends would spend the night here. They offered to pay for my stay. Blessedly, I hadn't seen a pale face the whole day and the temptation to go on was great. We didn't have sleeping bags, but the monasteries pointing the way provided blankets along with a spartan fare. Unfortunately, I could not even be sure Mona would have a roof over her head and I couldn't risk a night out with the boys.

But, oh, how I wanted to climb this stairway to heaven, so transported by the unceasing splendor of it all that the floor I slept on could just as well be cloud nine. With an increase in altitude the crowd, like the air, would get correspondingly thinner. And if I could not lose myself in a crowd, I knew I could get lost in a cloud. Above the clouds I would see Buddha's Halo in the dawn's early light, Buddha's Lamp in the evening's western sky.

Mona could only play second fiddle to the celestial music that lay before me. I hungered after Emei like the hunter after his prey, but the hunter returned from the hill. Another fish that got away.

The pagoda's upturned roofs were like sails catching

the wind, prows riding the waves. Like the upturned branches of a tree, the curves allowed for communion between man and the planet and, by extension, God. Temples were an expression of worship, of reaching out, rather than overreaching.

My friends want to walk me down to the Nature-Tuning Pavilion and see me off on the last bus to Emei. The pavilion, I assumed, was where you tuned into nature. By the time we got down to the waiting bus nearby, I was so taken by an innate kindness that no amount of indoctrination could kill, that the person had become as important as the place. I don't know how many times perfect (double entendre) strangers have embarrassed me by their humanity, and this was one of them. They, in turn, were pleasantly surprised that I flew my flag at half-mast instead of waving it in their faces.

A wide ride down and around the mountain left me far below our hotel and the row of restaurants and stalls and shops that lead to the lower entrance to Mount Emei. Mona managed to get a room, paying with common currency, renminbi. But come morning we would have to come up with tourist money, which meant a bus ride into town. No way. Besides, it was the spirit of the moment as much as the mountain that had me enthralled. Love at first sight, the freshness of surprise and the opportunity to just keep on going and to be in the ascension for several days with friends.

The Golden Summit was more a precipice than a cone. Even the lower ranges revealed what appeared to be a one-sided approach to the summit, maybe a materialized metaphor for the Way. Or the edge of the earth, the edge of awareness, for far below the summit is the perpetually veiled void and like a voice from the past, Mao's thundering Tatu River, one of his greatest challenges in his murderous march. On the other side of that is Gonga Shan, topping 25,000 feet, and those Himalayan stairs to the stars.

Originally, the idea of heaven was a vision of such a mountain, modified by cherub-filled clouds replacing pinnacles occupied by gods as diverse as Zeus, first of the twelve Olympians, and P'an Ku. Actually the mountains were occupied by P'an Ku. And didn't Jesus and Moses and Mao himself come down from mountains with messages? The Greeks had more in common with the Chinese, believing that the universe created the gods. In similar fashion P'an Ku, the first being created out of the chaos by the dual principles of yang and yin, carved the world out of granite which had floated aimlessly in space. Aided by the phoenix, the dragon and the tortoise, positive symbols, this super Adam or atom, or should I say Michelangelo, brought about creation with his hammer and chisel. (Is this why sculptors are duped into feeling like gods and have an almost impenetrable shell?) P'an (as in Pan?) Ku, then, a kind of god or Father Earth, was transmuted into mountains and rivers, as his left eye became the sun and the right eye the moon. Actually, his eyes were out of this world. And he was a "he" because his beard was transformed into stars.

P'an Ku's blood became our rivers "while the parasites which infected his body, being impregnated by the wind, were the origins of the human race." Transmutation, transfiguration or even tran-substantiation comes about through the death of P'an. Compare this salt of the earth and stars mythology with our religious thinking – and you can see we are not chips off the old block.

A forgotten fact had unconsciously guided me to a place where other dissidents had not fared as well. Early in the Year of the Monkey, officials at a nuclear research center in Beijing very reluctantly confirmed that a highly placed scientist who had fallen out of favor may also have fallen to his death – when push came to shove. In any case, he disappeared while climbing Emei, briefly reported in the New York Times.

11

Leshan
In the Shadow of the Grand Buddha

I returned to our hotel at a magic hour, all the more enchanting for the garden under our window. Here was the universe in microcosm. If you couldn't read the language of the Chinese world, a sign over the gate of the traditional garden informed you that you were entering a sanctum sanctorum – as opposed to the leafy sanatoriums of the west without rhyme or reason or those grand straightjacket affairs with no light at the end of the tunnel like the Tuileries. In France, where a beautiful flower that grows freely is "souci," so-named because it grows as easily as "worries," you will see no sign marked "Harmony and Happiness." If it is Sans Souci you're looking for, that can be found over the door of the bistro.

A "door of all subtleties" as the Taoist said of the Way which ultimately led to the classic Chinese garden. An oversized keyhole or peephole looking out on the world without and within. Portals in the walls called "moongates" allow light and air to give a feeling of space to the enclosed area. Traditionally, all the plants and trees in the garden are symbolic and placed to enhance the yin/yang design of the basic elements. But as the soul grew out of the soil all is a representation of human character.

The spirit of nature seemed lost on the party faithful who baited us at breakfast. Such a hotel, seedy as it was, was reserved for corporate executives on an all-paid holiday with their families. One very nervous skinny character over-stepping the bounds of decorum, unable to quite make the switch

Unraveling on the Old Silk Road

from foreign devil to honored guest, pounced on Los Angeles and America's racist policies. Why was everybody picking on the Koreans?

Back in the garden the willows were not weeping and true to Chinese interpretation or representation were the embodiment of grace. Would we ever reconcile ourselves to China's fall from grace, aside from those pockets of purity that transported the soul? We were so attuned to what was. The cedar to which I'm particularly attracted has religious significance throughout much of Asia. In China it symbolized virtue, and it looks like a virtuous tree. There has been flowery verse about deciduous trees in the west, but it misses the fine points of pines.

But I'm also partial to fir, for I am that evergreen in the winter of our civilization who remains true to his color – and a little wet behind the ears. Or is that the morning dew? And if the Chinese is true to his tradition and my own taste, a bent and crooked path wends its way through his garden – disharmony or "evil walks in a straight line." Even if it is the shortest distance between two points. Because who the hell was in a hurry when transcendence was your magic carpet?

Interestingly, the west sees virtue in walking the straight and narrow, when such a road can only lead to a closed mind, which is why the simple wisdom of the East written on the wind, the rain, the trees and the rocks is inscrutable to a west locked into its alphabet. Didn't the Dalai Lama tell Thomas Merton (the American monk who was beginning to find his Way), you don't climb the mountain by taking a direct path.

Not surprisingly the Chinese spirit evaded the great German philosopher Hegel (*Philosophy of Right and Phenomenology of Spirit*), who was no Kant, and regarded the Chinese as superficial, "not yet succeeded in representing the beautiful as beautiful, for in their painting perspective and shadow are wanting." Like so many scholars his imagination is wanting. True, "Heaven has a higher meaning than nature," but it is often there between the lines.

Yet, hitting home, Hegel also wrote, "The writer must content himself with what he has been allowed to achieve under the pressure of circumstances, the unavoidable waste caused by the extent and many sideness of the time, and the haunting doubt whether, amid the loud clamor of the day and the deafening babble of opinion, there is left any room for sympathy with the passionless stillness of a science of pure thought." Aided by nature an eighteenth century thinker could take for granted.

Two or three bus rides later we found ourselves on the other side of the Minjiang River and climbing the steps leading to the Lingyun Monastery. I can't be certain how we learned of this monastery turned hotel. Maybe from our friend on Mount Emei. We had an amazing tendency to end up in a monastery when we were near the end of our rope, often being driven right to the door of some religious retreat we hadn't known of moments earlier. Things were not moving as smoothly in China. Here they worshipped the almighty dollar yet somehow we managed to get to Lingyun, site of the Grand Buddha, without changing a dime.

We weren't about to cross the river and return to Leshan for Chinese money, even if we had been aware of the ferry. So off we went hoofing it about these holy grounds, going up, down and around Mount Lingyun and crossing another river to reach Wuyou Monastery, still connected to the mountain by a chain bridge that may have been used by Mao himself and not seeing action since. Ferried across the river and caught up in the flow, we completely forgot about changing money until we met Wendy, a Chinese-American from Massachusetts. Wendy's uncle, the doctor, was more than happy to have our dollars and bought us ice cream.

It was just what the doctor ordered, judging from Mona's bare-bone "diary." *"So many ice cream pops...it was fun...we were like two kids."*

How could I resist that kind of enthusiasm for life? Actually, ice cream coming out of the blue in a crisis was the sort of succor you can only get at your mother's breast. Mama, manna from heaven, that taste of familiarity when you are beyond the pale and out of the pink.

Off the beaten path we found a priceless but primitive restaurant we had all to ourselves. Mona was ecstatic over a heaping bowl of rice and the still brimming basket it was served from at the side of the table.

Our hotel monastery was practically on top of Da-fu, or the Grand Buddha, with a beautiful view of the encroaching subtropics. The rain-stained Buddha below is nature personified. Da-fu amounted to a quasi-anthropomorphizing of the holy mountain, as well as a milestone in Siddhartha's evolution from a man to a godhead, arms, legs, etc. And if the Buddha had become God and bigger was better, the result in sandstone was a Big Brother – another holy man/prophet bites the dust and he who would show the Way becomes the show, the all-seeing Almighty, as man moving away from metaphor and meditation seeks something concrete to dominate his life. Golden Calf or the Almighty Dollar – it's all the same.

Down and out in Spain, I could no longer distinguish between the skyscraping statues (of concrete) of Jesus and the all-pervasive Franco on his pedestal. The omnipresence of humongous Buddhas could only intimidate the shan man, shaman, and those who would drink from the source. This mountain man was reduced to the size of a molehill, literally using the Buddha's fingernail for an umbrella. I was standing on his toes.

At least Da-fu is seated. Still, his overbearing size and stoney face is far from inspirational, even when I realized that the oversized Buddha served the same purpose as the undersized figure at the bottom of a nature scroll: the mite before the immensity of the universe. I needed no reminders, certainly not in China, and the overall effect of this stolid statue, chip off the old block though it may be, is far removed from the subtlety of a scroll or a more fluid Buddha. Resting on the banks of the Minjiang River, Da-fu is a Prince of Darkness, a gargantuan King Kong holding court at the edge of civilization. Were I able to climb up to his knee, I half suspect I would find a cute blond under his resting hand.

Buddhism has much in common with Christianity. Siddhartha's birth was also an immaculate conception. The Jesus story is little more than an embellishment of the embellished life of the Enlightened One. We know for certain this

Awakened One existed. Siddhartha, like Christ, was tempted by the devil or Mara the Evil One, but undeterred from his destiny leaves the Bodhi-tree to go about performing miracles, though none as improbable as those attributed to the man/God from Galilee. The major difference in their lives is that Buddha turns his back on a transcendent state with no end – an eternity of bliss or nirvana – to lead the way by simply being. Compared to this sophisticated reality, Christ's dying for our sins is a cop-out, one in that long line of sacrificial lambs that was supposed to give us absolution and negate our responsibility in the scheme of things and the need to make the ultimate sacrifice: our own egos. Carried to its illogical conclusion, the U.S.A.'s Christianity, or inanity, was saying you could have it all.

Siddhartha was born in what is Nepal and became the Buddha in India. But the religion was better suited to the more stoic Chinese than the sanguine Indian with his thousand-and-one gods. Eventually, the fluid Buddha of the subcontinent, as much to do with biology as metaphor, evolved into the heavy statues that became the epitome of epiphany. We were grateful that our monastery was not only out of this world, but also, apparently, not in the *Lonely Planet.*

As a hotel the Lingyun Monastery had likewise been mostly reserved for the corporate crowd and the revered guidebook of the trendy traveler wasn't buying into it. We left the day after the executives arrived, but again it was the little things that turned Mona on, meriting an entry in her diary: *"Secluded corner off courtyard. . . .light rain, lush plants. How exciting for me to observe artist painting in evening. Carvings in stone – a sage like my seal. Bamboo. All those things for me, made it worthwhile."*

The artist was painting what was a very popular subject in the Year of the Monkey, but more so now perhaps. Everywhere we went someone was painting a tiger. Were these artists saying that China has a tiger by the tail? As protests went, they were paper tigers. Or were the artists exulting in their own sense of power.

On the day we went to Leshan to change our travelers

checks, we breakfasted at a small riverside dive just beyond the walls of Mount Lingyun. Mona remarked a guy was "swimming." Not quite, unfortunately. Having fallen into the river, he was carried away by the swift current.

There were boats on the river, but the river was nearing the flood stage and it happened so fast. We were halfway between the ferry landing and the Grand Buddha. In a minute's time the drowning man had disappeared just feet away from Da-fu. The victim's last clear view of this planet must have appeared like a Grand Inquisitor looking down on him in judgment.

Several years later we would learn that tradition had it that Da-fu was made in the hope that it would stimulate Buddha, himself, to calm these turbulent waters. Drowning, as it turned out, was common.

12

Chengdu

July 12. Leaving Leshan on ferry many Israelis. There was Dreadlocks. . . . it had been sometime. . . .he was wearing huge cap; hiding the dreadlocks? A 9:30 bus on other side of river took us to another leaving at 10:00 for the five hour trip to Chengdu. On bus were three Australians and English girls. Crossing our path on and off most of the journey. Getting off bus they each had the Lonely Planet in hand but couldn't get to a hotel. We all stopped to speak with someone who spoke English. Tony asked about best hotel in town. . .they had a strange expression on their faces. At Grand Hotel we met Charlie of CIT and his cohorts. They ran everything from panda sightseeing to pandemonium – but we didn't want to get bamboozled. Charlie got us a cheap ticket for train to Chongqing when Tony carried on about other rip-offs. Tells us he's a Communist – trust him. But they got us anyway, 685 yuan each for "Love Boat" down Yangtze. It was difficult trying to figure out how they were going to get you. They were two steps ahead, especially when hot and tired. So I left China without seeing a panda – without seeing Beijing and what I truly wanted to see, Suzhou and Hangzhou. Went on wild-goose chase. . . .raining. Soaked, stopped in restaurant on other side of city just off the river – it was nice, and such a good feeling just sitting, resting, hot soup. Silence. I didn't mind being wet.   Mona

You can understand why the little things went a long way. I remember well that nightmarish day of being in and out of the rain, trying desperately, in an airline office, to book her passage on a flight to Hong Kong – before she was stranded somewhere. But we could only make reservations from whence we departed, and we didn't know when and where that time would come or where I was going after we arrived. We were still shooting for Suzhou and a marvelous departure point but it was not to be. . . .

With a two thousand-year history and a dam as old, Chengdu was another one of those Chinese cities that had some things worth seeing, and buying, like embroidery. But it just was not worth the bother with so many manic miles in between. So I can't tell you about Wangjianglou Park, which we may have passed on a local bus. But a few blocks away from the Grand Hotel there is a street where almost every stall displayed these vests so popular with fly fishermen in the States. In China the many pocketed vest is used as protection against anglers of another kind.

The road to Chengdu was flooded and one hell of a traffic jam. The Australian girls were taken aback by my interest in the best hotel in town.

Was I crazy? Deserting the ship, or some kind of imposter? Well, all of that, but dropping by a luxury hotel had also long been one of my survival tools. A break from the journey, a watering hole, a voice in the wilderness where information in English is available. In the old days after a long trip, English was the sound of music – before it became the lingua franca. I never prefer a ritzy joint over something rustic in the historic part of town, but sacking out in some dump in the heart of a sprawling city because it is de rigeur doesn't wash either. Of course, if you don't have the price of a decent room, you can't squeeze blood from a cliché – and yet I could not help feeling that the "Survival Kit" that dictated the group's every move was obsessed with being politically correct and that many of these survivors had passed up affordable hotels in favor of holes in the wall. The long and short of it is that our necessary pause in an island of opulence became for us another monastery at a price the girls could afford had they also been traveling with Charlie – and had gotten a writer's discount. Or was it a student's discount.

We parted company outside the bus station, never to

see the distressed damsels again, the last of the southwest China group swallowed up by Chengdu. And thus we began our trek to the Grand Hotel. But ours was not the grandest entrance, and though I may have seemed like I belonged in the thatched hut of Du Fu at the edge of town, something the cat dragged in from the Tang dynasty, we were the right colors, green as in dollars and white as in the Golden West, a most welcome addition where Americans are rare. The Grand could have been the best hotel between Wuhan and Tehran, yet I would have much preferred the hut of the hermit poet if only to be away from the noise. In our condition we settled for the best, spending the better part of a day and a half locked in our room. I could not bear looking for another hotel and just wanted to be on a boat. Ha! Oh, how I pined for that evergreen time of Du Fu, ensconced in his bamboo forest. Oddly enough the sage had dreamt of such a place as this, a glittering shelter, when he found himself without a roof over his head. My soul was with the poet, but my heart was with Marco Polo.

"Having traveled these twenty stages through a mountainous country, you reach a plain on the borders of Manzi. Here there is a district named Sin-din-fu (Chengdu), which is also the name of its capital, a large and noble city, formerly the seat of many rich and powerful kings.... The city is watered by many large streams, which, descending from distant mountains, flow around and pass through a variety of directions. These rivers range from a half mile in width to two hundred paces, and are very deep. A great bridge crosses one of these rivers within the city. It has on each side a row of marble pillars which support a roof constructed of wood, ornamented with painting of a red color, and covered with tiles. Throughout the whole length also there are neat compartments and shops, where all sorts of trades are carried on. One of the buildings, larger than the rest, is occupied by the officers who collect duties and toll from those who pass over the bridge. It is said his Majesty (the Great Khan) receives daily the sum of a hundred bezants of gold.

"These rivers, uniting below the city, contribute to form the mighty river called the Kiang (Yangtze), whose course, before it empties into the ocean, amounts to a hundred days's journey. On *these rivers and in the vicinity are many towns and fortified places, and numerous vessels in which large quantities of merchandise are transported to and from the city.*

13

Last Train to the Coast

July 15. Chongqing. I thought I'd seen the last of the iron cockroaches. It was not to be. Luckily we met a Chinese girl, an English teacher (we often met teachers or students studying to be English teachers) on the train. They always seemed happy to practice conversation. She said it was rare to have a westerner teaching – conditions always poor. They didn't stay long. She offered us peaches. We mentioned the train being crowded; she said it was not. Wait. The train became more and more crowded at each stop. Difficult getting through to toilet – yet they managed to get through. Hordes of women selling uncovered meat, peanuts and a variety of garbage which ended up on floor along with spit, bones and vomit. I wondered how any more people could possibly get on – but they did. Finally the windows had to be closed – they were coming through the windows. The teacher said they would pull watches from your wrist or anything they could get hold of. I think most just wanted to get on train any way they could. Tony said passengers ride on top in India. Two boys watched our every move. Squeezed onto our small hard seats. One on each side of us. Teacher had briefcase chained to luggage rack. Half-hour before our stop, people standing over us, practically on top of us waiting for our seats. We had to stand in the aisle, it seemed forever, in order to get off the train at Chongqing. Stuck near the toilet – stench in the heat was sickening. It was one of the most frightening situations I have ever experienced. We got off with teacher. Met by friend. Miracle. Mobs and mobs of people kept piling on the train, and as we walked away they kept on coming – it never ended – until finally it was all out of our view. We climbed hill and the never *ending steps in the heat until I was ready to faint. Tony could hardly carry my backpack but I could not, and I didn't care what happened at this point. I was so dry. When we reached the top, the teacher's friend bought drinks. They took two buses with us to hotel and were on their way. Angels.*

Mona

And not surprisingly. The province of Sichuan is known as the "Heavenly Kingdom" and if Chengdu is its "pearl" Chongqing was our oyster. What we needed was a scallop – symbol for the patron saint of travelers.

What can I add to Mona's diary? She was becoming an expert on Chinese trains. But maybe losing track of time. Mona had us arriving in Chongqing on the 15th of July, yet our registration card from the Chung King Hotel has us coming and going on the 14th and 15th. The card also strongly advised us to use the safe-deposit box. Even the exterior of the Chung King indicated this was a place for safekeeping. The hotel looked like a cement Fort Knox, a multi-storied mausoleum that held the high ground. It would be a faceless fortress if the Chunky hotel didn't have all the earmarks of Stalin and the triumph of Communism over the Nationalists. Internationally. The owners were in Hong Kong. At midnight with one foot in the grave, it looked great.

Chongqing, named for the enthronement of Zhao Zhun of the South Song dynasty, means double celebration, but I'll be forgiven if it came to mean double-cross when we boarded our Love Boat. Little was left of what became the Nationalist stronghold the Japanese flattened. Rivers defined this city. Before becoming a Double Celebration, Chong King (Chongqing) was simply Yu, the ancient name of the Jialing River. Although pegged the "Foggy Capital" for its weather, Chongqing was for us more like Hong Kong than Hong Kong – without the skyscrapers and sampans.

A beautiful, sunny day, and with our boat tickets in hand, we followed a winding lane and steep stairs to a riverside stall. Chow. Not a sign of the dark, sooty city, the largest in southwest China that writers complain about. Another lane, or rather alleyway, took us to a loading area behind the docks. There is a road out of this cul-de-sac, but narrow steps took us to a walkway just above the Jialing River. I wondered if the Japanese bombs missed this ancient alley flanked by tiny houses, tucked under the maddening streets above us. A bridge spans the river at the beginning of the peninsular, but near to where the Jialing River is swallowed up by the Yangtze, a cable is strung across opposite promontories. The cable car does not look promising. But it is far enough away and the growing haze distances this sign of the times even more, allowing the rivers to hold sway.

Houses clung to the hillside for dear life. Enchanted by our unexpected find but getting hot, we entered a doorway guarded by an old man. We sat down and ordered tea, but drew a blank from the venerable figure. The old man just stared. Cha, cha, I repeated and was finally understood. Strange place, I thought, reminiscent of McSorely's Ale House off the Bowery. Crammed with sundry memorabilia, it could pass for a mad collector's attic – and, in fact, there was a storage space above us. I was struck by a tricycle. This eatery was so unlike the uninviting places we had visited on the wrong side of the tracks. In this cluttered ambience, I felt very much at home – as I should have. But the hoary guy was probably used to being pushed around, and while somewhat confused, didn't much mind that we had come by for tea.

We left our host's house to the smiles of knowing neighbors. Time for something stronger, we stopped by a kind of general store with tables in the rear. I reached out and touched a tree that grew out from under us. The rickety floor extended beyond the cliff. We had fallen into a tropical backwater of another time and place. Elevation aside, Manaus came to mind. That oceanic feeling hundreds of miles from the ocean, that teeming port life in a bucolic backwater that leaves you with the strange sense you are stuck in the middle of nowhere. Involuntarily, I reached for our tickets.

The waterfront brings out the sailor in me – and called for a beer. I was taken by surprise, the only place I wanted to be taken. . . . quietly. This was the difference between seduction and being driven to drink. But this was apparently the beginning of the end of my Orient Express and I had little to show for my grand drunk tour beyond a slew of exotic beer labels. Memories of people climbing mountains of coal, isles of pines in a sea of rice paddies. . .and this going around in circles, leading to a padded cell. The round-trip travel that interested me was going around the world – the world was only so large and happened to be round and I had no choice but to end up where I started, if I went as far as I wanted.

Although looking forward to our cruise, we were going in the wrong direction. The true adventure takes you up the river, back to true beginnings – and endings, like the salmon seeking the life-giving source and the last hurrah. You can say that about the ocean, but I'll leave that to yesterday and the billions of people who populate the shores of that vast, faceless dumping ground – I need a place I can get my teeth into. I was not looking forward to visiting Beijing. I wanted to see the city, but I could no longer tolerate all that sound and fury signifying insanity, and it looked like I would end up there.

A trip down the river is bound to be anticlimactic, especially after you've seen a bit of it – and so it is with the climb down the mountain. The joy is in the ascension. When Mona and I sailed up the Nile, we were in the wake of explorers who could just as well have been on a pilgrimage. Similarly, a journey up the Ganges River takes the traveler to a spiritual source, where you are born again. It is downstream where people are cremated. You can't sail to the actual source, but the Upper Nile River was for me the ultimate metaphor for the hazards of the spiritual quest. For days we were lost in that maze known as the Great Sudd, a sea of papyrus that seemed without end. Most seekers simply get lost in books or crooks (gurus). The Nile was my river of no return because I was never again the same. Which is to say, I am a fish out of water.

14

Yangtze Love Boat

July 16?. Love Boat #2 (as in poo). Embarked from Jiangyu #5 for Wuhan. An old ferry carrying mostly Chinese passengers. (Tony said they couldn't get aboard the last train to the coast.) A three-day-two-night journey. We were lucky to have an outside cabin – many second class cabins (there are no firsts) are inside. Ours at the end of row of tiny cubicles – fenced off from dormitory class. On one side our neighbor was a chicken for a while, until she got off or was eaten. Our neighbors on the other side, three cabins before us, scientists connected with space exploration – they had been to the States, commenting that our government paid for their trip and a stay of two weeks at the Helmsley in Washington. Told not to wander around in evening because of crime. They had plenty of watermelon, never stopped eating, never offered us anything. We talked to a Swede we met at ticket office. He was sharing cabin with spooky American. White guy. Said he had been living in Switzerland. Something to do with an orchestra in Singapore. Conductor? Tony remarked that he was with CIA or had one Singapore Sling too many. Our Chinese neighbors showed us the ropes – and never showed up at the restaurant again. They, like the Swede, had a tin cup for instant noodles (they had uncooked noodles packed away; add hot water). Swede had been to China before and decided this was the best way to go. Tony says he's a Yangtze noodle dandy. Singapore Sling ate luxury class with Mr. & Mrs. Malaysia. This restaurant only touch of class on entire tub. Two German ladies went third class or fourth and spent all their time in our lounge. Off limits, but I couldn't blame them. A horror getting through to the restaurant – serving all classes. Walk-

ing between people sprawled all over deck – hot and sweaty. The toilets. We disembarked twice. The first time with the scientists – not in the Swede's guidebook so he wasn't going. Mr. S. Sling said he went but I never saw him. "Palace of Hell" worthwhile. Heaven compared to boat. Paintings of monkeys in one hall; seemed to be ruling a kingdom. I thought of the movie "Planet of the Apes." Tony bought bananas at the next stop. Terrible argument. But the Gorges outweighed all the craziness – including the "coffee."

Mona

The day was gray when we left Chongqing and the complete picture was not as picturesque as the village life along the embankments, the alleyways and the quais of the Jialing River. The Chaotianmen Port was a jungle of derricks and the more trafficked Yangtze waterfront had a junkyard look about it – with nothing as graceful as a junk to relieve a scene rendered grim by the grime. Gazing skyward I imagined looking upon Loquat Hill with those renown teahouses I never saw. I may have seen Red Crag Village, the former resident of Premier Chou En-lai, but no one seemed to be pushing that attraction and I could not even find it on my map. The combination brochure was obviously a guide to what was politically correct. Like the American Indians, the Ba "Nationality" seemed more popular dead than alive. Two of their graveyards are shown to be just outside Chongqing. The "City of Achievements" is relatively near to the "New Stone Age Ruins," – which did not augur well for the dam. But the last thing I wanted was a history lesson when I was about to sail through that heart of darkness, belly of the beast, known as the Yangtze Gorges.

    Abandoned pagodas commanding the palisades once kept the dragons at bay. Evidently, not all dragons were benevolent. Minutes later Chongqing was under a blanket of mist and we were sailing through a countryside that often ended abruptly at the water's edge. And then looming like an apparition above the north shore, Fengdu, "The Ghost City." Popular because of its "Palace of Hell," the ghostly city is a quasi-gateway to the deepening gorges and a metaphor for what to many has been a river of no return. The construction of the Gezhou

Dam in the 1970s and 1980s has lessened the threat of a Yangtze that could populate the planet with ghosts, but this percolating "coffee" with the swirling styrofoam was still a drink to be reckoned with as the day of the flood and the tricky currents is not over. But "before liberation, the four disasters, flood, waterlogging, drought and schistosomiasis, haunted the Changjiang River Valley." *(From the transportation map for touring Changjiang.)* Changjiang = Yangtze.

Appropriately a city devoted to the afterlife, prepared today's eastbound traveler for the perils that lie ahead. The "Palace of Hell" is what our tickets read in English, but this could be a mistranslation for shock and schlock value. This was limbo – which can be hell – of grotesque faces of man and beast. Later, I found a "Five Hundred Million" hell bank note, issued in "Hell." Its value was written in English and Chinese.

Fengdu itself is a lively town that stretches from the river to the foot of Mount Ming and the nether world of the seventy-five temples that grow progressively bizarre with altitude. Most of the Tang temples seemed to concentrate on the fates of those who don't quite make it to heaven.

Some of the more popular hells or halls, based on legends of the nether world, are the "Pass of the Ghost," the "Dividing Line of the Real World and Nether World" (which would seem like redundant temples) and the "Hall of the Ghost and the Hall of Ox Demons." The ox was the symbol for the demon ego. It's all nothing less than the Fun House in Coney Island. Or is that the House of Horrors – in America, redundant temples. Also a barrel of monkeys is the Tang mural that reminded Mona of the "Planet of the Apes."

It isn't all monkeyshines or maybe it is. In the Chinese zodiac the monkey represents an intelligent, enthusiastic achiever. People born in the Year of Monkey are able to influence dragons. But what the hell were these halls all about? The "Pass of the Ghost"....we were still in what was known as Thebeth during the Tang period. Had Tibetan Buddhism's concept of the Bardo seeped through Chinese legends unbound by dynasties? Is the "Palace of Hell" trying to tell us this: "I shall give thee the mystery of this doctrine; the which shall profit thee greatly to the beginning of ghostly health, and to a stable fundament of all virtues." *(From Orologium Saptientiae.)*

I was struck by a graphic depiction of hell: it was a flood. I had been toying around with the idea of writing a book and already the title "Hell and High Water" seemed to fit the bill, but now I could see in the ghostly lexicon writ large, the handwriting on the wall horribly pictured, that I was being redundant. On the Yangtze and the Indus Rivers, high water was hell. Fire is not the symbol of damnation but of redemption.

On the Yangtze, in the future, man would be doing most of the flooding, as usual creating his own hell. The "Three Gorges Project," as it becomes a reality, will have far-reaching environmental and archeological consequences. Dai Qing, a Chinese journalist, has gone to jail for protesting the building of the dam and killing two birds with one stone by reciting a Chinese proverb: *"It is even more dangerous to silence the people than to build a dam."*

For Mona and me the dam is déjà vu. We saw what the Aswan Dam has done to the Nile and the people who lived along its banks. As in Egypt, with Abdul Simbul, the Chinese dam will require that an important temple, like the people in the area, be relocated. Ultimately – new power generated not withstanding – the wholesale dislocation was deemed a failure.

Independent experts predict the same disaster for the Chinese, but on a scale so much larger than the damage done to Egypt. Sure to disappear with the damming, if they haven't already, are the white-finned dolphin and the Chinese alligator. The Changjiang River was home to more than three hundred species. What will happen to those fishermen patiently dipping their nets into the flow? (As in India, the nets are suspended from a pole.) To the Chinese leadership the electricity that will be generated is the lit candle replacing the cursing of the darkness, but as zero hour (long past) approaches the archeologists from around the world are descending upon the gorges as if the origins of civilization itself are about to go down the drain.

"Not to worry," said the Director of the Hubei Tourist Bureau in the *China Daily,* "a higher river will create new scenic spots."

Yangtze Love Boat

And the world's largest dam would do something for the ego of the deceased Deng and those who have come in his wake. As the nonsense about the Great Wall being visible from space evaporates, the government is looking for a replacement. The dam will create a 375-mile long reservoir, but the Director of the Hubei Tourist Bureau neglected to add that this artificial lake will be unnavigable because of increased sediment in an already very muddy river. Hence, an unprecedented number of tourists flocked, floated, to the Three Gorges in the Year of the Monkey to be on hand for the last hurrah. Yet a best-selling *New York Times* journalist doesn't know what all the fuss is about. He suggests seeing the terra cotta soldiers in Xian instead.

With sheer cliffs closing in on us, mountains rising ever higher, it was as if we were being entombed in the very heart of China.

But the context is everything and the magnificence of this grand canyon was overshadowed by the specks at the bottom of the scroll. While many paintings are subverted by their frames, this picture was spoiled because of the viewers. I could have been in an open can of sardines careening down the Love Canal, when this should have been the way to transcendence – immersion in the moment. This was something to meditate upon for days without end and I had only this fleeting glimpse of the godhead, ten thousand Grand Buddhas shaped by the convulsing planet.

If you can't beat them, join them. Steeped in my grand funk, I saddled up to a chunky Red Army officer standing by the railing. I felt as I had under the foot of the Grand Buddha. This guy had that same, dare I say it, inscrutable expression. But I was literally wilting away while he in his gyrene-green and red uniform was as cool as the jolly green giant, even cracking a smile when Mona pointed the camera in our direction. Our photo projects the classic juxtaposition of East and West, one cool as a cucumber, impervious to distractions like heat; the other, a burning ember, brain cells gone up in smoke. My mostly liquid diet was not helping. Instant "coffee," instant dysentery. My cup of mud was the poorly filtered Yangtze.

Unraveling on the Old Silk Road

Full moon or monsoon, I've always been like a body of water played upon by the wind – a reflection of outside forces. My sinking feeling reflected that sinkhole that had swallowed our ship, soon to be coughed up in the boring boondocks. I had that harried, hari-kari mien of one on a one-way trip.

Anticipating the downhill ride that awaited us, I felt the same way when our Nile journey was over. And the spirit of Africa loomed large in these gorges (though the scenery could not be more different). Earlier in the century, on the Yangtze, there was that same elemental response to the elements, with everybody getting into the act to propitiate the ever threatening forces of nature. At a time when passengers and crew were steeped in superstition and engines were rare, a passage through the gorges was accompanied by wild dancing and the beating of drums, a fearful entrance into a Palace of Hell.

Swiftly drifting downriver on a junk was like a ride on a trackless roller coaster, but the journey upstream was a grueling, hell of a long haul where man was the preferred beast of burden, literally pulling anything that floated against the current, often clinging to the cliffs for dear life. Slavery existed in these parts until the Communist takeover.

No sooner had we emerged from the gorges, than the locks of the Gezhouba Dam opened. Our descent into a lower Yangtze revealed that the tamed beast is far worse than the wild one. The difference between the harnessed horse and the stallion. Yichang, our next port of call, was already upon us, but I wanted nothing more than to stay put and digest the Gorges, and perusing my map to fathom what I had just seen. Not so easy. The Gorge of Liver and Lungs was one of the last highlights. . .how about the Gorge of Sword and Books? The only recognizable site was the one to be flooded, the temple of Zhang Fei, a famous general of the Shu Kingdom revered for his fortitude and forthrightness. It figures.

By the afternoon of the following day, we could have been approaching the Great Sudd, a wide expanse of sea with none of the upper river ferocity that had dogged us since Dukou. Water buffalo like hippos were grazing in the blazing sun in the distance, the only sign of life on an undefined horizon known as the "oven." The earthen color had been baked out of a river indistinguishable from an ashen sky, and soon it was clear we had sailed out of the belly of the beast into the sultry mouth of the Amazon.

We were restless, but not enough to go ashore at the next port of call. I usually take liberties aboard a ship, but was too much at sea with myself, too disoriented to rise above my mal de mer and the galley life aboard the #2. I had also been discouraged from being out-of-bounds by the military-like regulations and restrictive life aboard trains or anyplace under the control of the government – which, when push comes to shove, is the Red Army. But once underway, we roamed around topside, in what seemed to be the officers' quarters. Pausing before a ladder (stairway) leading to the roof and the beckoning sky above. Little of this ferry did not have a deck above it – including this highest rung of the occupied ladder. An out-of-uniform officer materialized from behind a clothesline. We were overwhelmed when permission was granted to get above it all.

The boons and cranes, the iron works and warehouses fade from memory and I only recall a Yangtze bridge flanked by the Turtle Mountain and the Yellow Crane Tower – but the Turtle supports Wuhan's answer to the Eiffel Tower – spelt *K E N T.* The scientist, knowing how I felt about this nouveau pagoda, would only say that the government got a pretty penny for it and that Kent, like the cigarette it was selling, was suckered. Somewhere between Kant and Kent was the real China.

But there were no passengers up here, above the #2's bridge, and as the crew began to hose down the roof of our love boat, we thought this was heaven compared to what was, wistful about what might have been. But *"Tis as inevitable for life to over flow in sorrow as for the waters to flow to the east."* (Tz'u poem of Li Yu from Five Dynasties.)

15

Hankou

Heaven reigns but does not rule. *When it reigns, it pours.*
Confucius Cammarata

July 18. Wuhan. We arrived about 6:30PM. The Chinese scientist had his driver take us directly to a hotel. He said the best. Telling us on the way how important the three of them are. Ticket to Hong Kong my immediate concern. Hotel not changing money so we moved. I don't know how the hotels are in same category. I guess they pay off officials. Nightmare finding open ticket office. They couldn't change money because it was Saturday, the bank wouldn't change either. Ticket office closing at 11:30. While filling out info at new hotel, a well-dressed Chinese guy – Bermuda shorts, sun glasses, the entire get-up (wondering afterwards who put him together) standing next to me. Didn't realize he was watching me fill out registration. Came into elevator with us. Asked where we were from as nonchalantly as if he were another tourist. Followed us down hall and stopped at our door saying he was a coin collector. Showed us his scrap book. We told him we were very tired – no time and would see him later. What was his room number? He said he was not staying in the hotel and could not come back. We must have been crazy – we were! – but also in the back of our mind we wanted to make some extra money, everyone doing it in orbit of Lonely Planet. We were "crazy Americans" because we didn't change money on the black market. Tony said the market came to us. He gave me a lot for my Kennedy half dollar – he was so sharp to spot another one in my change purse (I didn't remember having *it). I had brought them with me to give as gifts, along with the chewing gum, which only I consumed. (Haven't chewed gum since I was a child.) I finally got my ticket and we moved a third time – Qingchuan Hotel. Between river and Tortoise Hill, trees, famous Qing Chuan Pavillion below. We can see the graceful Yellow Crane, but no desire to visit. Tony as spunky as a turtle, just wants to look beyond the river and watch CNN. We took a walk through village and it was very strange – everyone friendly, smiling – what I expected China would be like. . . .*   Mona

The Passenger Terminal in Wuhan's port of Hankou is world-class, especially when compared to the floating docks of Chongqing. Actually, it is out of this world because it accomplishes what airports do in most countries. Wuhan is a city of 8,000,000, the New York-to-be on the Yangtze (and vice versa).

    I suspect that the lift our shipmate gave us to the Jianghan was as much for his benefit as ours. As typical Americans, we would be impressed with a chauffeur-driven car. I don't know how his colleagues got out to the university; they were staying in the wilds of Wuchang.

    The Jianghan Hotel also came as a surprise – like the opera house in Manaus, a bit of Europe so far up the river. Wuhan, in the middle of the Middle Kingdom, may be the "Passageway to the nine provinces" and the capital of Hubei, but the candlelight wasn't meant to be romantic. The Jianghan was famous for its power failures, and was catering to the colonial powers at the turn-of-the-century when it was named the Ming, and Dr. Sun Yat-sen was leading his revolution on the other side of the river.

    Wuhan has been around since the Neolithic Age, but most Americans learn about the city through an adoption agency, as well as a travel agency. The tri-city's many orphanages have become a virtual cottage industry. Baby makes three. The government makes a lot of money and the hotels become testing grounds, nesting grounds, as prospective parents must care for the tots, sometimes for as long as three weeks, while their papers are processed.

    I can not be certain why we left our own moldering nest,

all that roomy elegance gone to seed, for the smaller Xuan Gong Hotel, but Mona seemed to know. It was centrally located and cheaper, but after we had purchased our tickets out of Wuhan, we realized we had enough to splurge – if I were to make my way to Beijing from Xian to where I would fly. I had no desire to be up in the air, but figured that if I were going to be in an airport to see Mona off, it would be too much of a comedown to go back to the old grind without Sancho taking some of the heat. Nor can I be sure why I chose Xian when I had my fill of war games. But I do know why. Xian was the only destination between Wuhan and Beijing (relatively speaking) not booked for the day of Mona's departure for Hong Kong. I was really playing darts. Playing roulette. Russian roulette, when you fly in China.

More than any desire to live in style for a few days, was our need to have a view of the river – from the proper altitude. This amounted to stopping the world and getting off. I like a Manhattan, a mixed town in the U.S., but I want China to be China (as seen on a scroll) and enough was enough. Pickpocket artists were so commonplace that Mona had neglected to mention yet another excursion or rather exploratory venture into my trousers. I wonder if the manager of the Xuan Gong had arranged for the coin collector to follow us to our room – and set us up at the hoodlum hangout in Hangkou.

He had recommended a "nice" restaurant. It was a streamlined affair with foreign beer at Paris prices, but evidently the guidebooks were telling the foreigners to go elsewhere. We were the only ones who had not gotten the message, which would be okay except that this was no place for any misunderstanding about the check. Nobody spoke English or any other language I threw at them and we left while I still had my shirt on my back.

We left the jet set bistro for something down-to-earth, crash-landing in an airy eatery – suitable for a quick getaway. Mona was wondering why a boy with no food before him, sitting at a nearly empty table, was practically leaning on me. Ha! I turned to the waif's table and could have grabbed him, but while preoccupied with what to do with the young thief, somebody more experienced could have ripped me off. He got nothing, so I let this curious visitor exit as casually as if his hands had been in his own pocket.

Young men hanging around banks waylaying foreigners foolish enough to make legal transactions provided overwhelming proof these illegal money changers enjoyed police protection – as well as German beer. I don't think these flighty fellows actually go into banks, but the sidewalks outside are a virtual gauntlet for any passerby who looks like he or she might be carrying dollars. And carrying our backpacks on our way to the Qingchuan Hotel was a sure sign we were ready to do business.

An old fellow who gave us directions warned us about speaking to young men. They can't be trusted, he said. He had been taught English by missionaries and seemed to recall his school days fondly. We thought what a great opportunity to learn what Wuhan was like before the Cultural Revolution, but our minds were set on getting out of Hankou as quickly as possible, passing up yet another golden opportunity because we were objects in motion.

Taking a bus to the Qingchuan Hotel was easier said than done, especially when the skies opened up at the transfer point, and we end up taking a pedicab, but not before we tried to hone in on the Kent Tower when the buses as well as the rain had stopped running. It was at this point that Mona looked upon the most "beautiful" melon she had ever seen and damn near went bananas when I would not stop to buy it, but my need to get off the street – we had even attempted to cut through Turtle Mountain Park – was greater than my concern for her welfare or my own thirst. I was driven – but never it seemed by a taxi. Not with four wheels, anyway. And it was not simply a question of having been taken for one ride too many and not being able to relax. It's just so out of character for the true traveler.

But at that moment, Mona was summing up my style with one word, which sounded like a bird. We were sloshing through the puddles of a dirt road in the back of a pedicab bound for the Qingchuan Hotel. Mona kept repeating that it was such a beautiful melon. Not buying that fruit was one of my biggest regrets. Little things mean a lot.

> *If rim and spoke and hum were not*
> *Where would be the chariot?*
> *Who will prefer the jingle of jade pendants if*
> *He once has heard stone growing in a cliff!*
>
> Laotzu

16

Palace of Heaven

Broad, broad
  through the country flow the nine tributaries
Deep, deep
  from north to south cuts a line.
Blurred in the blue haze of the rain and mist
The Snake and Tortoise Hills tower above the water...
In wine I drink a pledge to the surging torrent.
The tide of my heart rises as high as the waves.
                    From Mao's Yellow Crane Tower

The village, tucked under the shell of the Tortoise and wedged between the Hanjiang and Chiangjiang, was settled by the Han people. Arriving in this cradle of civilization on the rivers was almost like coming full circle, as we were on the same longitude as the White Swan in Canton. But our room with a wider panorama was at the desired altitude just as we were on a higher latitude. And if we had not journeyed far enough north to suit my overheated psyche, I had only to look upon that menthol cool tower atop the Tortoise – which also added that necessary touch of reality to assure me I was still in China and had not died and gone to heaven.

Thanking my lucky stars as we entered our room, I joked about our television having CNN as if I were asking for the moon and not budging, but sure enough we were connected to the outside world and cable became my umbilical cord – after I ate a huge plate of peanut butter and noodles with Mona. For peanuts. Mona went wild. I went.

Who knows what tipped the scales, though there is no

denying I used one greasy chopstick too many, in one smoke-filled room too many. It was the chopstick that broke the camel's back, but it was my lungs that were really bothering me.

Off the lobby of the Qingchuan Hotel is a doctor's office. When it was established that I had a bad cough, worse than anything I ever had, including pneumonia and dysentery, the doctor could only ask what else was new? He tried to sell me some pills. The lobby itself, when I was not upstairs, became my waiting room. For whom? Godot, the flight out of here? But I wasn't complaining. The sparkling lobby was like a biblical version of heaven, replete with a misty mural of the Three Gorges and bureaucratic cherubs floating about with their perennial jars of tea. Glittering pillars reaching for the stars heightened the effect of paradise – the name of the cruise ship that dropped anchor at the hotel's dock.

Wheeling and dealing Americans had probably seen better, if they saw at all. At the Information Desk a seasoned American was chewing out a clerk, promising heads would roll because someone, the competition I presume, was permitted to listen in on his high-powered conversation. The culture that Mao could not erase with his whacky "Revolution" will be washed away by flooding from the dam and these Americans downriver getting in on the first floor. The Yellow Crane Tower across the river was one of the "olds" that the Chairman demolished when the Long March developed into a power trip and egomania ruled the waves. Had he any idea, killing the thing he loved, that he would murder what he memorialized, literally tossing out the cradle with the baby and the bathwater?

Kent, lighting up the way, was the beacon that would bring home the bacon.

Returning to my room, I was an elephant finding a suitable place to die. Maybe I was simply ready to be ill – the only way I could get off the treadmill, as my revved up engine could not idle and I had to break down if I was going to go on. But a wider view shows that I was also like one of those caged birds hanging from trees we saw in the Canton Park. They were a long way from home and their ancient owners giving the birds some air might take them here and there, but they were still in a cage. China was a very large cage, yet I was not free.

Endlessly, I looked out my window at the Yangtze, the depressing haze from the oven around it. As a fish out of water, I've eluded the Information Net, kept my head, but global headhunters have shrunken the earth to the size of an informed insane asylum. Yet my despair ran deeper than that. I had enjoyed an intimacy with Mother Earth only experienced by those who have gone a long way slowly, and able to account for every varied mile of a journey to get a true sense of just how small our planet really is – beyond the clichés, anticlimax and the feeling that comes with a jet to a far corner. And it is nothing to celebrate, today.

I wanted to return to Marco Polo's time, when the Yangtze was a floating market festooned with the trappings of trade and a passageway for junks laden with pekoe bound for the China Seas. And it seemed you could see forever.

Old soldiers fade away but sailors and less sanguine travelers find other worlds to conquer, with love. The conquest becomes a quest for meaning, and no one can doubt I have been to the frontiers of inner space, but still the nagging knowledge that the world was not boundless affected me in the manner of mortality. The feelings of loss, the limits of the round-trip from infancy to senility, the battering of the I, in the batting of an eye. Aye, yae, yae. The I of the storm.

A very long journey is a kind of immortality as we go beyond the bounds of self – and obviously I could not get far enough away from myself and the jumble and jungle of my roots, though liberation is in direct proportion to distance. A surface reason may have put me on the road, but my love for the boundless voyage springs from that fountain of youth we call the subconscious or the collective memory and stems from the time when we were all nomads and the love of wandering was necessary to our survival, and a trackless journey could take centuries. Endless cups of tea, perhaps, transported me to Morocco.

My trip with majun, a mix of hashish, dates and nuts, came to mind, or what's left of it, and may put all of the above into perspective. This tasty dish is a regular breakfast cereal of "champions" with a kick like a rocket that sent me into space in a manner beyond words and the experience of few living, but the Moroccan who bought the majun had a telling word for his own celestial encounter: "Sputnick." The Soviet spacecraft that made history a few years earlier, he was trying to tell me, provided a similiar voyage, but I don't think that I can relate the power and glory of my own story – until I began to sputter and, like Icarus flying too near the sun, fell into the sea. I had become unglued.

If ever I left a part of me in another country or space itself, it was on that late afternoon in May, the longest day in Marrakech, that a Rolling Stone got satisfaction – but more than he bargained for. It is taking me a lifetime to digest that bowl of majun, and the nearest known experience to my star trek that I'm aware of is the near-death one being bandied about on bestseller lists, but the bird's-eye view of earth I have come away with can only be likened to an astronaut's and those few navigators with the right stuff who have seen that it is indeed a lonely planet, in need of a survival kit that reads like Lao Tzu. (Pinning our hopes on living in space is simply escape and the antiseptic stuff of dreamers and big business preparing us for a plastic future on a luney planet.)

> *These are the four amplitudes of the universe*
> *And a fit man is one of them:*
> *Man rounding the way of the earth*
> *Earth rounding the way of heaven,*
> *Heaven rounding the way of life*
> *Till the circle is full...*
>
> *One who has a man's wings*
> *And a woman's also*
> *Is in himself a womb of the world,*
> *And, being a womb of the world,*
> *Continuously, endlessly,*
> *Gives birth...*
> *And, being a valley of the world,*
> *Continuously, endlessly*
> *Conducts the one source....*
>
> Lao Tzu

Palace of Heaven

And endlessly flowed the "Long River," 2700 miles from its source to the sea, and my own streams of consciousness like the Yangtze's seven hundred tributaries contributing to the flow. But my metamorphosis from Luney Tunes to Lao Tzu could only be accomplished by swimming against the current — for this is the only way we salmon may lay our eggs.

To mix my metaphors, I had undergone the seventy-two metamorphoses of the Monkey King in his "Pilgramage to the West," before storming the gates of the "Palace of Heaven" — which is also the Palace of Hell. The monkeyshines of this Chinese classic are based on the Western Travels of the seventh century reformer monk, Hsuan Tsang. Not in a million years could I dream I was headed his way. And like the earlier pilgrim be arrested by the authorities in China's far west.

Or following in the steps of Lao Tzu, fed up with the ways of men, going off into the desert — in his case, to die. According to legend, a gatekeeper in northwestern China persuaded Lao Tzu to write down his poetry for posterity, instead. I would like to think that the old Gatekeeper in the sky convinced me to put pen to paper for the same reason.

17

Interrupted Journey

> *But eternity is his who goes straight round the circle,*
> *Foundation is his who can feel beyond touch,*
> *Harmony is his who can hear beyond sound,*
> *Pattern is his who can see beyond shape:*
> *Life is his who can tell beyond words*
> *Fulfillment of the unfilled.*
>
> Lao Tzu

With a little prodding Mona managed to get me out of the hotel and up the Tortoise Hill. My ever romantic wife could not accept so dismal an ending to what was to have been a made-for-television journey. Ha. Well, at least not this lingering, malingering woe is me in Wuhan. And so I made this gallant effort for old time's sake for a Sancho who had been pretty much through the mill with me – even if she had enough sense not to tilt at it. Granted, the Kent Tower was not the Yellow Crane, even if it had some tobacco stains, but it would have to do and the winding road seemed like an appropriate end to our China journey.

    The slow going gave me the opportunity to search out those smiling faces we had seen the other day, but the mask had fallen and all we saw was the old face of China. Maybe we were too far from the cozy enclave between the rivers for a friendly show, as the foreign tourists and those who catered to them were not trekking up to the Tower. In the village we could pass for a couple in the market for a baby.

    We noticed more bare-bottomed children in Wuhan than in the rest of China. Actually, pants without backsides. It was a lot less messy, but why not let the little tykes go naked instead of going about half-assed, as we used to say. And yet anybody preparing to adopt a child was required to change diapers. Was it because foreigners could afford to?

After my torturous crawl up the snaking road, I was ready to do a Kent commercial: a walking Surgeon General's Warning. And there it was looming high above us, the Kent television antenna. Our admission to the belle tour was three times what the Chinese pay, unless they were overseas Chinese who pay a little more than their mainland relatives. We opted for an empty restaurant nearby, that, like us, had seen better days and probably the likes of Chiang K'ai-shek. Who cares?

Chiang's only poetry came from the barrel of a gun and should be relegated to the dustbin of hysteria, and yet the monumental "Timetables of History" ignores Mao, while treating the Generalissimo as the major player in twentieth century China. That is akin to summing up America but ignoring Lincoln while expounding on a Reagan – which is why we got stuck with him in the first place.

We must show history its proper respect by rewriting it. The sixties was more objective about Mao, but as liberalism became a dirty word and our most popular writers were really talking dirty and nothing else, idealism like Islam with its surrender to God, became the major threat to a global consumerism hostage to the almighty dollar. We reach for pie in the sky and wonder why we have egg in the face.

Mao was no Lao Tzu and his poetry itself may have been a power trip. It's easy to say, with the destruction of the Yellow Crane and thousands of other landmarks, that the later Mao was showing his true colors, but the pagodas and the superstition that went with them were symbolic of the suppression of the human spirit and an impediment to equality. Would an art appreciation class have tempered his fanaticism? Hitler demonstrated, like no other artist, that the arts are not the true foundations of civilization but all too often only the masks for a lot of bad actors.

I was as still as the sultry air.

"What are you thinking about, Tony?"

Our marriage seemed to parallel our travel. I stared into the gray haze and drank my tea.

She knew me when. And it was a long way from Marrakech (1964) to Wuhan, and that was not even the beginning. I was divining the past and cursing the present. I cringed at the garbage that turned up on the travel pages of the New York Times, written by couples not even born when I was being born again and again (born yesterday?), in turn giving birth to sui generis, no sooner in an agent's or editor's office than it was being ripped-off and watered down. Ah, to be on that slow boat to Casablanca.

Yes, there was a time when we lived on love and little more. But Africa had had one affair too many and the ship that took us there was no more, just as the flag it flew under was gone with the wind. Mona was holding up, but you can read the lines on my face as you might the Dark Continent – roads that don't seem to lead anywhere in particular. The before and after photo of the traveler is worth a thousand words. It tells us more about his journey than the stamps in his passport.

This wasn't what the doctor ordered, but I was out of the sun, out of the way of mad dogs and Englishmen who had probably eaten them, thinking they were Big Macs, and the two waiters looking out the window with nothing better to do could wait until the cows came home.

Legend has it that Lao Tzu was immaculately conceived to a shooting star. Carried in his mother's womb for sixty-two years and born white-haired, he was with his celestial ancestry, the harbinger of his own birth, more than six hundred years before a comet signaled the coming of Jesus. It is a fact that Lao Tzu was born in Xenan or at least became the keeper of the imperial archives at Luoyang, the provincial capital near the Yellow River, and, like Socrates who perhaps did not want to be pinned down to anything, never put pen to paper. More than 2,500 years before the Beatles said let it be, he had done just that and drifted down to Wuchang and meditated at a spring, and, oh, how the birds did sing!

But Mao said philosophy without action was an idle

music score and the site of the spring was included in a mopping up operation. Making his own kind of music not even the birds were spared. A pilgrimage out there would have made a fitting end to this chapter, but out of Mao's, man's obsession to bring order out of "chaos" has come catastrophe, the apostrophe and this book itself. Proving perhaps, that Lao Tzu had the right idea, most things are better left unsaid and the proof is in the pudding head. But it is in self-effacement that we see the face of God – if you will allow me that slice of hubris.

Far from a beginning, the word is the way of deceit. That which is worth saying cannot be communicated. Thomas Aquinas, perhaps the greatest mind of the Middle Ages, had to write his Summa Theologica and literally bury himself under his tombs, before a moment of truth or resurrection revealed that his words were as empty as the straw he slept on, though not as beautiful and certainly not as useful. Saying let the publishers be damned, the enlightened saint did not write another word.

While I may cast pearls before grasshoppers, I have proven the quantum leap is within everyone's grasp. And if my divining rod can lead the way to holy water, it is something I must share, though there is the remotest possibility that my journey will come to fruition – for even if the spring has run dry, the salmon must lay her eggs. To that extent the traveler goes home again.

And so I must disagree with Lao Tzu and let it be, for we must undo what has been done and doing it my way, with "Old Blue Eyes" say do be do be do. The last word in philosophy. That we must do as well as be, and that the words must be put to music – the lingua franca of the gods and Frank Sinatra. (May he rest in peace.)

About the time that a star is born, the people of the Yangtze valley were communicating with their ancestors – quasi-gods – through the temple-filling sound of bronze bells. Decorated bells (crested birds often top an abstracted mask motif), are among many of the funerary objects from the 2,700-year tomb of Jin Zhou. The hammered out notes were meant to travel across the chasm of the nether world appeasing forbears who controlled the destiny of the living. The bells have that om or omni ring to them that is the meditative sound of eternity.

But I am afraid that the ringing in my ears is the sound of the here and now – not so much experiencing Lao Tzu's eternity as I was the vicious circle. I did not feel that the wild, blue yonder was before me. Not then. My real liberation was in an end to my worrying about how Mona was going to leave China. Finally, I was done with the hassle of helping her get reservations, carrying her backpack on and off, with no thought of my own fate beyond where I would get my next cup of tea. How very British!

A couple of weeks passed before Mona completed her China "diary." Thousands of miles from the scene of the crime.

. . .went to airport. Tony was still ill. The heat was overwhelming and I couldn't imagine how he would make it. Saying goodbye was very sad. . .sweat pouring from his face.

But separations or departures have been the glue of our marriage. As our favorite Prophet said, "Let there be space in your togetherness, and let the winds of heaven dance between you." Two years down the road I am writing this little ditty:

> *We never thought it would last*
> *Sinatra would say it's a gas*
> *It's still me and you*
> *Do be do be do.*

Part 2

JOURNEY TO THE PURE LAND AND BEYOND

18

Departures

Where have you been, oh wandering soul?
I have journeyed far and wide.
I drift to a home in any port.
Drift out upon any tide.

                                    The Ocean Tramp

We shared a taxi out to the airport with a French woman who had been to China ten years earlier. She liked it enough to return – mais jamais, never again. "Next time I go to Mongolia." Apparently everybody and his mother was going there, including me, I thought, when I arrived in Xian. The legendary trading city up near the Yellow River was my immediate destination. By default.

I planned to travel to Beijing overland, but wanting to see Mona off reasoned I might as well fly out of Wuhan, myself. It did not matter where. Not that I had much of a choice. But I was jumping out of the "oven" (as they call Wuhan) and into the fire. Xian brought me no nearer to the capital, but closer to this likely embarkation place than any other flight out of here with available seats. I really didn't know where I was going.

The French lady was frustrated. France, also, had more than its share of rip-off artists. But at least they were polite. While madame mourned the passing of the good old pre-free market days, I was grateful that I was not on the train that shared the bridge spanning the Yangtze that we were crossing. It is part of that north-south artery that makes the railroad the real lifeblood of China – which you can appreciate when you arrive in the airport. It is little more than a freshly painted hanger that appears to have survived World War II. Not a sign of a plane until Mona's takeoff.

I accompanied Mona as far as Immigration, attempting to enter the waiting room with her. That failing, she fell apart. The officers were moved, even a little flustered by her pleas to allow me to continue, but they held their ground. And yet, in that long month of drifting about China, this was the only display of warmth I had seen emanate from a uniform.

We hugged and she was gone, the first time in all our separations that she was more concerned about my welfare than her own. In the past I was apparently out of harm's way, but the last few days seemed to indicate my luck was running out. I would miss Mona but with the departure of her plane, her backpack, if not an albatross, had lifted from my neck.

Miraculously the restaurant was air-conditioned, mercifully it was relatively quiet. I had about eight hours until boarding time, but I could not think of a better place to spend my day. Enough green tea and I would be in a stupor. I sat in a corner under a cooler. A few feet away Christmas lights and a display case gleamed beneath this good, if incongruous, cheer. Are my wires crossed? My past appeared to be merging with the present.

Some hours into my wait, my staying power was sorely tested and I came up on the short end. Teddy Boys, hooligans – punks as we used to call them before the computer geeks aptly co-opted the term – descended upon me like the Golden Horde. I don't know which held the greater attraction for these would-be travelers, old money bags or the proximity of the cooling system. I could cool my heels for so long – but they were enough to get my goat and I was up and running like the hoofer I have always been.

Now I didn't have to feel guilty about not having seen the Yellow Crane Tower. I took the bus out to the lofty pagoda. When two students on the ticket line struck up a conversation with me, I cravenly suggested they buy my ticket. I was beginning to resent paying three times the price of admission to any attraction. I would reimburse the boys later, and went ahead of

Departures

my new friends.

But if Marco Polo could pass for a "Tartar" twenty years down the road, I still had some catching up to do. The ticket seller knew a foreign devil when she saw one, and the older boy was soon overtaking me, pleading with me to return to the entrance or he would be in great trouble. With visions of a summary execution for the Samaritan student and chastising myself for such a radical transformation in this otherwise happy young man, I quickly returned to the entrance. Old eagle eye had told my friend that I was his responsibility, and that I had to pay the going rate for foreigners or be gone.

The Yellow Crane Tower is on the Snake Hill that Mao alluded to in his poem. Recalling a side entrance when I got off the bus, found a shady spot and considered calling it a day. Workmen renovating buildings off the street paid me no mind, as I entered the grounds of the "Revolutionary Army of Xinhai Rebellion," which was holed up here.

Defiant as I was, I could barely slither up the hill. All I wanted to do was gaze out over the Yangtze River. I was not moved to poetry. In my line of vision, dwarfing the Yellow Crane and every pagoda ever built, stood the Kent television tower. Still visible on the far side of the river, the letters K E N T extended from top to bottom. The bottom line. . . .

Hunger and thirst drove me towards the pagoda and the promise of refreshments. Coming my way was my benefactor, restored to his former self. I was relieved that his part in my attempt at unlawful entry had apparently gone unpunished. Sitting before us was the top of the original pagoda, which had survived the Cultural Revolution. We briefly chatted as if I were just another American tourist fishing for answers he would soon forget – or never get. I continued appraising the stupa, symbolizing Buddha's mind, as the student went on his way, never imagining how I had materialized before this heap of balls.

And now as a foreigner, who had ostensibly paid his way, I was gaining entry into an upper level of the Tower and those halcyon days of the last dynasty, when the Yellow Crane was not just another dollar-making tourist attraction – but the revolution put an end to such royal splendor and the chickens came home to roost. Literally. Mao's poetry not withstanding.

With the "success" of the capitalist revolution and all the corruption that came with it, this symbol of dynastic decadence is less a cultural attraction than an incentive to the new empire builders, a replication of the spit and polish they aspire to. The nineties Chinese viewing the interior of the Tower could just as well be Americans touring the Hearst mansion and thinking I should have a place like this. It is not in the ancient scroll as much as in the lacquer finish that the middle and upper classes see their reflection.

It was time to return to the airport. The first bus went as far as a transfer point, a station, where buses slowing to a stop were ensnared in a human net. Most of the passengers were seated before the bus came to a halt, the more agile jockeying for a place as the bus rounded the corner. The peculiar thing about this ambush was that a local bus with seats to spare had become the last train to the coast.

I returned for a bite in the restaurant I had come to know so well. But not before I anxiously retrieved my bag at the airport sales counter, which seconded as a baggage check. Or was it the other way around. Fortunately, the clerk was unable to sell my backpack. I need not have worried – the gyrene-green thing was made in China and what is more it was government issue: The People's Liberation Army. This sack with straps is easy enough to rifle, but no self-respecting thief would go near it. And I'm not just having a little fun here – my backpack could not be less stylish. My past experiences and even the experts have demonstrated that with the advent of the free market, everything is up for grabs and anybody with the connections – quanxi – to get such a coveted job, had sanctioned access to the black market.

With all the planes departing from the same gate and the preceding flight being late, I almost boarded the wrong plane. But at that point it did not matter. I had been drinking boiled water in the waiting room and I was beginning to get a little steamy myself. And what the hell, I had not the slightest interest in going to Xian – and the world-famous terra cotta soldiers made this destination even less desirable. That is to say a half-baked army guarding into perpetuity an insane emperor was something your average American tourist could get his teeth into, and I reasoned the ancient city would be seething with pseudo sinologists.

Anyway, the flight was just what I needed to lift my spirits – no matter how hackneyed that sounds, for there is nothing like getting above it all to get above it all and sometimes only a cliche will do, or an airplane. And the cool cabin led me to believe that a northern destination promised cooler weather and a fresh start. A practical way to leave the miasma, I thought, and if I was given a fan instead of food on the plane, I was still congratulating myself on my smart move until I boarded the airport bus for Xian proper.

China had turned me off trains and onto planes, if only temporarily. Napping stewardesses, tired after proffering all that soybean milk and other liquid refreshments, sat just in back of me. I was in the next to last row, but I had an empty seat to my side and a taste of blessed privacy. And the planes fly low enough when they don't actually crash, to really get the lay of the land. The patchwork quilt became a little lumpy when we approached the ancient capital, but gone forever were the sugar loaves and the lush sweetness of the south.

19

Xian

> *Sa-yan-fun (later to become Sian)...is a great center of commerce and extensive manufactures. The inhabitants burn the bodies of their dead, and are idolaters. They are the subjects of the Great Khan and use his paper currency. Raw silk is there produced in great quantity, and the finest silk cloths, intermixed with gold, are woven. Game of all kinds abounds. The place is amply furnished with everything proper to a great city, and by its uncommon strength it was able to stand a siege of three years, refusing to surrender to the Great Khan....*
>
> Marco Polo

Xian (Sian) was the Chang'an of the Qin Dynasty. Qin Shi Huangdi was the founding father of China, the ruthless ruler who wanted his terra cotta favorites to watch over him through eternity (the excavated army was not buried in the emperor's tomb, but his real-life personal attendants, knowing the entrance to Qin's intact tomb, were interred with him). Censorship being somewhat less subtle two millennia ago, the emperor burned the books and otherwise disposed of the writers who would not satisfy his monumental ego. In America the powers-that-be simply bury radical writers.

If historic texts are to be believed, the emperor's tomb is actually a city, which might explain why this underground kingdom which boasts of palaces with pearl-studded ceilings and floors inlaid with precious gems was never excavated. Among other things, we have Qin (Ch'in) to thank for "China," the country and the crockery – and crock.

Tongue in cheek – or was that foot in mouth – I claimed that the country was named for tea or "chi" drinking Chinese. In fact the lingua franca Mandarin pronunciation is "cha," though the Indians say "chi" or "chai" like the Russians. Early on, perhaps, the English also said "cha," but we say "tea" because European traders sailing to southern China picked up the Fujian pronunciation of Amoy, "deh" or "teh," which sounds like the southern Europeans "té," which evolved into the English pronunciation of later years.

Let me quote Edgar Snow. When it came to China, Snow was truly a modern Marco Polo and may have known Mao as well as Marco knew the Kublai Khan. Mao, incidentally, admired Qin.

Snow writes, *"The region we had flown over is hallowed ground for the Chinese: the valleys of the Wei and Lo Rivers, the cradle of their civilization. Great battles for supremacy were fought here thirty centuries ago, west of the bend of the Yellow River, between armies equipped with bronze spears and shields, riding in two-wheeled chariots. After the period of 'Warring States,' the great imperialist Ch'in Shih Huang Ti (259-210 B.C.) prevailed and built his fabulous palace."*

But for those scraps of information that befall the serendiper, so much was lost on me. But perhaps my own information highway is more reliable than the electronic one. Snow is soon talking about a swimming pool being built at Lintung, the supposed site of the emperor's tomb. Mind you, this is around 1960. *"After its completion the park area was to be further expanded to include the tomb of Ch'in Shih Huang Ti – if tomb there was."*

And there you have it – and it wasn't. The Chinese wanted desperately to excavate the tomb. They detonated the bomb without us knowing about it. It is likely that they bombed with the Qin tomb, too, and that the tomb of his clay-fired army was all that the government was able to come up with.

The Han dynasty, coming immediately after the Qin, is known for most of China's great achievements in everything from astronomy to the wheelbarrow. (Many nationalities live in China, but the people we think of as Chinese call themselves

"Han.")

I had not escaped the heat – and the packed airline bus passed through a virtual desert before nature's near barren landscape gave way to a toxic wasteland and the civilizing odors of my boyhood. The industrial desert extended to Xian itself. Two hours later I was dropped off near a darkened marketplace, another twenty minutes to a recommended downtown hotel. It was also the closest hotel, named for the Ming Bell Tower, in the middle of an adjoining traffic circle. The rickety tower, one of the few remaining relics from the fifteenth century, is an island of grace lost in the haze and maze of traffic and tacky buildings.

Absurdity, culture schlock and a certain amount of luxury took the edge off my grand funk. I had checked into a Holiday Inn. The hotel boasted of its high-tech management. The comedic desk clerk, speaking good English, offered a "discount" that wasn't a discount.

I disliked paying for a double room at American prices, with American service, no less – which is no service. And this was the greatest shock, to step off the elevator into an empty hall, a floor devoid of wardens, gorgeous and not so gorgeous guards with a monstrous thermos of hot water at the ready. The idea now is to buy coke.

The next morning I bought a box of spoiled crackers in a store off the lobby. It was probably a "Friendship" store, but this was the last straw. I could have been eating straw. I don't know how many times I bought dated goods without recourse, but I was now on hallowed ground and putting my foot down. I found just the situation for my malaise. I couldn't get around the traffic circle, never mind going miles to see the life-size soldiers – no matter how expressive they were.

Intending to have tea and crackers for breakfast, all my delicate stomach could take, I was beginning my rebellion on empty. The saleswoman disappeared as the stale crackers spilled out over the counter and I began shouting for the return of my money. I had gotten off to a late start, but could wait until check-out time. I was good for nothing else but bed, and that was not my idea of a "holiday." Ho, ho. I was beginning to draw a lunchtime crowd and many laughs, but a few sympathetic souls agreed I should be reimbursed and the returning clerk had gotten the message.

I put away my phrase book. I had been repeating "jingcha, jingcha," police, police, waving my "Pocket Interpreter" just as she had probably waved Mao's Red Book in the face of the recalcitrant twenty years earlier.

Nobody wants to get the short end, but rip-offs are the trade-offs, damaged goods or just plain cheating, part of the tourist tax and the price you pay for getting out of bed. What makes overseas cheating so hard to swallow, if you are a free-lance writer, is that you are in very familiar territory – and where's the fun in that? But parsimony is par for the course and Marco was a trader till the end.

Marco Polo died in Venice, a materialist, but in fairness to myself I had less than two thousand dollars on me, very little material, with no departure time or place, much less a ticket back to the States. Or even Europe for that matter. With that in mind and an eye to a quick getaway out of Xian, I took a bus to the Jiefang Hotel, opposite the railway station.

The great expanse of space between the station and the hotel served as a plaza or grand piazza. A Ming Wall opened on this emptiness – but for that ever-present mosaic of races that camped out on the pavement, not necessarily waiting for a train. The battleship-gray bulwark, once keeping this motley crew at bay, stood in stark contrast to the now peaceful invaders. Many of these people Marco knew as Tartars, but I thought of the India that I knew, before American poverty also spilled over into railway terminals and bus stations, removing the exotic patina from what, in my more calloused days, I once viewed as mostly colorful.

Xian was best known to the West as the start of the Silk Road, but centuries before that appellation stuck, it was a paradigm for imperial splendor, and as Serametropolis (as it was known to Byzantium) the largest city in the world, perhaps. Yet, by the time of Marco's questionable arrival here, the city was already in decline, only to make a comeback in recent years. Before the Polos traveled the Imperial Highway, no merchants are known to have gone the distance – seven thousand miles from the Mediterranean shores to Xian. A journey of ten months.

European merchants in the market for China's riches would generally make the purchase in Samarkand or Kashgar, as the Chinese traveling the same caravan routes in stages, would exchange their silks for the silver and gold of the western lands. Mostly interested in cooling off, I was headed in the opposite direction.

I realized that my only feasible escape from heat was to be found in altitude rather than latitude - though certainly attitude, mine and the Chinese, had a lot to do with keeping cool. After wasting a day wasting away in the Jiefang, my nerves jangling, I took the morning train to one of China's most sacred mountains.

20

Journey to Hua Shan and Back

Inexperience, I believe
Will give little credence to my song.
                              Journey to the East

The holy mountain was not forty miles down the track – to the east. And my trip was not without that double-edged experience that cuts through touristic stereotyping. Eyeing me like a vulture as my water bottle approached empty and the advertisement for soda mocked me – it was the only thing on the train to drink – a late middle-aged man with a basket of grapes made his move. To be fair, I had cast a covetous eye towards his grapes and that was the encouragement he needed to proffer his unripe fruit, when the sun was at its zenith and I had reached a new low – heightened by the semi-arid land that did not augur an inviting climb into cooling mists.

The peasant wanted a dollar for a fistful of grapes. I played the waiting game, thinking he was relenting for a more reasonable price, when I realized he was trying to trick me into eating a grape – at which time he would have sprung on me for the full dollar. Trying to sell part of his lunch, my fellow passenger wanted the equivalent (Chinese) of maybe ten or twenty dollars, when he should have been happy with a nickel. A ripe grape may have been worth all the tea in China, but I would have choked on these raisins. I thought the old buzzard would be happy with half a dollar, but he was having a little sport – all or nothing at all – and what he really wanted was blood.

The sport sat opposite me in a booth that seated four, but he wanted me all to himself and chased away a boy who wanted a ringside seat. My two or three yuan remained on the shelf with my neighbor's untouched grapes – which he was urging me to take. He must have assumed that a foreigner would be willing to pay a dollar for something he wanted, no matter how unreasonable the price. When I finally motioned for this bird to shove off with his cotton-pickin' grapes, he had himself a good laugh.

I had played to another lunchtime crowd, a captive audience this time, but now I was getting more than moral support from the spectators. A man in his twenties viewing my vexation, left his seat to offer me a bunch of grapes. Ripe ones. "Duoshao qian? How much?" I asked. Nothing, he replied, with his hands. He refused to take a dime. This unexpected twist wasn't enough to wipe the smirk off the face of my now standing tormentor. Perhaps, the whole performance was predictable, not least of all a good Samaritan coming to the rescue.

The train, a relatively uncrowded local, rolled on, inching its way above the Wei valley towards that big bend in the Yellow River. If there is a cradle of civilization, I was on it, rocking to and fro, for every cradle has always been portable and whatever neolithic civilization took root here had been transported from the south. But the north has always looked down on the south – since it has been able to conquer it – and history has a way of bending in favor of the one who rocks the cradle.

I was barely aware that we passed the site of the funereal fun. But I was in no mood for a tomb, excavated or otherwise. Yet, see how we travel from the cradle to the grave, in need of one when we are ready for the other.

No, I had my sights set on higher mounds than the tombs of Qin emperors. Huashan is one of that quintet of holy of holies and now it dominated the land as far as the eye could see – which was not very far on this hazy day. To the north I looked down on the Wei valley. We were above the foot of the mountain, I would say the ankle, but rising above the railway station was a parched ravine without a hint of holiness or a shading tree and I could see my brain scrambling faster than an egg.

Journey to Hua Shan and Back

When nothing less than the alpinesque would stir my blood; there was no sign of a cloud and not even a trace of life to boost my spirits.

Siesta time and I was under the volcano! And I was going to climb it? It was a challenge to make it to the nearest makeshift restaurant, one of a dozen or so eateries and tea parlors running parallel to the railway station and owing their very existence to pilgrims already on the mountain or in bed – the latter having a much greater attraction for me. And this is saying a mouthful when you consider my love for mountains and my disdain for napping – under a flea-bitten mosquito net as it turned out, my cubicle costing little more than the free market price of grapes. I let the fan play on me, but could not sleep, leaving me with no alternative but to get drunk and float back to Xian.

Anyone else would have called it a day, said what the hell, I'm not well, and packed it in. I was going in the right direction, even if I wanted to go to Inner or Chinese Mongolia, before going on to Beijing. If I just continued down the track there were truly sacred mountains up ahead with mandatory clouds, but this was the hottest weather in the cradle's seven thousand year history, and hysteria won the day because for the first time in my life backtracking seemed preferable to forging ahead. But it amounted to the same thing.

This was more than a question of knowing that I had only to detrain in Xian and walk a few hundred yards to a comfortable room when continuing ahead could result in an unmangeable hassle. It was more than succumbing to the human need for the known. For me fulfillment comes in knowing I have arrived at the end of the road. Just as some people must climb a mountain, which I was obviously in no shape to do, my own dementia is defined by distance – and Xian was only the beginning of the road. Beijing? The Forbidden City could wait. I could not return to the States in this wretched condition – not before I had had my last hurrah. As far as I was concerned I was like the defeated Jack Kerouac, California dreamin' at the other side of the Lincoln Tunnel.

Continuing on to Beijing, even via Inner Mongolia, was

Unraveling on the Old Silk Road

like Kerouac's throwing in the towel and heading back to New York, because it meant the same thing, that I was washed-up. Mongolia was passé, neither a beginning nor an ending but a place to pass through – even if enchanting. If I was going to be buried in Asia, let it be where Marco himself had not visited, and let a decent mountain be my tomb. And madness it may have been, but I preferred that to the ignominious defeat of having come so far without experiencing the exhilarating freedom of the road.

I dressed. No one was around to accept payment for my one hour, maybe two, for the use of the room. If they wanted me, they should have known where to find me. Where does a wild-eyed gringo go? I was your quintessential Consul heading for the essential cantina. Apparently the time to climb Huashan is very early in the morning. But as far as sacred sites went, this was a ghost town, and I sensed that the mountain was not the attraction that other holy mountains were. I could understand why, since the sacred was always esthetically pleasing and the pickings were somewhat slim in this neck of the woods.

Yet I would have given anything to be in Huashan's mountaintop monastery and wake to a new morning and attitude. Huashan, like a shaman, would be able to transform me, but without the benefit of a cloud the ten miles to the summit could have been a hundred – walking on my knees, as befits any pilgrim worth his salt; which was becoming very scarce indeed in the temple of my soul. It may have been medically incorrect to treat heat prostration and prostation with beer, but the proof is in the malt and I was feeling no pain, as just about everything the Chinese drink is medicinal.

Chinese beer cures guilt associated with afternoon drinking. I imbibed enough to swallow the inflated bill without blinking an eye. In fact I was soon out on my feet, near sleep and waiting for a train that I thought would never come. Fortunately, I had crossed the tracks to wait at the appropriate platform, for within minutes of the arrival of my train, a freight train parked at the first platform where I had preferred waiting, blocking access to the westbound train to all but the most athletic travelers. Even if you didn't, as most did, climb up, down

Journey to Hua Shan and Back

and under the cars, the walk around this interminable train was beyond my capacity.

It is true we were pilgrims, mountaineers, and eschewed the easy way, yet I had not eschewed on much else that day and my fast had caught up with me. And here was another train bereft of vendors when I really needed them. I did steal a few winks and probably could have slept through to Xian, had it not been for the playful couples enjoying their Saturday outing.

Back at the hotel, I was apologetically offered a windowless room, which normally would have affected me apocalyptically, but I was lucky to have that on the weekend and counted my blessings. Besides, I preferred this to a dreary view and the noise that a less insulated room promised. I was no worse the next morning, but I was no better either. A closer look at my room revealed that previous occupants had been less philosophical about their accommodations. Attempts to allow a little light into the room left the walls bashed in in several places.

Judging by the checklists in even the best hotels, the Chinese have themselves a hell of a night on the town. It is unlikely that a foreigner is being advised that shooting off firecrackers in the room is prohibited. I had to put tracks between me and Xian if I were to keep my sanity – but not because Xian was worse than any other city. You can say differences diminish with dementia, still they were few – except for a wall here and a monument there, the common denominator is the demoralizing mess in between. We call this progress.

There is much to see here, but when a city becomes a station of the cross, you must move on to the next railway stop. The most inviting city is a way station, an appealing place only when the open road, a mountain or the ocean is not easily accessible and a museum becomes the world in a nutshell – and the nut can come out of his shell. What is most attractive about this miniature Old World is that it is still free of cars – amazing when you consider that is just the place for some entrepreneur to install or rent golf carts (though I would have preferred roller skates on my first trip to the Louvre).

Like Jerusalem, Xian is one of the true crossroads, connecting the north with the south as well as the east with the west. The Qin emperor himself was a Tartar and it was his Mongol roots (an oxymoron) that put China on the map of the world. Hooves really, but daring horsemanship definitely carried the day during the Tang dynasty, also. The Chinese still make a big stink out of an abducted stone horse, one of six that guarded the tomb of a Tang queen. This particular sculpture sits in a museum in the City of Brotherly Love, unless Philadelphia has recently given it back in return for a panda. The symbolic value of the sculptures to the Chinese government lies in their likeness to the valiant steeds that helped secure many victories for the warring emperor.

    The Communists evened the score in 1936 when they kidnapped our own stone sculpture, that old gray nag Chiang K'ai-shek, when the Generalissimo did not seem to have China's best interests at heart. It is said Chou En-lai was responsible for his life being spared. Somewhere in Xian is a kind of theme park that marks the spot where Chiang was taken prisoner by his own deputy commander in chief – unless the changing times have erased this piece of history from the map.

    Getting to the Wild Goose Pagoda seemed too much of a Wild Goose Chase, but that is unfortunate because one of the great peregrinating pilgrims of all time came here after he returned from India with the Tang equivalent of the Holy Grail – or true cross. Not only was the monk Xuan Zang (Hsuan Tsang or Tripitaka) the author of the Records of Western Travels, but he brought his Sanskrit Buddhist texts to the Pagoda to be translated. Its three canons resulted in the nickname "Tripitaka."

    California dreamin', I would go to the mountain, westward-ho, westward-ho, gung-ho for Huang-Ho, as the Yellow River was once called. I went to the station, intent on getting beyond the western bend in the river.

21

Journey to Lanzhou

*I sound my barbaric yawp
over the roofs of the world.*

Walt Whitman

I decided to go to Xining. At 8,000 feet above sea level and a Titacacan lake nearby, a habitat for 20,000 migratory birds, it seemed to fit the bill – if the Chinese propaganda was not misleading. And if the shores of Qinghai Lake were a gulag, the Chinese Siberia until recently, I did not know that. A large lake was a suitable destination, Bird Island, a quasi-Land's End that could probably quench my thirst for that oceanic feeling that said it was okay to turn back. The party was over.

Also trying to purchase tickets to elsewhere was a bodybuilding teacher from Springfield, Massachusetts. He was with a couple of other bodybuilders (from Belgium) – and you need all the body you can get when you take on China. This was the teacher's first time on the loose, a little vacation time away from his Chinese students. Although the fellow from Massachusetts spoke very little Chinese, he said the job was easy to get.

The teacher had had China up to his ears. Push had come to shove on the bus to the station and his opponent had drawn a little blood.

We had been waiting on line more than an hour, when he laid his money on the counter only to have the ticket window close on his enterprise – just when his destination seemed within reach. It was fifteen minutes before closing, but the ticket seller didn't like what she saw. Two rabid Americans and

Unraveling on the Old Silk Road

two bulky Belgians, who may have had regrets about giving up the Congo. The teacher was trying to get tickets for panda land, Mianyang, I believe. He and his girlfriend were going to hike the valley to an alpine hideaway, "No place like it in China," but this dream-place seemed to have gone up in the smoke of his anger, not an hour later.

"Who needs China, the people are so rude! We have the Rockies without all this crap! She wouldn't have closed the window on the Chinese."

Considering his condition, I was impressed that the teacher hadn't cursed. As for myself, it was a curious situation to see the shoe on the other foot. Maybe even entertaining because it had been some time since I saw a fellow traveler freaking out, even if he wasn't half my age. Just then his girlfriend showed up and pulled him away from the counter before he put his fist through the window. We both tried to calm him down; his girlfriend encouraged us to take a walk.

Walking across the Tartar tarmac commons under a barely bearable sun, I was bolstering my own will as much as my young friend's. For I had as much will as the Designer's pencil. I was a pawn, prawn, in the hands of fate and only wanted to keep out of the fisherman's net. But my pep talk appeared to have worked and not only was preppy to hang in there, but I was to be hanging by my thumbs with him. He had talked me into going to happy valley with him and his girlfriend. We hurried back to the station before she bought my ticket for Xining.

We had our tickets. But this was real California dreamin', and the more I thought about it the more I realized that panda land might as well be somewhere over the rainbow. The last wild panda was probably in somebody's pot – or Philadelphia. I wondered what I was getting myself into when a train ride alone would be an effort. Not only would I be basically backtracking and backpacking – but there were also twenty hours on a bus involved. This was the trip to make from Chengdu – to which I would have to return, if they could bring me back alive.

The snowcapped mountains my new friends painted for me were a magnet, but true north had a greater pull on me and after we parted I reasoned I had better follow my own nose. I returned to the Jiefang to check out. I could not spend another minute in my claustrophobic cage. And we had hours to wait for the train to Sichuan province. The teachers had returned to the university where they were able to secure cheap accommodations and now rest, but getting the bum's rush at my own hotel, I learned I could not even get a cup of tea.

Opposite the reception desk and open to the lobby is a tastefully turned-out cafe or lounge that was appropriately dark and as airy as the nearby mosque. Just the ambience to take the edge off the heat and administer to my unsettled stomach and psyche. But they had not so mysteriously run out of tea. How much could you charge a foreigner for a cup of tea when you can charge a fortune for a coke – and the lounge did a brisk business with Americanized cliental.

"No tea in China?" I shouted, the ugliest, perhaps the only American about. I was referred to the Jiefang's restaurant, where I had just eaten, but they were also out of tea. Demanding that the lounge serve me tea, I rushed the reception desk and voilá, té pour le monsieur. I sat glaring at a group of Parisians having more fun with Coke. They could have been on the Left Bank or the West Bank. Did it matter?

Teatime was all the encouragement I needed to make tracks out of there and make a beeline for the helpful assistant manager. I asked her to write a note in Chinese requesting that my ticket for Mianyang be changed back to the earlier departure for Xining. And to add that I was a V.I.P., somewhat under the weather, and that no effort should be spared to secure for me a comfortable accommodation. And I'm not trying to be funny. With her, I also left a note for my new found- and-lost friends, really feeling quite guilty about abandoning ship at this crucial time in their voyage, but there just were not enough lifeboats on this lollypop and it was every man and woman for themselves.

The rush hour at the Xian station made Grand Central Station look like a milk stop – and everybody seemed to be getting on my train. No sleeper was available, or rather, no bed. Boarding the first class sleeping car, I showed the conductor/manager my message from the hotel. I imagine he was much more interested in my ticket; he seemed to be pointing to the rear of the train. I passed a few cars and again presented my note to a conductor. Apparently he wasn't impressed with my status, because I soon found myself in the caboose, straining under my bag and considering the distinct possibility that I would be standing the entire night.

I had to do something dramatic. At the end of each car is a small conductor's cabin. The conductors drink tea here, make announcements and play cassettes, tapes. Taps, reveille, etc. I sat in one of the seats and refused to move, indicating through the most graphic sign language that if I got up, I would throw up. A guard showed me to the door. Now, I was frantic about this damn train leaving without me. Life-saving adrenaline flowing, I ran up to the sleeping car – first class, of course – and sat down in an aisle folding seat opposite a compartment. I was shown the exit.

Desperately, I pushed my way back into the car and cried out, "Does anybody speak English!?!"

If anything, I expected a response from the military or bureaucratic brass, but lo and behold, I hear a sweet accented "I do" floating down the aisle. The sound of wedding bells as an attractive German woman materialized behind the melodic but reassuring voice. What is more, the helpful fraulein has been studying Mandarin in Taiwan. But can she speak Chinese well enough to convince someone with authority that this highly questionable V.I.P. needs a place to sleep? She can. And her looks alone are enough to convince the all-around manager who sent me packing the first time.

It is not unusual for the super-conductor to come up with a spare berth after the ticket seller claims they are all sold out, but my German benefactress is assuring me that there really are no available beds to be had. Not to worry though, if I was content to sit on an aisle seat that had taken on all the splendor of a suite. Like a front row seat on opening night on old Broadway. Nor would I have to share my compartment with three other people. Sleep was another matter, but when I considered the alternative, it seemed like a frill, a luxury I could do without if I could only keep from falling out of my seat.

Journey to Lanzhou

The young woman returned to her compartment. Well, I couldn't expect the moon – unless it were full. Savoring my privacy, my victory, my escape from the deluge, and the peach preserves I picked up in the Jiefang lobby, I considered myself the luckiest man in the world.

Or were they apple preserves. At least I had the presence of mind to buy the fruit and hold on to the empty jar. Chinese style, I intended to use my container for tea. Or whatever came my way. A young officer out of uniform pulled down a seat, opposite his compartment. He offered me some of the noodles he had brought with him for the trip and poured water from his compartment's thermos. I was getting blood from the proverbial stone.

The fraulein realizing I did not know whether I was coming or going, left her Lonely Planet Survival Kit with me before retiring. She made a point of Xiahe, just a couple of hundred miles up the road. On this vast China Beach, this Buddhist shell was left behind in Tibet's ebbing tide. Basically a monastery, it seemed like just the place for a mad monk, she must have reasoned. So did I. Beyond this outpost of the faithful, the official Tibet beckoned. What need of I to plod along with a guidebook, when my plot had already been written in God's Book.

Beholden to alms, wasn't I unconsciously priming myself for this pilgrimage; weren't the obstacles merely the stepping stones to the summit? And wasn't the *Journey to the West* the Chinese rendition of the *Journey to the East,* in which Herman Hesse like Thomas Merton, later in his own real Asian Journal, talk about "going home?" Not the home of trendy travel writers, but that place of the soul, the journey of Hesse's "eternal strivings of the human spirit towards the East, towards Home . . .Where are we really going? Always home!" The real romance of the road is in the rendezvous with God.

The "home" of the sixties icon Hesse, and the "home" of the twentieth century saint Thomas Merton, also a household name during America's authentic Cultural Revolution (perhaps assassinated by the C.I.A.), is the bottomless source of Buddhism.

Anyway, if I wanted to go to Xiahe, I would have to detrain at Lanzhou, which was where my fraulein friend was getting off – three hours short of my original destination, Xining. Did I really want to forego the wild west for yet another Magical Mystery Tour? It was a foregone conclusion when I heard that Xining, with its pickpockets, had little more going for it than its altitude and that a journey to Qinghai Lake would be like going into exile – very much like going home (to the extent it is my birthplace) in New York. Later, I learned that Golmud, at the end of the line, was the real gulag. This was the last stop for Tibetan dissidents. Not Qinghai.

By nightfall I realized there was no way I would remain in my seat without a safety belt. Little did I know that I was under scrutiny and that a guardian angel was waiting in the wings. A young man from the adjoining second class sleeping car, the hard bed carriage, escaping into our rarefied retreat now and then, had observed that I seemed to be carrying sightseeing to an extreme. There was little to be seen beyond my window at the start of the journey, and less now.

"Don't you have a bed?" The concerned "student" had joined me. I explained. He wasn't very tired, he said, and offered me his bed.

"What about you?"

"I will sit at your feet," came the reply.

Not looking a gift horse in the mouth, I accompanied the Chinese student to the other car and plopped into a lower bunk. Surprisingly, the other five bunks in the open "compartment" (for want of a better word) were also occupied by English-speaking Chinese. Maybe the man in the third tier did not speak English. What is more, they appeared to be genuinely friendly. My circumstances may have thrown them for a loop, just as their knowledge of English gave an unreal edge to my experience. Life becomes a dream when you are deprived of them. What was happening speaks of a quantum jump, that leap of faith that enables the evergreen voyager to get over the hump. And doesn't our faith determine our fate?

Lady Luck had materialized in flesh and blood. Again, of the two women in our group, in that space between the two rows of bunks we occupied, one was a doctor administering to her first American patient. She gave me two types of pills, one to be taken before I go to sleep and the other with meals. Had I been eating and sleeping properly, I wouldn't need the pills in the first place.

The absurdity weighs heavier and heavier with each passing mile if there is no reader to share the burden of the reality beyond the fiction of ordinary lives. Marco Polo was not a sharer, he simply found himself a prisoner of war in Genoa and idled away his days in jail telling his tale to a prisonmate who happened to be a writer. The end result of this encounter was an honest, if flawed book that went unread or simply was not believed. Until it was safe.

We remain in the Dark Ages. For every book that is a milestone in our journey to the east, for the singular *Travels of Marco Polo*, there are a thousand *Travels of Sir John Mandeville*, a fifteenth century bestseller, typical of the myths John Q. wants to hear, the Loch Ness monsters so dear to our hearts.

Avanti! I expressed surprise at the kindness of my Chinese comrades: "Many foreigners feel alienated, uncomfortable." In defense of the Great Wall that seemed to exist between them and us, the student said, "You must know the Chinese for a long time before you can become a friend. The family comes first. You must know somebody. But the Chinese are really very kind." Knowing the language helps.

In the countless times I've been helped by passing strangers, in my down and out days in Europe, I don't know how often the response to my gratitude would be, "But anyone else would do the same."

While my days at home, wherever that happens to be (usually in America) seem to flow by on an even if edgy keel, my time on the road appears marked by these pronounced swings from bummer to bon vivant or rather chance (as they say in France), evening things out. The student went back to his computer or pocket electronic game, but soon "lights out" boomed out over the loudspeaker and a somewhat more quiet barracks on wheels rolled on towards morning.

22

The Golden City

*A man's life of any worth is a continual allergory –
and very few can see the mystery of his life – a life
like the Scriptures, figurative. . . .*

                                                               Keats

It was about 9:00AM and I was still on a roll. We had spent the night going up and away from the Wei valley and had arrived at the upper reaches of the Yellow River and its "Golden City" of old – on one of those crisp mornings that belie the day that lies ahead. The German girl had regrouped with friends and put me on a bus that would pass the Friendship Hotel. The Germans knew better than to stay there.

    Lanzhou was essentially a place where you slept and made arrangements to move on, at least since General Huo Qubing passed through here on his expeditions to the western regions some two thousand years ago. Tripitaka also slept here on his pilgrimage to our East. Marco Polo, on his way to his first encounter with Kublai Khan, was bearing north, coming upon the Yellow River where it meets the Great Wall.

    What became of my Chinese benefactors? Having seen my ticket, they were perturbed or at least puzzled by my precipitous escape from our mobile stalag. The local bus made very few stops and my hotel was not one of them. This practice of stopping every half-mile was perhaps influenced by the nomadic stock of the passengers.

    The hotel had been named for the "Friendship" that had existed between the Chinese and the Russians who helped them develop the northwest passage that opened up the Soviet frontiers. The hotel as well as the friendship had that Stalinist stamp on it, but its antiquated sprawl imbued the dump with a charm lacking in these less friendly times. And, most important, European gardens, even a bit of an orchard, provided a buffer between the street and this monument to Big Brother.

I didn't know where the melons outside my room came from, but Lanzhou is now known as a "city of melon" and I helped myself to a big succulent white-green fruit. A half melon, some crackers and tea out of the way and I teetered over to the bus station – which was near enough to the Friendship to recommend it as a desirable place to sleep for tourists catching the early bus to Xiahe.

Because the Tibetan enclave is popular with tourists who probably would not be making the much more expensive flight to Tibet proper, and there was only so much that could be charged for a bus trip under ten hours, local authorities had come up with the most scandalous way to skin the cat yet. All foreigners going to Xiahe were required to purchase accident insurance, which killed two birds with one stone, as the insurance requirement soaked the intrepid while prompting the more timid to opt out for the more expensive bus tour or taxi – which was perhaps more dangerous than your standard, much slower moving, standing room only conveyance but had no insurance requirement.

But accident insurance was only available at a downtown tourist office and I couldn't buy my bus ticket without it. Unable to be at the tourist office before everyone was out to lunch, I headed towards the Yellow River, stopping in a dry goods store for some nuts. A huge hospital stood between me and the river. The misspelled English sign that identified this medical complex was so memorable that I could not imagine forgetting it. It read something like "Communist" rather than "communicable diseases." I was coughing up more phlegm than the Chinese. Should I enter the admission office?

I simply made my way through and around the hospital grounds, arriving at a riverside stall in a state of near collapse. I had the Yellow River blues, or should I say "browns?" It seemed so long ago that Mona and I shared our happiest moments in China in a riverside restaurant. The only thing that remained of that time was the heat that was a little slow in arriving up here.

A stretch of the strand below me became a Chinese family's day at the beach. In a matter of days the shore would be no more. The air was as oppressive as the water, as much nature's doing as the pollutants in sea and sky. The river was still wide at this point, but hinted strongly at the high hinterland from whence it came. I pictured Mao attempting to swim to the other shore.

A bit downstream, topping the palisades of the opposite shore, is the White Pagoda. Like water under the bridge, the Yuan temple seemed to represent the inaccessible past.

Upstream has always held the promise of the pristine and my instinct was to go against the current. Walking metaphor that I am, making my way along the Yellow River I went against vehicular traffic bearing down on me. And just a few miles up the river the Liu Jia Gorge Hydroelectric Power Station sapped my own energy without my ever seeing it.

Walking away from the river, I hailed what looked like a taxi or an ambulance. It was the latter. No problem. The driver and the medic recognized an outpatient when they saw one. I showed them a slip of paper with the address of my destination, the downtown travel/insurance agency, and we were on our way to the appropriate bus stop – which didn't take too much time away from more urgent calls.

Already, bamboo scaffolding seemed out of place, and my ride down Xigu Road was brightened by a mosque and the Mongol influence that was now felt, but the population of Lanzhou was approaching a million and a half and its future seemed reflected in the downtown glass and steel. And the scam I was about to buy into:

The People's Insurance Company of China
Policy of Travellers Accident Insurance for Tourist Agency

    A. Scope of Cover.
        The company will pay the indemnity subject to the clauses of Travellers Accident Insurance for:
        1. Death or injury.

    C. General Conditions.
        Whenever an accident should occur during insurance period, the insured shall give an immediate notice to the company...in a rapid way in the same day...

I imagined having a problem collecting the few thousand dollars or yuan I had coming to me if the ride to Xiahe was more than bargained for. I followed my nose to the food stall outside the tourist office, where a young German out of a Hermann Hesse novel struck up a conversation with me. My faraway look gets them all the time. Hans was studying Chinese in Taiwan. I thought he might know my benefactress from the friendship train, but he informed me that there were many Germans studying Chinese in the Formosa, the mainland considered a suburb.

    The graduate student brought home the fact that Americans were jogging before they learned to walk, playing at being teachers while the sophisticated, usually prepared German remained the perennial student. There were skinheads in Germany, but they seemed to be outnumbered by the eggheads who traditionally trekked to the East – physically and metaphysically. American teachers would blunder about China, antagonizing the natives, while the Germans made a kind of dry run in Taiwan – getting their feet wet in the more western island "nation" before making the plunge into the Big Enchilada.

    Hans said he was also going to Xiahe, but tall, bespectacled and determined, he had no intention of paying for accident insurance.

    "How do you get around that?" Aptly phrased because that was exactly what he intended to do, going to Xining first and take in Qinghai Lake before making the less touristic run down to Xiahe. I could not say if such a route really existed, but if it did, the idea of accident insurance hadn't caught up with it. There just would not be enough foreigners to bother.

Bird Island alone seemed like it was worth the trip, One of three sanctuaries in all of China, it was not something you took for granted. Not many birds were spared the Chinese purging of the skies, because if they weren't considered pests that had to be eradicated, they were eaten, but I was already sold on my Tibetan outpost and a likely place to recuperate for a week or so.

Not wanting to be in the same fix as Mona, I tried to buy my airline ticket out of here – anywhere in the general direction of Beijing, but Xian. Even attempted to buy a ticket for Shanghai, but Xian was the only available destination out of Lanzhou until September, or so the sales person said. It was obvious the government was banking on those baked figures in Xian and had rerouted flights that were bound elsewhere in their compulsion to kill the goose that laid the Golden Egg.

A dozen or so protesting foreigners in the airline office, in the same boat as I, hightailed it out of there, while I could only succumb to that sinking feeling. At least I was able to purchase a bus ticket for Xiahe, and went to sleep early. That was one of the great things about being beat.

But on the other side of a glass door that opened on an adjoining conference and game room, something was afoot. This explained the pile of melons outside my door, though the manager assured me that this odd chamber was not being used. Ah, but it was midnight, a new day. I was damn near blasted out of my bed by a blaring television. For a few confounded seconds I thought I was under attack, and then surmising the source of the bedlam, I went berserk, screaming and rattling the glass door. No reaction.

Even for China, this nocturnal emission was provocative – and this probably the only television set in the Friendship Hotel. I could not accept at face value – two-faced, as it might have been – that the two characters next door were simply boors or hard of hearing. The "friends" were even smoking. Boy! did they have my number! If they weren't agents, literary or otherwise, the racket was really a ruse and that these racketeers expected me to hastily run off to see the manager leaving something of value behind. If there was a phone, which I never found, it wouldn't be working.

Still, I reasoned that if I left my room and closed the door, I could not reopen it without an attendant, who might not be around. What was the difference, when my nocturnal neighbors had only to open the glass door that led to my room and help themselves to whatever was laying about. But if these guys were having a little sport, the ball was in my court and carrying it for all it was worth, I ran through the corridor and down the steps and stormed the Reception Desk to the horror of a bespectacled clerk. Beating a hasty retreat, she barricaded herself in the office. Reinforcements appeared. Two seasoned veterans, probably on hand for the Russian invasion and perhaps appreciating a little action on a dull night, received me as if it were checkout time and that I was calmly paying my inflated bill, which had been paid.

Reassured that I was not entirely rabid, one of the old hands disappeared. Thieves or not, I was now convinced that my next-door neighbors were working for the hotel and were enjoying the standard break. Again, somebody was maintaining that the room was not occupied, never was, and noise, if there was any, was coming from elsewhere.

"I can see through the door," I shouted. The clerk's expression seemed to say that I was just another spoiled westerner imagining things.

"The room is empty," the clerk demurred when I demanded we go up the stairs to my floor.

"The manager has the key."

" Then get the manager!" I managed, almost apoplectic. A disheveled manager appeared and we went up to the game room. Obviously it was empty. The television had been turned off and the only sign of recent occupants was the lingering smoke. But that was not enough proof of the room having been recently occupied and as far as he was concerned, I had been hallucinating. Could they all be such great actors in on this little game; had my now-absconded neighbors been bureaucrats who came and went as they pleased?

I did not sleep, afraid my wake-up call would be a long time in coming and I would miss my 6:00AM bus for Xiahe. On my way out of the hotel, I ran into a Japanese and a couple of eastern Europeans, who had no complaints. They had stayed in the much cheaper dormitory, which should have been even friendlier, but the Japanese said they had a quiet night. Sure, what enterprising Chinese was going to muck about those unpromising accommodations – and I'll bet they weren't within earshot of a television. You get what you pay for.

The Japanese said he had intentions of passing himself off as Chinese making his way into Tibet. He appeared to have a problem just making it to the bus station, but on we trudged in a light rain, the oppressive humidity of yesterday a thing of the past, and my fading nightmare just another Late, Late Show. I was going to the mountains and that was all that mattered.

23

Arrival in Xiahe

Friends, you are welcome to Gansu!
(Title of my brochure!)

It was a long and winding road out of the Yellow River Valley and then a mostly uphill ride all the way to the Gansu gateway to the "grasslands" and forbidden Tibet. The often poplar lined road was also the bustling main street of the Muslim towns that ultimately gave way to the bastion of Buddhism above them. Except for the last leg of our journey, where we climbed into a sometime evergreen valley, my ride to Xiahe was the safest yet.

If anyone needed accident insurance, it was this mixed race of Muslims bedecked in their pillbox-shaped brocaded hats, who used the thruway as a sidewalk, and whatever stray animals crossed the road. Many westerners, all too quick to see Muslims as madmen, may have seen a terrorist threat behind the insurance requirement. As for the road being a sidewalk bazaar and a pedestrian walk, that was par for China, and did not pose an unusual threat to life or limb.

Xiahe itself is a one-horse town with considerably more donkeys, and carts that should be pulled by either, but these buckets, actually the back ends of bicycles, are really cycle-rickshaws. I no sooner got off the bus when one or two were dogging my footsteps. The third person to debus, I followed a pair of English tourists, apparently racing towards the best hotel in town. Fearing the remainder of the passengers would be hot on our heels I breathlessly arrived at this all but empty concrete palace that was facade and little else. Townhouse on the outside and outhouse on the inside courtyard.

Two bicycle-drawn "rickshaws" converged on me as I left the hotel. As I continued up the road, both rickshawmen shouted out what was evidently the name of a *Lonely Planet* choice, but I had enough bumping around for the day and decided to hoof it. The drivers realizing I did not know better tagged along until they made me understand that I had one hell of a walk before me. I piled into one of the wagons like a sack of potatoes, without the foggiest notion where we were headed. I just didn't want to be French-fried.

Bouncing along, I wished I had spent more time with that borrowed "Survival Kit" when I was on the train, on the other hand my bumbling was preferable to being overbriefed and destroying that all important sense of discovery, spice of life you experience when you stumble upon the unexpected.

Within minutes we were pedaling by a magnificent monastery that pressed a long suppressed button. My camera. I was a little slow in sizing up a picture. Showing his disapproval, a Chinese soldier is shouting and gesticulating. I read somewhere that photos of especially sacred places were forbidden and that an irate monk might rip the film out of your camera, but this was ridiculous. What, I imagined, would a soldier do to my camera? I only prayed that nothing would come of my indiscretion and that my driver would pedal for all he was worth.

The soldiers probably thought I was filming them and the road they were working on. We had gone over a small bridge – and east of Turkey, where they guard the very stones, a bridge or its photo is classified information and considered a likely target in the event of an invasion. Of course, the Chinese had done the invading. We pedaled on and up towards the setting sun and the Shangri-La at the end of this rainbow- colored ride.

The hotel, named for the Labrang Monastery about a mile downstream, even looked like it and I was tickled pink and some of the other richer colors that flapped in the wind in this neck of the woods. But my joy was short-lived when I discov-

Arrival in Xiahe

ered that I would have to share a ground floor room with a young Belgian couple, fresh off the bus and already digging in. The honeymoon was over – but not for this couple. Had I been in the young man's shoes, I would have decked the desk clerk, but these innocents were far from indignant and never very far from home, for home is where the head is.

Sharing their room with an over-the-hill hobo was the Belgian couple's idea of an adventure. I was probably the only American staying in the hotel. Exotic. But who turned loose all these Belgians? If they were trying to get away from all the tourists who crowded into their small country, they had come to the wrong place. Maybe they were really Israelis. No, it was Tuesday, so they must be Belgians.

A double bed fit in the room comfortably, but with an extra bed tossed in for good measure (and profit), our concrete cubicle took on the ambience of yet another barracks. I was sitting at the foot of my bed, my feet halfway out the door, when the manager, in search of space for new guests, stopped by.

"Is there room for anybody else?"

"At least five more!" I shouted. "The more the merrier."

Cheaper by the dozen. He got the message and cheerfully went off in search of other guests to pester. Actually, it was not cheaper by the dozen. The Labrang Hotel was the only place in the area with bathrooms and the Chinese owners knew they had us by the pampered balls.

But I had my age going for me. To the tourist I may have looked like a balding relic from the sixties, a real live hippy, but on the sly I was doing my V.I.P. number, with the promise of payola in return for vastly improved circumstances. Paying a few days in advance the next morning, I managed to move into a riverside room in the main building. Top floor. And I was paying just about the same as I was for that cramped bed of the previous night. I could not believe my good fortune, eyeing the extra bed with foreboding, but there was no question of the room being mine. Alone.

Senility aside, my emotions have never kept pace with my years. I have outraced time or allowed it to pass me by. But

Unraveling on the Old Silk Road

there was no forgetting my age. The bus that took me from Lanzhou to Xiahe also bore the date of my birth on the license plate.

Time is a circle and if I were going to go around in circles, what better place to be than in Xiahe, where prayer itself was poetry in motion, concentric merry-go-rounds in and around the monastery, the prayer wheels the wheel of life, the clockwise motor central to the Tibetan community. Poor metaphor for a people who travel from here to eternity on the wings of their faith.

I was finally anchored enough, sufficiently moved to put pen to paper. One of a dozen pens and three pocket-sized – stamp-book sized – note pads. My first literary effort since leaving the States. Maybe it was more a question of still not having enough energy to go on day-long treks, but there I was mooring myself in the moment when movement had been my cup of tea. What was truly a joy was that otherworld view from my window and the music of eternity under it that kept me there – the mesmerizing om of a fast flowing stream that carried me along with it.

Part of the stream had been diverted to turn the paddles of an ancient mill – which also housed the miller. Amber waves of barley lapped at the shore, grew to the very door of this motley structure. Beyond this mill, like islands in this sea of barley, were tents that marked the early arrival of the harvest festival celebrants. Serendipity. And above and beyond the barley fields that filled this tiny valley, were the earthen homes that climbed up the opposite mountain under a cluster of evangelizing evergreens and a sunburst of prayer flags. This piney promontory and the Tibetans' embellishment of nature marked a sacred place. Essentially to invoke protection of the mountain god.

I fancied that the colored strips of rags intimidate evil spirits and are a sort of scarecrow perched upon long poles. A large bunch of multi-colored flags graced the top of a tall pole just in back of the hotel, but unseen by guests it is unlikely that the sacred display was a tourist attraction. A Tibetan part-owner of the hotel was probably playing it safe, while

Arrival in Xiahe

the feelings of the Chinese, who did not want the festooned poles on their property, was "let the devil take the hindmost."

But it's what comes around, as much as what's blowing in the wind, that had me in its thrall from the evening I arrived. Fleeing my room, racing the sun in its own imaginary orbit, I got caught up in the clockwise flow that orbits the monastery, like the earth circling the sun, a time traveler on the run.

Following the river down to the monastery, before a more direct way had me walking through the upper village, I was suddenly besieged by pleading youth yapping "yuppy" at me. At a loss to explain this obvious case of mistaken identity, I quickened my step and was soon on Terra Sancta, entering the Labrang precincts by way of the enormous prayer wheels at the western end of the monastery that seemed to provide the necessary impetus for the pious peregrinations of the Tibetans, their shrunken circle a contained continuum of the ancestral journey to the tip of South America, a clockwise journey to the east down the ages.

In a few moments time the bottom line life of China – linear progression – had been transformed into one vivacious cycle and the transmigratory existence of another world. Nomads dressed for another season and altitudes higher than Xiahe. Their long coats were allowed to drop below their bare shoulders, but trudging along the upper rim of the monastery, occasionally prostrating themselves, they were oblivious to everything but their journey without end.

The magic circle, much older than the Buddhism it was an integral part of, was the way out of life's own endless cycles. Sharing this social whirl with me was a time traveler who could have stepped out of the pages of "Seven Years in Tibet." The only other foreigner making the rounds. The working class German had returned here after an absence of five years to basically hang out cheaply until he was compelled to return to the more common vicious cycle. He was taking his evening walk.

I wondered how Xiahe had survived the Cultural Revolution. It had not – but the resurrected monastery was experiencing a hands off attitude, to a point, and at a more desirable

Unraveling on the Old Silk Road

altitude than Lhasa, which made Labrang less forbidding, a real-life Shangri-La – when the golden stupas and the bow-shaped roofs emerge from the morning mist and maroon-robed monks under yellow hats scurry to their temple.

I fear it is a matter of time before the monastery is little more than a Magic Kingdom, but for the time being Labrang does not suffer from that sanitized look so common to theme parks and tinsel towns that promise a germ-free excursion into a never-never land never far from a Holiday Inn. There is real magic in the chant that reverberates through the prayer hall. Glistening in the early sun, the monastery is the chanted, enchanted "jewel in the lotus."

A visitor. A face that has the stamp of the State Department. She said she was staying in one of Xiahe's toiletless hotels, a middle-aged woman to boot.

Yet another American claiming to be a unilingual teacher. She said she had come to Xiahe with one of her students, acting as a guide, but was not very clear about where she taught in China.

If she did not confess to snooping for the Holiday Inn or other insiders, I considered her jig up when she rhapsodized about what a friendly place China is. One big Friendship Hotel, I said, adding that the general consensus seemed less enthusiastic.

The teacher accompanied me on my evening walk to the monastery. A rag-tag army of children closed in on us, but this time I was prepared for them, having learned the Tibetan word for pen. I pointed an accusatory finger at my companion when the children shouted their "yuppy" refrain.

"You see, even they have your number," I wildly laughed before giving the little urchins their pacifiers.

Early on, I considered myself a kind of Johnny Appleseed, distributing pens I really never did get to use, to youths who looked to ballpoints as if they were magic wands, the end of learning itself. In an incarnation of a great saint or Bodhisattva, the founder of the "Gelupai" or Yellow Sect (hence yellow hats), is shown with the Sword of Truth and the Book of Wisdom, but I suspect the "yuppy" yapping was a yearning for learning as much as it was a lusting after a status symbol. Was there anything more enviable to children in the Third or Fourth World than the sight of a foreigner writing a postcard?

There was one potential foreign rabble-rouser in Xiahe, a young Swiss man living in the monastery's hostel, who enjoyed a special relationship with the Tibetans. Or the Chinese, since he could be so blatant in his support of Tibetan independence. His T-shirt said as much.

Labrang has lost much to the Cultural Revolution, many monks had been killed and quieted on Tibet's eastern front, but lately there had been an undercurrent of protest, mostly surfacing in posters or letters. But how much was bait? There really are informers about and it seems the instinct for independence has been pretty much checked. Oh, the Chinese will toss the Tibetans a crumb, just as we will appease the Native American now and then, but nobody seriously believes we will give Manhattan back to the Indian. In a sense the monastery was a casino that made everyone happy and really not much of a gamble. The Chinese were using the velvet glove and were not about to kill this Golden Goose – until it seems capable of flying away.

The big difference between an Indian casino and Labrang Monastery is that ultimately the casino is a betrayal of Native American values and a symbol of an empty society (on both sides of the door), while Labrang is as much an image-maker as it is a moneymaker – Free Market freedom of religion. What Labrang and the casino have in common, if you forgive me, is the wheel of fortune, or simply wheels, both places being where, mixing the sacred with the profane, the player and prayer come together. Which, come to think of it, sounds like a Catholic Church. Bingo!

24

Of Monks and Marx and Mona Lisa

> *The milk of the lioness is so precious and so powerful that if you put it in an ordinary cup, the cup breaks.*
>
> Tibetan Saying

In a spirit of reverence and play – ideal prayer – I leaned into the mounted cylinders of copper and color so reminiscent of a children's ride. I was enjoying myself, yet open to the idea that these prayer wheels, almost in perpetual motion could very well be a force for good– preferable to mindlessly mouthing a Hail Mary.

But meditation is the hallmark of the Buddhist even if the Catholic church pontificates about Buddhism being "atheistic." The Church's hostility to the true peacemakers – as opposed to the moneymakers – raises the question of the "accidental" electrocution of Thomas Merton, the outspoken Trappist monk who had come around to the idea of individual responsibility and a truly catholic faith at the time of his death – at the height of the Vietnam War, in Bangkok, before he was to give his lecture on "Marxism and Monasticism."

The C.I.A. (maybe a literary agency?) would have done the dirty work, but not without the silent blessings of a Church embarrassed by a bestselling monk/author chanting "give peace a chance." Like that other enchanter, a decade later, singing let it be. . . . "imagine" a world without borders or wars but with strawberry fields forever. Also pushing daisies.

With his prized possession, Evans-Wentz' *Tibetan Yoga and Secret Doctrines* in his suitcase, Thomas Merton was looking forward to his meeting with the exiled Dalai Lama. Yet there was still much about Tibetan Buddhism that was foreign to him, and in preparation for his visit, the monk found himself meditating on a mandala that was "on close inspection. . . .full of copulation. I don't quite know how one meditates on it. It might be a paradoxical way to purity."

Sexual union in "secret assembly" is an aspect of yogic meditation depicted in statues and thangkas. But hankey-pankey is apparently relegated to the Bodhisattva and his consort and is basically a symbolic representation of "enlightenment" – the marriage of wisdom to compassion. "Compassion," oddly enough, perhaps, represented by the male.

You would have to look hard to find signs of sexual overtones in the sacred cloths and sculpted images of Labrang Monastery. Nor was I interested in more than an overview and saw nothing sexy in the rumbling horns and seeming chaos and color that brightened up the darkened halls of Labrang. I contrast this with the order and light of Catholic monasteries and cathedrals that seem to have a more celestial calling. (When Christendom attained esthetic heights.) The difference, generally speaking, is between the earthy and the ethereal. A subterranean world and heaven. The nitty-gritty of life and death issues – as one – as opposed to a vague mythical life after death. Like heaven.

The music says it all. Ordinary church music or hymns drive this sinner up the wall, while the droning sound of a Tibetan monastery takes me to my very roots.

Tibetans still venerate the Lord of Soil by planting a stick topped with colored flags in the earth – the Bon (Pon) underside of the Yellow Hats, pretty much demonstrating the roots of the Gelugpai prayer flags. Much of what is not indigenous, like Buddhism itself, has been transported from the subcontinent with its million and one gods and its super sanguine surreality. In her wrathful form, Sridevi (Sri Devi), the chief guardian goddess of the Gelugpa sect, is shown mounted on a mule with an eye on his haunch, fangs bared and flaming hair, riding over a sea of blood. In India she denotes the fearful Goddess Kali.

A monk I befriended, talking about the often macabre mandalas, said that the grotesque mix of blood, guts and bones are meant to scare worshippers out of their egotistical wits. Emptied of pride they become a vessel for the spiritual.

Ironically, the thunderbolt symbol of the Tibetan Gelugpa may very well have been sparked by the Aryan Indra, the God of Thunder and Rain and the patron deity of war. The formerly warlike Tibetan could have related to such a protector. On the other hand, the clutched thunderbolt of the "compassionate" male side of enlightenment may also spring from the Hindu belief that the diamond (likened to a thunderbolt), like infinity, is a many-faceted reality.

More than in any other living religion, death is the bedfellow, as the shaman's apron could be Shiva's neckless of skulls – but, then, Shiva is the granddaddy of the granddaddy of all organized or rather disorganized religions, and Shiva's Hinduism the mother of all. I can't say how far Shiva penetrated Tibet, but after the mother goddesses were relegated to consorts, it was in God we thrusted.

Little did we know when we were boys calling someone a "prick with ears," that we were describing the driving force of India: Shiva. This misplaced insult is an accurate description of one of the New York Metropolitan Museum of Art's more graphic lingams – which may sound like baseball, but is in fact a hands-on sport as old as the hills it was meant to fertilize. In his Vedic beginnings Shiva was not a hard-on but a "howler," accompanied by the divinities of the storm, sending down lightening – which seems to be a divine theme. But if lightening is a symbol of the destroyer (and orgasm a kind of death), the flashing sky is also accompanied by a life-giving rain – just as there would be no babies without the mother of all battles.

Shiva is often shown as the Lord of Dance crushing a dwarf, the symbol of ignorance, underfoot. The tantric strain of Buddhism – Tibetan Buddhism – that so interested Thomas Merton, evolved from the teachings of the solitary Shiva ascetics, or siddhas, who wandered about Northern India, and if not a physical, was at least a philosophical movement in Tibet. These Tantrics of the "Left Hand" who believed in the transvaluation of all values – and were truly a howl – were devotees of an esoteric tradition that stresses the ability to achieve sudden illumination. Lightening-quick enlightenment.

Even so, a famous Tibetan thangka shows a sword-wielding deity standing atop a conquered Shiva representing an obstacle to enlightenment. But that can't be so.

From the time of the Upanishads asceticism emerges as the highest form of religious life, ascribing the stability of the universe to the powers generated by a penitent – the ascetic abstaining from sex in that Himalayan fastness that extended to Tibet. Jealous gods and goddesses would try to seduce the ascetic from his meditation and cause him to expend his accumulated potency – but how many days' abstinence constitutes penitence?

In Northern India (1973) I stopped by a Shiva temple while waiting for my train to Nepal. Much smaller than the station's teashop, it was at the foot of the platform behind a gate and a beckoning chilum-smoking sadhu, in sack cloth and ashes. Actually, loin cloth and ashes; red, white and yellow ashes, as a matter of fact, and hair to shame a sixties hippy. But even the hashish-filled peace pipe that was passed around was par for the course and I was on my way to becoming one hell of a penitent – even before my train pulled into the darkened railway station; due to a power failure that was a projection of the lights that went out in my own head.

Yet, what was most unnerving about that day and night is that I had been drinking from a bottle of "Monk's Brandy" before my destiny led me to the railway station's penitentiary. And I'm not talking about the bad trip that often comes with mixing booze with hash, but my propensity to outfox fiction. Divine Comedy, indeed. It bears repeating over and over again that it is this series of incredible "coincidences" or connections – synchronicity or symmetry – that the straight shooter finds so distressing; the divine dimension that the uninitiated call dementia.

For a better understanding of my circular reality, I must

add that my Indian summer or grand drunk tour (de force) ended in kaput or Kapit, Borneo, where I was forced to leave Christ Hospital because I could not pay for my room. The parting words of the American missionary doctor were, "Funerals are expensive in Borneo."

My reply to the mercenary doctor was, "I won't be paying for it." At any rate, in my *Travels with Shiva* – I discovered people and customs similar to the ones I had left behind in Nepal.

But what do I know? I am only an amateur anthropologist and as the anthropologist wrote in his letter to the *New York Times Book Review,* he had never heard of an "amateur" anthropologist. That may well be, but I have heard of idiot anthropologists – the whole scholarly crew who until recently claimed that the Mayan Indians (returning to the other side of the world) had developed a peaceful or non-violent civilization, when only a moron could make such an oxymoronic observation. Every peace movement begins with those beyond the pale, the puffery of the threatened professional with a stake in his smothering security blanket.

An anthropologist should be the last person in the world to mockingly object to amateurs when civilization was built on the backs – broke the backs – of the "primitives" who had no word for their poetry or art because they were doing what came naturally.

My gut feeling tells me that compassion is a part of wisdom – but it makes more sense to say that knowledge and compassion add up to wisdom and that beyond the semantics of this algebra, the creative pursuit of truth results in illumination. Being lit up like a Christmas tree – without the Christmas cheer.

My cup runneth over with the milk of the lioness – though granted it has sustained a few cracks from a very bumpy road and the corrosive effects of drinks less celestial. White lightening was more thunder than anything else, and absinthe – when mixed with water was only the color of the milk of the lioness. But I am living proof of the power of transcendence – it's just that I leak too much.

The Dalai Lama advised Merton that the ax of true doctrine must be used to cut the root of ignorance, but that harm can come to you if you don't know how to use the ax.

A Bodhisattva and his consort are often shown clutching, besides themselves, their respective symbols for enlightenment: the bell and the thunderbolt. The sweet sound of the bell and I imagine the shape (the only valid bell curve) represents the female side of the equation (when I was a kid an old man always asked me if I had rang the bell lately). The male has also co-opted the female's "wisdom" and relegated the wiser side of human nature to only a soothing sound and touch, which is actually more in line with the supposed "compassion" of the male. It's as clear as a bell.

Ultimately, Thomas Merton experienced his epiphany in what on the surface seems like a kinder and gentler nation. Many pilgrims seeking what is seemingly a higher or less esoteric form of Buddhism end up in Sri Lanka. It was called Ceylon, in 1967, when unfamiliar with Augustine's admonition, I came there by sail. But then, I was not searching for God.

I did not know Merton from the man in the moon and while we were covering the same ground at about the same time, we did not see the same thing. Merton was bound to find what he was looking for in the peaceful faces of the Buddhas – that sacred Void so far removed from the mumbo jumbo that Marx called the opium of the people – that oceanic feeling that connects those islands called men and women.

(Dalai, actually, means a vast ocean but this has less to do with the depth and expansive nature of Buddhism than it does with the Dalai Lama's exalted position as the reincarnation of a revered Lama. He told Merton that Buddhism can be compatible with Marxism – and isn't the monastery the highest form of Communism – but that the problem lies in its Totalitarian nature.)

Merton felt that he had gotten beyond the ambiguity of Mona Lisa's smile. The silence of extraordinary faces were filled with "every possibility, questioning nothing, knowing everything, rejecting nothing. . . .I know I have seen what I was obscurely looking for. I don't know what else remains." All roads lead to home. In Tao fashion, Merton had gotten "beyond the shadow and disguise." Ironically, he had been meditating on statues.

I've always been leery of a destination. I want to be a work in progress. Such a profound sense of arrival could only mark the end of the road.

25

Yak to Yak, Belly to Belly

The province named Thebeth was laid entirely to waste at the time that Mangu Khan carried his wars into that country.... A scandalous custom, which could only arise from the blindness of idolatry, prevails among the people of these parts: they are disinclined to marry young women so long as they are virgins, but require on the contrary, that they should have had previous relations with many of the other sex. This, they assert, is pleasing to their deities, and they believe that a woman who has not had the company of men is worthless. Accordingly, upon the arrival of a caravan of merchants... those mothers who have marriageable daughters... entreat the strangers to accept their daughters and enjoy their society so long as they remain in the neighborhood....

Here are found the animals that produce musk, and there are so many that the scent of it is diffused over the whole country....

These people have no coined money, nor even the paper money of the Great Khan, but use salt for currency. Their dress is homely, being of leather, undressed skins, or canvas....

Among these people you find the most skilled wizards, who by their diabolic art perform the most extraordinary marvels that were ever seen or heard. They cause tempests to arise, accompanied with flashes of lightening and thunderbolts....

They are altogether an ill-conditioned race. They have dogs the size of asses, strong enough to hunt all sorts of wild beasts, particularly the wild oxen called beyamini, which are extremely large and fierce.

Marco Polo

Unraveling on the Old Silk Road

"Marx! Marx!" Two Tibetan monks had me by the beard. So that ruled out Groucho. Also Chico and Harpo, for that matter. I was at a table outside my favorite eatery having yak yogurt, when the passing monks couldn't resist seizing upon this recent symbol of oppression. Twenty years earlier in Florida, I was accused of looking like Castro, so I suspected I had moved up in the world. And it wasn't the first time that the good natured Tibetans had a little sport with me.

"No, no, not Marx! Santa Claus! Hemingway! Abraham Lincoln!"

But none of these people rang a bell. I definitely needed a trim. With Communism's fall from grace, Marx was almost as much a pariah to the Chinese as he was to the Tibetans. I could be a persona non grata, as much for being a true socialist as a free spirit – for when the free market is the rallying cry, anybody upsetting the apple cart is suspect, and all it takes to send an apple rolling or to be a threat to transnational interests is to be a free-wheeling transcendentalist on the loose. Ironically, the last officials to make an issue of my beard or maybe just my Amnesty International-look were some Argentine soldiers in 1976. By then, the beard, as a symbol of liberty, had been outlawed.

The business-minded monk (not an oxymoron, unfortunately) could find himself in the same boat as the Chinese. The major difference being that the darker skinned Tibetan was compelled to travel deck class. Labrang does call to mind a ship anchored off a far shore – since 1709 when the Yellow Hats had already been a dominant force in northern Buddhism for three hundred years. Tson-k-a-pa is the Tibetan reformer, "the man from onion land," (Manchuria) who did the most to turn this "ill-conditioned race" into perhaps the most playful, prayerful people on the planet. It's all a matter of energy – and a great saint is the other side of a great warrior with the will to see the light. Tibetan, Mongol....it's more a matter of semantics than anthropology and with the fall of the Mongol Empire in the fourteenth century, Mongolia accepted Buddhism, and a Genghis Khan, transmuted, transmigrated, becomes the Dalai (Mongolian word) Lama. The Devil's horseman becomes the lord of the oceanic experience.

The man from onion land was said to be an incarnation of the Bodhisattva Manjusri, and probably came from Manchuria. Regarded as a great saint, Manjusri is a deified culture hero of the northern Asian tribes, especially the Manchus. The Manchu emperors of China were followers of Tibetan Buddhism. Physically and metaphysically it is all connected.

The most intriguing symbol of the linked cultures can be seen in the Vajraurhi mandala of eastern Tibet – the interlocking triangles that the West recognized as the Star of David; derivative of ancient India. Forming the matrix of the creation of life, the upward pointing triangle represents the male essence, as the triangle pointing down symbolizes the female side of the equation.

Adibuddha is the cosmic concept encompassing all time and space – and perhaps shape. Shiva, Mahakala, "Great Black One," though a Hindu deity, can also be a wrathful manifestation of Avalokiteshwara, the Bodhisattva of compassion – of whom the Dalai Lama is the incarnate representative. But I'm getting in over my head. If I haven't actually drowned.

Genghis Khan is an unlikely cultural link of the Silk Road and its tributaries, as well as a promoter of Tibetan Buddhism. Scholars have now determined that his purpose for sparing the weavers from Damascus to Xian, in his rampage across Asia, was to have the captured craftsmen transform precious silk into tapestries emblematic of Genghis' power and rule. As Marco Polo related, gold was sometimes woven into these valuable cloths, some of the most remarkable, emblazoned with dragons, coming out of Tibet.

Central Tibet is somewhat defined by the limits of the yak-inhabited plateau – and explains to an extent why the Tibetans would choose to live in an often cold, mostly barren land. The first nomads to ascend the Asian highlands discovered that the yak could serve most of their needs, though the more adventurous – the ancestors of Attila and the later Khans – walked to lands end in those more connected times, the tip of South America.

Chief among the many tribes to migrate over the Bering

Unraveling on the Old Silk Road

Land Bridge were the Mongols with their vast capacity to travel. And when they could no longer bridge the ocean – great wizards that they were – they descended upon western Asia and Europe like the horsemen of the apocalypse. This is the source of the stored energy, the thunderbolt of the Tibetan Buddha. Their tour de force.

History and geography, possibly, nearly repeat themselves as the shamanistic wanderers pick up where they left off, on America's high plains. And our own rocky Himalayas. Surely, the song in their hearts so many miles from their steppes was, "Oh give me a home where the yak roams" – and there, just east of the Rockies, they discover the accommodating bison or buffalo (though it is likely they grazed on both sides of the Great Divide). Could this shaggy symbol of the American West be the evolved yak? Like the yak, the bison provided food, shelter and clothing. And fuel. Yet, in continuing south to the Alto Plano of the Andes, the Asian nomads found themselves in a land so much like the one their ancestors left behind that they settled into an existence almost indistinguishable from some of today's Tibetans. The llama, rarely found below 12,000 feet (at least near the equator) became a near substitute for the Tibetan sheep, though they are to the South American what the yak is to the Tibetan. The cultivation of potatoes replaced barley.

Cowboy hats are foreign introductions and the braids under them interwoven into many cultures, but there is no getting around the fact that the "indigenous" faces of the Americas have that made-in-Asia-look. The Native American of western Canada does not buy the anthropologist's Asian connection, responding, "They want to make us second-class Chinamen," preferring totemic ancestors to the Chinese. But would they be so hostile to the idea of descent from the Mongols? Genghis Khan also claimed totemic ancestry and there is a wolf somewhere in his bloodline. Descent from the wolf and bear is common to the cultures on both sides of the Bering Sea.

In the mountains at this time of the year, and maybe always in this corner of Gansu, the sheep were more numerous than yaks. At Labrang, apparently, they take on the significance of the lamb of Christ, and seem to be an emblem. Almost as serene as the sheep gracing the thangkas or tapestry over the entranceways to the temples are the dogs who mostly confine themselves to the prayer route.

The sight of a dog not destined for the kitchen table – uncaged and unscathed – struck me, on first encounter, as an apparition. And disorienting, only strengthening my South American connection – for after more than a month of roaming around China, I don't ever recall seeing a dog, while in the Andes the lay-abouts are part of the landscape and if they are in the kitchen, they're waiting for handouts. If I expected to see a dog, it was one of those monsters that so impressed Marco Polo. These I would see later in the "grasslands."

A monk informed my Swiss friend that these monastic mascots were the incarnations of monks who had gone astray themselves. And who could doubt this, watching these placid beasts sleeping under the mounted prayer wheels they may have turned in a previous life. The monks, the dogs, the mostly earthy prayer halls, were as natural to the landscape as the sheep to the undulating hills – and when the basically Chinese tourist buses left Labrang, I had the monastery to myself and felt as much a part of it as the temple's burning cedar; a kind of spirit that drafted, drifted about the hallowed grounds. The handful of stray tourists, including myself, blended into the woodwork like the dogs.

But as bucolic as this mosaic could be, it was still an extension of the town, or the other way around, and I could only take so much of the valley when the cooler heights beckoned, and welcoming tents had sprung up like strawberries after the rain. Still under the weather, despite the yogurt, when I struck out for the grassy plains, I took the mountain passes high above the road and the last adobe abode. Many tents were scarcely visible in the "grasslands" opening on Tibet. I was transfixed by this panorama of the distant past when a barebreasted woman holding a fungi appeared out of the glorious blue. An old lady giggling embarrassingly, she raised her folded arms as she passed, probably hiding her breasts from this bearded apparition – and then disappeared as mysteriously as she had appeared. Was this the Tibetan's much vaunted magic at work? It was as if I had eaten the mushroom – though I really can't speak to their hallucinogenic properties. Yet, the improbable sight left me so stoned that I allowed an extraordinary photo to pass me by.

    The fish that got away. Climbing the carpeted pasture my only company was yaks. A leery encounter as I did not know how the grazing bovine would react to my presence. But if these shaggy beasts were Marco Polo's feared oxen, they were about as unperturbed as cows. And there was a touch of the cow in the local yaks, product of mixed ancestry. Like the mule. Perhaps I just had not encountered any males. Were yaks the descendents of water buffalo left high and dry – and cold enough to grow their protective mats?

    Not an hour into a gulley off the road I came upon my first tent. A barking dog was quieted and a man bid me to come out of the rain. Grateful as I was, this was quite a comedown from the sunny grasslands spied from above. Some tea braced with yak butter and I was out of the ravine and onto the road. More tents. A messy affair for a caravan that had evidently run out of steam.

    The rain marked the beginning of the festival and the harvest. Wanting to reap what the Tibetans had sown, the Chinese had created their own version of a celebration a little further up the road and at least ten miles short of the beckoning vista I had seen off in the distance early in the day. A kind of Coney Island – with the emphasis on con – this hokey honky-tonk was designed to waylay tourists bound for the real thing. One method of diverting the tourist flow was accomplished by the Chinese owned vans and jeeps that would charge a steep price to take the unsuspecting visitor to this acoustic nightmare, seemingly at the end of the road.

    I ended up here twice by default utterly exhausted, though I confess this artificial carnival had me fooled on my first visit. Bedecked with loud banners to match the music, could the gayly festooned grounds be anything but the festival? This tourist trap had everything but a yak – and I gave little thought to the distinctly Chinese flavor of the noise that boomed over the speakers. I expected the Chinese to have a hand in shaping a Tibetan festival or anything else, and they are in fact busy bastardizing their music to reinforce the government's claim that Tibet had always been part of China. In every way they can, the Chinese are watering down the differences between the two cultures.

An "engineer" from Lanzhou claimed he was here to repair the dam below us, but considering the information he gave me, he could have engineered this spectacle himself. As so often happens, I was the unwitting spy or witness who comes in out of the rain. The engineer whisked me into his tent, asking me what I was doing here. What the hell did he think, I thought, slowly realizing that this Chin dig had nothing to do with the Tibetan harvest. I was given food, but no sign that the Tibetans were already setting up their main camp up the road. The engineer warned me that I was forbidden to go beyond this point. He was gracious about the whole thing, saving me the trouble of going to one of the dingy stalls or shacks to buy food and drink. He even led me out of the soggy grounds to a waiting bus about to take the Chinese merrymakers into town. Other foreigners had yet to discover this gem.

Perhaps the engineer and these Chinese tourists really didn't know about the Tibetan festival. At the least discouraged from partaking in a freebie with its evocation of freedom and a past, a culture, distinct from their own. But I guess the main idea was to separate the people from their money – what economic progress was all about. And this was accomplished in the damp, cramped enterprise above the dam in the shadow of the mountains.

Nature cooperated on my first trip to the main Tibetan encampment. I was completely blown away by a fleet of tents in a sea of grass. A glorious sun, the billowing tents catching the wind out of the mountains, carrying me along, I was suddenly stopped in my tracks by a woman with a red umbrella gliding above an expanse of yellow flowers. Although I unconditionally accept nature, the woman, the tents were to these wavy plains what sailboats were to the ocean – enhancement to the point of enchantment.

A common design on the tents is a quasi-arabesque curlicue of blue, a brilliant hue that seems to be an emblem of sky people. But the tents themselves mirrored the movement of patchwork clouds across the wild blue yonder and seemed to embody their spirits. The Chinese had killed Tibetans in this corner of Gansu, imprisoned them – put them on reservations and to work in factories – but they never took the wind out of their sails.

I fancied that the revolutions of the prayer wheel reflected the spin of the planet, the clouds following in its wake and the endless cycles in the lives of those who still regarded the canopy of heaven as their real home. Whatever the actual reason for the festival – sacred and profane – an opportunity was afforded the town's people to indulge their instinct to live under the open sky, as many of the camping celebrants lived in Xiahe. Even their distant relative Kublai Khan preferred his tent to the summer palace. The nomad's summer romance.

Above Xiahe, domesticated yaks followed in the wake of the melting snows. In passable terrain, tents are transported on carts. These portable accommodations commingle in the native American tepee. At about the same time the Chinese were engaging in the forced settlement of Tibetans, the Canadian government compelled its indigenous people to resettle in prefab communities, often far from their homeland, fishing and hunting grounds, but close to a packing plant. The Canadians could not understand why these salt of the earth people would often wreck these artificial houses or Quonset huts in an effort to get closer to nature – even in the coldest weather.

Following their own internal clock, Tibetans had come from miles around to attend the festival – which was sanctified by prayer and performance at Labrang, and was almost a culmination of the celebration. I had a foretaste, a strong taste of the holiday, in a tent buried in the barley field opposite my hotel. It beckoned to me from the beginning, and early on I gingerly approached this moveable feast, wanting a little more than a close-up of the nomadic life. Which was at odds with a barley field.

When the man of the house or tent took notice of me, I was invited to dig into a pile of lamb that was washed down with white lightening. The booze tasted like the firewater I had in Nepal (and less exotic places as a matter of fact) at a celebration in honor of the Dalai Lama's birthday. Recalling that everyone had asked for a photo of the absent pontiff, I thought it strange that these party-goers showed no such interest in the Dalai Lama.

My host was a roly-poly man, but looked like he could be a nasty drunk. I saw no compassion in his thunder, wondering if he owned the barley field and the vehicle that brought him here. I asked him if he was Tibetan. He said he was Chinese, but a well-healed Tibetan would toe the party line out of fear of being considered a "separatist," the Chinese term for Tibetans who won't kowtow to the oppressor. Like the Kurds of Turkey, the Tibetans were considered the black sheep of the family and were discouraged from crossing cultural boundaries which weren't supposed to exist in the first place. Maybe I could not make myself understood, but I met few people outside the monastery who would admit to being Tibetans.

Song and rot-gut dissolved our differences and it wasn't long before I was three sheets to the wind and dancing with my rotund friend. Back to back, belly to belly, I don't give a damn, I don't give a helly – let the devil take the hindmost. It was not Chinese music his son was playing; I would not have been able to dance. Whatever my host thought he was, his hospitality never wavered – though I must say if he would have stood still for a second he would have fallen on his face. My fat friend would not be happy until I was out cold – and it is the custom, of course, to literally drink your guest under the table. Less than a foot high, it was the right height for dancing the limbo. Surviving this ordeal by firewater, I was able to make it back to my hotel under my own steam.

Days of whiskey and wild flowers were rudely interrupted when I payed my rent the next morning. Part of the deal for keeping this room with twin beds all to myself was my promise to stay on beyond the festival and to pay three days in advance. The payola or bribe was really voluntary. Discouraging the favored treatment I was enjoying – a room to myself at a reasonable rate – gratuities were forbidden. However, the desk clerk I was dealing with didn't bat an eye when I slipped him my Maine T-shirt and a unisex thing that Mona left behind in Wuhan.

I concluded I was in like Flynn, but now my main man, my partner in crime, was informing me that the owner of the hotel had given him hell for allowing me to have a private room, when he was forced to turn away guests. Although I was still unwell and with a hangover to boot, I felt guilty about anybody being turned away on my account, but sobering up I realized that the manager would fill up the lobby, after the guests were hanging out the windows, before he hung up a no vacancy sign – which I never saw. Most of the guests were used to dormitories anyway.

My young friend was advised that the extra bed was already broken – probably the only reason I had been able to enjoy my solitary confinement as long as I had. Lulling myself into a false sense of security – making me feel very much at home – I had laid most of my clothes on the spare bed. A testimony to my sense of territoriality. Don't tread on me. Or my threads.

Demanding to speak to the owner, I reminded my Maine man that I was a V.I.P. who could ultimately promote or demote the hotel. He replied that I had gotten this prize room, in the first place, because he knew I was important, and that the matter was out of his hands. Who was kidding whom, I wondered, but when you have a pot to piss in in Xiahe, you are not unimportant. I left the desk clerk (maybe he was the manager) with the threat that if anybody but a pretty woman shared my room, I would check out of the hotel.

I became disconsolate. I would call the consulate... but those days or countries were over. Never had I felt more at home in a hotel. Maybe I could bribe my Maine man with my Berkshire T-shirt. I was in my fifties, I paid my dues, I deserved my own room – and a pot to piss in.

My mind had slowed down to the speed of my evacuating bladder, to the point where I could write, ionized bubbles from the broiling brook carrying me aloft, along. I was being swept away by the current, the currency of my words. And yet... the day my journal is more important than my journey, I'll be writing my obituary.

Which I seemed damned close to doing – even if I could go up a mountain, when someone else in my condition would be climbing into bed. I was in this Proustian position when my mind raced ahead of any line I might want to write – which I didn't. I can't shake that old habit of expecting the unexpected – the milestones – to be as indelibly stamped in my memory as the border crossings in my passport. But even that was becoming a rarity – even when it was required.

I headed to town with a pocket full of pens. I could not contemplate sharing my room with anyone, even if the price of privacy was the dregs. There were actually two hotels in Xiahe, and the monastery annex. I had already checked out the annex. My Swiss friend had been living there about a month or so, and not only shared his hot plate with me but also had invited me to take the extra bed. No, this was too much like Swiss Family Robinson. Worse, because it had one very, very busy outhouse that looked out on a faded fountain that hadn't seen water since the deluge. I thought he might have some ideas, but he was out hiking with a monk.

I got no further than the lobbies of the hotels. The déjà vu was just too depressing. With sinking heart I slinked into the monastery and making my way to the outer circle, an angel cast out of heaven, searched for an angle. I did not get very far on my Via Dolorosa, the upper prayer path, when my clockwise drift brought me to the door of Labrang's health clinic. Xiahe also had a hospital on the main road near the monastery's annex or hostel. But the clinic is a small concrete block that mostly dispensed a wide assortment of herbal pills. The doctor, a monk, took my pulse and very little money for the pills that would fight my cigarette cough – that sapping souvenir from the lower altitudes. He had no cure for a hangover.

Labrang doesn't really have a wall, but the upper way hugs the mountain and looks down on the monastery – and out on the opposite heights. The view is better than the tail of the dog that bit you – an expression that doesn't sit well where there are docile muts about. Completing my circle I ended up in the monastery's hostel.

A couple of Canadian brothers were now staying in the annex. They are not to be confused with a North American religious order, but were two young teachers on a sabbatical. Like my friends from Massachusetts, the brothers had come to China to teach and were learning a lesson they would never forget. The younger Canadian was forever running the fifty yard dash.

A toilet bowl had taken on the dimensions of a throne – and I decided I was not about to give mine up to any usurper.

The afflicted Canadian took things in stride, but was less forgiving about the Chinese, "a yellow plague," that had apparently effected his mind. One of the main attractions of Xiahe was getting away from the Chinese, but now the teacher was unhappy about the young Tibetans who were taking over the hostel in anticipation of the official festival. With the door of his cubicle open on the courtyard to get some air, he had become a sideshow for the curious. He did not appreciate being caught with his pants down.

His sanguine brother also could only talk about the Chinese and was fighting mad. "We're accustomed to people being polite in Canada." And if "please" didn't achieve the desired results, a fist, it seemed, would.

"They are so rude -- why, look at the way they treat their own people. And the spitting! I tell my students, college material, that spitting isn't allowed in my classroom, and you'd think I was preventing them from breathing. Where do you spit in Canada, they ask." He was foaming at the mouth.

We were joined by a young dude from California, a college student, who had the hottest shades in all of China. He was asking if I had any dope.

"I stopped smoking," I told him.

"Why?" he asked.

"Well, for one thing, I thought it was illegal." Standing tall, he looked down on me. "They'll shoot you if they catch you."

I thought that was reason enough to quit, but one-upping this California dreamin', I told him I get higher on a beer than he could on a joint, and the next thing I knew the three of us are heading for the only "Tibetan owned" restaurant/bar in town. The way the student saw it, we'd be striking a blow for freedom and were on a kind of pilgrimage.

26

Hello, Dalai

Land so high, made so pure.
Without equal, without peer.
Land indeed! Best of all!
Religion too surpassing all!
                    Tibetan poem

The Long Island-born Californian came to China by way of Pakistan. He suggested that I leave China the way he entered, which was also the cheapest way out of here. "Three days by train and two by bus..." What about the nights, I asked, but he was still briefing me. "You get a temporary visa for Pakistan at the border..." Jesus Christ, I said, "I can hardly make it down this street, which isn't all that noisy or crowded or hot and you're sending me to Pakistan!"

In the restaurant we were joined by an aging yuppy passing himself off as a cowboy. Another Long Islander, this character had taken his law practice to Texas.

"And what do you do, hoss?" I was at a loss. I could have answered "to be is to do," but he may have read the handwriting on that wall in Dali.

Beer is to me what peyote is to some Native American tribes – but never on a sunny day. It's like holding up a candle to the sun, an insult to the sacrament and my liver – and drinking with Americans (if the Canadian will pardon the expression) in this corner of the world only heightened my sense of sacrilege and amnesia, with a lawyer, no less!

This taste of camaraderie was a rude reintroduction to

the society that is the impulse behind my travel and travail. Diverse as these travelers were, I could only be the odd man out. They would return to normal lives, or what passes for normal in America, while my own journey would continue in the country that just happened to be my place of birth.

I grew up trying to straddle two worlds, one leg in the country I was growing up in, and the other in the country that my parents never outgrew. Now, one leg was in America, if that's how you would describe a tentative toehold, and the other in a world developing into what I was trying to escape. Is it any wonder I was a drowning man clutching at straws trying to keep afloat on voyages past.

One beer and I was sailing up the Nile, "Who was that guy who wrote about the sixties dropouts sailing up the Nile; he was writing about me and my wife. . . ."

"He's still writing that stuff," the UCLA dude interjected.

"That was my book, *The American Voyager,* I lived it, I wrote it. . . ."

The lawyer cut me short with a snort. An old loser wasn't supposed to the steal the show. "Hey, this is Xiahe, 1992!"

He was overruled by the student. "Let him talk, it's better than listening to who barfed where."

The Dalai Lama had complained to Thomas Merton about the ladies in tight pants and purple hair who were indulging in the latest exotic fad. The religion of the month. A few days later I would see the lawyer subtly mocking the chanting monks. Long Island had a very long reach indeed.

As so often happens, I ended up *Tramping to Jerusalem.* I gave the lawyer a quick rundown.

"Sounds like you wrote something anti-Semetic."

"I wrote about the Israelis what you guys say about the Chinese. What's the difference between Israel's occupation of the West Bank and China being in Tibet?"

"As far as I'm concerned, the Palestinians already have a homeland."

"What's that?" I asked.

"Jordan."

In the future, I would venture no further into Xiahe than Labrang. Nothing came of the threat to put another guest in my room. The owner probably reasoned that it was more profitable that the extra bed remain empty and I stay on beyond the festival, than have me leave and have both beds free when the celebration was over in a couple of days; with no tourists to fill them. Nor did he wish to make the V.I.P. unhappy.

Management had enough problems with normal guests raising Cain. While I was waiting in the lobby for my call to Mona to get through, a French couple were complaining at the reservation desk.

"What is the matter with this hotel? Yesterday you don't have a bed for me, and now I can't have breakfast!" And now hysterical, "Is zer something wrong with me?!?"

My Maine man responded, "But the restaurant is closed."

"You said the restaurant was open until 9:30. It is now 9:30, and I paid for my coupon yesterday."

I didn't know the Faulty Towers used coupons but then I never ate in the restaurant, though I once managed to smuggle a bowl of rice out of the kitchen. No, the sullenness of the restaurant staff was no way to start my day, and I had found ways to stave off starvation.

And the cafe was no way to end my day either, when I needed a cup of tea. With the Xian affront fresh in my mind – that mysterious shortage of tea – I asked for a cup of China's lifeblood.

"You can have Coca Cola."

"I need a hot cup of tea." My voice rising, "You're not going to charge me ten times as much for that carbonated crap."

Foreigners, Europeans all, aghast at this un-American outburst and my assault on their tastes, turned away as I countered their startled glances with an accusatory look that said they were subverting the character of China. Leaving the Cafe Disco, I spat for good measure. I had gone native. En toto.

As with the tent in the barley field, I finally succumbed to the lure of the primitive mill opposite the hotel. How could Don Quixote resist? Even if it was water operated. I don't think I thought it was more than a hut. A fellow hermit appeared to live there, as irascible as myself and busy shooing strangers away from his turf. But the old man had a soft place in his heart for birds and that was part of the attraction of the ramshackle hogan on the river.

Every morning the miller hung his caged creatures from the limbs of trees growing on the river bank. Before I saw that the hermit had a part in the birdsong, I thought I had indeed arrived in paradise, their singing heard above the rush of the water, a sign that this was a place where men and beast found sanctuary in China. Visiting the birdman one morning, I was surprised to be so warmly welcomed and invited inside his sanctuary for tea. It was little more than a raised bed, as is the custom, heated by the stove.

Opposite the bed was a second door. He opened it and bid me to enter another room. Crossing the threshold of the millennia, I watched in wonder as a great stone, ever so slowly, ground the grain. In the way of eternity, the millstone was turned by the water wheel below, its rumbling rotation a sacred drone that produced the staff of life. Like manna from heaven, answered prayers. Haltingly, the amber-colored flour formed a termite mound on the floor. It was periodically poured into a sack. Getting me more tea, fortified with yak butter, the old man then took a ladle to the freshly ground barley and mixed the mess into an impromptu breakfast. Voila, stampa (tsamba). The consistency of mud but slightly tastier and the breakfast of champions.

The barley had grown up to the miller's doorstep, but was now cutting a hasty retreat as a woman with a scythe was reaping the ripe plant. Kernels were left out to dry in the sun before the rains came and the cycle was completed – signalling as much as the moon the start of what had once been a harvest festival, in the good old days of the Bon religion.

"Are you going to watch the monks dance?" My Maine man was greeting me in the lobby and was actually wearing my T-shirt. I remarked on what a nice shirt he was wearing – and under a suit jacket no less. The manager replied thank you, as if he had bought the thing himself. Wearing my shirt, he was acknowledging that he owed me, and would not have the audacity to thrust a stranger upon me I hoped. And maybe my shirt was the flashiest glad rag he had to show off for the celebration. Relieved, I headed for Labrang and the main event.

Like a great magnet, the monastery was drawing Tibetans, the salt of the earth, from the four corners, out of the hills and into the valley. Walking, on horseback, men and women of every stripe, in baubles, bangles and beads streamed past me. Warm as it was, more than one pilgrim was wearing the spotted coat of the snow leopard, and many were swathed in a wild array of hats and fur coats, and the wine-colored toga of the monk, sometimes topped with inventive turbans.

I reeled like a drunk. And on they came, in great boots, amulets and anchor-shaped hatchets hanging from their belts, worldly possessions on their backs, coats draped from bare shoulders, exposing the richest color of all. Copper of their faces, complementing the inner glow of those who have been to the mountain. Trickling down the gullies, the alleyways and byways and every path that led to Labrang, they carried in their wake a hobo tramping to yet another Jerusalem, until reaching the flood stage, I was beached at my favorite restaurant.

Pushing on I was eventually before the grandest prayer pole, like a great tree planted before the principal temple, in the very heart of Labrang. Enough flags were fluttering to frighten the Devil himself. At its root the great stake could have been a Maypole. Tibetans and tourists alike occupied its foundation for a better view of the activities, but it was not central to the occasion.

Like Times Square on New Year's Eve, the air was electric with expectation. Then there was the distant rumble of thunder and horns accompanying the drums. The droning was followed by a drama as old as the hills, as masked performers, all monks, whirled about the human circle of spectators. Demons and deers, horned creatures harked back to the more sanguine days of animal sacrifices. A time when only humans would propitiate the gods. A key figure in the opera was a white bearded wizard who could have been Father Time himself. I believed, mistakenly, that the hoary one could have been the

Buddhist saint who brought enlightenment to the Tibetans.

I had no playbill, but I think that few really knew the score. It may as well have been a circus – with the most garish clowns and ghoulish freaks to boot. One bizarre hybrid in a silk costume of red and gold appeared to be a prancing bear at the command of the whip-wielding ancient whose painted face was distinguished by a red crescent craddling what could have been a miniature sun in the middle of his yellow forehead. Shades of Shiva! The bear seemed to represent the malleable worshipper at the beck and call of the priestly figure.

The colors alone were deafening and becoming annoyed by the actual clamor, I made my way to the roof of the major temple. My spectacular surroundings were a harmonious relief from the interminable din below. And V.I.P. tourists trucked in for a grandstand seat of the performance – or ritual. My camera and chutzpah countered any interference from monks guarding the access to the more rarefied atmosphere of the roof. Senior monks or lamas were seated in an enclosure above the entrance to this great prayer hall. I stopped short of joining them.

The roof was highlighted by golden nubs, stupas reflecting the brightest sun in the brightest sky. A kind of Asian baroque, but the mostly earthen temples tempered the overlay of gold that only complemented the alpine scenery above the purifying cedar or juniper smoke (that helped neutralize the stench of urine from the drainage ditches towards the rear of the monastery, subtly employed when a quick leak under raps was in order). Even the evergreens the Chinese spared were for show. But the steeply rising valley remained tantalizing and what was in my line of sight would one day soon be my lifeline to the monastery.

Only a peasantry starved for entertainment could have sat through the entire performance – even if they understood the allegory behind it. The enraptured audience became my own entertainment, but I was anxious to get out to the grasslands and the secular winding down of the festival, which included a payoff to monks for arcane spiritual favors.

I piled on a waiting bus that had already seemed like an

eternity to the American girl who had been there from the start. Her patience evaporated with the disappearance of the driver, who had apparently absconded with our fares. Tired of protesting to no one in particular – few beyond the sang-froid Germans and myself understood her – she began beeping the horn for all it was worth; maybe the only thing that worked in the damn bus.

But the blasting horn barely penetrated the general cacophony, and the ensuing street symphony only succeeded in unnerving me. When even the Tibetans tired of waiting, she tried to hijack the bus as I cheered her on. It was no go.

"Do you have any ideas?" She was hovering over me, consulting the senior tourist. "What's the word for police?" she added as if she had the answer to our problem.

"The bus driver is probably the police."

But undaunted, she pulled out her Chinese phrase book and began screaming, "Jingcha! Jingcha!" to the unmindful throng. Shaking her "bible" like a crazed evangelist, another tourist bit the dust.

By the time the show was on the road – on a different bus – I was halfway through my water. But I was more concerned with breaking away from the tourists than replenishing my water and I debused short of the tents, slightly after an abandoned compound. This ugly blot on the grasslands had something of a concentration camp air about it. A reservation. There is no reliable guidebook on the cultural revolution.

Crossing the meadow, I found refreshment at the edge of the encampment. I was welcomed like a long lost brother, but I could not resist following a stream, as it was still early in the day and I knew this would take me beyond the contaminating present. Beyond the human turds, and the one or two fishermen, the grass had given way to the unforgiving rock of higher ground. But still I pressed on, fighting the temptation to drink from the stream, even when the tents were tiny white flowers being consumed by distance.

A hamlet seemed deserted. Walking up to the dwellings on the low ridge, I was approached by two young men and then an unfriendly fellow who did not like what he saw. I shook my almost empty canteen. I thought the brute would shake his fist, but I got the message, never getting within a stone's throw of his crude digs. Heading towards the stream and the first cluster of adobe homes, I now noticed smoke. A peasant appearing at her doorway eyed me with more caution than curiosity. And her chained dog was barking – and by the looks of him, he was no incarnate monk but the devil himself, straining to take a bite out of my hindmost. I held my throat. "Cha, cha," I croaked. I wouldn't dare ask for water.

She motioned that I follow her to another mud house, the line outside festooned with strips of meat drying in the sun. This scene was a step-up from a cave, but similar to what I had seen in eastern Turkey. Another beast straining at the bits came to life. Evidently, I was fair game. The lady of the house came to the door. Avon calling, I mumbled. The first lady with a mocking, almost hysterical laugh and mimicking me, informed her friend what I was all about. She held her throat, "Cha, cha," the dog is barking, children have appeared in the doorway and the hot sun is beating down on this bedlamite dance. Backing up and begging off, I said to myself I better sit this one out – and hightail it out of here.

But no, the second lady bids me to enter her darkened hovel, and when finally the water had boiled on the dying embers, I had my tea. I really couldn't blame them for having a good laugh before demonstrating their rarely failed hospitality. Still, I was soon beating a hysterical retreat – flabbergasted when I realized the dog was free of his leash and gaining ground on me in a kind of attack and backup scenario that had me scrambling over the badlands for rocks to toss. This was carrying a joke too far – much further than a stone's throw from my missing hostess. Much worse than my encounters with the curs of Columbia. Dancing with wolves, indeed.

When the beast was within twenty or thirty feet of me, I was mad as a junkyard dog myself, and firing salvos with as many arms as Shiva. Incensed by my stones the dog circled, barely restrained by the invisible leash that inhibited this half-domesticated animal from going for my throat – and maybe he realized he had bitten off more than he could chew. He bugged off.

27

Strawberry Fields Forever

Arriving at the festival in a froth, I walked down to the stream to join some Tibetans sitting around a friend playing a guitar. The music was of no particular nation, but as boundless as the sky. One of the young men opened a beer for me. If this didn't carry the day, two camera shy women astride a yak forded the stream – I captured them for posterity anyway.

Now, I'm sitting outside a tent focusing on a long stacked stove against the darkening sky, the teapot so much more defined with the color drained from the day. Embers burned away. Twilight and an omnipresent jar of tea sitting aside the enormous kettle. But I have never seen a Tibetan with a jar of tea. This new group that has invited me into their tent has lived in the city. I may as well be reading tea leaves for all I know, but it doesn't matter.

Young monks have forded the stream and are hurrying up the bank. Their robes blending into the burgundy-streaked sky behind them. Something is in the air. I leave the tent. Drums are growing louder and now hastening my step, I see a bonfire, a kind of torch being passed as the leaping flames have replaced the retreating sun, and·this great fire must carry this long day into night. Circling the eternal flame in the timely fashion, singing dancers go back to the beginning of time. Human kind.

In many tribal cultures, including the pre-Buddhist Tibetan, perhaps, the circle itself symbolizes the greatest fire of all, the sun. Food, warmth, in its eternal rising, a faith in the future, infinity. God.

These are not performing monks. Many of the dancers are women in long black skirts and red sashes, apparently ceremonial dress that was nonetheless topped by the perennial broad rimmed hat. With a drumbeat and song as insistent as the stars, they danced through the night, far removed from the clamorous opera at the monastery. Was anything more elemental than fire, this Bon fire that lit the Mongol's way in their journey to the east?

Shiva's cosmic dance of fire in the circle eternal. The deadwood leading to enlightenment. The Apache spirit that keeps home fires burning, like the transported flame of the ancient Persian. It is all connected and in the understanding of our connectedness – political correctness be damned – will we close the circle, will we be whole.

Like Christianity, Tibetan Buddhism had incorporated or absorbed an earlier paganism, and the Yellow Hats seemed the happier for throwing them into the ring (they wear their eighteenth century admiral-shaped headdress on the monastery grounds). I was feeling no pain myself as I boarded the bus for Xiahe. Most of the passengers happened to be monks on this particular bus and they exuded a non-alcoholic aura or air. A lighter-than-air laughter that was sobering, a levity that was uplifting. Little more than that remains with me, but an outsider will bask in the remembrance of their unquestioning acceptance, dance. As they accepted life, they accepted death, their Book of the Dead, an esoteric counterpoint to their playfulness. Their survival kit in the nether world or bardo between lives. Is it joy that sustains the soul, provides the light at the end of the tunnel? Through the tunnel to another incarnation? Laughter lights the lamps of the world, but compassion enables us to see.

Ritual laughter is employed to train young monks. In the monastery, I heard and saw a class haw-haw an erring novice into correctness. The joke was on me the next morning, when with more smoke than fire and little else, I got off to a late start. The grasslands had left me low and dry and I had drained the huge thermos of most of my water, left to cool in several glasses. Confident I could fill up on tea at the mill, I brought along my empty fruit jar to mix barley into breakfast, before taking a mountain path to the monastery. But the mill was closed, the door locked and the old man nowhere to be seen.

With one more card to play, the joker crossed the balding barley field and headed up stoney gulch to the tiny hamlet that had provided succor in the past. Once before I had eaten tsamba with an elderly couple tending their yaks in the mists above the valley. From their hut, today, I would be veering off in the opposite direction of the grasslands, mostly playing it by ear. Shamefully, I had counted on the aging yak herders. But this happened to be the day that my one-eyed friend was taking a donkey load of yak dung to the village or Xiahe itself. I met him about halfway to his hut. It was so dark inside that I had not realized my friend was blind in one eye, but, now, greeting me, this did not lesson his smile. Knowing I was thirsty he urged me to continue on.

The cluster of hutches was almost deserted. Only the old man's wife was home, looking out at me from her dwelling and looking none too happy at my arrival. It was an expense and an effort to make the customary tea and guiltily I turned away, regretting I had put her on the spot. They would never take money and my pens were as worthless to them as they had become to me. Perhaps she was afraid. Stoney house, stoney kraal (now bereft of dung), stoney silence – but a heart of gold. The fool may think that God provides, but he is often inconveniencing a good Samaritan.

Children were drawing water from the nearby stream. The women were simply making themselves scarce. Not like the good old days. I motioned I needed something to drink, meaning tea, but the young Tibetans, doing the obvious, pointed to the fast flowing rivulet. I was afraid of drinking water beneath the yak line, but I could get no higher than a yak and eventually the ancient mariner succumbed to its teasing presence. And it may as well have been salt water for the damage it did me down the road.

I did not drink more than a mouthful, yet going out of my way to see the mountain's most prominent prayer flags. They were loud yellow and red, but one could only wonder how such a happy array of colors could ward off evil spirits – unless the devil is impotent in the face of joy. Were evil spirits little more than invisible crows scared by the beribboned rag dolls (no matter how tall the pole)? A Tibetan guide with young French tourists in tow wasn't talking. This was the first time I had seen outsiders above the tree line. The educated Tibetan, the age of his charges, and ashamed of his heritage identified the towering talisman as an ancient marker from the time that Tibetans had no roads.

Climbing higher and higher, I passed the tent of yak herders who had followed their animals up the opposite mountain and were calling to me. The monastery was nearly in sight of my flower-clad pyramid but I had emptied my canteen and strayed from the path. Baking, I could only consider the closest distance between two points and lowered myself into the carpeted chasm. Astounded, I saw strawberries. No, I must be hallucinating. It was almost mid-August. Where I was from they were ripe by July. They were red leaves. And then I saw tiny strawberries, one, two, three. . . .and they were getting larger and larger and this whole steep slope untrodden by man or sheep was blanketed in the most succulent fruit. And down I went hand over fist, foraging as much as I was descending, eating and holding on to this plant for dear life, in making my way down the mountain, staving off dehydration. The berries could not have been more accessible if they had been handed to me on a platter. In one tricky place I was actually grazing, enjoying a hand-to-mouth existence.

By the time I crossed a wooden bridge and was walking along the river towards something more substantial than strawberries, my head was spinning like one of the rickety prayer wheels at the low end of Labrang. A curled up cur cocked a knowing eyebrow in my direction. See you later, alligator.

I was in bed and before my television earlier than usual, still hopeful I might see myself on the screen. On the roof of the monastery, yesterday, I was interviewed by a Chinese television crew assuming that my commanding view of the performance spoke to a high position. But I would have to wait until the yaks came home before seeing myself on the other side of the boob tube. We were getting only one or two stations in Xiahe, enduring a nocturnal diet of Olympian Chinese copping just about every cup or gold medal there is, and quiz shows and documentaries heavy with the military.

    Not many uniformed soldiers were about in Xiahe, until they put on a little parade, but the few Tibetans who could afford television were not forgetting on which side their bread was buttered, and forgoed any ideas of independence. In the blatant, prescribed adoration of the army, government programming left the viewer with the impression that Tianaman had never happened. The army was the strongest, if not the only remaining symbol of the Communism that was – that legendary Long March to the People's Republic. Now it was Communism. It was China. It was brainwashing nostalgia writ large. Hail, the conquering hero – and you better believe the Chinese Army is eating their rice but feeling their oats. I did not have to know the language to know the military brass had all the answers. It was enough to discourage the Dalai Lama himself – now being criticized for not being more aggressive about independence.

    I had invited an American girl to watch my television with me. We would meet at the Cafe Disco after I got the strawberry juice out of my beard. Like the first American I met here, she was just curious about the hotel, and like the first woman seemed too accepting of China. But she exuded innocence and her youth gave me pause. Writing this gives me pause. What would I be getting into? Absent minded possessor that I was, I could forget my age and my significant other. Strawberry fields forever, a roll in the hay? But watching the army go through its antics was better than counting sheep. I wasn't in my room very long before sleep shaped my destiny.

    Every mountain here had its own character. Not a mile from the hotel, beyond the crematorium and the tents beyond that, I set my sights on yet another prayer flag. Not resting long on the knoll above the tents I noticed that a man with binoculars was trying to get a fix on me. He appeared to be a Chinese soldier, slightly out of uniform, not likely to be keeping tabs on the sheep high above me. I had to bypass the prayer flags, but in good time was in the midst of the most beautiful sheep in the world. Half black and half white, they engulfed me as they followed their noses back to the valley.

A chasm had widened between me and the flags and was revealing ruins that had almost returned to nature. Getting a closer look at the rubble, I spied a cave. I only wanted to get out of the sun and look out on the sacred ridge. Cooling off and calming down, I felt the presence of something beyond me. Clumps of clay were beginning to take on human form and low and behold, I had uncovered a cache of terra cotta figures. Baked reliefs. I expected to see Buddha, but sunlight revealed a sort of Lord of the Soil or Shiva, himself, with that octopus reach of the Cosmic Dancer.

These small figures were probably talismans meant to ward off evil spirits. The size of a tiny bottle of aspirins, these tablets were not relics but of recent vintage. Had I walked into an underground religion, the underside of Tibetan Buddhism that was living proof of Bon? Unthinkingly, I took two tablets, an easy fit in the palm of my hand, and continued my ascent.

Clearly I could have benefited from enrolling in Labrang's Institute of Thinking While Hearing or Seeing, instead of being at the mercy of impulse. With new sights to behold I gave little thought to my find. Not a day went by in the mountains that I didn't stumble upon a sacred site or sacrificial fire or campfire surrounded by surviving remnants of a rite. Nearly always these took the shapes of large postage-sized prints or pictures that showed a steed of heaven against a background that was less stellar than stygian. Maybe it was only the quality of the print revealing a tiger.

Circling the crematorium, I returned to my hotel stricken with Shiva's revenge. Perhaps I was overplaying the Shiva card, but Sanskrit is basically the written language of Tibet, introduced with India's religions. . . .I needed expert help. It was not until 1995 that I decided to do something about my little shavers. I had already moved twice, beginning to resettle in New York (to the extent that is humanly possible), when I telephoned the Museum of Natural History. It can be considered a monument or at least a dedication to Teddy Roosevelt, the Bully Boy president who not only shook his "Big Stick," but also shot up a good part of Asia and Africa in the name of science and sport. Speaking to a curator, I inquired of my tablets' significance.

"I would like to donate one of these things to the museum."

Madame Curator was not pleased. "You say you found these things in a cave."

"Yes."

"That's looting."

"Wait a second, there is nothing rare about these things. They were made in a mold, they are still in use."

"That is still looting."

"China is trying to keep these things in the dark, they might have anthropological worth. Aren't you curious?"

"China is very concerned about preserving its culture. I urge you to return the figures."

"It's not China's culture to preserve. They'll cast everything in their own mold to reinforce their hold. Xiahe is really Tibet."

She would not discuss the matter any further. Please, I said, at least recommend a book that could be helpful to me understanding what I found.

"Foreign Devils on the Silk Road," she answered.

"That was me, I guess."

She laughed. "That's all of us."

Today their plunder is more sophisticated than in the Great White Hunter's day, his likeness looking down to us from the celestial ceiling of the museum, big stick in hand surrounded by trophies. It was poetic injustice that I who had petitioned the Cloisters of the Metropolitan Museum of Art on behalf of Cuxa Monastery in southern France for the return of its capitals, had the shoe thrust on the other foot, on the other side of Central Park. Maybe I could palm off my tablets on the Met. The way things were going for me I was less concerned about breaking a Chinese law than having brought a curse upon myself. On the other hand who knows what harm could have come to me without my clay amulets.

28

Foreign Devil on the Silk Road

This was not the best time to shove off, but I was running low on cash, and the hotel and no one else for miles around would change my travelers checks. The maid was not being very cooperative either. I asked her to change my sheets and she takes my toilet paper instead. She returned the toilet paper and when I asked for clean towels – much of the communication through sign language so there is no misunderstanding – she brings me more toilet paper. No soap.

The newly arrived tourist bus parked outside the hotel restaurant was becoming less of an eyesore and beginning to interest me when I considered what was involved to get back to Lanzhou – the only destination for departing buses. I focused on the shiney bus as if it were my only way out of Xiahe. The alternative with a regular bus was the de rigeur advanced purchase of my ticket. That meant, with the 6:00 A.M. departure, I had to take my chances of being out of the hotel by five-thirty at latest, to be at the bus station in time for takeoff. The manager said I could get a ride to town on a tractor for two dollars, but with a fresh stirring underfoot, I would walk or trot first. And I knew what he meant by a "tractor." I asked him about the tourist bus.

"It's leaving tomorrow."

Where are the tourists from; what country? I questioned, my hopes rising.

"Spain." Adios, partner.

Somebody had tacked up a thangka depicting the wheel of transmigratory existence. At the hub of the wheel were the three root poisons which bind us to existence and rebirth. Ignorance, one of them, is symbolized by a pig – an animal the Chinese are ambivalent about. Especially in Taiwan where hog farming is a big industry. Desire is depicted as a cock. The third poison, hatred, is symbolized by a snake. The band around this inner circle of sin shows human beings moving up to a happy rebirth, clockwise being chased down to a hellish incarnation. The highest realm we can be born into is shown at the top of the thangka, a kind of Olympus or Shangri-La of the gods, and oddly enough this mountain range-shaped heaven bore a striking resemblance to the high Pamir, just above the Karakorum at the far edge of historic Tibet – awaiting me far up the road.

Was this depiction the ancient mythical Kingdom of Shambala? Was this the inspiration for Lost Horizon? Also located in Central Asia.

At this time I still thought I was heading toward Beijing and was not considering any destination beyond Lanzhou, not crossing any bridges before I came to them and as likely to swim across the river. A Spanish tourist had probably put up the thangka, sensing that La Bu Leng Temple Hall (the old Chinese name for the hotel) was lacking something. The hanging, which looked like a replica of a thangka I had seen at Labrang did not stay put very long. My goal was to find the guide. She was a Julie Andrews, sound of music type woman who instantaneously brought out the cock in me. A young, bright blonde who had ridden her bicycle across China before getting her job. It seemed like half the tourists I had met cycled about China, but I remarked it was a rare senorita who would so spin her wheels.

"Pero, no soy española, Señor."

"Si, de donde vien?" I asked, struggling through America's second language.

"Soy Svede."

"Swedish," I replied, switching to English and anxious to get the show on the road. She spoke English better than I or me, and could appreciate my situation, but "you must convince my group and they are a lot more comfortable speaking Spanish. Introduce yourself."

They were a daunting flock. My oldest and still vivid memory of Spain is of the flack my beard drew. Who was I to go around imitating Christ, seemed to be the tenor of their hostility.

"Por favor," I addressed the group, "Soy Don Quixote." Pronounced Don Quishot. No, I better play it straight. "Soy Americano, soy infirmo y es muy dificile por me ir a Lanzhou con autobus locale, loco."

That I was infirmo or infirm nobody doubted, but the knight of the woeful countenance looked harmless enough and I must confess to some nonsense about being an escritor de viaje. It's usually unwise to say you are a writer, but I picked up the habit when I was an unwilling traveling salesman, and in predicaments like this it explained away perhaps threatening eccentricities.

I passed muster. "Be ready to leave at 5:30."

I wasn't and had hardly budged before the angelic Swede knocked on my door gently reminding me that they were ready to depart. I was up much of the night with a runny tummy and never felt so bad about imposing upon someone. Especially since I did not want to look like another spoiled or soiled American: the world could wait while I got my act together. Ever so prompt, normally, I was doubly chagrined at holding up the Spaniards. Mañana should have been good enough for them. My room was a flurry of papers and clothes, memorabilia that was less packed than dumped into my sack-like backpack. Half-dressed, I scrambled down the steps as if my life depended upon me boarding that bus. Maybe it did.

Everyone looked like they were ready for siesta and quite forgiving. They were, after all, Spanish, but my seatmate, a professor of literature and instantly recognizing me, insisted Spain was now a different kettle of fish. The past, even Franco, was no more. It was less. The professor lamented that only crime kept up with the rising prices, but as I could plainly see, they were more tolerant. Wasn't I on the bus? They had come to Xiahe for the "Seventh Month Festival" as this fiesta was officially known, the new year beginning in February. Yet they were unaware of the ceremony or performance at the monastery. The trip had been arranged in Madrid.

I could understand this new Spanish get up and go, but I asked if getting up in the middle of the night wasn't overdoing it.

"We have a train to catch."

Maybe Julie said as much. How could it register? "We have taken the Silk Road Tour." The Spaniards had barely rediscovered the Americas, and here they were joy riding to the end of the road – without their bus? The staid, stay-at-home Spaniards?

"No more bus?"

"Only the guide."

I asked Julie about their tour.

"Dunhuang. Turpan. . . .you should not miss the Silk Road."

But once I got that far there was no turning back. Pakistan was a pipe dream I associated with that pot-smoking student and I could not imagine unraveling all the way to Karachi.

"You're really not ditching this bus, are you?"

"It's a long ride." The bus lacked a toilet for one thing. And we soon made a "lu stop" as the Aussies say. I thought about the "Sundowner" tour bus I hitched a ride with in India. As in the subcontinent the rules of the road dictated men and women find their own bush or tree when nature called. A kind of call of the wild, but oh, how I preferred a silk road to the red tape. My return to Lanzhou left me so disoriented – the word was beginning to take on a special meaning – I could barely pull away from Julie's skirt. Oh, good shepherdess, don't throw me to the wolves.

I did not know what to do at first. Should I find a hotel? The group was staying at a hotel out of my class, but it was next door to the tourist office that sold me my insurance. I told Mona I was going to Beijing via Inner Mongolia, I would be home soon. I had to cover some ground while my bowels were holding up. Again, they were trying to sell me insurance. Was this a new policy? Was there no destination without great risk?

"My insurance is good for fifteen days, and I've only had this for fourteen!"

"That is too bad, the conductor will not allow you on the bus with this old wrinkled insurance."

Just then Julie barged into the office. "Guess what? There is no space on the train for my group, and we've had reservations for weeks." It was her turn to raise a little hell.

They would be stuck in Lanzhou for at least a day. Had I not been torn in so many directions, I would have seized the moment, held on to her silk skirt, but I was beyond the sound of music and found myself in the street – facing the music. I hadn't gone a quarter of a mile before I knew I would be damned if I let the sun go down on me in Lanzhou. It had more going for it than most Chinese cities, was the capital of petro chemical pollution, but after my sojourn in Xiahe I required something a bit more pristine. Beneath a headline in the China Daily (July 18th), I read, "China's birthplace, the Yellow River, is set to be reborn." The river was almost inflammable already, and they are rhapsodizing about the green light for the economic rebirth. A photo next to the article shows a family bathing in a river. Bliss.

Stopping at a hotel near the station, I headed for the tourist office. The operator – and a cool one at that – just happened to be going to lunch. Would I join him? Who is paying, I replied, realizing he saw me coming. Sitting in this overpriced hole-in-the-wall, he asked why tourists spend a thousand dollars to go to China and then spend peanuts on food. "I eat better than the tourists."

"By the time the tourists get to Lanzhou," I responded, "they have little money left to eat."

The operator could not give me train information and said I would have to go to the station. A bus was out of the question as far as Inner Mongolia was concerned. But I didn't have the heart to deal with the railway mafia. In the lobby of the hotel, I debated what to do. Where there were tourists there was a way, but the pickings were slim. Desperate for feedback, familiarity, I sat next to a middle-aged German woman. The stodgy stereotype. Was I mad? She could barely understand me, though no language was necessary to see I was at the end of my rope, if not shoestring. My map wasn't holding up very well either and literally fell to my feet in pieces. What better symbol for the fragmented world I inhabited than my made-in-China tourist map?

If I expected a lift on another tour bus I was mistaken, but she took out her made-in-Germany tourist map and when she had shown me where she had been, bid me to keep it. I weakly demurred, but she was on her way to the airport and insisted I take her map. If I didn't know where I was going, I had a better idea of where I was – and that is half the battle.

I returned to the tourist office, determined to get some service. In the same boat, but going in a different direction, was a girl from Hong Kong. She suggested we go to the railway station together and stop wasting our time. The operator was fishing for a bigger lunch. Supper. It was getting late. Suzie waited on one line and then another, but learned nothing about Inner Mongolia. I was on my own. I shoved my German map under the ticket window, trying to point to Hohhot and shouting "Hot hot," the city where I wanted to go to, with a Freudian accent because I was only getting hot hot under the collar. Televisions were blasting away above the heads of two of the tellers – who were not saying much. Television may not have been very practical, but the noisy distraction looked a hell of a lot more modern or progressive than a fan humming away, of which there were none.

Suzie hadn't gotten much further with her own destination. She was able to tell me that the Beijing trains were sold out for about a week. Sizing us up had been a ticket scalper. Breaking the so-called law, this perhaps off-duty policeman bought tickets in bulk and sold them to tourists at a much higher price, leaving the Chinese travelers out in the cold. Suzie, considered a foreigner, was going to Jiayuguan, the end of the wall, stirring up in me an all but forgotten hankering for the ultimate symbol of China, or even Asia. Did I have a choice? I had missed the last train to the coast.

My Hong Kong friend did not know if she was experiencing resentment or was misunderstood. Or if it was understood that foreign devils were reserved for the scalper, a vulture waiting until all hope had expired. Suzie finally gave in. At least he didn't want blood. And now for the second time in a railway station someone was asking for the displeasure of my company – for nowhere does misery love company more than in Asia. Suzie beat me to the punch.

In fact, I attract fellow travelers like an old boat draws barnacles. They don't consider that the damn thing is sinking. While I was waiting for Suzie, a group of Israelis got on the line next to me. Surely I had descended from one lost tribe or another.

They were young and vibrant students who had come to China to study everything from cookery to history and could not conceal their enthusiasm for their broadening horizons. I did not have the heart to ask them about their government or more accurately the policy of the majority. Were there really that many Israelis in China that I couldn't go anywhere without running into them? Was no one holding down the fort? Or had my intimacy with this strange land created a magnetic field that Israelis found irresistible? Not everyone could be with Mossad.

I had forgotten to change my travelers checks. Overriding concerns had sidetracked me. Luckily, I had just enough cash to take me to Jiuquan, the station before the Great Wall, or rather, the recognized end of it. And digging into my pockets and my bag, I was able to come up with enough loose change to reserve a hard bed. Suzie was traveling first-class.

Waiting for the scalper, we drew a crowd at the outdoor cafe, right off the parade ground or great open space that fronts the railway stations of the larger western cities. These eyewitnesses to the criminal transaction about to occur made my Hong Kong friend very nervous. I made matters worse by dragging out our exchange with my harried antics and a messy accumulation of bills and brochures and those sundry items that find their way into the collector's sack. Our audience could not have been more riveted if I had been pulling rabbits out of a hat.

Nor could I have felt more magical when we had actually pulled off this deal and were getting the hell out of here – with not ten minutes to spare. The China Daily winks at the travel intrigues with the article "Small Tricks for Travel Headaches," but the newspaper fails to mention the most important one.

Separating on the train, I was relieved to be solo again. Suzie was just what the doctor ordered, an emergency procedure, but how much medicine can a man take. She was not the Miss Wong you would like to meet on a high and windy hill. As for Julie and her Spanish charges, I had absconded on the train for which they had reservations. I could have taken two Julies and gone to bed and never bothered with calling the doctor in the morning. Instead the old sailor managed to crawl into the top bunk by himself.

Rack and roll, rack around the clock, but we had a long way to go before it was dark, gaining ground on the sun in the process. And since all of China – ah, the symbolism – runs on Beijing time (at least officially) my days would get longer as the season shortened. Lanzhou is on about the same latitude as Washington, DC, yet about three hours into our journey – at about 9:30 P.M. – it was still light on this mid-August night.

China was turning out to be either semi-tropical or semi-desert. As the terrain got sparser and sparser it seemed as if China was going to be that perennial iceberg, that one-eighth of its visible portion bearing little resemblance to its vast unseen bulk – which in China's case is the sparsely populated arid north and west. My sense of discovery was heightened by my fifties and sixties brainwashing that dictated that the dictatorship of Taiwan was the only China, and that if you sailed beyond this Formosa you would go over the edge of the earth, falling into a kind of black hole inhabited by monsters. Which, come to think of it, seems, sometimes, like a fair description of the People's Republic. Maps of this terra incognita were hard to come by.

As the train rocked on through the night, occasionally coming to a jerky stop, I could spy a glimpse of the Great Wall, a fragment here, a portion there returning to dust. Much of the wall is mud, ruptured ramparts put to other uses when not actually crumbling away. Contrary to Mao-inspired propaganda, the much touted symbol of China snaking its way across the Asian badlands was not visible from outer space. I could barely make it out from the window of the train.

29

Journeys to Jiayuguan

Campichu, the chief city of the Province of Tangut, is large and magnificent, and has jurisdiction over the entire province. The bulk of the people worship idols (that is, of Buddha), but there are some who follow the religion of Mahomet, and some Christians. The latter have three large and handsome churches in the city. The idolaters have many religious houses, or monasteries and abbeys, built like those in our country.... Those persons amongst the idolaters who are devoted to the service of religion (the lamas of Tibetan Buddhism) lead more virtuous lives.... They abstain from the indulgence of carnal and sensual desires.... Their maxim is that if advances are made by the female, the connection does not constitute an offense, but is held to be such when the proposal comes from the male.

The laity take as many as thirty wives.... They do not receive any dowry with them, but on the contrary, settle upon their wives dowers of cattle, slaves and money.... They take to their beds cousins by blood, and even espouse their mother-in-law. Many other mortal sins are regarded by them with indifference, and they live in this respect like the beasts of the field.

In this city Marco Polo remained, along with his father and uncle, about the space of one year, which their business required.

Travels of Marco Polo

Monkey business, more than likely. One account of Marco's stay in Campichu has him ill for over a year, but I can't say with certainty where the capital city is or was, much less speculate on his connections. We do know that whatever the

Polos were up to, it was a family affair. My best calculation places Campichu, changed to Kanchau and Changyea, where Zhangye is today. Stopping in Zhangye after midnight, I felt the spirit of Marco hovering over my bunk, but more concrete evidence is hard to come by.

For better or worse, if you get the gist of things, I research my book like I travel: what I stumble upon is grist for the mill, but I still stack up my instincts against the experts. The famous Blaue family map has Campichu somewhere above Beijing, near the Arctic Circle, and our history of China is as hazy as their seventeenth century geography.

One expert's explanation for Marco's failure to mention the Great Wall, when he was sometimes living under it, is that his references to Gog and Magog in describing the Tartars or Mongols, is an Old Testament allusion to those beyond the pale. Somehow, this ties in with the Alexander legend that has him building a rampart to keep out these invaders, that goes without saying, because the knowledgeable Marco would assume Alexander's rampart is the Great Wall. It's Greek to me. Only those who have not been there can speak with such authority. As I may have said earlier in this book, walls were such a fact of life in his time that they were beneath comment. As with other omissions.

A bus was waiting outside the Jiuquan railway station to take the passengers into town. Debusing at the outskirts of Jiuquan, I headed for the newest and only hotel for foreigners. I was the only foreigner staying there. Checking into the hotel, it struck me that my visa would expire in a few more days. As an English-speaking tour operator materialized behind the Registration Desk, I inquired about having my visa extended at the nearest police station, which is the not uncommon custom of die-hard tourists.

I showed the young woman my passport. My visa was valid for sixty days, but the most prominent date on it was September 13th, three months from the day I purchased my visa. Regardless of what day I actually entered China, I had to be out of the country by then. The tour operator seized on that date and said I could remain in the country until then.

"It is not necessary for you to go to the police station." This was something I wanted to believe and she was attractive enough to turn anybody's head.

Like a million people who assured me of one thing or another, she, too, would prove to be wrong, as Gullible continued to travel, listing September 13th as my expiration date whenever I registered in a hotel – when a little arithmetic in this nation of mathematical geniuses would have shown that my visa, which hotel clerks spent so much time pondering, expired on August 19th. Even I knew this, but a billion Chinese can't be wrong. But I get ahead of myself. My visa had not expired – yet.

I walked out of the Jiuquan Hotel into a light drizzle and the China beyond the countryside and its myriad villages. The typical middle-sized city where the first thing that strikes you is the billiard table and players blocking the sidewalk. And maybe the billiard tables weren't as common as they appeared, but that God was telling me "look who's behind the 8 ball!" One Muslim in a skullcap, unfazed by the rain and bicycles streaming by, was hunched over the table for a good minute before shooting, his ball careening off the walls.

The only sizeable thing of antiquity within walking distance is the Drum Tower in the traffic circle. A little to the north of the city is a satellite launching center that makes "Jiuquan well-known as a city of space flight...The vast desert makes you carefree and joyous...and acclaim the nature as the acme of perfection." My brief guide to Jiuquan shows photos of "the hunting and the hunted," one a magnificent but bloodied ram in the arms of a tourist.

The advertised argali, bharal and wild oxen had been hunted to near extinction, but who gives a hoot when you are "carefree" in the trackless wastes of the Gobi? I never saw so much as an antelope in my journey to the west. The people of Jiuquan were friendly and seemed surprised to have a foreigner in their midst. The hotel was everything I could ask for and, in fact, the tour operator lent me money until the exchange counter opened in the evening. I was even invited to her apartment to repay her, thinking I was about to rendezvous with a single woman. Her husband and his friend could never have suspected that this honored guest had anything but the most honorable intentions, that the hunter wasn't yet home from the hill.

Morning. I had checked out of the hotel and walked the couple of miles to the side street where I would pick up my bus for the "Great Wall." It was by far the worst vehicle I had ever seen anywhere in the world. A garbage-strewn rusting crate on wheels. The only solid thing on this mobile coffin were the bars behind the bus driver. It was a blessedly short ride to Jiayuguan, but the Great Wall was nowhere in sight and I had hardly extricated myself from the death trap when I was being hustled by fledgling entrepreneurs in a frenzy over the live one who had fallen into their laps.

That symbol of land's end, the edge of the civilized world and that dreaded outpost of every Chinese soldier, had become the Golden Fleece. Luckily I arrived at the wall before the tourist hordes overran what was meant to stem the Mongol tide.

30

Beyond the Pale

*The Huns have no trade
but battle and carnage.
They have no fields or plowlands.
But only wastes where white bones
lie among yellow sand
Where the House of Qin built the Great Wall
that was to keep away the Tartars.
There, in its turn the House of Han
lit beacons of war.
The beacons are always alight, fighting
and marching never stop.*
                      Li Po (Li Bai), 7th Century Poet

    Upon leaving the district last mentioned, and proceeding for ten days east-northeast through a country where there are few habitations and little that is worthy of remark, you arrive at a district named Succuir, in which are many towns and castles...The inhabitants are in general idolaters, with some Christians. They are subject to the dominion of the Great Khan....
    Throughout all the mountainous parts of it (Tangut) the most excellent kind of rhubarb is produced in large quantities; and merchants who buy loads of it, convey it to all parts of the world...The district is perfectly healthy, and the complexion of the natives is brown.
                                             Marco Polo

Unraveling on the Old Silk Road

Jiayuguan is Marco Polo's Succuir. Succor. Most likely he passed through Jiayu Pass, "The most magnificent pass in the world" at the western end of the Great Wall. Beating the crowd out here, I was truly carefree, able to walk along the top without interference and revel in the lunar landscape beyond the ramparts and the Wall as well. With its lofty watchtowers, palace and temples, this last section of the Ming outpost is more like a castle. Stretching away from the remote fortress, the much older and smaller Han wall seems to go on forever. A half-mile away, through an opening in the wall, a freight train is chugging up to Mongolia.

Passing through the gates, I found myself between two towering walls that took me back to Marrakech, and looking down this corridor of time, saw intermittent walls snaking their way across the deserts of two continents, rebuilt reminders of man's interminable intransigence – and the ever encroaching wasteland. Like a mighty dragon rising out of the Bo-Hai, the waters north of the Yellow Sea, the Great Wall winds its way more than 1,500 miles into central Asia, defining China as much as defending it, lengthening with imperial glut, with the march of time, until it peters out far beyond the pale.

The Chinese, scrawling their names on the Wall (perhaps they may have also invented the Roman graffiti) say, "You are nobody until you have seen the Great Wall." This is obviously hype coming out of Beijing, since it is only in the last century in the 2,400 year history of the Walls, that any but the slaves and conscripts made to construct and garrison the Great Wall would go near the damn thing with a ten-foot pole. The only other small parts of the wall accessible to the public are in the Beijing area. These two fragments really are overrun by the tourist hordes.

The Jiayuguan "district," once famous for "rhubarb" and the poisonous plants that caused the hoofs of horses "to fall off" when eaten, is still sparsely populated with less than a million people in more than a 100,000 square mile area. Most of the inhabitants are the Hans who run the oil refineries and the space center, and the Mongolians, Kazakh, Yugu tribes – Huns – that the Hans tried to shut out with the wall.

Beyond the Pale

There are not many people in the northwest corner of Gansu scrambling to scribble their names on the wall – they are preoccupied reading the handwriting already there. When I headed for the other wall, the desert ships still outnumbered the tourist buses. These were the first of the furry two-humped camels I saw and they seemed somewhat out of place, if not sorts, when the temperature had hit eighty and was climbing. I had barely begun my trek towards the disconnected wall above the oasis when I was suddenly struck by the severity of the unveiled sun. I had hoped to hitch a ride to my destination, but even the mad dogs and wild oxen were out to lunch, and a peasant family leaving their melon patch were about to join them. With my canteen already on empty, I ambushed the farmers before they could leave their plot.

"Cha, cha, cha," I sang, once again performing my tea dance, waving my canteen as if I were chasing flies. A veritable saint, letting his family continue on, bid me to follow him back to his own field of canteloupes and watermelon, and then sliced a Godsend into manageable pieces. There is nothing like slaking a desert thirst with its own miraculous produce, "allowing you to suck the marrow of nature." Not so corny when you are bone-dry and you think you'll see a mirage before you taste a melon.

Each melon patch was watched over by an elevated hootch or doghouse-sized thatched hut – and there I sat in the blessed shade wagging my tail for all I was worth, more bathing, drowning in this manna from heaven than eating it. Patchwork canals through the hardest hardscrabble had created a little green paradise. Thus refreshed, I passed beneath the scattered tombs with a surer step, when nearing one of the burial sites I was transfixed by the sparkle of multi-colored minerals scattered before me like diamonds and gold nuggets. Fool's gold, but if you see the universe in those grains of sand, who gives a damn. Jui Quan means Wine Spring. And I was headed there.

I walked about two miles before I got a lift to the oasis at the foot of a solitary wall, An earthen wall, which offered me shade leads up to this tourist attraction, of probably Ming extraction. I walked along the top of this no-frills rampart to the upper base of the black, barren mountain – and here the wall ended abruptly before the most forbidding natural elevation I've seen anywhere. Who needed a wall? This was the end of the world the Chinese viewed with foreboding. It could not have looked very inviting to the nomadic invaders either. Even poisonous plants would not grow here.

What a little irrigation had wrought, wrung out of the wastes, is something else, though wine is one miracle that the earth did not cough up. Grapes, yes. "Grape wine," as the Tang poet said, "is in luminous cups" – the precious drinking vessels manufactured in this neck of the desert. I settled for some tea in an opaque cup – inside a literal hole in the wall. The guard also rustled up some chow for me. Moving out to the shaded area by the irrigation canal, I plopped into a reclining chair.

Sitting at a table nearby, a Chinese girl began reading Pushkin aloud, in English. She asked me to read to her from the same passage to see if she was getting it right. A Colorado Indian in Ecuador came to mind. He had asked me to read to him from the Old Testament, which American missionaries had left with him.

"In the beginning. . . ." the wheel of repetition begins to turn. The girl introduced herself as a "taxi conductor." She had helped shepherd a van load of Spanish tourists out here. I was put off when no one recognized Don Quixote. But then, I didn't recognize them. This was not the group that gave me a lift to Lanzhou.

Did the Spaniards have a monopoly on the Silk Road? Was it the Wine Spring that lured the only tour out here? When they returned from their walk on the wall, I squeezed into their van, and sure enough, my pushy friend was collecting fares. Left off at the bus station, I tried to make a reservation for any westbound morning bus. The conductor told me no reservation was required, which I found very odd, and could have attributed to a language barrier, but she had also assured me that it was only necessary to arrive at the station an hour before my 8:00 A.M. departure.

I had dragged my bag around the whole day, only to end

up in a dump, the only hotel in Jiayuguan – a guest house of the same name. Welcoming spittoons flanked the front desk. I could have wept when I thought of the hotel I checked out of in the morning. I did when I entered my room. The guest house is a cavernous concrete block with concrete cubicles – four guests to a room. Unless I paid for the four beds. Which were actually boards. Room and board? The mattressless slabs and a wash basin in the corner constituted my furnishings. With one addition. I did not want to piss in the basin, so I swiped a spittoon from the stairway.

I could not tolerate the communal life at the end of the hall. It was a "head" out of boot camp.

Driven into the streets, I gagged on the stench of the oil refinery, my view from the window – under which there were workmen raising the dead. In fact, the move may have saved my life.

Walking down the main drag, I was serenaded by crooning customers. It is the custom of the sidewalk restaurants that anyone with the urge can step up to the mike and cry away a storm. Avoiding the dirge I went down a side street and ate delicious raviolis, or whatever the locals called them. They were just like mom's, really. The main attraction on the main street, directly across from the guest house and almost identical to it, in outward appearance, was a department store. Too beat to socialize, I opted for the sorry alternative to returning to my sordid quarters. I would only go back under cover of darkness – the only cover I got.

What the hell, maybe all the odds and ends would serve as ballast for my light headedness. Keep me on an even keel. I had been very careless about having adequate water with me the deeper and deeper I was going into the desert, but making no attempt to complement my canteen and jar. And now with no purpose beyond escape, my wandering eyes are held by a canteen sitting up on a shelf. Not a duplicate of my Boy Scout "be prepared" toy, but a huge Chinese Army Humpty Dumpty that would withstand any fall. With a strap to boot, the full bodied aluminum container would become as much a part of my life as my Chinese Army backpack, bought in Canada. Like my gung-ho bag it was gyrene-green. I was delighted as the family purchasing an odd television set.

A crimson sky brought down the curtain on my day, but predictably a man with a jackhammer looked like he would be drilling through the night. The yard had been lit up for this encore, but he was out of there by eleven, and I was up at dawn and down in the street before seven, enjoying a moment of serenity in the traffic circle. Old folks went through their graceful motions – but the future was gaining ground on the avenue, as young joggers enjoyed the brisk morning air.

I hadn't gone a couple of blocks when I walked into a group of young and old alike engaged in follow the leader. The last of the tai chi. A glimpse of snowcapped mountains and I had a spring in my step, if autumn in my sole (though not quite down at the heels), and summer in my heart. I arrived at the bus station with more than an hour till departure time.

But Gullible had been suckered again. Now, I was being informed that I had to buy my ticket a day in advance. How could I believe it could be any other way? Beaten, I was about to buy my ticket for Anxi, when suddenly coming to my senses, I stormed out of the office. Standing by the van or minibus, was the taxi conductor who just happened to be going my way. Next to her was the proud owner of this conveyance. With the cat in the bag, the enterprising entrepreneur was quoting me a fare in dollars. A fair price by American standards, but telling him to shove his chicanery, in the universal language, I strode into the street like a man possessed.

I was hitchhiking to Pakistan, there were no two ways about it. Come hell and high water, this was a one-way trip. Letting off steam, I could not think of my map, much less read it, as I headed in the wrong direction, the mountains, the Danghe Nan Shan stretching to the northwest. Within walking distance it seemed, at the speed I was moving, was the Qilian Shan itself, shimmering in the sun. With the sun on my back, I was pointed right as the crow flies, but ruffled feathers not withstanding, the Alps-high mountains were beyond my range.

With no cars going my way, I stopped a pedestrian. Tonight's goal was Dunhuang, to my ears sounding like the elusive "Don Juan." He went that way. I steamed back past the bus station and on to what my German map refers to as the "Silk Street." Street of dreams.

The first of the great dreamers seems to have been Chang Ch'ien (125 B.C.), who failed to acquire the "blood sweating horses" of Ferghani, somewhere north of Afghanistan. He was an envoy of a Han emperor trying to defeat the Huns. In a less sanguine pursuit, in his own journey to the west, Tripitaka, the greatest tripper of them all, came my way, perhaps even stopping in Dunhuang on his way to India. Confused by seventh century China's false prophets of Buddhism, this ultimate pilgrim sought the true word at its source.

Pointing to Dunhuang on my map, I approached several youths at a fork in the road. "Don Juan," I said, pointing to one road and then the other. No go. They pointed to the bus station. "No, no, I'm hitchhiking." I stuck out my thumb. I might just as well have stuck our my tongue. I made a motion to walk. I patted my backpack, and then actually walking with my extended thumb, I went up the busier road, looking back for reassurance. "Far, far." Again, they pointed to the bus station. I was obviously walking to Dunhuang.

With the tourist site two hundred miles away, the young men had cause for concern. I had better luck up the road where people were waiting for westbound buses. As I walked off in the direction of Pakistan, a young Chinese thinking I wanted a bus, cried out, "Here! Here!"

I stepped lively. This was the standing room only crowd, which tourists weren't supposed to know about – and right now, I did not want to know about it. Outside of town, I paused for a good view of the mountains and allowed puzzled bus drivers to go on their manic way. Stopping for me was a van packed with workers on their way to a factory in Yumen. I am not even certain if I waved them down. It was that thumbing motion that threw people off. Apparently, I was shaking my fist at everyone.

In minutes I was taking my last look at the Great Wall, that Ming part of it running south to the mountains, boxing in China. I didn't feel so much like a traveler passing through the wall, as a convict going over it. I had seen little of that once great barrier reef, but it was a wall and a symbol of the constraints China places on the free spirit.

    I left the van near the almost invisible turnoff for Yumen. Most Chinese believed that those who passed beyond this wall endured a kind of death, but for me it was more like being born again.

Labrang Monastery. Costumed monks ready for their performance.

Bai women going to the market. Near Dali, just off the Burma Road.

Passing ships in the (near) night of the Yangtze Gorges - much of it now submerged.

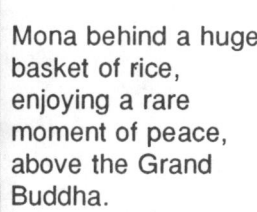

Mona behind a huge basket of rice, enjoying a rare moment of peace, above the Grand Buddha.

Tibetan house at the edge of "grasslands." Family is seated below drying meat.

Tibetan "grasslands." Camera-shy women astride yak ford stream to partake in festival.

The "Pure Land" of a lama invaded by the author's camera.

The end of the Great Wall.

Upper Swat. Abdul outside his restaurant - above author's hotel.

The grand abstraction of the Taklimakan. The desert of "those who enter never return."

Yurts overlooking Kara Kuli Lake where the Pamirs meet the Kunlun Mountains.

Tajik horseman and mount. Muztagata in background.

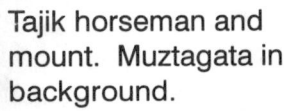

Fabled Khyber Rifles, guarding Afghan border with Pakistan. Author in front row.

A path of Shangri-La. Upper Hunza in Northern Pakistan.

Upper Swat. The faithful after prayer. Mosque in background.

Afghan refugees returning home.

Part 3

THE ROAD TO SERENDIP

31

Off the Wall

Twenty miles into the desert, I was drinking up the myriad minerals that go into the luminous cups of the area, but hardly touching my water. I was intoxicated by the intricate rock shapes that littered the hard earth. Ancient travelers coming out of the east would have been struck by the luminosity of this terrain, gateway to more of the same. Was the green in the stones jade? The sun still at a reasonable angle, I was not at all anxious about getting a lift to Anxi and the promise of shade.

But there were mostly buses going my way, and not many of those, so I boarded the first one that stopped for me. The bus was still cool. Incredibly, I had a comfortable seat in the sun and just laid back, almost falling asleep. Wind-driven propellers, turbines lined up in military fashion seemed to be sweeping down on China out of Mongolia. Acre after acre of the Gobi. These tiddlywinks, the modern sentinels of the desert, catching the easterly, were Gansu's cactus. Not a true windmill, but enough to get Don Quixote's lance up.

We went down a side road to Chijinpu, one of the few oasis towns off the Silk Road. This leafy retreat was chock-full of Bactrian camels. Caravans were still outfitted here. What a pleasant sight after the mind-blowing turbines – harmless alternatives to coal that they may be. Back on the main road I debused at Qiaowan, conveniently deposited outside the outhouse.

"Don Juan, Don Juan." I was directed to go up a steep long hill. Commandeering a truck. I realized I had done it again. Here the poor fellow thinks he has done me a favor, and I'm standing outside the bus station yelling at him, pointing to my feet and then pointing in the direction of Dunhuang. I'm bending my arm at the elbow, apparently quaffing an imaginary beer, but it is all a demented pantomine to him and he reassuringly leads me into the bus station as if it is an insane asylum.

Reasoning there is no outrunning the Greyhounds of heaven, I reconcile myself to a bus out of here. But the ticket seller is motioning me to climb up a flight of stairs and I am let into an office. Leaving his desk, a beaming rotund man in uniform meets me halfway and vigorously shakes my hand. Trying desperately to speak English, he is shuffling a pack of cigarettes under my offended nose. I had to demur three or four times, each time more forcefully, until coughing up some phlegm, he had finally gotten the message – or so I thought.

He realizes he is not making much headway on that front, and I am unable to make heads or tails (about what must sound like a tall tale until you are in my shoes) of this encounter. But it must be important because he is now boiling tea and shooing away would-be visitors. Am I in army headquarters? I am wondering. Why the red carpet treatment – when I may have broken the law? I'm repeating, Dunhuang, Dunhuang, very careful with my pronunciation.

"Yes, yes." He is smiling, but the water is taking long to boil and I am doing a slow burn myself. Trying to calm me down, he is benevolently looking me over and stroking an imaginary beard. He points to my beard to make certain, I understand.

"Good, good," he is saying.

"Good God," I am saying. The guy is a lunatic. He is shoving a pack of cigarettes in my pocket. "No, no, for Christ's sake, let me out of here. . . .wait, wait." I'm dying of thirst. Cha, cha. I allow him to pour whatever water is remaining in the kettle into my canteen.

Walking out of his office, it occurs to me that I have been the guest of the Transportation Commander, and that he is so happy that he is gay. I hop on a bus and return to the bottom of the hill where the fiasco began, and simply trudge out of town. This is a Silk Road under a thick blanket of coal dust and enough chunks of black gold to heat up Qiaowan. But in no time I'm getting a lift and riding along the Shule He, the Nile valley of the western Gobi. Here, unfortunately, mile after mile of this snaking oasis is choking on industrial pollution. The river, until recently the lifeblood of the desert cultures, was now slaking the thirst of monstrous smokestacks, angry dragons rising out of the lush farm land.

I was on a roll. Nobody with room in his vehicle could pass me by. Was I Claudette Colbert? Drivers didn't know and didn't care if I was fish or fowl or simply a fool – even if bumming a ride was illegal. And as poetry will have it, pickup trucks seemed to be my best bet. Was I on Route 66? But never was I more welcome, even if one or two pick-me-ups expected payment. It was as if my walk across China was the most natural thing in the world, that I was as much a part of the Gobi as an Asiatic wild ass who wandered from his "horde" and chanced upon the road. No questions asked – though the language barrier could have something to do with that.

32

The Adventures of Dunhuang

One of the wonderful things about this wild west is the wide open space. Inside and out. I made it to Anxi in time for a late lunch in an airy restaurant with murals. Meals are the least of my concerns. Not a dozen diners, half of them in uniform, are having a very leisurely lunch. Each soldier had at least a couple of large beers – with a kick like a mule. Good service, friendly people, but it was too early to call it a day.

Walking in the direction of Dunhuang, I go into a bookshop in the dashed hope of finding a detailed map. A few doors down I stop in a shop for something to drink. Nothing I want, but I'm shaking my canteen, and the woman behind the counter takes it and disappears. She returns in a new blouse and is carrying a watermelon. She is not Chinese and her own cantaloupes fill out the blouse nicely. I'm now in the chesty part of China. She hands me a slice of watermelon and I sit back on the decrepit couch with visions of sugarplums dancing in my head. This pretty one seems to be enjoying a taste of me, also. Which begs the question – if I look and feel like that couch I have sunken into, why is this beggar the most popular man west of the wall?

My floating feeling is enhanced by the paper covering over the ceiling billowing in the breeze. Blessed coolness. She leaves me to retrieve my canteen – hot to the touch. She is no ice cube herself, but I have a date with a Buddha, and I strike out on the wrong road again. I've gone beyond an army post before I retreat to the shade of a tree, directly across the road from the small base. Siesta. I'm part of the scenery – and making as much headway. This is the silt road. I follow a horse and cart up to the main road.

A businessman and his family are going to Dunhuang. There are several crates in his van, but I have plenty of room and willing to be part of his business. My contentment is short-lived. We are eastbound. I'm disoriented, but I recognize old ground and the sun has sunk low enough for me to have no doubts about knowing which end is up. Again, Don Quixote is shouting, "Don Juan! Don Juan!" Again, a portly fellow is reassuring me that we are indeed going to Dunhuang. And I'm being pacified with fruit, which is a great step-up from cigarettes, because the van has been baking all day, and I'm just about done.

We have merely gone out of our way to get gas. But the paying passenger is edgy, looks like he will abscond before he actually pays, and I am feted with drinks. Fortunately, because I need every drop I can get and more, for with blazing saddles, we are headed into a blazing sun and are enveloped in a white heat. The palest blue sky complements the shimmering desert, before we arrive in torrid Tianshujing. The family chows down in a road stop, but I can barely move, drinking soda (which I never touch), eating fruit, turning into a prune. A mother and child are taken down the road for a small fortune.

Masked women, laborers, are keeping the ditch along the side of the road clear of blowing sand. We are entering Death Valley, and I am a little concerned about keeping alive, my canteen long on empty, but there is a song in my heart (and sand in my mouth) for I am out of the labyrinth, free at last, and singing *California, Here I Come*. Lending itself to the spirit of this inferno are the graves, burial mounds off the side of the road, as this is the gateway to the Taklimakan, the place where "those who enter never return" – and the sinking sun does not keep the scorching heat at bay.

Suddenly, like a mirage, a city rises from the sands and we have arrived at a kind of Las Vegas, where the only game in town is the caves. The grottoes, actually, are some miles from Dunhuang. We have passed the turnoff, and I am not happy at the thought of backtracking.

I am a burnt husk, but now the real fun begins. I check

in and then out of a hotel after I've seen the room. A better place is full. I protest, as if I had reservations. The desk clerk returns with a Chinese student who is working away her summer in the gift shop. Speaking English, she commiserates. There is a new hotel up a side street. Not as nice as this, but beggars can't be buggers. She makes a call and the owner is over here in a shot.

We pile into a mini-delivery van, an open tin of sardines on three wheels that has become an instant "taxi." The owner wants a dollar to look over his place. I tell him where to get off, and I bang on the walls like a cat on a hot. . . .asking to be let out myself. My student guide/friend/translator says the ride will be free after all, and in a minute we are at the edge of Dunhuang. It is a Taki hotel, but I am undeterred by the dormitory at the top of the stairs, continuing down the hall like an officer unexpectedly reviewing his desert troops.

I am brought to the most lavishly preposterous room on the premises, or anywhere else in the world for that matter. The premise being, I presume, that I would settle for nothing less than this bridal suite, with its cascading curtains and fatuous furniture. I explain to the student that I did not need these frills, she should tell the owner, "We are not on our goddam honeymoon! Nothing personal."

Shown a more modest room, I immediately checked in, and dropped by the Muslim restaurant across the road. It actually spilled out into the street. A couple of beers under the clearest sky and it was all worth it. A devil moon rising out of the desert. Cat's eye, round and yellow, full moon, strange bedfellow. In its slow ascendancy of the heavens, now bathing my darkened hotel (due to a power failure), in the most beatific glow. My own glow had more to do with being beat, but with the moon, I was seemingly suspended in another time and place and considered myself the most lucky man on or out of the planet. I would be sleeping alone, but the honeymoon was not over.

The bathroom ceiling was bursting at the seams, and its walls had become waterfalls. Beyond the physical threat, I pondered the metaphysics of the very same situation in my mother's bathroom, where the ceiling actually caved in before I left for China. High as the moon and no doubt under its influence, I weighed the inconvenience of moving out and perhaps jumping into the frying pan if I found another room, opposed to the alternative of holding fast, and battening down the hatches. After a little damage control, putting my bag on a chair in the event of high water, convinced I would be above any mishap, literally, I took to my bed. I really felt I had no choice. I was so wasted that the threat, the sound, of impending disaster was drowned out by the loud but tranquilizing rush of water. I knew I would be asleep within seconds, and even if I remained so for only a few hours, I was, barring a serious catastrophe, better off holding my ground.

Someone was pounding on my door. Rescuer or robber? it was all the same. I screamed, "Go away!" but now the nocturnal intruder was unlocking my door. The latch was holding, but I sprang up to the door with my last ounce of energy, pulling in my wake a couple of chairs. Thus barricaded, I returned to bed and blessed oblivion. Hadn't I learned, that like everything else in China, a private bathroom, etc. had hidden costs. My assets were liquid.

Much to my surprise, I woke high and dry – though just barely. Curious about what sounded like a snow shovel in the corridor, I emerged from my room to see that the floors had been flooded and that cleaning up operations were underway. The whole damn building, apparently, was a dam that was about to burst – built in the recently adopted spirit of laissez faire. Anything goes – and the first to go is the plumbing.

I could not believe the view from my window. Beyond what looked like a North African village and a palmless oasis, was a sand dune as high as a mountain. With little thought for sacred grottoes and yet more Buddhas, I set out for the desert, foraging along the way. Spreading away from the dirt road was every vegetable under the cobalt sky – and orchards contrasting surrealistically with the shifting landscape beyond the farm. Trying to make sense out of me, a young farmer dissuaded me from tramping any further. He plucked an unripe pepper for me and insisted I take his photo. I don't recall receiving his address; rather it was as if he wanted an opportunity to reach out to the world and show his place in it.

    I was soon on the road to Mingsha Mountain and the Crescent Moon Spring. Squat whitewashed houses and flowering trellis were dwarfed by the "Whistling Sand Dune" ahead of me and the new hotels encroaching on the adobe houses just as surely as the desert. Further on was a Daoist temple, with its upturned eaves, a colorful echo of a China fading away into the mists of impaired memory. I was surprised by this reminder of The Way, in this out of the way place, where Buddhism had held sway. Or was this a hybrid?

    At this distance the camel-colored dunes could be a series of cresting tidal waves, about to engulf the sacred compound. A Laotzu look-alike, a monk in a brown robe, clanging a cymbal, is standing on the back of a fuchia festooned truck. Drums are sounding. A festival is underway and the guest of honor, with crossed-legs, is sitting under a tasseled umbrella. It is an ashen statue, a kind of phoenix, rising in this arizona so far from Beijing.

    The next day at the Mogao Grottoes, I asked a guide about the celebration. She claimed she was unaware of a temple, let alone a festive occasion. I said there were trucks, many people, or rather, participants. Of course, Tripitaka hallucinated, also. There was no mention of this temple in my brochure. The guide finally dismissed the event as Japanese inspired, as if it were a plot of some sort. But Japanese tourists always look like they are on their way to a Florida golf course, and cameras are part of their uniform. I didn't see any of that. The ceremony looked to be home-grown, a living religion and an apparent threat to the misguided woman of Mogao.

    Everyone who goes to Mogao raves about the fantastical frescoes on the walls; everyday resurrections, flying Buddhas and a Western Heaven, where clothes, if not money, grow on trees. A perverted version of the Pure Land. That is more a state of the mind than a place, where the East meets the West. Both peoples have looked towards the Kulun Mountains. But the grottoes were dark and dank, lit by the stiff guide's flashlight and further dampened by western students of arcana. I

The Adventures of Dunhuang

was more interested in what was above the cliffside caves.

Yet it was to this monastic oasis that pilgrims from the West, India, Tibet and Cathay made their way since the fourth century. Their scholarly toil made archeological history at the turn-of-the-century, when a monk discovered long-discarded scrolls, eventually sold for a song to the British Museum.

I had gotten off to a late start and by the time I left the departing pilgrims, I reconciled myself to simply reconnoitering the shallow edges of the vast sandy sea until later in the day. The Chinese claim that much of the desert had actually been reclaimed, contrary to the prevailing tide.

China also claims they were the desert's earliest inhabitants, justifying their occupation of neighboring Xinjiang Province – despite much recent evidence to the contrary: European mummies and clothing that bore no resemblance to anything Chinese. Authorities found one archeological dig so disturbing that there was proof of decapitation. In the least, the Persians and European offshoots predated the arrival of the Chinese by centuries. Eurasian traffic has long been both ways and paved the way for the Silk Road.

And it turns out that these people invented the wheel – not the Chinese.

33

View from the Top

The town of Lop is situated toward the northeast, near the commencement of the Great Desert, which is called the Desert of Lop. It belongs to the dominions of the Great Khan, and its inhabitants are of the Mahometan religion.

Provisions for a month should be laid in, that time being required to cross the desert, even in the narrowest part....At three or four of these halting places the water is salt and bitter, but at the others, amounting to about twenty, it is sweet and good. In this tract neither beasts nor birds are met with, because there is no kind of food for them.

It is asserted as an established fact that this desert is the abode of many evil spirits which lure travelers to their destruction with the most extraordinary illusions. If, during the daytime, any persons remaining behind on the road, either when overtaken by sleep or delayed by natural functions, until the caravan has passed a hill and is no longer in sight, they are startled to hear themselves called by their names, and in a tone of voice to which they are accustomed....at break of day they find they have been led into danger. Sometimes these spirits assume the appearance of their traveling companions, address them by name, and try to lead them out of the proper road....Marvelous indeed and almost beyond belief are the stories related of these spirits of the desert, which are said at times to fill the air with the sounds of all kinds of musical instruments, and also of drums and the clash of arms, obliging the travelers to close their line of march....Such are the excessive troubles and dangers that are inevitably met in crossing this desert.

Marco Polo

View from the Top

Leaving the desert, I entered a restaurant and did what any other sane man in my burning shoes would do. I took them off and waded into a large beer and a bowl of rice. What a way to waste daylight, I thought, but I had decided to follow the conventional wisdom of attempting the ascent when the sun was below the gracefully curved summits of these Lop-sided sands. That was fine if you remained in the evening shadows, but if you were climbing to the top, the rising heat would be with you longer than the light, and even a traveler worth his salt – of which little of mine remained – would be easy prey to the evil spirits. And, of course, beer would speed up my dehydration, so I headed for the garrison or fort turned museum, just up the road.

It may have been too hot for mad dogs, but a bus load of Desert Foxes, finished with their North African campaign, descended like locusts on the museum. I imagined I saw Rommel himself, but the rest was no hallucination and I retreated to another beer – to be joined by a Chinese artist from Lanzhou, who tried to pawn off his paltry abstractions on me. I preferred the real thing and ran off to the greatest abstraction of them all, those shifting horizons at the end of the road.

At the sandy base of the first mutable mountain is the Crescent Moon Lake or Spring. With reeds and desert plants leading up to a temple just above it, I mused about this fascinating archeological find. Who built it? When? Why? It turned out that this particular plot or prop really was Japanese inspired. I was admiring the set of a Japanese movie. But the oasis is real enough and it must have been a welcome sight to many a thirsty traveler. Real temples were destroyed by the Red Guard.

Leaving the camels in the dust and plodding past the last tourist trap, I set my sights on the loftiest heights. Once I had climbed the dunes immediately before me, it seemed like easy going along a slowly ascending saddle or wavy ridge that fell back before the shifting turret of my sand castle. But, Great Wall, great balls of fire, it was hot enough to take the starch out of Chinese laundry and convince me that setting out for these castles in the air had to be one of the dumbest things I had ever done.

But the ghostly Mount Blanc lured me on, the siren seducing Odysseus. The only signs of life were a few burning bushes and the strangest camouflaged lizards, little buggers that survived for want of enemies. One day they would compete with dune buggies. I got beyond an oceanic swell and into the shaded bosom of the dunes to take my bearings, and drink my still hot water. Birds appeared to be riding the currents above the showy summit. Certain they were not vultures, I continued on as effortlessly as hot air rising. And sure enough the updrafts had swept the desert floor clean, and my sea gulls, seemingly in pursuit of some higher truth, turned out to be merely swirling debris. Yesterday's newspapers flapping their pages like bats out of hell.

Had I known that the beacon for the great beyond was a lodestone, a magnet for litter, catalyst for literature, and that I was not looking at birds but the garbage I tried so desperately to out-maneuver – failing in this in the great outback – I would have gone back to my beer before I reached this point of no return; high in the grainy saddle, looking out upon mile after mile of rolling swells, cresting to an altitude of a thousand feet or more. And to retreat was to walk into stinging sand and the ascending hordes who would get nowhere near my Singing Dune – if it was indeed Mingsha Mountain I had homed in on. And so I continued to climb the cascading incline, until reaching the 1,500 foot (!?!) summit. How do you measure a mountain of shifting sand? I looked upon the Jade Gate and gazing upon the phantasmagoria or the phantom Lake of Lop (hundreds of miles to the east of Lop) and across the infinitude of the Taklimakan, I had some feeling for the fools who passed this way before me.

The first great Seeker in these parts, apparently, in A.D. 414, was the monk Fa-Hsien, on his way to Bamiyan in Afghanistan. The monk Xuan Zang continued on to India. In his *Records of Western Travels,* Xuan Zang or Tripitaka notes, "At night ghost shadows dance amid will-o-the-wisps...During the day, gales whip up sands to fall like rain."

Sections of the Silk Road, however, bustled with activity from the second century B.C. to the twelfth century A.D., traffic coming to a virtual standstill, when the Great Khans went out of business and the brigands had the road to themselves. In his *Record of a Historian* (c. mid-second century B.C.) Sima Qian wrote, "When Marquis Zhang Qian went to the Western Regions as imperial envoy, his entourage included three hundred people, each with two horses, ten thousand head of cattle and sheep, and a great amount of gold and silk." Marco Polo was not as meticulous in his bookkeeping. Though surely the Marquis did not cross the Taklimakan with such an entourage

Two threads unravel from the Silk Road and skirt the "Great Desert" or Shamo that lies before me. One track, via the Jade Gate, runs to the north of the lake, the other to the south, and whichever the traveler chose, he was dependent upon the "wandering" waters of Lop Nor for his survival. In the early 1900's a Swedish explorer, Sven Hedin, helped solve the mystery of the lake's location by proving that constant silting of tributaries and evaporation resulted in relocation. Which sounds like the story of my own life.

The lesser Silk or Silt Roads close the circle around the Tarim Basin, in Kashi or Kashgar (different spellings for the same, sometimes nonexistent, places). This is the far west, north of where Marco Polo or his ghostwriter began the narration of his chapter. The village of Lop, then, is on the southern thread, east of Pakistan, and is for all practical and impractical purposes the beginning of the Gobi – which simply means "Great Desert," and encompasses that vast swathe of shamo across Northern China and the Mongolias – including the Tarim Basin. The Taklimakan Desert.

Somewhere out there, due west, in China's Nevada, nuclear testing is being carried out. Israel's Wilderness of Zin comes to mind with its own testing site. Always this mixing of the sacred and the profane – or just plain desecration in the name of defense. But I must say for all its beauty in the dusty dark, no place lends itself more to the end of the world scenario than the sands of the Taklimakan. And those desert countries, the three horsemen of the apocalypse, will be responsible for the impending Armageddon. But oh, my God, why must I be the messenger and the metaphor, in the eye of the sandstorm, now insulted by this cyclonic pummelling by newspapers – all to be taken with a grain of sand.

Why? Because it is the Year of the Monkey (1992) and mad monk that I am, I am the hero of *Journey to the West*, the fictionalized version – of Tripitaka's travels. The main character, of course, is a monkey or a metamorphosed monk whose horseplay is the stuff of transcendence and salvation. But this is only my pedestrian interpretation of the eighteenth century Chinese classic.

Yet had I meditated on a lone shrub a minute longer, it would have become a burning bush, and taken on the quickening glow of the western sky. I looked towards the Crescent Spring, and there, above it, like a swarm of red (capitalists?) ants, Chinese tourists had materialized to gaze upon the wonder of the crimson tide. Surely, I thought, some would continue their ascent, but they went nowhere near my pulverized pinnacle.

Shaking off the Delphic dust, actually sand, I began my descent, with my size 10½" boots surfing these shifting Berkshires in a matter of minutes. Pausing above the tourists, I looked up to the head of my shamo Sphinx, and wondered how in God's name could they remain in the shadows, when another mile or two would have put them in back of beyond.

This was yet another corner of the globe where sunset was cause for that twilight ritual that is celebrated from the sea level of Key West to the heights of Nimrod in eastern Turkey, Masada in Israel and beyond. Sliding down the last dune was like lowering the boom. An onslaught of tourists, an undertow, emerging from some Hades, hellbent in the face of blowing sand, were trying to scale the paw of the Sphinx. And getting a shamo shampoo in the process. Let them grovel at its feet, you must go fearless into the faceless desert before the Sphinx reveals itself. Beyond the signposts until intuition rears her lovely head, like Minerva out of the shell – after you've had a taste of hell.

34

Revenge of the Monkey King

Morning. It's not yet 9 o'clock and I am already talking to myself. This is the right road, but does it dry up, like the river. I buttonhole passersby and people at a local bus stop to direct me to Hami, but all roads lead to the bus station. I get a ride back to where I was picked up, and flag down a truck that is actually going to Hami. But I don't think the truck has arrived there yet. It's chugging along at a glacial speed, and I ask the driver to deposit me like a moraine in the middle of the desert.

Not to worry. There is a vehicle passing about every fifteen minutes, and I have calculated that one out of three drivers will give me a lift. I am a walking, talking, divining rod – at least when it comes to troubled waters. For I have been left off near the invisible turnoff for the Jade Gate, the long gone track for Loulan and beyond. There is enough green here to suggest the course of the now dry Dang He and evidence of Lop or "The Lake that Wanders." I wandered among the ruins.

Time stood still here, there were no shifting sands, but to travel through Yumen Pass was to go back to before the era of Christ, and the melting pots buried by time. Sand, time, was the last frontier. There were no borders, only buried links, rivers gone dry and quasi-Hellenic civilizations gone with the wind. In 1990, an international team of explorers set out from the ruins of Loulan in search of the lost cities of the Taklimakan, "the place from where nothing living returns."

Though they had the most modern equipment, the explorers themselves were almost claimed by the desert. Armed with the maps of Ural Stein, they were trying to rediscover the ancient cities of Niya and Miran, which were nearer to India and Pakistan (Kashmir) than they were to Dunhuang. Now, after seventy-five years had passed since the Austrian scholar had absconded with the treasures of the Taklimakan, the explorers were looking upon a Greek culture that had rested on Corinthian columns of poplar. Stupas, also shaped from this "palm tree" of the central Asian oases, neither here nor there, were part of the cosmopolitan landscape. But there are no poplar trees here.

Here, where the rivers once flowed, there was fusion and flux, the first western inroads in China. And in Buddhism's journey to the east, the lotus flower blossoms into concrete Buddhas and China's penchant for abstraction becomes formalized. But Dunhuang's murals show Buddhas with broad shoulders and the narrow torsos of the Indian. Many of the holy books plundered here were written in Sanskrit, but the scripts of many lands made their mark in the march across the desert. Maybe the best proof of Niya's origin is the mummified Indian couple that was uncovered here. But their clothing revealed Chinese characters. It was in the desert that the east met the west – before Alexander was turned back at the Indus River.

Aside from ruins, there are towns on the maps of China that are presently little more than modern watering holes without a gas station, that could not get on a map of Death Valley. I was just to the south of such a town, listed on one map as Xihu, when my own explorations were interrupted by the sight of a northbound bus that looked too good to pass up.

A CIT bus was going to the railway station at Hongliuyuan to pick up some tourists and take them back to Dunhuang. CIT was my nemesis, but was obviously giving me a lift. The tour bus was empty but for the driver and a guide who spoke English quite well. Painfully, slowly, I explained my situation and asked to be left off at the Silk Road. But here we were leaving my international highway in the dust and the driver was refusing to stop the bus until we were at the railway station and I was asked for the price of a tour. With memories of their south and southwest China rip-offs as fresh as yesterday,

I said in no uncertain terms, with the assistance of sign language no traveler could fail to understand, that this was one time these running-dogs of capitalism had bitten off more than they could chew.

I'll spare you the usual comedy of errors getting there, but it was close to noon by the time I was back on the Silk Road. I parked myself under a post offering a sliver of shade. It is noteworthy that *Journey to the West* is based on official attempts to prevent Tripitaka from going to the Western Regions and on to India. The monkeyshines of the Monkey King of this novel are a fantasized version of the reformer monk getting around the edict, "all Prefectures and counties should keep a close watch to arrest him."

It is also a fact that in his *Record of Western Travels,* Tripitaka notes that he was approaching Hami, when he became a wanted man. In this area he was nearly captured by soldiers when he stole their food.

35

Through the Land of the Salamander

Next to the district of Kamul follows that of Chinchitalas, which in its northern part borders on the desert and is in length sixteen days' journey. It is subject to the Great Khan and contains cities and several strong places. Its inhabitants are three sects: a few of them confess Christ, according to the Nestorian doctrine; others are followers of Mahomet; and a third worship idols. There is in this district a mountain where the mines produce steel, and also zinc or antimony.

Also found here is a substance of the nature of the salamander, for when woven into cloth and thrown into the fire, it does not burn. The following mode of preparing it I learned from one of my traveling companions named Zurficar, a very intelligent Turkoman, who directed the mining operations of the province for three years. The fossil substance procured from the mountain consists of fibers not unlike those of wool. After being exposed to the sun to dry, this is pounded in a brass mortar and is then washed until all the earthy particles are separated from it. Having thus cleansed and detached the fibers from each other, they then spin them into thread and weave the thread into cloth....

Of the salamander in the form of a serpent, which is supposed to exist in fire, I could never discover any traces in the eastern region....

Marco Polo

M arco may have learned how to make asbestos, but Chinchitalas or present-day Xingxingxia is not in his line of march, being about one hundred and fifty miles from Jade

Gate and his road to Cathay – in the opposite direction. It is in mine, however, about one hundred miles up the original route or something like it, because in 1992 this rutted desert track bore no resemblance to the red ribbon passing through Hongliuyuan on my map. The real Silk Road is two miles to the south of town. An hour passed before the second westbound vehicle to appear on the horizon stopped.

Three nouveau capitalists in their tin mobile had come to the rescue. We didn't go a mile before my benefactors were pulling up to the side of the road, at a barely discernible turnoff, which did not exist on my map. The only thing that distinguished this track from the rest of the desert were the signs of human intrusion. We followed in the grooves of vehicles and hoofs until the driver lost control of the car and we rode up an embankment and into the brush, narrowly escaping a flip over. I expected each jarring bump to end in a shattering finale, but only the jumbo thermos and my glasses were the worst for wear. No, the other rear passenger was slightly injured. And I was convinced this Chinese Volkswagon wasn't going anywhere, soon.

It occurred to me that I did not have much water and that my companions had lost half their tea, as the sliver littered thermos had been emptied of its contents. This thermos was almost double the size of anything I had seen in China. Strange as it may seem, I was not terribly concerned about the fact that I was stranded in the desert with three strangers and there was not so much as a salamander in sight, or likely to be. But our little Beattle had maneuverability and we simply started the thing up and went rolling back over the walls of sand and onto the route.

A little further on a passing train afforded me the opportunity to do my thing. A standing room only crowd waved me on. I believe that this was the only time this train was to cross my path. Had I an accurate map, I could have walked down the railway track and started hitching here. I would have arrived at this spot much sooner. We were traveling due north now and at a considerably reduced speed. Down from thirty miles an hour to about fifteen. Our Beattle was almost lighter than air, with little traction, and speeds surpassing a turtle's had us airborne. I waved as our last link with civilization rolled on down the track.

Nondescript badlands gave way to Dakota Badlands, the improved scenery apparently owing much to the desert flood and the rich sandstone hues left in their wake – and all that antimony and salamander painting the desert. Gritty abstractions abounded. And blackened mounds stood in stark contrast to a day on fire. Eureka! We were hot on the trail of the elusive salamander. Onwards our Beattle crawled, up, down and around colorful gully and ruddy ravine, swallowed up in the surreality of the shamo, bumping and grinding, winding our way deeper and deeper into the desert – and into the earth itself, as I think we were below sea level, and perhaps had fallen into one of Zurficar's forsaken mines.

Alexander in Wonderland! Street of dreams, screams, lunatic landscapes – no escape. But here and there we saw forbidden stretches of the new road, still under construction, and then a few miles short of Xingxingxia, the remains of ramparts commanding the not very high ground. Here, surrounded by the ruins of castles of mud, we got bogged down in a befouled spring. Maybe the heavy road equipment had exposed the water table, or just the passage of time and less weighty things. Hell and high water, I had found the home of the mythological salamander and my discovery was all the more delightful because I had no foreknowledge of the find. Only a rod, which divines.

Xingxingxia was a zinger. Maybe a half-dozen buildings, half of them abandoned, and what was still in use looked no different than what was defunct; in particular, the restaurant that could have served Tripitaka. The meat hadn't been around that long, but if this place had a legacy, it was inherited by the wind. My business-minded friends showed their contempt for this bit of history by pushing away bowls from some last supper and berating what or who we could charitably call the waitress, out to lunch herself. Regrettably I was too tired to dig out my own chopsticks, and like my benefactors simply poured boiling water over our utensils.

Through the Land of the Salamander

If this was not a ghost town, it had at least two feet in the grave, but the real Xingxingxia was in the pit from which we had emerged like the salamander, a phoenix rising. But the completing of the new Silk Road spelled prosperity, and tarmac or asphalt if not asbestos lay before us. I should note that *"It is said that they preserve at Rome a napkin woven from this material, sent as a gift from a Tartar prince to the Roman Pontiff as a wrapper for the sudarium of Jesus Christ."* (Marco)

At the first bend in the road providing a little shade, we came to a halt and the driver unceremoniously took a siesta. And didn't the Chinchitalas of which Marco wrote sound like a city in Mexico?

We were now, in fact, in Xinjiang, the Uygur Autonomous Region, and China's last frontier, occupying a sixth of the country; till this century the eastern regions of what European maps referred to as Turkistan. The fact that only now a real road was being built seems to indicate that we had been traveling through a no man's land and that Anxi had been the western frontier of Cathay.

> *Rain falls at dusk on the frontier town*
> *wild geese fly low....*
> *Countless camel bells ring over desolate sands*
> *Caravans travel to Anxi city*
> *with rolls of silk.*
>
> Zhang Ji

36

The Rules of the Road

Kamul is a district within the great province of Tangut; it is subject to the Great Khan, and contains many towns and castles, of which the principal city is also named Kamul. This district lies between two deserts; that is to say, the Great Desert already described and another of smaller extent, being only about three days' journey across. The inhabitants are worshippers of idols and have their own peculiar language. They subsist on the fruits of the earth, which they possess in abundance, and are able to supply the needs of travelers. The men are addicted to pleasure, and attend to little else besides playing upon instruments, singing, dancing, reading, writing, according to the custom of the country, and the pursuit, in short, of every kind of amusement.

When strangers arrive and desire lodging and accommodations at their houses, it affords them the highest gratification. They give positive orders to their wives, daughter, sisters, and other female relations to indulge their guests in every wish, while they themselves leave their homes and retire into the city....They consider the hospitable reception of strangers, who (after the perils and fatigues of a long journey) need relaxation, an action agreeable to their deities, calculated to draw down the blessing of increase upon their families, to augment their wealth, and to earn them safety from all dangers, as well as a successful issue to all their undertakings. The women are very handsome, very sensual, and fully disposed to conform in this respect to the command of their husbands.

It happened that when Mangu Khan held his court in this province, he learned of the above scandalous custom and issued *an edict strictly commanding the people of Kamul to give up this disgraceful practice, and forbidding individuals to furnish lodging to strangers, but to make them stay at inns. In grief and sadness the inhabitants obeyed for about three years, but finding that the earth ceased to yield the accustomed fruits and that many misfortunes befell their families, they resolved to send a deputation to the Great Khan to beg him to permit them to resume the observance of a custom solemnly handed down to them by their ancestors from remotest times – especially since their failure to offer this hospitality to strangers had brought ruin on their families. The Khan, having listened to this application, replied, "Since you appear so anxious to persist in your own shame, let it be as you desire. Go, live according to your base customs and manners, and let your wives continue to receive the beggarly wages of their prostitution." The deputies returned home with this answer to the great delight of all the people, who, to the present day, observe their ancient practice.*

Marco Polo

Three government cars sped by and we resumed the road to Hami (Kamul). Hongxing was the first real town I had seen since morning, and from here on in or out, poplar trees would be harbingers of civilization. This had been so for a while, actually, but now these sentinels of the oasis were more obvious. The poplars lined the roads like the sycamores of France, but without their royal canopy, just barely shading the traveler. The Chinese call the poplars the trees that never die, for even in death they may stand for a century. Hongxing was yet another long green ribbon in a landscape or sandscape where a little (Ho Ho) hospitality went a long way. We were in Hami before dusk.

Through my phrase book, I was able to learn that the Mexican-looking driver owned a chain of clothing stores throughout the province and that he was making the rounds. I was relieved to know this because the other passenger in the back seat was fingering his pants by way of communicating his boss's profession. My real destination was Turpan, and I simply wanted to break the journey, now hoping I would be able to tag along with these characters in the morning. But Hami, apparently, no longer catered to foreigners in the accustomed style.

Of course, I didn't hang around that long. Hami was a fair-sized city and there appeared to be more black than green in this patchwork. It was time, finally, to catch that train that had cut us off at the pass, when my well-dressed friends were unable to get me into their hotel. Hardly more than concrete barracks, the accommodations were probably the best Hami had to offer and the thought of leaving these secluded grounds to size up the city, compelled me to do the unthinkable. Leaving the sartorial splendor of my friends, saddened but harried, I hurried through a small, wooded area to the main road and hailed a cab.

With twenty minutes to spare to catch my 7:00 train, I was frantic, but the woman taxi driver's soothing sounds made me to understand no sweat. The train was, as usual, late, three hours late, which really is understandable. A piece of cake compared to the three course meal that waiting for a train in India is, but I did not beat the system that day after all.

This was déjà vu or Dostoevski, because again I found myself on a night train without a bed, only this time I was rescued by a Russian emerging from his sleeping car to investigate the commotion of our boarding. He was wearing a stickpin identification button in his lapel that read "Moscow Convention." It was of course Greek to the Chinese, but it spoke of authority and he was given wide berth. Wide enough for me to sleep on. His badge was from last year's convention of railway scientists, but he was now returning from a meeting of Russian and Chinese scientists in Lanzhou.

Traveling with the Russian was his blonde assistant or secretary who spoke no English. The three of us sitting on the mad scientist's bunk, I once again considered myself the luckiest man in China, for after my smoke had dissipated and I passed out, I could have been easy prey to the standing room desperados still on the train who watched me void earlier in the day. Good fortune isn't necessarily what happens to you, but what you are able to avoid, often unbeknownst to you – which is why the worst road is sometimes the better one.

The Rules of the Road

But this changing of horses in midstream was too much, even for me, and I found myself beyond time and space. I could adjust to this port in a storm, but a Russian captain was the last person I expected to meet aboard this train. If Russians went anywhere, it was to America, yet Dostoevski, actually, was a physicist and the convention was devoted to maintaining, to the degree possible, a stress resistant train. I saw this as analogous to the wear and tear on a passenger and thought that ours was one more conversation beyond forgetting, but if my writing is a trip to the lost and found department of my mind, the memory of this encounter, aside from musty recollections, remains unclaimed.

It did take me back to the Russia I knew in 1964, through the innocent eyes of that time and place, when you were accepted for what you were. Today, I had to consider that my popularity had more to do with being an American – a passport to freedom – than with simply being.

I feel traitorous to consider that our encounter was less than fraternal, but from there on I appeared to be a potential bankroll for the have-nots. I wanted to renounce my citizenship for years, a means of protest, but now principle was entwined with practicality because foreigners confuse Fort Apache with Fort Knox, and if I remained green, it was behind the ears.

I detrained in Turpan, shortly after dawn; the nearest rail town actually. It was as if I awoke from a dream and was adrift at the edge of the world.

If Turpan is known as the "Furnace City," a hell at five hundred feet below sea level, I had landed in limbo, a few feet above sea level.

Lending itself to a nether world is the candlelit hovel that passed for a bus station. As push came to shove for the remaining tickets for Turpan, I walked to the mouth of a tunnel or an underpass that descended into the fiery basin below. My God, the entrance to Hades!

37

Turpan

Hungry, I entered the last chance cafe, but didn't have the patience for the pleasant but befuddled Uygur couple. Did I want soup or nuts? I stepped outside in time to flag down a bus – for as Bion said the road to Hades is easy to travel. A scarred, salted earth marked our descent into the furnace, but it would be some time before the sun stoked the ashes. Standing on the bus, I saw a few familiar faces. Was there no escape? A train afforded me some leeway, but running into a tourist in a cramped bus was like looking into a mirror.

Crossing the salt basin, I had looked in vain for signs of irrigation. Even the Dead Sea had water, but the miracle in this desert lies underground, in the canals that helped drain the Divine Mountains to the north. Surface irrigation would only end in evaporation before the water went where it was needed, but the tunnels that led to Turpan provided this baking oasis with a variety of melons and an umbrella of grapes and the necessary bacchanalia to take the sting out of the sand.

The two thousand-year-old subterranean aqueducts are known as Karez. Because of the receding glaciers, most of the oases was reclaimed by the desert. In this inverse universe the underground became heaven. A back road to the Emin Minaret, at the edge of the old town, revealed cellars used for siesta as well as storage.

Sleepwalking, I found myself eating gratis grapes in the trellised courtyard of a family that was Armenian in appearance. The land of Noah's Ark. And climbing Mount Ararat, Noah's Ark was as ephemeral as the Promised Land. But the

Pure Land has always beckoned.

It was as if I had entered a dream as old as our settled existence. A beautiful young woman, very camera shy, was rocking her baby in a tiny cradle atop a table – an ancient cradle that had all the color of a Sicilian cart (before my parents set out for their own promised land). And I thought, this is your cradle of civilization wherever there is a baby rocking under an arbor, in a harbor of grapes. A sanctuary on the sunnyside of the mountain. Rock-a-bye-baby in the tree top, the baby will cry when the cradle does stop.

Wearing an embroidered dopa (a square cap) and a full skirt, she was probably Uzbek, descended from the dispersed Golden Horde. You would think these Turkic people would be more at home on a horse, with goats rather than grapes. But desert folk are a goat/grape group and they are not mutually exclusive. As a volunteer worker in the Golan Heights, I will never forget coming upon a stone relief of a grape cluster that both Arab and Jew lay claim to, and, of course, it is a mutual inheritance, predating the tribal differences fostered by the high priests of ignorance and greed. Problem was they didn't get high enough.

Perhaps the grape promoted the harmony enjoyed by the exiled Manicheans and Nestorians. Somewhere in the Middle East or Persia, Zhang Qian or a near contemporary, around the second century B.C., came in contact with the grape (and date) and returning to China introduced viniculture to Cathay.

One of the more infamous foreign devils to come down the pike, Albert von Le Coq, was in the wine business before he was carried away by "Orientalism" and ended up in Shui Pang, outside Turpan, where he found fragments of St. Matthew's Gospel and writings on the visit of the Three Kings to the Christ child. In the Kizil Caves, above Kucha (unbeknownst to me on my itinerary), von Le Coq discovered a blue pigmented fresco of King Ajatashatru taking a bath in butter, when he learns about the death of Buddha. This sounds like Nero fiddling while Rome burned or von Le Coq being very fond of La Grape. In fact, the linguist returned to his native

Germany, where he became Director of the Berlin Museum.

Before dreaming of going to China, I saw some of his antiquarian spoils, believed to have been destroyed in World War II bombing raids – several decades after his discoveries. But that story, the obliteration of his valuable thefts, is only part of the fiction of the Silk Road – mostly for the consumption of the outraged Chinese authorities, and armchair travelers who like a neat ending.

Like the people of the Old Testament and the Hunza, the natives of Turpan have a reputation for longevity. It's the grapes in this land of milk and grapes that does it. The climate is as cold in winter as hot in summer (temperatures pushing 150°), with the salt lake to the south freezing over by January. This Dead Sea places production of salt right up there with wine. Islam may have brought an end to booze as well as Buddhism for the faithful, but we must consider it has something to do with long life, or that the people are getting high on God.

Is it simply the good stock of the Indo-Europeans who made these deserts bloom before the Three Kings set out for the Holy Land that accounts for all the pensioners, or are the Chinese trying to market this Arizona to easterners?

Who knows who or what emerges from so ancient a melting pot as the Turpan Depression – this basin for that heavenly ring of ice that nourished it since time immemorial. I can not find it in my own edition of Marco Polo's Travels, so I won't swear by it, but at least one expert claims that whoever was living in Turpan at the time told Marco that their original king was not born of human stock but arose from a tuber generated by the sap of a tree. This almost sounds Germanic. People as old as the hills. Ancestry can't get more ancient than that, although the Uygur branch of the Turkic tree claims descent from a she-wolf, which sounds like the origin of Rome. My own theory is that the Turpan allusion to its family tree has its roots in Buddha's sacred tree. Given the dolce vita of the time, in the Tarim Basin, we can assume that when the Venetians (I refer to the Polos) were here, the baby had been thrown out with the bath water. And though wine is available, I cannot say these Muslims imbibe.

Do archeologists really know or acknowledge when or where legend ends and reality begins? By the 1920's ripping-off the Silk Road ruins of Xinjiang was so lucrative that the locals got into the act by forging texts and sculptures, and even invented an ancient language for the benefit of the hoodwinked scholars with money to spare. With facts stranger than "history," there may be more than a grain of truth to the myth of Mu, the buried Shangri-La of the shamo.

Cathay may have looked to Xinjiang the way Rome looked to Egypt. The Chinese even found a Cleopatra there. The biography of King Mu and the Book of Mountains and Seas, written in the Warring States period (475-221 B.C.), describes the story of Zhou dynasty Emperor Mu Wang's meeting with the "Queen Mother of the West" in the tenth century B.C. Long before that real or imagined encounter, before Asian and Eurasian tribes journeyed to the Americas, the cry had been, "Go West, young man!"

I didn't read this biography, but the author of the *Lost Continent of Mu* did, and it is another piece of the puzzle that has fallen into my lap. This Mu showed Asia to be the surviving Empire of the Uygurs, the Motherland of Man that was swallowed up by the Pacific at the time of the Biblical Flood – the author's answer to Atlantis and an embellishment that appealed to the Age of Aquarius, when this 1931 book by James Churchward later became a bestseller paperback in the sixties. The New York Times wrote that "... *thanks to the writer's researches, the sunken Pacific continent now takes on an interest beyond that called up by shear geology or the surmises of archeologists.*"

Well, I don't know what lies under the Pacific, but perhaps The New York Times was looking in the wrong place, though clearly the Tarim Basin is a different kettle of fish. Much of what Churchward claims must be taken with a cup of salt, yet it is obvious that the long-dried up rivers of the Taklimakan make this the real Middle Kingdom – long before the Chinese Kingdoms to the east were trafficking in silk or learning about grapes. It was not the Garden of Eden as Churchward purports, but the Turkish word for home is "eve" – which seems to point to some

Turkic connection to a motherland.

Anyway, buried in a tomb fifty feet below the surface of the ancient ruins of Karakhoja or what the Chinese prefer to call Gaochang, a Professor Kosloff discovered artifacts that appear to attest to the universality of the entombed symbols. Connections that cancel out by a long shot the accepted second century B.C. origins of these ruins, not thirty miles from Turpan. We know about the Han and the Rouran people who ruled here, but Colonel Churchward, who made his own finds in an Indian temple, concludes that "Karakhoja" was just another ray in the first Empire of the Sun.

Certainly Club Med will contest this finding. A few days later in Kuqa, without a clue to Mu, I came across one of Kosloff's unearthed symbols on the back of a pushcart. I remember it because I thought this sunburst was interesting enough to photograph, but connecting it to nothing in particular. Now I see that the eight pointed sun also happens to grace the bottom of those Sicilian carts and other parts of the planet's four corners. This still amounts to a hill of beans, even if the gaily colored sun with its eight cardinal points is also a representation of the eight-fold Noble Path of the Buddhists, and this, their lotus flower, happens to be the floral symbol of the "Lost Continent."

My own understanding of the lotus is in Ulysses's lotus eaters and myself finding a kind of Nirvana in what was really hashish. There may be no more significance in all this beyond synchronicity, but in my book it is a sign I'm on the right track and I am certain the piece will fit into place soon enough (even if I must shape a corner or two). It is amazing how people with an axe to grind find the "evidence" to fit their axiom. But this is not the Tantric Buddhist's "axe of true doctrine," which is honed hacking away at the root of ignorance.

The ancient Chinese thought that Buddhism was a bastardizing of Taoism – which in a way it was, for the Bodhi-tree took root in China and Japan as it never did in the Hindu-inspired chaos of the subcontinent. A chapter in *Journey to the West* reflects the Tao in Chinese Buddhism.

After the fictionalized Tripitaka and his monkey friend (and other beastly associates) acquired the holy writings, they discovered they had been stuck with blank scrolls. They came all the way to India for this? The monk and the monkey complained to Buddha, personally, and speaking to the Taoist tradition of the chartless way, Buddha replied that these were the true scriptures.

This view is echoed in St. Augustine's confession that all that he had written was straw compared to seeing the jewel in the lotus. But again, all roads lead to the Pure Land if that is what we are really seeking, for there is no "Lost Continent," but only the "Lonely Planet."

If there was an Empire of the Sun, it all boils down to the desert kingdoms being buried when the glaciers began melting away with the first global warming. As in all things, we just haven't dug deep enough to find the remnants of what was basically a series of nomadic settlements. Only recently have we uncovered evidence that the Native American has been around a lot longer than the accepted ten thousand years, and if he came to America, some tribes could have traveled to the Taklimakan, much closer to home, before ending up on the other side of the Pacific Ocean. I don't know if the Kazakhs still retain the custom, but like many American Indian tribes, they named their child for the first thing the parent sees after birth. History marks their beginnings in the southwestern Gobi, and yet their land extended to the Caspian Sea in the heart of Russia.

Most of us were Asians before we became Europeans and Americans. Before that we were all Africans. Egypt's eye shared the same vision as Nepal's all-seeing stupa. Novus Ordo Seclorum, indeed. Some Armenians can pass for some American Indians. So can some Asian Indians. Columbus was right after all. Native Americans can no more be categorized with their different languages and customs than the people on the street where I live. There are just too many connections, including the pizza one. Pizza, pita, chapati, tortilla flats. Nan is the Uygur word for bread, which is pan in Spanish, but it is really pizza without the frills. Connecting the circle of humanity we are all brothers and godfathers.

I continued up the dirt road, the mud-brick houses low to the ground. Nothing moved faster than a donkey and cart – a mile of low mud dwellings, and then like something that had sprung up on the Mesopotamian plain, I was looking at the Emin Minaret. A tower of beauty that had about it a primitive but passive sensuality. The floral design could have been a grape trellis or the vines wrapping themselves around the minaret. And like the houses that had given way to vineyards and corn fields, this mosque was of the earth. Smooth, sunbaked earth that grew out of so substantial a base that the Muslim beacon was more a breast than the phallic of a more defined structure.

This was the nipple of Mother Earth, and it was to her that we submitted. The design of this temple was as old as Diana, old as Sumeria and the summer of man, similar to the "mare's nipple grape" that was introduced here more than two thousand years ago. Corn is a much more recent arrival to China, coming here via the Americas. Karez irrigation came from the same place as the grapes, although the Chinese might dispute that. The Karez is one of the subterranean connections with the Mediterranean or Persia, linking the deep wells that are the underpinning of the culture. Even the vineyards are sunken.

Back in the village miniature mosques stood off the road. They are humble family affairs topped by a crescent, symbol of Islam and Turkey. In the 1930's the short-lived Republic of Turkestan was declared in Khotan. Despite autonomy Muslim protests persisted in Uygur. I don't know who is counting today, but at least one hundred Muslims were killed in 1990 and things seem to be heating up. The "New Dominion," Xinjiang has been a military reality since 1949, but Beijing has been sending immigrants to the far corners of Uygur homeland in increasing numbers. Fearing the fate of Tibet, the Uygurs (Uighurs) by 1998 had mustered an underground army of thirty thousand or so young radicals, responsible for a series of bombings in Urumqi last spring, as well as in Beijing. The Chinese have retaliated with the closing of hundreds of mosques and cultural centers.

The quasi-official symbol for Uygur or Xinjiang (as the Chinese know it) is an airborne horse. The Uygurs were important middlemen for silk, buying Chinese goods in exchange for their prized horses.

Is this the blood-sweating horse of Uzbekistan that Cathay so desperately coveted to maintain its empire, the sacred steed of Turkmenistan, or the dragon horse of Kuqa in Xinjiang? This steed is the offspring of lake dragons and wild mares. An alternative origin for the symbol is the heavenly horse of Kushan. I would not bet on any of them. Unless they are all one and the same. Possibly Alexander the Great in his bloody journey to the east carried with him the tale of Pegasus – the greatest horse in mythology, sprung from the Gorgon's blood. But the horse remains the lifeblood of the Turkic people, although Turpan, on this dusty road, relied on a distant cousin, the donkey.

I was stopped in my tracks by a lively refrain emanating from a harbor of grapes. An old man pleased by my show of appreciation beckoned me to enter the leafy enclosure, from which he plucked a healthy bunch of the desert manna. He bade me to take a seat and as the music played on, he rose from his chair like a hawk riding a thermal current – and then, warming up to his audience, breathed the air of Persia or even Armenia. Carried along by horn and drum, he began shaking like a leaf in the wind, a more refined than frenzied arabesque of outstretched arms, come-hither charms. From here to the Atlantic, this was the sound of the oasis, where the arid zone was also the erogenous zone. And as the music thundered away and the old man twirled, I wondered if this was Turpan's milk of longevity – openess. I had another cup of human kindness and went on my way.

38

The Northwest Passage

At last! The great adventure for which my whole life has been a preparation was under way. The Northwest Passage – that baffling mystery to all navigators of the past – was at last to be ours!
                                                           Roald Amundsen, Explorer

Although it was not my intention to read about Roald Amundsen's voyage to the North Pole, I had been having a problem researching my book. I wanted to read *My Life as an Explorer* by Sven Hedin, one of China's more notorious Foreign Devils, but the local librarian did not know the Silk Road from the Silicon Valley and she picked up on Amundsen's book of the same title, instead of Hedin's.

Just as well, since we explorers are of the same ilk and God knows Amundsen was speaking to my Silk Road when he penned the above. My whole absurd life has indeed "been a preparation" for the troubled waters that lay before me, as poetry would have it the northwest way out of Turpan. Though I must say that pushing the age of fifty-six on the bumpiest road, I was, perhaps, overprepared.

Had the temperature been fifty degrees cooler, I would have remained for Turpan's Grape Festival, but I beat a hasty retreat from the record-breaking heat and did not let the sun set on my weary body. Was it one or two days I spent there? My memory of Turpan is like the waves rising off the boiling tarmac, a kind of merging.

Morning was something else. I left the hotel under a cool gray sky. The main thoroughfare was under a canopy of grapes, arching trellises forming a tunnel of love – at least this is what the billboards seemed to promise, with an alluring maiden more European than Asian reveling in the Tarim Depression's most popular produce. Unaware that I was liable to a fine, I contented myself with picking a few grapes as I made my way to the edge of town. Already last evening was like a dream, the hundred small fires and smothering smoke of humongous cookouts of kebab, a stygian scene in a nether world that was neither east nor west.

    This was China's West and the seductive woman could have been the Queen Mother of Mu, certainly bigger than life. Every West had its Golden Gate, or courtesy of Puccini, Golden Girl. A short ride found me tumbling from the rear of a tiny tin pickup truck to the cheers of my young Chinese companions. They were heading east and I was back on the Silk Road, my thumb pointing north northwest. I was on my way to Urumqi. Then, I would play it by ear.

    A van transporting a bureaucrat to my destination pulled over to the side of the road. I could have a lift for a price. I scoffed at the offer as any self-respecting tramp would. The van continued on its way, only to make a U-turn and return to the living, breathing, balding statue of liberty. This time the price was right and we were on our way. Why I was hitchhiking at the edge of the Gobi did not seem worthy of inquiry – though only a handful of foreigners trusted or thrust out their thumbs in that Year of the Monkey. The bureaucrat's major concern was to impress upon me who he was – and to that end he showed me identification, which was, of course, Greek, or even Chinese to me. But Turkic brass and even those of less brilliance are godfathers who spare no effort demonstrating they are top dogs.

    A few minutes passed before the godfather's pretty girlfriend joined me in the back of the van. The local custom earlier in the century – and millennium for that matter – of lending your woman to a foreign guest came to mind. The treasure-seeking orientalist, von Le Coq, got more than he bargained for after he had been working at Karakhoja for some time. Dignitaries from Turpan indicated that it wouldn't do for a man to live alone. And lo and behold an official's daughter was ready to "marry" him. When von Le Coq protested that he was already married, the reply in today's parlance was "no problem." Old customs die hard and fearing my indifference to my seatmate could be considered offensive, I wondered if a little hankey-pankey was called for. On the other hand, the wrong move could be considered gauche. What to do? Sitting my ground, I watched the pretty thing disappear under a blanket.

My spirits lifted with our gradual ascent out of the desert and the refreshing breeze of the mountains. I had no sooner removed my sweater, in deference to a rising sun, when the proximity of Tian Shan had me bundling up again, ever so happy to be leaving the scorched earth for the promise of "beautiful pastures" – the translation of the Mongolian Urumqi. But something has been lost in the translation and that sea of grass and wild flowers has been mostly consumed by China's Golden Calf. The Mongols found pasture elsewhere.

There were about three more hours of hard driving between us and Urumqi. For the moment my way was a trip to December – it was that cool – and I was like a little boy looking forward to Christmas. Though a deepening gully was pink with flowers awaiting the autumnal flow. Oleanders grew wherever water had lingered, deep roots following receding water tables. A few miles from Balyanche, the only village in our climb to Urumqi, a lone man foraged in the riverbed. Perhaps he was looking for jade. There is no more delightful contrast in the desert than wadis where coursing water has left a snaking oasis and no stone unturned in its life-giving wake. Especially in China, where at every turn nature had been shaped by the hand of man.

And suddenly the mountains appeared. Too often they might as well be a mirage, evaporating snow, the misty dream shown on a scroll. Inaccessible. But Tian Shan with its glacial crown was within walking distance and the grasslands swept up to the mountains like a green skirt trailing away from the desert floor. A welcome mat extending from beyond the fringe of the Taklimakan to the foot of Bogda Feng. In the middle of the Divine Mountain is the Heavenly Lake that had no outlet until the eighteenth century when one was dug out so that the desert would bloom. But for me, China's mountains would remain a tease, forbidden fruit just out of reach. Or with a big bite taken out of it. That first unforgettable panorama so rich with promise that so greenly greets the traveler emerging from the desert would soon fade away like a dream.

Oddly enough the least successful of the *Foreign Devils on the Silk Road,* by Peter Hopkirk, was the American, Langdon Warner. Perhaps he was too much of a romantic: "Imagination flouts the counsels of prudence. . . ." He rhapsodizes about "holy men from India crossing the roof of the world. . .travel older than history. Our eyes would not be denied."

Other plunderers, like authors commuting between bestsellers, kept their eyes on the prize. Actually, by the time Warner arrived on the scene there just wasn't much treasure left to be carted away on those two-wheel carts that still cluttered the road. The heyday of the Silk Road had already passed. Asia was in the grip of revolution and foreigners who had been greeted warmly a few years earlier had by 1926 become devils. For several years White Russians had been streaming out of the northwest and the welcome mat trampled in their escape from egalitarianism or just plain ism and prison.

When we pooh-pooh China's paranoia about foreign devils, remember that there was hardly a treasure hunter – there were no true scholars scavenging about Xinjiang – who wasn't also playing the Great Game. The Chinese were treated as second-class citizens. It wasn't bad enough that Europeans stole China's history and even some of her geography. Sven Hedin who was also a great mapmaker made no bones about being a spy for one great power or another and eventually was in the service of the Chinese Nationalists. The Swede often left the loot to the less adventurous.

And so the digging and cutting and the hauling away of statues and frescoes was the Little Game being played out in the shadows of the Big one. Though this "archeology" was mostly confined to the fringes of the Taklimakan, it helped make the reputation of a number of museums around the world. The rules of the game were simple enough. Beyond the spheres of territories that reflected the larger Game being played out in

China, it was mostly a case of who got there first and left with the most; which, after all, is what cutting up the larger pie was all about. The western Europeans dug the Turpan region more than anywhere else, while the Russians were digging Kucha (Kuqa) to the west. There was nearly a shootout when the Russians arrived at their digs only to find a German finger in the pie.

Following the advice of the curator at the Museum of Natural History, I finally got a copy of *Foreign Devils on the Silk Road*. You will recall I wanted to donate and define my own meager find. My accidental discovery of a small cache of fresh terra cotta figures seemed to be a surviving form of the Serindian culture that dominated the Taklimakan and – if my Shiva-like shaver is an aspect of it – extended much further to the east. They seemed that commonplace and I could never dream that I was guilty of "looting." (Serindia lasted until the eighth century.)

I've known about the Great Game for some time, but had little idea of the size of the playing field. Certainly it was not level. It is no secret that to the west the great powers had been trying to carve up the Ottoman Empire since before the time of Victoria, but through my own ignorance or the West's interpretation of history, I was unaware of just how often Great Britain surfaced from the subcontinent. Or how bloody a road it was to Mandalay, where the flying fish play. Most of us have heard about the Hindu Kush, had seen the film *Four Feathers* and know about incursions into one oasis or another in England's journey to the east. But little-play has been given to the attempt to carry the White Man's burden into northwestern Xinjiang, at the very gates of the former Soviet Union.

In that far corner of China, Below Kazakhstan, beyond Mongolia, that other Great Player, the Russians (soon to become the Soviets) were digging in. They were outgunned, but in a sense they were coming home. The Tartars put Moscow on the map and their czarist heirs (scratch a Russian and you'll find a Tartar, the saying goes) had slowly made their imperial way to central Asia and the very Pacific itself, long before Communism was a dream and an excuse for conquest. The czars familiarity with the terrain, the cards they were playing with, persuaded the British to back off. By the turn-of-the-century the Russians were justifying their incursions into Xinjiang with the need to block future Tartar – Mongol or Chinese – advances on the Motherland, as in days gone by; since the days of Attila when the Gates of Dzungaria were a northwest passage opening on the inviting West. Greener pastures and all that. But it is like the United States justifying its presence south of the border because of fear of a Mexican invasion.

For a perhaps pro-Chinese look behind the cloak and dagger, I have Jan Myrdal to thank. In his own *Silk Road* this Swede's insight into foreign intrigue extends to his knowledge of the little-known Swedish missionaries in Xinjiang at the turn-of-the-century. Demonizing the Islamic populace made it that much easier to justify the "civilizing" efforts of western imperialists while China was still reeling from the Opium War. Beyond this déjà vu, Myrdal clearly showed that the Great Game was still being played out. The players have changed since the book was written in 1979, but the stakes have remained the same. Perhaps that is why China is still playing its nuclear card in 1998.

An interesting development in the Game is that Kazakhstan, no longer in the Soviet circle and a wild card amongst changing players, is coveted by the United States and Israel, extending their source of oil and market for their arms. Myrdal thought that the American century ended with Vietnam and our closing shop in the pivot area of Peshawar near the Afghan border, but that hornets' nest was still buzzing when I got there even if the aircraft were temporarily grounded. Myrdal did not know the Soviet Army would invade Afghanistan on Christmas eve and that the United States would side with the mujahidin – even though these fundamentalists had kidnapped the U.S. Ambassador to Afghanistan earlier in the year. You must wonder about the true nature of the envoy's death because this result of the kidnapping gave us cause to meddle with the Soviet satellite, and the rest is history.

39

Between a Rock and a Hot Place

> *No one enjoys life in Urumchi, no one leaves the town with regret, and it is full of people who are only there because they cannot get permission to leave....*   The Gobi Desert

Mildred Cable and Francesca French seemed to be speaking to me; and to every traveler who has passed through Urumqi since these wandering missionaries penned their book more than a half-century ago. Nor did statesmen have a picnic. By the time the intrepid pair showed up in town, banquets were known to serve up coup d'etats. In 1935 Soviet troops were invited by the Chinese to bring stability to the area. The wild west had become a hotbed of Muslim discontent. A strong Russian influence continued here until the Sino-Soviet split in 1960.

    Urumqi has another claim to fame. It is the furthest city from the sea in the world. At least fifteen hundred miles. So I knew it was more than that to the port of Karachi, my likely way out of Asia. The mountains receded as my northwest highway connected with the northern arm of the Silk Route. Pastures shriveled up to the predictable industrial park and those heraldic smokestacks of every large city. Or small. To my surprise I was deposited at the outskirts of Urumqi.

    A bakery, little more than a hole or oven in the wall, beckoned and I had what was like a hot pizza sans sauce. This pizza or pita bread was the Muslim staple and a welcome addition to noodles and rice for breakfast. I hopped on a local bus, asking as best I could to be let off at a hotel – and hopefully the adjoining tourist office that would point me in the direction of least resistance. Passage through Pakistan was a last resort, really.

The bus driver motioned for me to get off when we were in view of a large building. It had the feel of first-class and my fellow passengers were nodding their approval. There could not be that many hotels that catered to tourists. Just outside the building I crossed the path of two young men who had that air of missionaries or C.I.A. agents about them. Squared away, as we used to say. They had flown here from Beijing and knew where they were going. Kazakhstan. They were looking for a travel agent. I said there was probably one in the hotel across the road, but they knew better and stole away without disabusing me of my delusion. My hotel was a government building.

A very short march away was a parade ground or lot. Soldiers were drilling. A little reminder to any Muslim malcontents that this was still China – though nobody seemed to speak English. I finally had some luck after questioning about a dozen waiters and waitresses in a restaurant. I was directed to take two buses to what was probably the Overseas Chinese Hotel. When I asked about a taxi, an attractive Eurasian left the restaurant and accompanied me to the bus stop. A note for the bus driver indicated my transfer point.

It remained sweater weather until about noon. A glacier cooled wind, the atmosphere itself gave this town the air of the northland. A mish-mash of cultures and nationalities filtered through a modern maze. It could be 1,500 miles from the desert. But all too soon the surrounding alpine scenery would seem like a mirage, a fabulous freak of nature in the eternal sands of Asia. In the interminable rock and hot places.

The hotel (old annex) used to house Russian guests and the lobby of the ramshackle building remained home to the unsinkable Aeroflot. Early on I had considered returning to the west on the Trans Siberian Railway and now saw the possibility of this materializing with a short hop over the border. Considering my alternate escape (I could not even think about returning to the United States via eastern China), I found myself bursting into silent song: *you don't know how lucky you are, boy, returning to the U.S.S.R., boy, the U.S., the U.S.S.R., boy, you don't know how lucky you are, boy....*

I did not think a visa was necessary for one of the newly independent Islamic Republics that were still serviced by the Russian airline, and assumed I could get a Russian visa wherever I ended up.

Leaving China this way – on a magic carpet – bypassing the hassle of a border crossing had not occurred to me before stumbling upon this tiny Aeroflot office. But I was only to get my hopes up. The office never opened. This was apparently a one-man show and today was the day of the once or twice weekly flight to Tajikastan, or was it Kazakhstan, and the Aeroflot personnel had closed up shop to be at the airport. And the C.I.A. was probably on that flight. Perhaps I could have bought my ticket at the airport and been on that plane, but the first rule of Serendip is not to go out of your way for what is supposed to fall in your lap.

Fly when there is no other way. Like Horace Walpole's *Three Princes of Serendip,* my own serendipity is limited to accidental discovery.

Across the small lobby is a CIT office. I would travel to Pakistan as planned, but I would need some help getting out of town if I was to avoid the usual merry-go-round. No matter that the Pakistani consul had absconded. I had completely forgotten that my Chinese visa was about to expire. So, all I wanted from this operator was to help me get back on the main trunk of the Silk Road – via the inviting mountain pass indicated on my map.

Although the concept of hitchhiking may have been beyond this fellow, his knowledge of the English language and the bus station was good enough to understand that I wanted to avoid the latter at all costs. He really spoke English quite well, and there could be no doubt in his mind that I was out of mine, come to think of it. After all, the only way I could get my point across was by giving him the thumb. Walking. I spelled out I would be relying on whatever was going my way, but it must have smelled to the high Heaven Mountains – which were my destination. The western, probably restricted range, off the tourist track.

For all that, the operator went to great pains to trace

my projected route on the local map/brochure he gave me. This would place me a good ways out on the open road pointed in the right direction, perhaps. My trip would wait till morning. A few bottles of beer would tide me over. I would have my Aeroflot, after all.

Waiting for the local bus that would get me beyond the apartment blocks, I looked across the road in amazement. Waiting for the bus that would take her and her Spanish charges in the opposite direction was the lovely Swede who had suggested I go to Urumqi in the first place – jumping-off point for the Heavenly Lake. The guide and the Spaniards were on their way there. This was the end of the line for most of the Silk Road tours, the reason I was heading in the opposite direction. They were cheering me on. It seemed so long ago that we had met in that Tibetan enclave. But they remembered my name. "Don Quixote! Don Quixote!"

I was their alter ego. Their Silk Road Tour was supposed to be the adventure of a lifetime, and there I was on my own, old enough to be their father, but carrying on like their son. A father, son and Holy Ghost. In some small way they would live my solitary quest when they thought of that character who bummed a ride on their tour bus before they headed west on the train – a lifetime ago. For movement through space is the essence of time and I had covered a lot of ground. I therefore travel at the speed of sound.

But if one or two of my amigos envied me my adventures, I felt a momentary pang of longing, belonging. Leave the driving or conniving to someone else – a confident Julie Andrews (was how I referred to the guide) who knew where she was going. Following the impossible dream was becoming impossible, and for one sane moment I actually considered crossing the road and going up to the Heavenly Lake with the heavenly Swede and listening to the sound of music. I got static instead.

Debusing at the edge of town, a wooded suburb, I walked westwards. A distinctly Chinese man, a distinguished cadre perhaps, driving an expensive car, heeded my extended arm. I showed him what a fellow cadre, the CIT operator, had written on my map. He continued a very short distance before we were making a U-turn. Within a few seconds the promise of the pristine was shattered by the receding greenery, a wider road and larger buildings – and yet, fool that I am, I was surprised when the tipped-off government official pulled up to the ubiquitous bus station. The government-owned hotel knew when, where and how I was going on my wild-goose chase. I had permission to leave Urumqi, but only on the government's terms.

I could not blame them. An American hithhiking in a sensitive area. Rebellion was in the air. I was somewhat less philosophical when I left the car. A young Hong Kong Chinese came to the rescue. Hong Kongese are a different kettle of fish from the mainlanders. With them I felt as I did when I used to meet a fellow American in a foreign country – before I became an alien in my own. In the same boat or bus station, we were experiencing the automatic or instantaneous bond of the outsider. He would appreciate what I was trying to do.

"Hitchhike? What is hitchhike?"

I tried to explain. "You know, waiting for a car, a ride at the side of the road." I stuck out my thumb. Again, it might as well have been my tongue. The tall, bespectacled youth was dumbfounded.

Hong Kong was too small a place to hitchhike, it just wasn't done. But didn't this quasi-westernized kid go to the movies?

"Haven't you ever seen somebody hitching in the movies?" And again my thumb went out, but this time I tramped through the crowded terminal. The end of any road. "Auto stop, auto stop!" I repeated, using the European term for beating the system, but also absent in the lexicon of the then Crown Colony.

"Where do you go?" he asked.

I mentioned far-off Kashgar.

"Too far to walk!"

"But a car, a truck, something, will stop and give me a lift." I wasn't getting through to him. This was like trying to explain the spirit world – free spirit – to a non-believer.

"We are going to Kashgar, too." His friends nodded.

"It is better if you go on the bus with us."

"Okay, okay, just get me on this bus, please, and I will get off when we are out of the city." But I could not get on the bus without reservations. I thrust my map of China in front of the conductor, running my finger along the yellow ribbon on my map. She explained to my young friend that I would have to go to another bus station to get on the less traveled road.

I had no choice. The Hong Kongese, with only a few minutes to spare before he boarded his own bus, heeded nature's call, his toilet paper trailing behind him. I bring out the best – and worst – in people. In no time he was back at my side, despite his own discomfort, concerned about my welfare. He left the terminal with me and pointed in the direction of the other bus station, and then looking very grave, removed his compass from his pocket.

"You will need this." He pushed his direction finder upon me, with no hope of ever seeing it or me again. I demurred. I had only to follow the sun. But it was the road that was errant – Don Quixote wasn't going anywhere.

A decade earlier, down and out in Europe, my problem was getting off the road, finding the right exit. I had the location of the "bus station" written down. A mistake, because I had gone far enough to show the address to someone, and ended up going a mile out of my way. Back on the boulevard of dreams, I was soon outside an engaging People's Park and a waiting bus for the mountains.

The day was so beautiful, the beckoning park such a break from my maddening routine that I hoped the bus wouldn't be leaving for awhile. This idyllic location for a bus station was unlike any I had seen anywhere in the world, and there was only the waiting bus and a ticket booth. A well-dressed man traveling with his family spoke English. I pointed to my map. Yes, the bus was going there. Where was he going? Why, to where the bus was going, of course. But what was the bus's destination? It turned out that I was on a tour bus bound for what was probably the popular White Poplar Valley – also known as the Southern Pastures or Baiyang Gou in the southern spur of the Heavenly Mountains, and my now projected southwest passage was through the town of Balguntay and my resumption of the Silk Road.

I thought these passengers were too well-dressed for your run-of-the-mill bus – though not well-off enough, perhaps, to be on the Heavenly Lake bus, which had evidently left for the foreigners' preferred choice of tourist spots or traps a little earlier. It would have been a real comedown to have run into Julie and the Spaniards after they had just cheered me on in my escape out of here.

There were no Hong Kongese on this bus, much less Europeans and if it was a tour bus as far as I was concerned, I was on a one-way trip. A few minutes out of town Tian Shan rose behind flaxen fields forever, a celestial Switzerland that stretched from the edge of the Gobi to Kazakhstan. My informer said he and his family had come all the way from Beijing to see the shimmering shan beyond the farms and factories. The scenery here, I was assured, was like nowhere else in China and anticipating the Shangri-La that lay before me like a naked lady, I was in heaven.

The southwestern range of the mountains loomed higher and higher, the fields fairer and fewer between, until the only green was evergreen and I had been transported to an Austria where chalets had been replaced by yurts and the esthete was spared yodeling. But it was downhill from there. Trying to milk this tourist attraction for all it was worth, the government had butchered the dragon that layed the golden eggs. Yurts of skins – igloo-shaped tents – had given way to concrete lookalikes that gave the valley the air of a tacky motel in the Rockies and that unfinished look that is more pronounced where mañana is good enough for them and montana is given little thought.

A road cutting through the mountains appeared to correspond with the one on my map and my way out of here. Yes, the Way is often a circuitous route. But the Beijinger assured me that this was not the way to Balguntay – or Serendip. He said the bus would be heading in that direction once we extricated ourselves from this trap. Tourists were already climbing up to the spur of the mountain above us. This was the upward stream of pilgrims I had seen all over China, down the ages following the path that would invariably lead to a temple – the crowning glory of every sacred mountain.

But in yet another trope for modern China, the winding way leads to an outhouse. If not a house of prayer, a place where one could think, if not sit. This must be the picnic area, I thought. And sure enough, lunches were unpacked and people who had traveled a thousand miles to experience Shangri-La did what came naturally, as the poetry of the Tao got lost in the excited chatter of the extended family. A ball materialized, practically at the precipice. Anyplace the Chinese gathered became a home away from home.

Down at the restaurant I could not persuade the waitress to accept my funny money. Hungrily, I scrounged around a food stall, undecided about the fruits I would buy, when I was shooed away. Flabbergasted, I approached an English-speaking woman and asked what was the proprietor's problem.

"No problem. He says you have no money."

The word had traveled from the restaurant to the marketplace. Did I look like a Russian? With rubles. Nobody wanted my Foreign Exchange Certificates, worth more than the regular exchange, and they didn't know dollars from donuts, though these nouveau entrepreneurs would not part with a crumb for a starving man.

This was particularly hurtful because this alpine valley had been home to the hospitable Kazakh. No relation to Cossak. It has been said you can not leave a yurt without drinking fermented mare's milk, but business is business, the oldest profession after politicians, and many men who will cheat you blind in the marketplace or slit your throat will offer you the eye of a sheep looking out from the business end of a knife, when you are their guest. I do not know how many times I have been regaled by people who would be just as comfortable robbing me if they thought I had money. Robin Hood is alive and well where there is still honor among thieves. But that sheep's eye is baloney.

Below me a stream rushed on to Urumqi. Kazakh horsemen better known for "chasing the girls" or "goat snatch" from the back of their horses forded the fast moving water with tourists clinging on to them for dear life. I don't know if it is played in these parts but chasing the girls is the sport of the steppes, a sort of polo where the object of the game is to score a goal with a decapitated goat. Did Marco Polo returning from his travels introduce the game to the Europeans who gave it their own spin and his name?

Backtracking a bit, our bus headed north until it stopped before a gate. We could go no further until we left the bus and payed a fee. This subtle form of highway robbery seemed to sit well with a Mongol or Kazakh riding tall in the saddle and armed with a scythe. The Scythian had taken time from making hay to observe the new crop of tourists entering their Southern Pastures. Surreal indeed, this grim reaper, horseman of the apocalypse past (future?) mounted against a backdrop of icy peaks. The gatekeeper instructed us to enter a shack just off the road and took our toll, the second of the tour. Ascending we rose until the grass was a patchwork of felt yurts, themselves patchworks but a welcome mat to one who had intimations of spending the night in one up the road.

But further on a fleet of buses were parked where the horsemen once played goat-snatch. Could purse-snatching be far behind? How I yearned for the day when this welcoming sight was untarnished by tourism. But the tourists were setting camp here and there and were an attraction in their own right. I was offered kebab in exchange for a hello and when a beer followed, I realized I had better make tracks if I was to get a ride out of here. Continuing up the valley in search of my southwest passage, I ran a gauntlet of boys wanting to rent me a horse. And then the pied piper was beyond the last artificial yurt, even a hotel, and I had left the gaggle of giggling children in my distant wake.

But then the road petered out into a path and I knew that I would indeed be making tracks if I followed the Beijinger's directions, for my route could not possibly correspond to the yellow line on my Hildebrant Urlaubskarte of China. My map notwithstanding, I barely resisted the temptation to keep on trucking, trust to fate and let the devil's horsemen take the hindmost. There had to be yurts up this leveling valley, shelter, and sooner or later I would be on the southern side of the snowy ranges. Mutton and mare's milk would stay me until my descent. The mountain air would be just what the doctor ordered if it didn't kill me.

Trudging along, pondering the frigid night that awaited me, I came upon a couple of surprised young men. They knew a thing or two about yurts – of which, apparently, there were none – but could make neither hide nor hair out of my Karto Grafik. My first instinct had been to go through that gulch where the bus made an initial stop and this is where I gravitated when I got beyond the parked buses, abandoning ship for the first ride that came along. Left off at a likely hitching post, I was soon landing a lift with a truck and barreling for all we were worth, rocking and rolling into a steep canyon, feeling in my arthritic bones that this was going to be authentic.

The canyon opened on high pasture and the scenery took on a wild and woolly look as a man on horseback carrying a sheep rode past a yurt. I was certain I had seen the last of the pollution and polluters, glory be nothing more toxic than horseshit awaited me. I cast a curious glance at what appeared to be chunks of coal on the road, but surely I was on the high road and I regarded the black rocks as a natural phenomenon, whatever they were. Snowcapped mountains imbued the earth with a pristine purity and if I wasn't entering virgin territory, I was finally on my way. All those dead-end, end runs, off the wall wandering into left field, why it was all part of that valley without which there are no mountains.

I had gone in wide circles to unwittingly find the straight and narrow. I had simply been mired in the bullshit without which the magic mushroom will not grow – and evidently I was on a bad trip, for materializing as suddenly as fungi when the fun is about to begin were smokestacks, a sprawling spewing coal mine cheek to jowl with medieval hovels, like some horrid hallucination. I could not believe my eyes, could not believe that workers could live in such wretched conditions and that this profanation of people and the pristine could be a part of the Heavenly Mountains. I had wandered into Dante's Inferno without benefit of a Virgil, while my own map seemed to show

Yongfengu.

Surely the tour operator back at the hotel and the Peiking Man knew what was waiting for me up here if I was unlucky enough to find my way to this hellhole. The CTS agent had said something about the pass being snowed in on occasion, but this was yet another snow-job hiding or obscuring, whenever possible, the reality of China by a cool operator.

Yongfengu had the air of a company town. Everything was blackened by a patina of coal dust and my mood was as dark. A young official approached me. "What are you doing here?"

"I'm taking a piss, if you don't mind." I explained my travel plans.

"Oh, too far! Maybe five days to walk to Balguntay."
"I'm actually waiting for a truck."
"What truck?"
"Any truck," I replied.
"There is no truck."
"Then why is there a road?" I had him.
"Maybe tomorrow." I said I would wait for a car.
"What car?"
"Any car."
"No cars," he countered.
"Then I'll walk."

I was more angry than hungry, but I thought I had better have a big hot meal before I moved on. All the food in this greasy spoon was served with pepper, but the coal dust was the least of my worries. I had my own chopsticks; they are de rigeur for the China hands, but I couldn't find them and sans souci picked at raviolis sans sauce, with the restaurants own sticks. With the help of my phrase book, I was able to satisfy the curiosity of the waitresses. They urged me to return to Urumqi. One waitress's gestures seemed to say everything: bandits, snow leopards, who knows what was in store for me.

But what finally discouraged me from tramping more than another mile was the fear of other coal mines up ahead. This bleak upper valley speaks of loss and violations, cries, and is all the more mournful when contrasted with the blue skies. I returned to the greasy spoon utterly wiped out and unaware that I had found the yellow brick road on my map.

40

The Return of the Conquered Anti-Hero

A cup of tea, and with renewed determination I sought what I had already found – that seemingly elusive yellow line on my Carto Grafik. What the hell was it doing on a German tourist map I'll never know. Were the mines owned by Europeans? I reasoned the road must be just outside of Urumqi – and maybe it really is for that matter. Luckily a taxi was loading up to go there. The driver was a quick-change artist who said ten when he meant one hundred yuan. I told him where to get off when I got out, giving him the ten in FECs, when he arrived at my hitching post.

Within minutes I was boarding a coal truck. Unnecessary for a man doing a slow burn. I looked desperately for a more likely road to Balguntay, but we only got closer and closer to Urumqi. Did it slip by me when I was diverted by an army truck that was moving slower than us? As we approached this military jalopy a soldier standing in the back waved a red flag. How gung ho, I thought. The east is red and all that. This was Mao territory after all, and, in fact, his brother, active in various campaigns in this area, was executed by a local warlord. Had I not been so burnt-out, I would have been quicker to realize that the soldier posted on the bed of the truck was signaling a passing vehicle to his driver. Or vice versa.

Left off at the outskirts of town, I boarded a stalled bus and immediately became the life of the party. Unfortunately, I could not share the passengers' enthusiasm for my sudden appearance. An old man speaking fluent English, a by-product of his war years, assured me there was no road to Balguntay over the mountains. I must return to Urumqi, but was welcome to join their group.

I arrived in Urumqi as brokenhearted as that early French explorer returning home after his failure to find the Northwest Passage. As shattered as Carl Furillo coming out of right field after dropping that infamous fly ball in the World Series. As defeated as Jack Kerouac returning to New York, when he failed to get a westbound ride out of New Jersey. He never did see the light at the end of the Lincoln Tunnel. Nor would I be able to face my own fans, returning to my homey annex as daunted as Don Quixote himself at the end of his road.

Why didn't I follow that sane instinct – fleeting to be sure – to accompany the young Julie Andrews and her group up to the Heavenly Lake, where the hills were alive with the sound of music? Now I could not face the music – nor did I have to since the guide and her group would be staying in the hotel itself, if they hadn't already caught the night train to Xian, the end of their quixotic tour. I would write to Mona, "Went bananas trying to hitch a ride out of the 'home of melons and fruits.' "

It is after experiences like these that I am convinced that my subconscious – my conscience – is running the entire show and that I'm led wherever I must go as the perennial penitent. Can there be a worse punishment than obsession with truth? But this is not to be confused with masochism, for the diminished – demolished – ego provides a clarity that is ecstasy after the facts and reason enough to be a bungling stumble bum.

Writing my way to the lost and found department of my mind, I now recall that the Russian engineer, Dostoevsky, had said the track to Russia was now open to tourists. Had I not forgotten that, I probably would have gotten a train out of Urumqi for Alma Ata and seen my alma mater – for better or worse. It can always be worse. And apparently Mother Russia was not in the cards. Serendip – Sri Lanka – was the only place where my Unraveling could end, and there was only a one in a billion chance that unbeknownst to me it would be.

41

Pushing On

The dread of spending another night in the same hotel turned to gratitude when it sank in that the mania-go-round was over for the day and that I would be spared shopping around for a place to sleep. And I was absolutely overjoyed when I was able to check into the same seedy room, for a tree (a little the worse for wear) was outside my window and I had slept like a log the night before. If my room had seen better days when the Russians were here, it was as comfortable as an old shoe. Not a chirp was heard out of anyone in the cheaper annex, while the well-heeled would raise hell in the hotel.

I was up early enough to get the worm. Hightailing it out of here, I scoffed at the poetry of the "red phoenix crying in the morning sun." It was a new day! I was caught up in the morning rush-hour and swept along with jacketed young men (mostly) hurrying to work. I saw very few road signs in China, and making matters worse for the hitchhiker is the fact that many places have several names or at least different spellings. The post office referred to Urumqi as Wulumuqi (formerly Urumchi) and Turpan was also Tulufan, but there was no mistaking my connection with the Silk Road.

The flow had placed me on the desert road with its bevy of pushcarts. And pullcarts. Mostly melons were being sold, as Urumqi lived up to its reputation. I was in a swarm of fruit peddlers when suddenly I was struck dumb by a hauntingly absurd but familiar sight. A man selling fruit was a double for my father-in-law. He sold produce in his younger days and probably would have remained in the fruit line had he stayed in Russia. Through their wandering over the centuries, Jews are the most mixed people in the world. And this was a true crossroads where I found myself, for Urumqi is yet another fork in the Silk Road, its prongs sticking into the melon of Central Asia, out of which spilled the "minorities" who populated Xinjiang and gave the "Western Territories" much of its flavor.

This mobile marketplace at the edge of town was the place to load up on liquid refreshments before making the descent into the Taklimakan and is one of the few sizeable roads in these parts not known as the Silk one. Beyond the pushcarts I seized the day, when lunging from a muddle of peddlers, I hailed a car going my way.

"Kashgar! Kashgar!" I cried out.

"Tuksun!" came the driver's reply and praying this was not another name for Turpan, hopped into a real automobile. The fast moving car lessened the pain of backtracking much of the ride, and in two hours time I was in Tuksun and following the sun.

On a roll I jumped aboard the first passing conveyance. Unfortunately, it was a bus, and after enduring about an hour of this nonsense, I debused at Kumux. Enough was enough. The roads were being dug up and a good part of the town was under construction. Making a dusty exit here, my memory mercifully fails me. . . .

Ah, but I should be so lucky. It all comes back. That antique truck chugging along at walking speed had gained ground on me, and thinking if I can't beat the truck, join it. When I was out of the midday sun long enough, I resumed my own trucking. I tried to ignore a passing caravan of Mack trucks and trudged on until I was stopped in my tracks by the sight of reeds and brackish water. Was this a mirage? I bothered little with my inadequate map and was totally unprepared for Lake Bosten – which I assumed would be yet another one of those wandering lakes or phantom bodies of water that so confounded the foreign devils of an earlier time.

And it probably will be a phantom when the Chinese are finished pumping it for all it is worth. When I finally read the English language magazine I had picked up in Urumqi, I learned that ". . .after the big pumping station has been built. . .Bosten

Lake will become even more beautiful." Like a desert. The drying up of the lake may have resulted in more reeds, which seems to have provided a curious boost to the economy and explains what all the reed mats were doing piled up and spread out in front of the houses.

There are two types of fish that were native to the lake. One with a big head and the other with a long mouth. Many varieties of carp had been introduced, and crabs, shrimps, muskrat and mink now make their home in and around Bosten. Surprisingly, this is one place Marco Polo did not write about, but Xuan Zang came this way and bested St. Patrick in his own encounter with water snakes by turning them into fish.

The lake gets its name from the outraged lover, Bosten, who, in a quarrel with the covetous Rain God, withholding water until he has his way with Bosten's girl, is killed when he disrespectfully shoots an arrow into the sky. A sympathetic goddess pushed down the God of Rain's calabash while he was in a drunken sleep and rain poured down for three days, turning the center of the Yanqi basin into the large lake that now bares its honored victim's name. The lake's actual source is near King Coal, where I had been the day before. Still, the existence of this inland sea in a bone-dry basin seemed mythical in itself.

Coming to a shady tree, I resumed my riding stance. I could just as well have dropped down from outer space, out of some God's gourd, maybe my own, for all the curiosity I aroused. Every household within a mile, apparently, had sent an envoy to look me up and down. Fish or a newly introduced fowl was the question. Once again I was a one-man road show and the crowd was cramping my style, compelling me to flag down a bus. Of all the rickety rat traps on wheels it has been my misfortune to ride, this cage took the cake, for it was carrying a cargo of tires on which the passengers stood. With my bent head bouncing against the ceiling, I was fit to be tied. Eventually, I got a seat, but my feet were still atop a tire, while my chin rested on a knee.

Adding insult to injury, the driver was stopping every quarter of a mile. When I came to my senses and fled this tiresome bus – and some – pushing some FECs at the driver as I gingerly extricated myself from this nightmare, the flabbergasted brute began shaking his fist and yelling what I could do with my funny money, Chinese legal tender though it may be. But what was an independent traveler to do when the people in the boondocks wanted no part of it? Ah, but that was the name of the game, the way to keep the tourist on a leash and his money in the government's coffers – for if the only currency he received in exchange for his dollars or marks were certificates that an honest, independent businessman could not accept, his buying power was limited to government-run enterprises; unless he went to the black market with his FECs and got real money in exchange for it. *Renminbi.*

Abused, I debused somewhat the worse for wear. I once responded to a challenge in no uncertain terms, but escape was the better part of valor. Passengers were an afterthought on this portable garage and this driver's real business was transporting tires. However, my bruised ego was not long in recovering, but it would be some time before my greasy boots would lose their newly acquired black sheen. The coal trucks were squeaky clean compared to that grease pit.

What the hell, beggars can't be choosey. My deflated state made me more receptive to the show of shore birds, and I was filling myself up on this quasi-oceanic experience when I realized I was plumb out of drinking water, and it was getting late in the day. The traffic was decreasing, and with a thought to any port or truck in a storm, I waved down everything on wheels, demurring, however, when a receptive horse and cart came by. It would take that conveyance days to reach a hotel. But I hardly fared better when the slowest motorized vehicle in all of China rattled to a halt.

42

A True Believer

I was in luck. I had gotten a lift on a road better suited for a Bactrian camel than this battered truck (camel thorns did grow beyond the lake) but my parched appearance persuaded the driver to pull up to the side of the road and cut open those melons rolling around on the floor of his cab, I had been coverting. We had arrived in the river town of Yanqi, through which passed one of the prime feeders of Bosten (also known as Baghrash Lake and Bositeng Hu).

Yanqi, still known as Karashahr in Sven Hedin's day, has quite a history for a small backwater town. When this "Black Town" revolted against Han rule in A.D.11, General Ban Chao sacked the town and decapitated 5,000 inhabitants. It recovered to become the Buddhist Kingdom of Agni during the Tang dynasty; but by the seventh century it was under Tibetan occupation, and finally was ravaged by the great Tamerlane himself in 1389. When Hedin came down the pike – this track wasn't paved until the seventies, actually – Karashahr was still the chief economical emporium in the region, but the "dirtiest town in all Central Asia."

What better place to dig into a watermelon? I was' swimming in the ambrosia, when another thirsty truck driver approached us and partook in our pleasure. But this guy had other appetites to appease and I was appalled when he began smoking his hashish behind the open door of the cab. They shoot you for crimes like this in China. When it comes to independence-minded minorities, though, drugs may be unofficially sanctioned. He offered me a tote. I would sit this one out.

Unlike my benefactor this young Indo-European spoke a bit of English and with the help of sign language demonstrated what this stuff was doing for him. No explanation was necessary. I was relieved when this Yanqi doodle dandy took his pipe and drum back to his truck and we got our own show on the road.

The Mongol tents that greeted Sven Hedin sixty or seventy years ago were nowhere to be seen, not in my line of sight, limited to the northern rim of the lake. But the Mongols living in the Heavenly Mountains still made their winter home here. These skilled horsemen are the same Torguts who migrated to the Volga River in the seventeenth century and were in the employ of the czar until the Cossacks ran them out of Russia. These steppe people appear to have ended their migration from western Mongolia in the shadows of Tian Shan.

Possibly, this group of Mongols with their sheep and cattle, the original cowboys, are the same people who also summer on the lake, building shelters on the shore and fishing from small boats. I can't distinguish between Kazakh and Mongol, much less between branches of the same family, which extends beyond Nepal, where, incidentally, the national drink is raki as in Turkey, with its own connection to the steppes. Perhaps we should stop pigeonholing people and leave the labels to bottles.

We grinded on. In the failing light, I took a closer look at the young driver. Not a very expressive face of mixed race – which only describes much of humanity. As a hitchhiker, how many times with approaching dusk have I tried to plummet a man's soul. In his tough features that leaned towards the east, I looked for kindness, though I must say I felt a hell of a lot safer on the Silk Road than in the car of your average American.

I should have rested easier when I noticed the photograph of Chairman Mao dangling from the driver's mirror (Chou En-lai was on the other side), but his Yanqi friend was out of left field and I had to wonder about his own predilections. What did he make of me? But he was a true believer and if he didn't take me for a hobo, I was in the least a reincarnated Karl Marx, for instead of demanding payment for my ride this uncomprehending soul was proffering me a one hundred yuan note. At first I thought he wanted to change money, but why would anyone hitchhike, he must have reasoned, unless his passenger did not have bus fare, much less the equivalent of twenty dollars.

Like the revered penniless Communist who had made up China's Holy Trinity, my friend believed my coffers were empty – though it was obvious I had to have seen better days. With a dusty dusk settling in upon us, my friend demonstrated that I needed a place to sleep in the style befitting a foreigner. And if I wasn't going to accept his money, the only thing to do was to insist I sleep under his roof. I remembered with amusement that my bushy reminder of persecutory Communism had provoked the Tibetans to taunt, "Marx, Marx," while tugging at my beard. The most amazing thing about my friend's offer of money is that he would have been giving up a week or two's wages – unless he was transporting something more fragrant than fertilizer.

If a stretch of road before Bosten is called "Dry Ditch," then we were in "Dry Bitch," with enough minor ups and downs for me to be absolutely overjoyed as we went over the last bumpy hump and under a ripening sky winded down to Korla and a row of low houses. Really hovels, mostly held together with mud. Inside were two cots and a spigot in the rear of this noble soul's one-room home wind. The outhouse was about a block away in an even more dismal side of town.

I was surprised to learn that Korla is the capital of Bayinguoleng Mongolian Prefecture, when there are only about 40,000 Mongols compared to about 500,000 Han Chinese in the vast area that this Prefecture covers. Uygurs and Tibetans make up the rest of the inhabitants in a chunk of Xinjiang that ranges to the gates of Gansu. Korla has heavy industry and Americans are looking for oil south of the city. Beyond shipping tomato paste to the Japanese, the city's claim to fame is that Sven Hedin and his expedition were almost executed here by the Muslim General "Big Horse" in a rebellion against the Chinese.

A toilet in Xuan's humble home would have been as out of place as a throne, but in my present condition of infinitely more value. I looked at his earthen floor and then to my dirt poor host. Was there an angle to his hospitality? He brought me food, but I could not help thinking that he had to be fishing for something with his one hundred yuan note. No, there was dignity in those no-nonsense features and I wouldn't have hesitated to sleep in his hovel and stay out of a hotel had I been my usual self. Still, I could not completely accept my friend at face value until he accompanied me to a hotel near the entrance of the city.

Looking more the tourist than I, Xuan accompanied me to the newly constructed building. Yes, they accepted foreigners. After tea and the assurance that I had a place to sleep for the night, Xuan walked out of the lobby none the poorer for his encounter. But my cup runneth over – as we drank our farewells in the reception area.

With my friend's departure the price of the room jumped. Flying into a constipating rage, I ran after Xuan, pausing in the parking lot to get my bearings. The attractive manager was at my side.

"Where do you go?"

"To my friend's house."

She was shocked. "But he is only a truck driver!"

Mao was spinning in his grave. I told her what I thought about her class consciousness. Telling me to hold on, she told her boss of the latest development and returned to my side. The room was mine at the original rate, and what was more, I was welcome to view a troupe of Mongolian dancers in the auditorium.

I had become the gratis guest of honor in the auditorium – which, I imagined, had yet to see a Planeteer. I had not seen a tourist the whole day, and here I was with an enticing beauty at my table motioning for some audience participation. She was taking my hand, but there was just no way I could hack it – unless she carried me up to her room.

It would have been longer getting here had I taken the train from Urumqi. Korla is the end of the line.

43

The Road to Kucha

I walked to the Silk Road with little effort, but I was at the wrong end of town and left floundering in a swarm of traffic – much of it four-legged. The first rule of thumb anywhere in the world is to get beyond the jam, and the less traffic the better. In China you must be conspicuous – with no doubt in the driver's mind that he has come to the rescue. If they had only known. Even the buses would not stop for me. The fact that I am usually walking along the road confuses drivers, though this can be a point of curiosity in many countries.

Hopping on a cart, I remained on board as long as I could endure before flagging a taxi that was motorized. Korla was large. I was in and out of another vehicle before standing at the edge of what had seemed an interminal industrial zone – all the more grating, contrasting with the green oasis snaking its way through the desert below. A small river nourished pear orchards and cotton fields. Standing in scrub, I thanked God the driver had left me beyond the spewing stacks.

A fast ride took me to Yeyungou, with barely enough time to grab a bite. Rather, it grabbed me when a man opening a melon for his comrades, thrust a canteloupe under my nose. This was one of those wonderful juxtapositions – a desert town teaming with fruit-laden handcarts. A wave of my arm and I was on my way. This really seemed more like the fruit road. In fact, Russians hooked on rhubarb had a kind of extension of the Silk Road that they called the "Rhubarb Road." The Chinese had come to believe that rhubarb was so essential to the British diet that during the Opium War they considered banning its export to them in the hope that their enemies would be crippled by blindness and constipation. I don't think they had the heart to withhold tea.

Anyway, it was clear that the market economy did not take much reviving after the demise of Mao and that there was an almost prehistoric appreciation of haggling in the people. An eye to buy or sell when the opportunity arose. When the couple who had given me a lift stopped at a restaurant, the man disappeared for awhile. The woman, grabbing my backpack, my worthless grab-bag, made me to understand she wanted to see inside. I obligingly pulled out a pair of dirty socks. Close. Though I wasn't quick to interpret her hands running along her lovely legs. After all, I was still in hankey-pankey country where an absconding male meant the woman herself was up for grabs.

This was not the case, however; she was simply in the market for women's stockings. Did I look like that traveling salesman Marco Polo? The black market in nylons had been revived because Xinjiang had begun manufacturing stockings to combat it in the seventies. Maybe the local quality wasn't up to snuff. Surely I had something for sale. She fingered her jewelry. Unlike the truck driver, Xuan, these hustlers weren't fooled by my vagabondism. No photo of Chairman Mao dangling above their dashboard. The man returned to the car, asking to see money. Not the funny stuff, but "America, America."

We had arrived in Kucha (Kuqa). I regretted not aborting this mission at the last market town, when this enterprising pair turned off the road to water down their car. I had my doubts from the beginning and they gave me a little scare when they drove into the desert a bit, in the direction of a well. A regular Ganges flowed outside the town, bathing a chaotic conglomeration of man and beast that must have marked a market day. The marvelous mix spilled onto the Silk Road, creating a pollution-free traffic jam. Inviting.

But, Mao Zedong's revenge was cramping my style, so there I was in Kucha passing up a dormitory (never my style) and making my way to a motel at the edge of the old city. Two boys with less than twenty years between them, hustled me to their cart for the last leg of the journey. A pretty girl emerged from a little building at the gate and invited me into her combination curio shop and registration office. Formalities out of the way, I called it a day.

I never would have dreamed, or even cared, that Kucha was the center of the thirty-six kingdoms of the Western Regions. But this was one of the fifty Central Asian Kingdoms that fell to the Chinese when General Ban Chao defeated the Xiongnu in A.D. 91. By the fourth century this region was known or rather renown as the Kingdom of Guici and was a hub of Indo-European culture.

With an infusion of cultures from middle China, India and Persia, the kingdom was using the musical instruments of all Asia. The orchestras tended to be large and the choreography made the extravaganzas the Esperanto of dance. Dancing women in their flowing silks played stringed instruments as graceful as the performers. The famous Tang poet, Yuan Zhen, rhapsodized that music "reverberates wherever you wander... and thunders endlessly." The music followed him back to Chang'an (today's Xian), where the lutes, drums and reed pipes, the sitars and the sounds they made were adopted by the Imperial court. The performers, especially the dancing girls, had been following returning visitors from the Celestial Kingdom since Qing Luguang led his army on a crusade to the Western Regions in 384 B.C.

Today you are hounded by a different sound. It is often the background music for a Kung Fu movie, which thunders endlessly wherever you wander. I had gone into a rustic restaurant in the old city for an early lunch, but was compelled to leave before I could complete my meal. Perhaps I would find more peace in a mosque. The one I had my sights on turned out to be further from the restaurant than I had estimated, never realizing that this Uygur city of mud could go on forever.

Having taken the long way to the mosque, I made up for lost time by commandeering a horse and cart and remaining on board until I was certain I would lose my rattling screws. Then, intent on escaping an avenging sun, took up the invitation of a Chinese student to mount the back of his bicycle. My weight made it necessary to clamber aboard this light bike while

The Road to Kucha

it was in motion, and I can leave to your imagination the results of this running start. But I picked myself up, brushed myself off and allowed my young helmsman to peddle away, until walking seemed like the only endurable manner of locomotion. As it should be when one is on a pilgrimage to a holy place.

I debiked at a kind of taxi stand where all the transportation was four-legged and two-wheeled and vying with a herd of cattle for the use of the Silk Road. I had only to cross the road and walk a short distance to the mosque, but unfortunately, it probably had been closed since the Cultural Revolution. Had I come to the wrong mosque? Boys were lounging in its cooling shade.

I decided I must have a hat. Passing by a small shop laden with everything I did not need, I pointed to the old merchant's skullcap and then to my head to show what I wanted. The long and the short or the small of it is, I walked away with the shopkeeper's hat, the grizzled ancient beaming at my instant Islamic bearing. He would not take no for an answer, even if it did not fit. It is one thing, in a hot country, to give a friend the shirt off your back, but to give a stranger the hat on your head has to be the apex of hospitality. (In fact, a stranger, a foreigner in Singapore, lent me the shirt off his back so I could get a visa in the Indonesian Consulate, and that failing, I ended up in Borneo instead of Indonesia.)

By the time I returned to my hotel, I was ready for bed, though a late lunch should have been more like it. The pretty manager/receptionist had left her office to show a new arrival to his room. Apprehensively, I observed where she was taking her latest guest, since I had my room all to myself and had perhaps paid for only one bed. In answer to a question I could not make out but only imagine, I heard her say, "American." Afraid of instant popularity, I rested easy when I saw them enter a cottage other than my own and awaited the woman's return to her office.

She was really quite attractive in her innocence and beyond nationality. Where the west had met the east, she was a warm sight to behold. Charmingly, she gave me my key and I considered myself the luckiest man in all creation to be able to return to my tranquil abode and perhaps die in peace. Or better yet, I could picture a dancing sugarplum, and I really could not rule out the possibility that she would come by with her lute. Wasn't the foreign devil, von Le Coq, visited by damsels in skimpy silks playing stringed instruments?

Innocent, but wise in the ways of the east, she had all she could do to suppress her bubbling smile, which may have been her reaction to my newly acquired "yamulke," come to think of it.

You guessed it. The new guest was unpacking his bag in my room. My gear spread over the empty bed had not dissuaded him from making himself at home. A flimsy attempt at territoriality that he could have taken for untidyness. The young man was Japanese. And stung to the quick when I indicated he was not welcome, "For Christ sake, man, I'm sick; I'm crazy!"

Of no importance. In fact, that was what the Japanese liked about Americans. I was a lot more acceptable than a Chinese guy who in all likelihood would be his roommate if he checked into another cottage. But the student had his pride and I may have been more than he bargained for anyway. If, like most Americans, I carried a gun, he could not rule out the possibility I would use it. Dejectedly, angrily, he began packing. I apologized for not being able to be a more gracious host, but he wasn't having any of that; there was simply no excuse for my behavior was the unspoken sentiment, and no place for it in his "Lonely Planet."

Too stirred up to sleep, I decided to eat. But I could not even get a yogurt at the hotel restaurant. I confronted the key lady, but her smoldering look had me on the defensive – when it was my privacy that had been violated. She hadn't even warned me about my room being occupied. In any case I could not believe that this was the same butterfly who could melt a sailor's heart. She demanded I pay for both beds, but what hurt me more than this Silk Highway robbery was the fact that right or wrong I could have been responsible for this monstrous transformation in her. That I could be the object of such anger from this sunflower shamed me.

My attraction to this woman may have been connected

to my relationship with my wife; that same irrepressible warmth – which can turn to ashes as quickly as a dash of cold water on a fire. I left the registration office in a cloud of smoke.

I had only enough energy to wash my skullcap, which was really quite clean. Whiter than my own white hats when I was in the Navy. But this was a cotton beanie. Was I a Muslim or a Jew? Or both and everything in between. I arranged the curtains to allow just the right amount of light streaming through the trees to bathe my room. Beatific. Batton down the hatches and I'll be under way. No nocturnal visitors wanted, just enough space for air. My windows faced a backyard where the guarddog spent his nights. I laid down and soaked up the dying light and the muted sounds of the village. Nothing more disruptive than the gentle creaking of a horse and cart carrying me away. Blessed peace. Sleep.

And then it hit the fan. It must have been about midnight when I was under siege. Understatement. It was the enemy within, the yellow peril. I ran to the head just in time to unleash that frothy flood called giardia. But because my ideas of the norm had shifted somewhat with the course of my journey, the striking color seemed par for the course. I lay in bed until it was light enough to venture forth, gulping down the last of Mona's diarrhea pills – said to be ineffective against giardia.

But by the time I was on the road my giardia was just so much water under the bridge – which I had to cross before I was on my way to Kashgar. My brisk walk under the fading poplars and a sparkling dawn afforded me intimations of autumn. This wasn't so much the old city as it was town and country, wheat and corn, fields and plum orchards. The scene did not comfortably fit into the *Bower Manuscript* (named for the guy who found it), written in Sanskrit about 1,500 years ago. It was here that the Devils had their first intimations of the Indian influence on China and the ancient Buddhist treasures of the Taklimakan and Thousand-Buddhas caves to my north.

But ignorance was bliss and I cared not a fig for what I might have missed.

44

The Road to Kashgar

*Up on the passes and in the narrow valleys –
everywhere lie skeletons and skulls, grinning...
horse, camel, man?
It's not easy to decide as you rattle by.*

An Earlier Traveler

A few warm-up rides and I crawled into a pickup truck that was going all the way to Kashgar. Or so the driver said when I practically commandeered the thing. I had just abandoned a stalled vehicle and I wasn't wasting time as the hunter from the east gained ground on me. Joining an old couple and an odd couple, I shared the back seat of this massive truck with the younger woman, less particular about the lack of air in back.

Aksu suffers pretty much the same fate as Kucha, as this was yet another one of the thirty-six kingdoms to fall to General Ban Chao and be buried under layers of succeeding civilizations or depredations. But Aksu can boast of a river and after crossing this Styx, our Silk Road made Africa's Hell's Run look like a mere Purgatory. Much of the traffic consisted of convoys of trucks kicking up those clouds of dust the Peruvians call *pulvo*. Pulverized earth that looks like smoke rising out of the charred chasm into which we had plunged. Through this, I was kept busy rolling the windows up and down, trying to strike a balance between the necessary air and the choking dust.

Observing a number of casualties on the side of the road, I could easily picture myself dying of thirst from just a simple breakdown – mine or the truck's. I was short on water, and already terribly dehydrated from the giardia alone. I counted my blessings when we emerged from this hellish limbo with life and limb intact – I had been in Purgatory after all.

The lurching about had churned up an internal storm that would not be quelled. I realized it could come to this, that I might have to jump ship, but I had not given much thought to what I would do with my gear. Certainly yesterday's acquisitive couple had made me leery, and I wasn't very comfortable about leaving my earthly possessions with these imperfect strangers, and perhaps being caught with my pants down as they drove off into the sunset.

Throwing caution to the winds, I had little choice in the matter – I fled the truck, almost bringing the vehicle to a halt myself. My benefactors waited patiently – they had been there one or two thousand times themselves – and when we pulled into a nearby town, the older man pointed across the road. I seem to recall a red cross, something that indicated that the building was an infirmary or a dispensary. But it appeared to be closed and as I looked about the dirt-yard, someone on his way to the outhouse pointed it out to me. That's what the older man had in mind. Well, any port in a. . . .

Enough – yet what follows is of some social significance and I must report it. Practically on my tail, a man with a grin on his face, spies me in my corner and squats in the neighboring hole as if we were old buddies. And curiously enough, I was taken back to boot camp where we lacked stalls even if we had bowls. This cheek to jowl intimacy is what makes Asia and the service an extended family.

Our next stop appeared to be a barely converted caravansary, little more than a desert outpost with what may have been a gas pump out front. Inside there was a greasy spoon and a sink. Washing up, I was astounded to see a yellow fluid draining into the sink. Taking a closer look into the mirror, I saw that my eyes were the source of this foul substance. White mucous or whatever had been par for my obstacle courses, but that this secretion was the color of my excretion threw me into a panic. Had my wires crossed? I was absolutely haywire. What was the matter with these people? My eyes must have been draining like this for hours, without a peep out of them. This unseemly sight may have accounted for the standoffishness of the young lady.

If I am like the ocean played upon by the wind, I am also the stuff of the desert. Aksu itself lies at the bottom of loess cliffs, which extend across much of northern China, and I had become the Yellow River, or at least its source. But if my mucous was of the good earth, why was I the only person whose eyes ran yellow?

45

Star Struck

> *Awake! for morning in the Bowl of Night*
> *Has flung the Stone that puts the Stars to Flight;*
> *And Lo! the Hunter of the East has caught*
> *The Sultan's Turret in a Noose of Light.*
>
> Rubaiyat

With the sun fading fast, the young man had bought a bottle of white lightening and proceeded to get bombed just up the Silk Road. We had stopped before what resembled a mining company near the small town of Sanchakou and the turnoff for the older Silk Road and the ancient Yarkand (today's Shache), the better commercial route for Samarkand and Palmyra, when they were the desert pearls on that string of oases around the neck of Asia. Merv, Bokhara and Balkh, what are they today? The noose was too tight and the light was extinguished with the poets.

    Utter desolation, little traffic, and the driver is getting loaded in the shade of the truck – now considerable because it is getting late. With these characters alone I have already covered more than two hundred miles, but they have an appointment to keep and there is no need to remain parked while the bottle is passed around. But the older man is getting concerned and to the chagrin of his young driver, tosses his bottle out the window. He really doesn't require any more sauce, and his mood is expanding with the lengthening shadows.

    I was feeling no pain myself. I was in the back of the truck, in back of beyond, so thoroughly wiped out, a tabula rasa for the magic of the cocktail hour. Desert twilight – when and where the transcendentalist is most receptive to a natural high and the rocks in your head are converted to gold – a virtual Philosopher's Stone. Flaming mountains of the most brilliant colors seemed to keep the night at bay, but when day was finally done it sprang upon me like a panther.

That brief eternity of the defining desert evaporated in a twinkle. Total darkness. Only the stars to light the way of the wise man from the east. God knows who was driving now – or if anyone at all was driving, but we sped on through the night. By the time we stopped at a roadside stall for tea, I was crash-landing, coming down like a ton of bricks. All that had remained of that extreme exhaustion which had served me so well at twilight – the phantasmagoria of late afternoon – was an acute awareness of my vulnerability. A muted panic. Paranoia.

We had turned off the Silk Road and were driving into the desert. We stopped when the pickup truck could go no further. There was shouting. I was urged to leave the vehicle. I could hardly stand. Someone had a flashlight. Flash back. A man had come out to meet us and my mind went back to a midnight ride in post-Tito Yugoslavia, when I noticed *then* that the men who had given me a lift had a shotgun. My fellow travelers *now* were obviously visiting friends or relatives, but that did not rule out foul play.

The driver was remaining with the truck while the others were going off with the newcomers. I may have had a choice to remain with the drunk, but I was croaking, and the older man was coaxing me to go with him. But my bag! I turned to retrieve my backpack and he pulled me away indicating that the truck would remain here, not to worry. Ha! My gritty eyes strained to fathom my possibly threatening predicament. Had I the strength, I simply would have grabbed my bag, though I had no idea how far we would be walking. Everything down to my toothbrush was in it. I had only my Travelers Checks and camera with me. What more did I need, really? I could buy another brush; shirts and underwear were cheap enough. Goodbye to bad rubbish, I half thought, he who travels lightest travels furthest and faster. I kept my passport.

But that wasn't my reaction when, after stumbling one

hundred yards into the desert darkness, I heard the pickup truck rumbling into the night, headlights beaming toward the old slick road. My protest went unheeded. Body fluids draining from all my orifices and artifices, this was not a command performance and not about to influence the course of events.

How did I let myself get into this mess? Preparedness has never been my strong point, and if my courage was of the fools-rush-in kind, I always had a reserve of energy that kept my spirits bolstered. Oh for the balls of yesteryear, even yesterday, to keep the fear at bay. But it is more a question of joy cancelling out danger – ultimately boiling down to the energy it takes to get cooking.

I must confess to sorely missing those muscles – that false sense of security – that had fueled the Refiner's Fire. I am the sum total of every adrenaline depleting endeavor, energy consuming journey, that transforms coal into empathy's diamond. And burnout.

I really had become attached to my bag like the turtle to its shell. It was all I had going for me, or rather, with me. The natural, earthy color and texture of the bag, a chip off the old block. I hated the modern, more streamlined sterilities that were in such jarring contrast to nature. And like Picasso, I develop a strong attachment to any piece of junk that has been around me long enough.

Most important were the bits and pieces, the memorabilia that defined my fast fading trip. Crestfallen and leery, I made my weary way through a cluster of houses. And then a door opened on a lit and welcoming room. An elderly couple. I may have been robbed, but I wasn't being kidnapped, or was I? A bowl of ablution, water was passed around. I made a show of my eyes, hoping my host had some sort of herbal remedy for this desert malaise, or whatever I had been afflicted with. My discomfort did not make a dent on these hardened denizens of the desert. That mucky mucous flowing from my eyes was kid stuff.

What about my bag? I went through all the motions, tapped my back, put my arms through imaginary straps, put an imaginary toothbrush to my almost imaginary teeth. The leader of today's little expedition pointed to his watch and moved his finger from the present time of about 10:00 or 11:00 (I forget which) to midnight. By 1:00 the last slice of melon was out of the way and I was snug in a rug that had been rolled out for me, without seeing hide or hair of my bag.

Unable to sleep, I went outside before the women had fallen off and unrolled a rug. The man of the house brought me blankets. I lay motionless, mesmerized by the stars, a billion points of light shining through the greater blanket of night. Was I alive to the immensity, the intensity, of the moment? What more mattered? I could have used some sleep.

If I did not thank my lucky stars, I looked to the crystalline clarity of infinity. Comets streaked across the inky bowl, light-show of the ages. Cosmic handwriting on the blackboard of night.

46

A Knotty Situation

Up from earths centre through the Seventh Gate
I rose, and on the Throne of Saturn Sate,
And many knots unraveled by the road;
But not the Knot of Human Death and Fate.

                                                                  Rubaiyat

Tiger, tiger, burning bright in the forests of the night. I was brought down to earth by the sound of moaning. A so-human suffering that the blackest night could not conceal. And I thought about all the pain the desert held, so raw and exposed. In the place of my bag opened a Pandora's Box of insights. And then shedding some light on the night, the moon came into view. No longer a cat's eye, round and yellow, but blue moon strange bedfellow. I followed his westward journey until he was overtaken by day. Lassoed by dawn.

    I had gone sleepless, but was possessed of a maniacal determination. With the strength borne of surviving that longest night into light, I was button-holing my fellow travelers about my bag. The navigator had hardly roused himself and was totally unprepared for my metamorphosis. He pointed to 9:00 A.M. on his watch, giving me that "no problem" look. Breakfast was brought to me.

    My yellow crocodile tears seemed to be drying up in the clean, crisp air; but real crying had not disappeared as the anguish of night spilled into day. I believe the young woman traveler, my fellow traveler's daughter-in-law, had been told a relative had died. He motioned for me to follow him into the garden.

In the back of their mud-brick house was a veritable Garden of Eden. A large vegetable patch, and in the stead of apples, fig trees, pears and the already picked apricots. Oddly enough, the sight of the fig tree reminded me of my own childhood backyard in old New York, but nothing had prepared me for fig trees in China; the biggest, juiciest, almost white figs, I had ever seen. From Persia had come pistachio nuts and peaches, pears and dates, which were now grown in China, but never was I given a sign of this lush produce putting my own backyard figs to shame.

I can't be certain where these figs originated, but the Near East is in the air. We were but a few miles from Artux (Artush), near the Tomb of Satuq Bughra Khan, who died in 955. He was the first ruler in the region to convert to Islam. Legend has it that as a young man the Khan was confronted by an apparition that persuaded him to turn against his Buddhist faith. The alternative held up to him was Paradise, that well-watered garden attended by beautiful women. His subsequent Holy Wars converted the Buddhist States of the Silk Road to Islam.

Anyway, my questionable friend plied me with the green-white figs, these luscious laxatives that could reactivate my giardia. I recalled the story of a group of Chinese coming upon a man in his apricot orchard and being prevented from eating more than a few of the volatile fruit. They were offended until they realized the man was trying to tell them that should they persist they would succumb to the runs. Not feeling my oats it was obvious that it would not take many figs for me to be the pushover I had been the night before.

Lunch had come and gone and the bagman still had not shown up. Police, I said, police, using the Chinese word – probably the only one the navigator understood. I marched him up to the road.

Cars and buses streamed by. I repeatedly shouted police! police! Kashgar! Kashgar. . .! where I thought I had a chance of getting something done. He was pointing in the opposite direction, where the wheels of justice would have less traction. Hadn't he allowed the young man to drive off with my bag? But I seemed to detect a glimmer of sincerity, even certitude, in his changing behavior, and relenting, we piled on the bus for Sugun.

Leaving the standing-room only bus, we began what seemed an interminable walk through Sugun. Reaching my limit I ran up to a soldier and excitedly tried to explain to him that I had been robbed. The soldier was a fierce-looking Chinese and seemed to think that I was just another "minority."

"American, American," I assured him, but he must have known I was a foreigner from the very beginning, because no one else would have had the temerity to approach him this way. My friend explained his case, and then flagged down a pedicab. All the while we were going further and further away from Kashgar, until we were at the edge of town. I refused to go on. I whipped out my passport, asking for his own Identification Card, and then pocketing it, allowed the hapless soul to be peddled towards Beijing.

Sometime later my friend returned with my bag at his side. My sad sack had taken on a human dimension. But I felt less relief than remorse. Hadn't I been a bit hasty? Hadn't I learned (I had forgotten) in all these years that time is of no consequence in the lands of mañana, where the people live in yesterday and the truth may be stretched to tomorrow?

And even if this was not another of those cultural misunderstandings, and the two characters knew what they were doing, I had permitted my little comedy to intrude upon a morning of mourning. There was a bright moment in this clash of cultures. With my rug rolled up and out of the way, my grandfatherly host joined me on a mat as a woman of the house prepared breakfast under a warming sky. In his skullcap, the white bearded man appeared beatific. We made no attempt to communicate, there was no need to. But this was a moment to remember and as I unsheathed my camera, he gave me the OK. He removed his everyday head-covering and wore a larger, rich maroon-colored hat for the occasion. I was, after all was said and done, his guest!

47

Home of Melons and Fruits

At length you reach a place called Kashgar, which it is said, was formerly an independent kingdom; but it is now subject to the dominion of the Great Khan. Its inhabitants are of the Mahometan religion.... The language of the people is peculiar to themselves. They subsist by commerce and manufacture. They have handsome gardens, orchards and vineyards. An abundance of cotton is produced here, as well as flax and hemp. Merchants from this country travel to all parts of the world; but in truth they are a wretched, sordid race, eating badly and drinking worse. Besides the Mahometans, there are among the inhabitants several Nestorian Christians, who are permitted to live under their own laws and to have their own churches....

Marco Polo

Kashgar was one of the kingdoms that sided with the Xiongnu against the Han Dynasty, drawing the indomitable Ban Chao to Kashgar and beyond. The nasty general went as far west as Merv to expand China's sphere of influence. He spent most of his thirty-one years on the road quelling the rebellions of the Western Regions. The Chinese remained in Kashgar until the seventh century, when Tibet incorporated much of the Silk Road into its kingdom. Genghis Khan and family and Timur (Tamerlane) were among the conquerors to include Kashgar in their tour de force.

Assailed by the resounding sound of the smitty, shouts of drivers and the ringing of their donkey bells, I made my way through a throng of Uygur men in variegated caps and thinly veiled women. It was a road that seemed to lead somewhere. Further on is a hotel.

I saw nothing to distinguish it from a hundred other such hotels I had visited, but unbeknownst to me I had stumbled upon and stumbled out of the famed "British Consulate." The Qinibak or China Bagh Hotel had been built over the Consulate's garden (according to a sometimes unreliable guidebook I peeped in) while the Consular house itself in the rear of the hotel is reserved for official visitors. Like the old days when the British Consulate was the only game in town – not to be confused with the "Great Game" which the Russians were also playing on the other side of town.

In the notes I wrote upon my return from Asia, I referred to the British Consulate as a Pakistani hangout. Entering the lobby of this hotel, I went into a culture shock, for here were people of Hindu stock, flashily dressed, flashing eyes, dark-skinned businessmen who brought home the proximity of the subcontinent and the projected leg of my journey for which I was ill-prepared. Where were their trucks?

But they were nowhere to be seen, the kaleidoscopic trucks of these traders, these outlandishly decorated caravel-like vehicles, today's caravans of the Karakoram. Better suited for a carnival. I didn't know if this was poor timing or if relations with China had gone sour, but at least for the first few years following the completion of the Sino-Pakistan Highway, the Chinese government treated the traders as if they were going to rescue the Xinjiang economy.

To quote my Silk Road magazine, "The fleets of Pakistani traveling traders generally include from several dozen to one hundred trucks."

Going overboard, perhaps, the author of the dated article rhapsodizes that "whenever they hear the exotic music of the truck horns from a distance...south of Kashi, the people streamed out into the streets. Overjoyed children shout and jump about, old men smile and stroke their beards. With feelings of great joy, everyone welcomes these traders from far away." It was no wonder they gave away their wives and daughters to Marco.

Eventually, I would have my fill of those loud trucks. I can't speak to the reality of the late 1980's, but the Pakistanis I met were treated like they had brought the plague instead of the suits they would trade for silks. But official surliness was par for the course and the article is just another case of taking with a cup of salt anything written in an official magazine. It may be that the trucks are "gay and gaudy as a bride dressing and making up for her wedding," but the photo also shows people dancing around a truck as if it were a Maypole. As if it were staged.

I wanted to rely on a more reliable source for my coverage of the Karakoram Highway, but what I thought would be the definitive "Silk Road" (1992 British publication) has been snowed under with unforgivable nonsense. This guidebook states that the Karakoram Highway was named for the "crumbling rocks" that are one of the pitfalls of this high mountain road. With the word "kara" being one of the more popular words in the Turkic vocabulary as in the Kara or Black Sea or even the fabled city itself, Karakoram, or Black Sands, it is obvious to anyone who has traveled the luna landscape of the highway (and knows a bit of Turkish) that it has been aptly named.

The ruined city of Karakoram was the sometime capital of Genghis Khan, and is also associated with the legendary Prestor John, King of the Nestorians. The ancient Mongol capital is outside Ulan Bator, but the "Silk Road" has placed Karakhoja, the most famous ruins of the Silk Road, 1,000 kilometers away in its stead. And while I'm at it, this guidebook refers to Tamerlane as a relative of Genghis Khan. An Uzbek, the Turkic Timur – to this day a popular name in Turkey – would indeed be a distant relative. This man from Samarkand (or close enough) did trounce the Golden Horde descendents of Genghis Khan, and that is the extent of their relationship.

I was not disappointed when the manager of the former British Consulate could not come up with a room, for the helpful compass-carrying Hong Kongese I had met in the Urumqi bus station was once again at my side and recommending the former "Russian Embassy." He and his friends happened to be going there and the next thing I knew we were bumping along on a donkey-drawn cart past the formidable walls leading to the Seman Hotel – and the seedy high ceiling rooms that was the Consulate in the rear of it.

Paradise. Tree-lined bungalows and a bathroom fit for a czar. My ground floor window opened on the through-road of the compound, but I was so beat that I fell into bed pulling the covers over me like a bear ready for winter. I can't say if I was chilled or if it was my shade-cooled cavern that accounted for my late afternoon hibernation on what had been a hot day. Nor can I say if I slept through the morning or the month. Actually, it is even possible that I was up before nightfall and exited the old Russian grounds via the back gate to have a beer across the street. Measuring time after the fact is made more difficult by endless nights followed by days lengthened by observing almost every cotton-pickin' foot of your journey. Rarely is my grounded travel interrupted by distracting books or conversations; nor am I an occupied driver, driving away from it all.

The sounds of the street that were normally so annoying were almost soothing in their familiarity after my al fresco night in the desert. I have to be near death to nap in the afternoon – and dead to have remained in bed till morning – so call me a ghostwriter because I really don't think I went out that night.

Sir Aurel Stein (with unseemly bravado) could dismiss the Kunjerab Pass, in my path, as an "excursion for ladies" (before Women's Lib, of course), but Sven Hedin was the devil himself for whom no mountain was too high or desert too low; and there I was possibly sleeping in the rascal's bed. It was only natural that early on the pint-sized Swede would gravitate towards the Russians, but as the Game progressed, Hedin was up for grabs and as an ambassador-at-large proved that physical courage is inferior to moral convictions. It was one thing to sleep at the British Consulate when you have been in bed with the Russians, but the little devil was also in the employ of Hitler, whom he admired.

The history of the Silk Road reads like fantasy – especially when it comes to Marco Polo, who was bound to lend himself to literature. In his existential *Invisible Cities,* Italo

Calvino sees Marco not so much traveling from place to place as materializing here and there. Amazingly, this book fell into my lap when I found myself trying, once again, to retrace Marco's steps. Calvino has Marco trafficking in metaphors, accused by the Great Khan of taking a "journey through memories" and returning from his voyages with a "cargo of regrets." And then Kublai hits Marco – and myself – where it hurts. "Meager purchases, to tell the truth, for a merchant of the Serenissima!"

The book fictionalizes the relationship between Marco Polo and Kublai Khan, but there is no doubt that the emperor of the Tartars was influenced by his emissary; just as today's leaders would be enlightened by a later traveler of the Silk Road. But the spacey, spookey style of *Invisible Cities* does not capture the spirit of Marco or his journey, beyond the fact that the Merchant of Venice could have used a compass. And did seem to materialize. When Kublai Khan attacks Marco and demands, "Confess what you are smuggling: moods, states of grace, elegies," we know that through the metaphysics of travel it is really me who has been attacked; for it was I who was the poet, beggar and king of the road.

The most fantastic thing about the Silk Road was the silk itself. The fact that this was Rome's slippery slope to financial ruin; that the Chinese were able to keep the production of silk a secret until Nestorian monks, really the first foreign devils, in 550 were able to smuggle silkworms out of the Western Regions. The worms were brought to Byzantium, where the church monopolized the production of seres (or silk) and kept its lucrative secret until God knows when. With many facts stranger than fiction coming out of the East, it is not surprising that the legend of an all-powerful Nestorian king persisted to modern times.

How the worms traveled to Xinjiang is the real mystery, but if legend be believed, a princess from Cathay, engaged to the King of Heitan just down the road from Kashi (Kashgar) – smuggled the eggs in her hat. They are prodigious buggers. A silkworm's cocoon can net a half-mile of silk, but how the Nestorians got tangled in it is yet another mystery. But I guess the strangest element in the story of seres is that the Romans could never figure out the stuff – and rued that day, two thousand years ago in Syria, when they saw the silken banners of the Parthian troops and fled the unfurling "flames" in panic. And fascination.

There is about these fringes of the Taklimakan the dry air of musty discoveries. Victorian/Viceroy cloak-and-dagger that was the inspiration for Indiana Jones. A hundred variations of the Pharaohs curse, that for hundreds of years kept the deserts's many and often mummified treasures from crumbling in robbers' hands.

One of the more curious tales to emerge from the Taklimakan is the story of a man who falls into debt and goes into the desert to die – the usual fate of those who wandered among the cursed ruins. This blessed soul, however, stumbles upon a treasure that does not exact revenge. There is in this story a parable for every penitent who walked away from it all, and the Buddhist and Taoist approach or non-approach to life, that hands-off philosophy that suggests if you don't seek, you shall find. Everything falls into place.

Kashgar is a kind of last chance cafe for most travelers exiting China's western door. There are a few other places up the road where you can imbibe, but this was where you also said goodbye to civilization for a while. The favorite table in town is at the restaurant in the rear of the old Russian compound. A gate opens on the street. All the tourists I had tried so desperately to avoid came here to catch a beer in the desert air. Not too happy to see me either was the Texan via New York lawyer who had informed me that the Palestinians already had a homeland and it was called Jordan. I don't think he ever went on to Pakistan.

For the last quarter of a century I joked that all I want out of travel is to get beyond the reach of lawyers and lawn mowers, and for the moment I had half-succeeded. Another survivor of Xiahe and the Gansu Corridor was an amiable giant I had dubbed the "Flying Dutchman," because a part of him was above it all. He was not having an easy time of it, finding a welcoming port – or the man from the Low Country was engaging in one-upsmanship, for my Dutch friend, actually Belgian, was telling me, the hitchhiker, that he had been detained by the Chinese authorities. He had been removed from the international bus while his bag went on to Pakistan without him. It was at the bottom of a pile of luggage, but no problem, his girlfriend would look after it until he was able to rejoin her. He was bound to tell tall tales.

    I was outraged that this young man should be putting up with the closed society of buses when the open road beckoned, and berated him and his friends for not hitchhiking. I roared that the Belgian was only encouraging the Chinese with their restrictive measures. Gloriously drunk, I behaved as if hitchhiking, bumming a ride was my crowning achievement.

48

The Road to Kara Kuli

A blessedly bracing morning. The Flying Dutchman had told me about a Shangri-La that is the jewel in the crown of the glacier strewn Pamirs and I was on my way. A modest flow of rush-hour traffic outside the hotel. Workers waiting to catch a bus that would be going up to the Karakoram Highway, but there was no bus in sight, not even a donkey and cart. I tramped to the point where the Silk Road became the Karakoram before having a loaf of nan at a stall. Then, I bused to the edge of Shufu. It was time to hitchhike.

Imagining I was following the red ribbon on my map, I was surprised to learn I had taken the yellow brick road. Marco had taken the red ribbon, the south road that passed through Shule, the ancient name of Kashgar.

And then they went eastward, *"ever eastward, and the moons were born, grew wane and died... They passed through Khotan, where the divers bring up jade from the rivers, white jade and black jade, and green jade veined with gold...And they came to the town of Lob, and a new moon arose, and they entered the Desert of the Singing Sands."*

A jaded ditty from Donn Byrne's *Messer Marco Polo*. A dated ditty that may have inspired Italo Calvino. In any case, another book that had just fallen into my lap – when just across the border Harry Wu was preparing to enter China with his cargo of justice on the little-used Silk Road to the north of me. Like Tripitaka and other monks before him, Harry Wu had been to a Promised Land, where at least they make a pretense of justice, and with truth's sacred scriptures indelibly written across his soul, he had come home again. But you can't go home again, and the Chinese government wasn't buying.

Today's destination was a cluster of yurts off the road, overlooking the lake. It was a kind of base camp for Kongur Shan. Actually, Kara Kuli is located between Mount Kongur and Muztagata, the highest mountains in undisputed Chinese territory. A foot on each end of the eastern shore, both mountains would be a peak experience worth cooling my heels over. Standing over 7,500 meters, (about 26,000 feet) the Pillars of Pamir should be easy to spot with any luck. Though the mountains were marked on my map, I was afraid my ride would pass them by, for who would understand the Romanized alphabet?

(National Geographic shows the original Silk Road on the opposite side of the mountains – which may be – but the mountains have apparently moved also, as Muztagata is now located where my yurt was.)

But I had gotten this far with the Sino-language, and I walked a mile or so beyond the town until I arrived at a bridge. And there above the river the sky opened to the vast sweep of peaks that stretched some 2,000 miles, a silver crescent that reached back to almost where I had begun my Chinese journey. This was the corset that held up the underbelly of Tibet, with great strands that ran up to Tian Shan or the Heavenly Mountains, the icy fortress that almost came full circle and made China the Forbidden Kingdom. The High Pamir, a day's walk away, gave way to the Karakorum and the Kunlun, extending, spreading, expanding to the hoary Himalayas and the end of time.

If Kashgar was the last chance cafe, Shufu, apparently, was my luckless tea stand. Last stand. One horse and cart after another. Surreys with a fringe on top. Transportation for people and produce, an unhurried pace that gave me pause, peace. But the day was warming up and those distant high altitude islands of ice and snow were misting over. I walked back to a fruit and vegetable stand, and then nearer to the town, a bus pulled up. The international bus. What to do? Hold out or go to market with the sheep? I could see the resignation in the faces of the Planeteers – I didn't know they would be on the same bus in the morning.

One or two foreign tourists were grabbing a bite or simply goofing off at a nearby shack. I could not see any vehicles making the grueling haul to Tashkorgan any later than this – and anything going my way would go that far because Kara Kuli Lake was in the middle of a beautiful nowhere and there was nothing remotely resembling civilization between here and the Hunza River other than Tashkorgan, the last stop for the bus, and Mohammed Kashgeri's Tomb just up the road.

Kashgari was an Uygur scholar who wrote a dictionary of the Tujue people, a tribe within the Uygur family. The encyclopedic book, also translated into the dominant Arabic, was presented to the caliph of Baghdad in 1075. So renown did this dictionary become, revealing the extent of a Tujue culture the equal of the Arab, that Kashgari's whitewashed tomb high above the road is the only man-made landmark between here and the Stone City outside Tashkorgan.

A truck rumbled to a halt by the fruit and vegetable stand. I don't recall seeing another machine getting beyond the bridge the entire morning. The Chinese driver immediately busied himself taking on a cargo of melons. What was one more melon? Waving my map, I pounced on the heavyset fellow. He stuck up ten fingers. Holding up one and feigning refusal, I walked to the bus.

"Okay, okay," he called after me. We compromised.

As the bus pulled out and passed us, the Lonely Planeteers looked on in amazement as an over-the-hill hitchhiker tumbled into a lorry loaded with comestibles and sat on the roof of the cab – but what better way to see the roof of the world. I may have looked down my nose at those caged souls, yet this was not the self-satisfaction of yesterday's drunk but the absolute joy of the purist (relatively speaking) waiting for nature's caress. It was the only way to travel in China. I didn't have the time to walk – or the inclination, along the side of the road, and that was ditto for a bicycle, glued to the road, rider bent under an invisible load, or whizzing by like some souped-up snail. I wanted my head in the clouds, but my feet making contact with the earth, and if I was to ride, I would stand like Hemingway when he would write. Everything I have written is in the wind, but there is nothing like it except standing at the bow of a boat, when you're on the bridge of a desert ship. This was the satisfaction of a man ready for action (and the looney bin).

Over the river and into the trees, a well-watered area that was soon giving way to arid elevations and intimations of the Kara in the Korum, grainy rocks blackened by sun and circumstance. A planet in places burned to a cinder with the Gaizi or Kaxpar River coursing through it, and yours truly, a survivor of the inferno himself, leaning on the cab, leaning into the wind, barely able to contain my rocky mountain high. White water rushing below us was tonic for a tramp who had serendipitously discovered what he had really been searching for. And to think that a mountain man like myself could travel to China, ready to overlook this Great Wall, until my back was up against it.

A pristine Shan, the greatest cathedral known to man, rose high above the sand and the barren reaches of Taklimakan, that vast sea rolling on to Karakoram.

Marco, when he encountered the tribes of the High Pamir, wrote, *". . . .this region is called Belor. Even amid the highest of these mountains, there lies a tribe of savage, ill-disposed, and idolatrous people, who subsist upon the animals they can destroy and clothe themselves with the skins."*

The truck stopped for an elderly man in a great coat, boots and a fur hat who clambered aboard. A lorry bin had become the local bus and the driver seemed more interested in packing in his passengers than getting his melons to market. This was fine by me, a break from the rocking and rolling, and a chance to soak up the sun.

The captain summoned me below. Did he want me to ride shotgun, or think that his star passenger deserved more than this floating cabbage patch. He was amused when I insisted on traveling deck-class. And next to the ocean, I can think of no more romantic ride. Forbiddingly beautiful and in its extremity beautifully bizarre, a roaring river charges through an eternity of mountains washed by waves of sand, ice and snow. And fire. A cold day on fire. Cobalt blue. Camel- colored sand under melting sheets of ice, a commingling of the elements that seemed totally, even otherworldly barren and beyond comparison, extraterrestrial.

Of all nature's grand abstractions, the sand-filled lakes at the bottom of the upper falls are unique, but almost suddenly these rapids level out to an alpine meadow (contained as it was). On we bumped along, swaying to and fro, lurching like the camels in the distance. And then as we slowed for a turn, a group of workers appeared out of nowhere, some road-gang – or highway robbers may be more like it. Not succeeding in flagging down the truck, they gave us chase until another ascending bend in the road enabled these shouting savages to hop aboard the truck like stagecoach desperadoes of the Wild West. Unarmed and unwelcome passengers – stowaways – restricted their plunder to produce. They ate everything they could get their hands on and into their mouths.

When we were on level ground once again, the still-eating brigands disembarked, shrugging off the chewing-out the captain gave them. Maybe the driver had expected some assistance in fending off these marauders when he asked me to join him in the cab. Instead I slaked my thirst with a pirated sliced and peeled cucumber. Apparently they had arrived at their destination, a derelict caravan stop of old that may have appeared more desirable to Marco Polo. It was the size of a tollbooth, which may have been its real purpose. A guardhouse on the lookout for something more profitable than produce. Lapis lazuli from Afghanistan, perhaps saffron, perfumed medicine, wines and spices from Persia, came to China another way. Gazelles and lions from the shores of Arabia took the sea route bound for Cathay.

The road follows the rapids until they open on yet another valley. The driver had tried to dump me at the last stop, jettison me with the riff-raff. It was the bleakest part of the hundred kilometer run and there wasn't a yurt in sight. Emptying my pockets, I refused to budge from the bridge. I would go up with the ship – and lo and behold we followed a now boggish stream around King Kongur to its lapis lazuli source. Sparkling Kara Kuli is the basin for both Kongur and Mount Muztagata, "Ice Mountain Father."

The aquamarine lake is a deceptive Southern Sea in a sky-high, dry montana. Grazing sheep people this amazing space as far as the eye can see, but beyond the verdure of the valley and the reach of glacial runoff, the Grand Abstraction peaks. On the opposite shore, snowcapped Domes of the Rock rise from the lake, a row of yurt-shaped mounds carved from the massive mountain they seem to support. At long last Taklimakan was behind me. Practically flush on the border in disputed territory is Tajikistan. But you must be as sure-footed as a goat to cross this frontier, because the truck is very near a steep incline.

49

Muztagata's Revenge

> *For twelve days the course is along this elevated plain, which is named Pamer, and as during all that time you do not meet with any habitations, it is necessary to make provisions at the outset accordingly. So great is the height of the mountains that no birds are to be seen near their summits; and however extraordinary it may be thought, it is affirmed that from the rareness of the air, fires when lighted do not give the same heat as in lower locations, nor produce the same effect in cooking food.*
>
> Marco Polo

Kara Kuli is also deceptively pristine, because a few miles down the Karakoram highway, the authorities had constructed a wretched desecration but a stone's throw from the lake. This hovel serves as a hotel and restaurant. Nearby is a storage area and trading post, a junkyard softened by the stray camel that might come up from the lake. (Camel dung on the gold-streaked hardscrabble that surrounds this camp would be my bed for several nights.) The scene is salvaged by the half-dozen yurts to the side.

I had not arrived a minute too soon. My canteen had been on empty for some time and I was being sustained by the cucumber my thieving friends shared with me. Most of the yurts were unoccupied and grabbing a number of blankets from the hotel, I settled in with the understanding that I could be having some tentmates at any time. At this point I didn't care. All I wanted was water. But the tea here was served ready to drink – no thermos of boiled water. I was disappointed, but it was preferable to beer at this early hour, and with a canteen full of the Chinese perennial, I fled the chaotic encampment for the greener pastures from whence I came.

Green and black. Sheep turds gave this lake its distinct flavor – and the tea I was drinking. Getting beyond the rust and squalor, I paused atop a grassy knoll. I could not believe my shaded eyes. Before me was high-tech dementia in the form of two Day-Glo tents. Perched at the edge of the Kara Kuli, the modern monstrosities looked like they were a pair of circus balloons and as out of place on the High Pamir as the plaster and tin that defiled the site of the yurts – and detracted from the sight of these felt dwellings.

I approached the eyesores as a gorilla in the wild would. I kept my distance. But a shirtless yuppy (or a wolf in sheep's clothing) had spotted me. We were far from the trading post. What was I? The one that got away? Yet another Yeti? But he had read the guidebooks and knew how to approach the Himalayan wildlife (and we were in the link or lake that is part of the chain of shans). With a smile across his face as large as the slice of watermelon he proffered, the camper was bidding me welcome.

Who was more surprised by the encounter? I can tell you who was the more leery, for I was talking to an American Jew, perhaps paranoid about being a very, very long way from home on the edge of a vast Muslim sea – and if I was not Bigfoot, despite my size 10½, extra wide, he hadn't the slightest clue about the apparently stateless vagabond. My distinctly un-American canteen was overflowing with something he wouldn't drink if the lake dried up. In fact, the camper was drinking purified lake water, using one of those filter gizmos that had not, unfortunately for him, kept all the bugs at bay.

"Where are you from?"

"Persia."

"Persia!?!" I almost slipped from my rock. "You mean Iran?"

He paused. "Well, yes."

I looked at him. "You mean your parents are from Iran."

He was taken aback. "How is the Ayatollah doing? You're not a Muslim?"

Realizing I was probably an American, he confessed.

"Relax, man. These people don't know Palestine from Pakistan. On the other hand, how do I know you're not with Mossad?"

The former New Yorker was living in Boston, with his parents living but an hour from us. It is not that it is a small world but that no man is an island. Like the cities on a map there is a connecting thread through our lives, that may be threatening. Beyond the impossibility of getting away from New York or China, there is no getting away from what has become a part of you.

You can run but you can't hide. Drop me in the middle of the desert and I will land at that moment when the only noisy, polluting car for a thousand miles around is just starting up. A terrible analogy to apply to a guy with a bicycle, perhaps. Speedo said that he and his brother, Darius, had biked here from Sust, across the border. That was great, but he could not relax for a microsecond and I was put off by speed-freaks in the wild, pedaling for all they were worth like the hunchback of Notre Dame in a jester's costume, even if they were good souls.

Speedo told me to get a hat. Unfortunately, I left it in Kucha. He had taken off his shirt and, applying sunscreen, did not leave a square inch of exposed skin free of the cream.

"Just like Club Med, ah?"

"There's not much ozone at this altitude." He replied. I remarked with some admiration, he hadn't forgotten anything, conscious that my sunglasses were sliding off my nose. With a few screws loose, Mona's glorious shades that she had thoughtfully left behind fell to the earth. Not to worry, Speedo was a computer expert and was prepared for everything but the people he might run into.

"You are missing a screw," he said, " but I have a sewing kit in my tent."

His brother was still sleeping in his tent, downed by dysentery. The other tent was occupied by a young French couple about their age. He returned from his tent and did a damn good job of patching my glasses together.

We watched a lone tern dive. Speedo said how much he envied me. I said I had to go.

"Hold on!" He had more goodies in his grab-bag. Putting his sewing kit away, he came up with a made-in-Switzerland water filter that he submerged in the lake. In moments we had drinking water. Clearly, the old salt had overlooked a few things. Didn't my sunglasses say it all: I couldn't get it together.

Night. A rusty, trusty thermos of tea at my side, a tenuous link with the luxury of the east and the fuel that kept Mona and I going. This was such a far cry from those softer times that by the second night it was all a dream. Or nightmare. After trying to sleep fully clothed in the swirling sand, the tea seemed to me to be so out of place as to be back of beyond.

For the record, Beyond is a small village on the southeastern shore of Kara Kuli. Before I went in back of it, I tried to get some food and water, but there were more camels in the holding pen than there were people that I could see in the entire village, and I saw nothing to eat or drink. The Bactrian humps were in miniature, the lower mounds on the northern shore, that seemed the more practical destination, but I wanted to get as near as possible to Muztagata and was compelled to go on.

Nomadic myths abound with accounts of supernatural camels. The Kirghis of this area believe a herd of snow-white camels haunt the summit of Muztagata (Muztagh Ata).

I had to slog through a bog to get to the village, and I thought I would get close enough to melting snow to fill my canteen. I learned, there was another village in back of Beyond, where it seemed all these bounders had been, for several people were returning from that direction. The throughway is a rocky ravine with ankle-deep sand. Tired of plodding on and with a few drops to drink, I climbed a partially shaded ridge and draining my canteen, meditated on or perhaps hallucinated the hallowed mountain. It is possible I was headed in the direction of the ancient caravan route.

I had seen nothing like it. This magnificent mass of metamorphic rock and ice, intruded by Tertiary granites – or is the colossus Muztagh Ata, in fact, only a carboniferous pile of geosynclinal deposits and snow, with of course, Cretaceous overlapping – and one thirsty cretin looking on. I hadn't climbed very high, but the glacial crown was at eye level and teasingly near. Rising from below the opposite ridge with none of Kongur's intruding Pamir, I knew there was water to be had with an hour's trek – but I would have to be content in saying that I had seen hell freeze over. And white camels ice-skating.

A thousand glaciers extend from Kongur a little to the east, for two hundred and fifty miles across Tajikistan – including what was formerly called, for a brief time, Communist Peak. This blasphemy, in the Academy of Sciences Range, is near where more than one map shows a much larger Kara Kuli Lake. I wonder if that "Black" Lake is the same blue color as this Kara Kuli.

Pamir, if it is derived from the Persian pai mir, means foot hills and is a definite misnomer in the east and that part of the mountains that include the Hindu Kush, running through the Afghan-Pakistan border to Karakoram. Coming out of the west Marco would have experienced a wild range of "foothills" before climbing the alluring heights of the miles high thighs. Yet, he doesn't breathe a word of the jewel in the lotus, Kara Kuli. Maybe she was frigid at the time. But if I wax pornographic, you must remember that mountains and mountain lakes were my first love and man has long equated my hangup with heaven. There are worse fetishes. (That Marco is mum on the lake speaks to the old Silk Road being over the mountains, out of his line of march.)

Dying of dehydration and returning to Beyond, I was overtaken by a man on horseback swathed in animal skins. I held up my canteen, turning it upside down and tapped it. The grim fellow got the message, but staring down at me from under his Mongolian or perhaps Tajik hat – the icy image of a Hun, despite the heat – I could not be sure he was offering safe haven when he motioned to me to tag along. His solitary house was in the lengthening shadows of Muztagh Ata.

Removing my shoes, I entered a spacious room covered with rugs. Evidently this was a man of some wealth, even if it was tied up in tapestries. Only the ceiling was bare. The rugs appeared to be from Khotan, if not actually made there and could very well have passed for Indian. American or otherwise. The man's wife brought me stale barley pancakes and tea. She and her child looked on as I drank my fill. Motioning that I should go to sleep, the man fetched an extra carpet and indicated that he had to go out. After my night on terra firma, curling up in a carpet appealed to me, but remembering the hospitality in these parts, I could not be certain what was expected of me. The wife looked on, but she was about as appealing as the other dish that had been set before me.

If my host had something less hospitable in mind for his guest, it would have been sticky wicket picking my pocket. Besides there was a more subtle way to fleece the sheep that sleeps. Everything the merchant had was for sale and when he realized he had brought home deadwood, he put the bite on me. Maybe I was wearing the wrong colors. Light blue and even green were unlucky colors in the Tajik culture – which I thought quite strange when one considers that those other denizens of the desert, the Arabs, understandably have a propensity for green. Their dislike of the gentle colors may explain why the Tajik calls the kettle and what goes into it "black." For all that, my host may have been Kirghis.

Responding to his request for some exorbitant sum, I made a show of emptying my pockets. My questionable benefactor then brought imaginary food to his mouth. Was he making a show of dire straits or simply suggesting that I had not paid enough for his wretched refreshments. This was the first time in all my travels that a host demanded payment – nor was his existence anywhere as threadbare as the lot of most of the souls who gave me the shirts off their backs. I doubt if this hungry display reflected Tajik hospitality, even if Marco had few kind words for them. A few years contact with the modern traveler had not improved their social graces. The Club Merde on the other side of the lake was enough to bring out the shark in any man. Especially if centuries of conditioning in an unforgiving climate left a man with an almost instinctive need to plunder.

And yet, ripping off a tourist was no more plunder than the cat going for the mouse. Ironically, the cycling Samaritans told me how hospitable Beyond was. Was this off-color humor? Whatever the reason, for one split second, I thought he would kill me if I didn't buy a kilim.

The only softness in this upper valley, beyond the kilim, contrasting strangely with the brittle landscape, is the wetland that drains into the lake and reforms as Kara Kuli spills over on the opposite shore. This flowering marsh is harvested for fodder and at this hour and altitude is a haunting twilight zone of myriad rivulets. Leaving Beyond I made my escape through this bog to rest on a less amphibious shore and meditate on the turning terns diving into their turquoise sea. I was filled with the ocean, though sea birds and the fish they dove for were not part of the lore; terns were much more familiar on a tropical shore than on these mountains so far from the sea. Yaks roamed closer to the road. Kara Kuli, where the mountain ranges came together and there was that same overlapping of nature and cultures. This was Tibet as well as Lake Titacaca, and wherever I was.

Nearer to the hotel was a huge tourist caravan on wheels that had just rolled in from Tibet. The high-tech truck was busing a cargo of mostly disenchanted Germans. They had paid to go to Tibet's holiest mountain but near the sacred pilgrimage site was a river that had to be crossed first. The ferry attendant simply refused to take the tourists across the river. Outraged about the cost of the aborted trip, a middle-aged German woman was telling me that the ferryman was simply being "spiteful."

I suggested that perhaps their gargantuan motor home was too big for the crossing, but the indignant lady assured me that this was not the case. Better yet, maybe the ferry attendant was being respectful; something she would have known had she read the classic *Seven Years in Tibet*. Heinrick Harrer notes that Mount Kailas stands in majestic isolation from the rest of the Himalaya range and that when he first caught sight of it, "our Tibetans prostrated themselves and prayed. For Buddhists and Hindus this mountain is the home of their gods and the dearest wish of all the pious is to visit it as a pilgrim once in their lives."

But even the empathetic Harrer did not grasp that the presence of his impious group would have amounted to a desecration. "We, too, would have liked to travel around the mountain as the pilgrims do, but the unfriendly master of the caravansary at Barks prevented us by threatening to stop our future transport facilities unless we continued on our way."

Harrer had recently arrived in Tibet – and an infidel was not welcome in Mecca either. A pious Christian was expected to go to Golgotha on foot. Humble yourself. The "unfriendly" master of the caravansary not unlike the "spiteful" ferry attendant were keepers of the faith –barring the barbarians at the gate.

I'm just as choosy about who trods the forest floor. A cyclepath in the mountains should ride off a cliff. As for that proud airless abomination that transported the Germans around Tibet – the ferryman should have sank the damn thing – it was now desecrating Kara Kuli and the tourists' consolation prize, Muztagh Ata. Historical and physical Tibet was near enough for this new pilgrimage site to fit the bill.

Would the lady like some tea in my yurt?

She was not the type of person you generally see in so base a camp. Her grand tour had been sold as the ultimate in maximized, sanitized comfort. Even so, frauleins tended to enjoy slumming with the real McCoy. Adventurous Germans preferred the high road in China, since Heinrich escaped from a British internment camp in northern India and made his way to Lhasa, later to become, incredibly, the right- hand man of the Dalai Lama. The demigod, as Herr Harrer referred to him, was still a boy. Heinrich was Tibet's Lawrence of Arabia and more.

China sent the Dalai Lama into exile in 1959. He was the winner of the 1989 Nobel Peace Prize, but China has pretty much managed to muzzle the religious leader as far afield as the U.S. He was snubbed at the Fiftieth Anniversary of the United Nations, but remains the mascot who lets us feel good about ourselves. Trendy enough to attract the movie actor, Richard Gere. An asset forgotten Harry Wu lacked. Yet China prevented (by proxy) the Dalai Lama from speaking at St. John the Divine in New York.

And did its best to railroad the 1997 movie about *Seven Years in Tibet*. A year later, the Tibetan choice to succeed the Dalai Lama was still a prisoner of the Chinese government. They were grooming their own candidate (as is the custom, a child).

By the time President Clinton left China, the independence of Tibet was no longer an issue, much less the successor to the Dalai Lama.

The media was strangely silent. Tibet had become too expensive a toy for the corporate owners who saw big bucks in toeing the line. Lost in the hoopla and hype of the presidential visit was the real China, itself – beyond the showcase of the east. Our president had been Shanghaied.

50

The Party is Over, The Jig is Up

It was not yet dusk when I crawled up the steps of the last chance saloon. An expression that often depends on your stops and tastes and whether you are coming or going. Or didn't know whether you were coming or going. I had come to the right place. The restaurant was out of place. And I was having my first beer here. It could be my last beer in China and with Pakistan looming before me, my last drink in Asia.

Sitting alone at my table, I was eyeing the in-crowd near a window. The foreigners, actually, were more like drifters thrown together in the same lifeboat. A disparate, desperate bunch who seemed not to have left their table in several days. Chinese, the few who came here, sat at their own table. The bus made a rest stop here. A femme fatale, or fatal fraulein from the lower depths, invited me to the captain's table. (He had gone down with the ship.)

She and her mate, staying in one of the yurts, hailed from Berlin. Compared to the group parked by the lake in their space vehicle, these Berliners were from another planet. Like her partner, the girl claimed she was a taxi driver. Nearing the end of my rope or road, I was somewhat suspicious of her subtle advances. Her boyfriend was less than half my age, more than twice my size and more her speed. I was flanked by Fraulein and an Australian mother and child, also staying in a yurt.

The Aussie had a certain pixie charm about her – game obviously to be hitting the high road with a kid in tow. But she exuded a vulnerability that her boyfriend, and perhaps Fraulein as well, could not help exploiting. Looking at her traveling companion across the table, she said, "He is too aloof and noncommittal."

Fraulein sympathized, thinking what a sucker she is. The woman was so naive that she expected this Englishman's fling to materialize into something that lent itself to her maternal situation.

He was a cold fish – and had other fish to fry. In fact the Englishman was a journalist who may or may not have been on sabbatical and was at this very moment with his nose in a notebook.

Fraulein spoke about man's inherent inability to open up, but I sensed that her interest in a vulnerable psyche was that of the predator's. Easy pickings. She and the other taxi driver were following the sun – and usually at a lower latitude and altitude. They were going where the living is easy and the dope is cheap, hanging around till their money ran out. I had been to those places myself, once managing to hold out for a year and a half. I experienced a kind of Rip Van Winkle in reverse as I returned to a neighborhood where everyone had long hair.

I thought about those foreigners, freaks, who haunted the other side of the Himalayas in the sixties...until this day. My most traumatic experience in India, if you have forgotten, dear reader, was overdosing on hash and Monk's brandy (I drank the latter earlier) in a Shiva temple adjoining a railway station while waiting for my train to Nepal. In my helpless state my greatest fear was being robbed by a foreigner more desperate than I (not uncommon) until I thought I had already lost my mind. Laying in the top bunk I was experiencing this inexplicable pounding in my ears, even voices – until I realized passengers had not settled themselves on the roof of the train yet.

Talk about your bad trips. The conversation had become a celebration of leaving China. Everyone was so happy to be going where the people had to be friendlier, and if they weren't, the dope was so cheap that it did not matter. My concern was trying to survive in the subcontinent without beer. India, at least, had Whoopee Sparkling Beer to take the edge off the surreality that is daily life east of the Indus River, but Pakistan would not be making whoopee. If the Karakoram Highway was to be a dry run to the sober heart of Islam, I reasoned a less kaleidoscopic journey would be easier to handle. Even if the riotous trucks indicated otherwise.

"I give you guys a week," I lectured, "and you'll come running back to China." I was practically laughed out of the restaurant. "Listen. At least you know where you stand in China – and I've proven a tourist doesn't have to take things lying down." Which is partly true.

Fraulein went into the old refrain. "But we want to do as we like...."

This sounded like Xiahe at the other end of historical Tibet, though the similarity ended there. I looked out the windows – the only thing this derelict restaurant had going for it.

Nobody was going to confuse this place with the Japanese-built resort near Mt. Everest. I could imagine the amenities there – like a self-cleaning toilet bowl. The bleak base camp at Kara Kuli is as black as the name implies, with the motley crew imbuing the location with an end-of-the-world air – heightened by the lack of oxygen available at this altitude, about 15,000 feet above sea level. We were like survivors on some futuristic slope – without benefit of an ark. Or art. Not even a map on the wall to give a feeling of place.

Noah would not cultivate his vineyard here. Nor would we sons of guns be inclined to hang around till harvest. My fellow travelers, with little thought to where in Asia, would piss away their last dollars. We were shooed away from using the only indoor hole, which was privy to the Chinese occupying the rooms in the back of the kitchen. These exiles were unhappy here. Even the Irish have long held the belief that nothingness, death itself, awaited the voyager who reached the western most shore – and for the Chinese, this was it.

In this land God left to Cain, barely supporting grain, I could see that if there were any truth to the myth of the lost continent of Mu, this would be that ancient shore above it all when the oceans covered much of Asia. This would be where the races came together, without vineyards, not in Noah's Anatolia. On a similar shore Tibetans would create their Pure Land, finding a purity in the forbidden barrenness of the high

The Party is Over, The Jig is Up

altitude sands, creating mandalas that were metaphors for a land transformed by Buddhism – like every faith suffering the fate of a sand castle.

Before coming in for a drink, I went behind my yurt and snapped a prize-winning photo. A wavy expanse of Kara Kuli is framed by the inverted bowls in which we slept (those ancient domes that Buckminster Fuller turned into a modern fad and a reputation as a visionary), and their mirror image on the opposite shore. Because of distance, the towering domes above the lake appear smaller than the yurts and bask in a light denied the already darkened low foreground.

"How long have you been in China?" Fraulein was grilling me.

"Over two months."

"Did you have a problem getting your visa extended?"

I explained. Curious glances. No China visa. No visa for Pakistan. Even the journalist looked up. "Maybe they'll allow you to straddle the border," he offered.

A bearded dude or dud of undetermined nationality said, "No sweat!"

All the foreigners were here, now, but the cyclepaths. And the French couple. Too gauche.

This would not be the first time I was a borderline case. I went into a grand funk, thinking about the Boa Vista in Brazil. Despairing of the Venezuelan Consul ever turning up and issuing me a visa – he had been missing – I simply set out for the Brazilian border reasoning that I could get a visa for Venezuela at the frontier, since surely no one could expect me to wait forever for the disappearing consul. But this was not the concern of the border guards. I was compelled to hitch back to Boa Vista, a day's journey, and return to the American missionary camp where I had been staying, until a maniacal consul materialized out of the jungle. By this time the missionary, with no converts after ten years, had almost brought me to my knees. A chapter out of *Journey to the South*.

Blocking out the experience, having gone up, down, around and inside South America, I returned to Colombia with an expired Colombian visa, just getting in under the wire with my already expiring Venezuelan visa. When Colombian Immigration realized that my visa had expired, they turned me back. The Venezuelans pointed out that I no longer held a valid visa for Venezuela, returning me to Colombia. As my head became a volley ball between the two South American countries, I thought I might become the cause of an international war until persona non grata ended up in the Colombian court. But not before guns were drawn as my ranting and raving quite literally had the Columbians up in arms. Calming down, I was given Safe Conduct out of the country. Three days to get out of Columbia – but more than enough time to really screw up.

So, I can honestly say that I was prepared for anything but the necessity of returning to Urumqi to leave China – assuming that I could avoid going to jail first.

Another glorious morning. The east is red. Less cleavage is showing above Kara Kuli. Snow is descending even lower and many bosomed Artemis is wearing white shawls. Yet there is hardly a trace of its source and I imagine there is a snowman as well as a sandman and mother earth. It is not a sheltering sky. I need a cloud to cushion the sharpness of the emptiness. I'm wearing most of my clothes, but as I leave my yurt for the last time my backpack seems heavier than usual. A stowaway? Something I drank or did not eat? I had to come to the ends of the earth to resume my social life.

I was on the restaurant terrace drinking tea from my newly filled thermos, when the Australian woman approached me. Not a soul about. She is hysterical. She can't find her camera. I had a paranoid idea of who could have taken it, though I doubt if my suspicion had ever crossed the mind of this innocent. She was certain that she left the camera in the restaurant last night and that the staff was playing finders keeper. The manager stood his ground as the Australian threatened to call the police – though I never noticed if there was a telephone about. I didn't have the spirit to suggest that perhaps it was not the Chinese who lifted her camera after all. I simply joined in a search of the restaurant.

By now travelers and workers were trickling down to the lake to wash up. I could not be bothered. One of the joys of

The Party is Over, The Jig is Up

roughing it in the cooler climes is rolling out of bed or bag in the morning, and being ready for action. I would not have dreamt of undressing last night and I was not going to start now. Washing in the Pure Land seemed like such a waste. Splash a little of my cooling tea on my face and I was as good as new.

Below the trading post is another semi-camouflaged restaurant catering to the Chinese – anybody, perhaps, excluding foreigners. I was the exception. The cook looked meaner than a junkyard dog, but he had taken a liking to me after I passed by his open kitchen door one day and turned my Chinese Army canteen upside down, its cap dangling from a chain. We were about the same age, and he showed special consideration to a veteran – wounded in action, no doubt. On my first visit he brought me tea and dumplings, outside the kitchen door. As if he were feeding a stray. Someone separate from the flock.

It's hard to determine if a place is off-limits to foreigners (excluding "overseas Chinese") or if the restaurant is closed when the cook has a mind to close it. Often, when they don't like your looks. When I turned up this morning, two Chinese women tried to shoo me away. The cook saw it was me and motioned that I enter the restaurant. It lacked the view of the concrete block that catered to tourists, but had a touch of humanity that the high-priced icebox lacked. The higher, better placed restaurant was strictly functional – squeeze the tourist for his last dollar. And, perhaps, camera.

Still uncertain that I had been a privileged character, I called over a couple of undeserving tourists who were peeking inside. They must have seen me enter my hideaway. I don't know if they were ever served, for the cook gave me hell for letting the commoners come in. I walked away with my tail between my legs. I felt the same way the cook did about these travelers and it served me right. I guess I regressed – a carryover or hangover from the night before. In my weaker moments I want to belong, but I crossed that Rubicon long ago and inhabited that place of cooks, bakers, candlestick makers and those who set the world on fire.

"Hey, Tony! Mr. New York!" Fraulein was calling me.

I corrected her. "Ich bein ein Berliner."

"Oh, you are President Kennedy."

The taxi drivers from Berlin, as well as one or two other tourists from the round table, were going to Taxkorgan. They were waiting for the bus on the terrace, but I had enough and prayed I would get a lift out of here before I found myself in the same boat. It was still to early to expect anything going my way, but I went up the road, sat on a rock and drank up the lake from my own terrace. Not even a yak or a camel in sight to presage traffic.

The French couple turned up an hour later. They were waiting for the bus to Kashgar. The woman was really quite attractive. She tells me, "Vous a trouver le secret pour rester jeune." *I had found the secret of remaining young.* They were long gone by the time the Persians showed up. Delayed by dysentery, the ever-prepared brothers would never admit that something as common as Tourista could cramp their style.

In retrospect, I would have loved to be pedaling off into high noon with them. I didn't let them get away until I hit my jump-suited buddies for some anti-acid and vitamin pills. Our parting was cut short by an approaching minivan sagging under its varied and sundry cargo.

"Geez, here comes my taxi. . . .hey, don't envy me too much." I was waving like a castaway on a desert island who had not seen a ship in years.

The stunned driver stopped as Darius and Speedo pedaled away and left me to my own devices. The driver tried to fend me off, but this was an emergency. I climbed through the back doors, squeezing myself between foodstuffs and another passenger.

We drove some miles before snaking above yet more mountains and making an anticlimactic descent into a broader valley and more settled people.

Though used throughout Turkestan, I don't recall seeing any more yurts. The most endearing, enduring sight, on this two-hour run was a camel caravan that we passed up. A family that had pulled up stakes.

Then the inevitable. An army roadblock or checkpoint. Checkmate. The Sicilian Gambit had been stopped in its tracks.

The Party is Over, The Jig is Up

My Great Game was over. Documents had been collected. The unfortunate driver was the messenger bearing bad tidings – contraband cargo that was stretching his legs. An army officer was berating my defensive benefactor, who motioned to me with mimicking routine.

"Sick, sick," he was saying, in imitation of my own routine and what almost amounted to a commandeered vehicle. The inspecting officer had the goods on me. It is unlikely that the driver's command of English went beyond what he had learned from my entry into his van. My abused chauffeur was now transporting me to the police station. I had indeed hailed a taxi for Tashkorgan (Taxkorgan) and it was going to the very door of what I sensed would be my ultimate destination.

Siesta. But the word was out on me and an aide accompanied me to the nearest hotel to be certain that I checked in. The desk clerk was briefed that I was not under house or hotel arrest. Beyond the police station and down a winding hill, I found myself on what is reputed to be the original Silk Road. It passes by the ruins of "Stone City" – which, I believe, gave Tashkorgan its name and was known to Ptolemy as the western-most trading post of the "Silk People." Fa Xian came by here at the end of the fourth century. He was on his way to Sri Lanka via Gandhara, in what is now Pakistan. Marco taking this track, coming from the opposite direction, would have by-passed Kara Kuli.

I had been ordered to return to the police station at 4:00. A woman translator was on hand when I promptly arrived for my interrogation. First, I was ordered to make out a statement to the effect that I did not have a valid visa – and explain why.

"My visa expired."
"Where have you been sleeping?"
I told her.
"Kara Kuli Lake?? Where is your pass?"
"Pass?"
She was pissed. "Yes, pass, permission."
"Permission?"
Her temper mounting, the translator hissed, "Who authorized you to stay there?"

I stole a glance at the stolid chief. "I just went there."

"How?"

"I rode on a truck."

"That's not permitted!"

"Nobody told me."

Nor had anyone ever pointed out that a pass was required to stay at Kara Kuli. I had fallen between the cracks that yawn beneath the loner – though an idiot could have surmised as much. Yet, I like to treat people and countries alike and I so much wanted to give China equal footing. Even favored nation status. Maybe the Flying Dutchman told me about the pass, and maybe the Berlin taxi driver assumed I had one.

"You must confess that you slept at Kara Kuli Lake."

I was handed another blank piece of paper. I wrote that I regretted breaking any Chinese law, but that I was not entirely to blame for sleeping at the Lake, since the manager had checked my passport and had given me permission to sleep in a yurt.

"He shared some responsibility," I wrote.

The sharp woman read my confession. "What does this mean – 'responsibility'?"

"Blame is the same as responsibility."

That really got her Irish up. "Not right! Your responsibility!"

The translator/interrogator returned my confession. I crossed out the manager's responsibility.

I was charged with committing three crimes. But the hotel receipts I had since the beginning of the trip with Mona, and the exchange receipts held me in good stead. We had spent big bucks. I was turning fifty-six and had an obvious mental condition. The Health Certificate you fill out when you enter China poses the questions, "do you have a mental problem, leprosy. . ." etc., a questionnaire better suited to departure. The Chief tallied up my fine. I insinuated, given the circumstances, that this was highway robbery. The interpreter showed me a book with a list of charges and the corresponding fines. I could have been fined a hundred dollars and was really getting off quite easily. However, the forty dollars I would be dropping meant that I would turn up – if I were so lucky – with no cash of any kind at the Pakistani border.

I balked. The Chief told his interpreter I could always appeal my case in Beijing.

"But I'm going to Pakistan. Am I going to appeal this in Pakistan?"

Not only was my question insolent, it was misunderstood. The Chief was enraged. "Pakistan...! This is not Pakistan! This is China!"

The woman's translation carried the Chief's rabid indignation.

"Oh God, I know, I know," I explained to the translator, "I know this is China; I know this is China."

Geezus, he's going to send me back, my mind was racing. But the Chief sees I'm at the point of nervous collapse. He calms down. I am not Harry Wu, after all – nor does China need an agent provocateur on its hands. Let Pakistan have this fruitcake. He is issuing, or rather, the translator says he is issuing a new visa. For a price, of course. And whereas my expired visa in Columbia resulted in a Safe Conduct Certificate that required I be out of the country within two or three days, the Chinese, despite my criminal record, were allowing me to stay in China another fifteen days.

But China is not as easy to leave as Columbia. I assumed I remained just another tourist with those bottom line bucks to spend, but musing over my passport reveals that my visa was valid until December. Expecting to see September as the Europeans might write it, I traveled with this misconception – which really did not change anything as far as the tourist's requirement to report to the police if he or she is remaining in China more than sixty days. Though only August 28th, I had already been in China sixty-five days.

Yes, I was being short-changed, since the duration of a stay, the extra stay also, is good for two months. Yet, I wanted nothing more in the world than to be on the bus going to Pakistan at dawn. I left the police with no thought to what awaited me at the border.

I was no wiser than when I left Colombia. Not even mellower. I just burn out a little faster. But it is the fool who drinks from the fountain of youth, is that citizen of the world that Lao Tzu knew – when the only frontiers were in the mind.

51

The Great Escape

Something hidden. Go and find it.
Go and look behind the Ranges –
Something lost behind the Ranges.
Lost and waiting for you. Go!

                                            Kipling

Tashkorgan goes to show that there is often another Last Chance. It is in the opposite direction of the police station, beyond the castle that Marco marveled at. The unruly eatery caters to the Tajiks, he found beyond the pale, and I don't imagine it has changed very much since Marco's days. One beer was all I could take.

After bus fare to Sust, I would not be able to afford much more than that. But again, my Persian friends were coming to the rescue. They had just blown in, checking into my hotel when I was ready to call it a day. Had I eaten yet? Not really, and off we went to the civilized restaurant across the road. Speedo barely made it. Two more bushed brothers I had never seen. Speedo chowed down in record time and was off to bed. Nor were they very slow in getting here, considering, and I had to wonder if they had bummed a ride on the bus part of the way.

Darius was still in college and his learning was coming out of his ears. "You'll love Pakistan. They'll love you. They'll kiss you!"

"This wasn't what I had in mind." But I gave him something to think about when we checked out the dance hall on the hotel grounds. Only men were dancing. How romantic, I said.

"It doesn't mean anything," Darius said. "It's the custom here."

I asked him if he cared to dance.

"I'm tired," he politely demurred. I thought I was being funny in my fatuous way, but it was plausible that in the circles my friend traveled asking a man to dance was no joking matter. No matter. I told Darius I would appreciate it if he or his brother telephoned Mona when they got home. They would be flying back in a few days. Mona is not certain which brother called (Speedo visited us), from Boston, after Pakistan's floods, to say I was okay. She was absolutely overjoyed thinking I had already survived the disaster.

The manager neglected to give me a wake-up call. Anticipating that, I did not allow myself to sleep after waking at midnight. But I was still running late. Five hours to climb out of bed and there was still a possibility I would miss the bus. The light wasn't working and I was not up to fumbling around in the dark – yet this was the Hilton compared to the cheaper hotel that housed the ticket office and the Planeteers, who were like firemen, able to roll out of bed into the waiting bus out back.

I could not believe it. A hotshot American had just jumped ahead of me in the ticket office and was asking for the last train to the coast. The guy at the desk was selling him the last ticket. Had I no police record, I simply would have picked up the bus down the road – if there was nothing else going my way. A bus may run out of seats but it never runs out of space. No one was ever turned away from an Asian bus. Too frazzled to think clearly I imagined that a seat was my only ticket out of here.

As it turned out the American, another cyclist, was only going as far as the border – where it was downhill all the way to Karachi. This wasn't good enough for the ticket agent. He was interested in a larger fare.

The biker was going bunkers himself. "You turned me away yesterday. You don't expect me to spend the rest of my life here, do you!?!"

"No problem."

The Great Escape

I bought my ticket to Sust and went out to the bus. Passengers were pressing against out getaway. Escape hatch. Booby hatch. Instinctively I pushed through for a touchdown, almost coming to blows with a Pakistani.

"You are not permitted to do that!" someone shouted.

"Is this China, or isn't it? Where the hell have you been?" I was trying to board the bus. I could not feel secure, could not believe I had a seat until I was in it. And then I could not be sure that I was leaving – let alone getting across the border. "I have my ticket, so mind your own business."

"We all have tickets," a German woman was informing me. How could that be? I found the bus before the ticket office, and there was hardly anyone around. The woman was serious enough, but who did these slackers think they were kidding? And then it hit me! This was the international bus from Kashgar.

I was a pariah more than a passenger. They calmly boarded the bus when the driver was ready for takeoff. Not privy to mitigating circumstances, the tourists regarded me as stark, unraveling mad – at best. Oh, to come to such an ignominious end – to be herded on to a sheep car with Sophisticated Travelers cum the New York Sunday Times and Pakistani traders from Punjab. Had I come this far to take the crosstown bus over the roof of the world? Déjà vu.

No, most of the tourists had never been on a bus before; it was a novelty, part of the Asian experience – and then only for the short runs to Sust and Gilgit. What did these tourists know about sleeping on buses, arriving when it is dark and departing when it is still dark? The Stygian life of South American bus travel, etc. Old salts like myself should wear hash marks on their sleeve like veteran sailors. One stripe for every four years of service. It's not enough to wear your heart on your sleeve when nobody knows an unstrung hero from just another hobo.

A remaining seat was next to me. I had been quarantined – and near the desirable front of the bus. Maybe it was cheaper to pick up the bus on the road. (Perhaps someone missed his or her flight.) Among the stampeding tourists the bus stopped for were the taxi drivers and the American biker from California. The cyclepath, basking in his pseudo coolness, wasted no time bragging that his accumulating property earnings amounted to more than what he was spending on this trip. Downhill racer.

Ms. Berlin has filled the empty seat. I don't appreciate this because we are beginning our serpentine climb out of the valley and the higher we go the lower I get. Oxygen deprivation among other things is a factor, but I also connect a Berlin taxi driver with a New York cabbie, and I'm wondering if she is about to take me for a ride. She fingered my sweater, but there was not much else she could rip-off. Maybe I was being unreasonable when you consider that my bag looked like something the cat dragged in, yet if I am going to be in a bus and I can't be alone, I want to be with locals – and if they have been displaced by tourists, especially couples, I want Sancha Panza at my side. I missed her. She began this Asian journey with me; and it only seemed right that she should be in that seat as I approached what I thought would be the highlight of the journey.

A psychedelic train of trucks was snaking down the mountain. There was a certain amount of disbelief among the tourists, and reverence perhaps, among the traders who hailed from the other side of the Range, but no dancing in the streets. There were, in fact, a few nomads on this mountainside, but they had become like cows after the initial passing of a train.

I was sorry to leave China if only because much was left undone and I could not undo what I did. I had made a big point out of altitude early on, but this is where they cart out the oxygen tank on the Huancayo train out of Lima and at more than sixteen thousand feet above the sea I had reached the level (and age) of diminishing returns. And departures. On our first trip to the Andes, I did not know what down was and simply got sleepy. It takes energy to be happy.

Before coming to the first checkpoint, I spotted a caravan heading toward the Mintaka Pass. A similar chain of camels passed Marco Polo as he came out of the Hindu Kush to our west. But we stayed our southerly course until we came to the Chinese border post of Pirali. It looked like another dumpy trading post, a place to spend your remaining yuan on candy and not much else.

The American biker was not happy about being let off here, but he did not want to spend another dime to continue. He pleaded poverty but when I offered him a few coins to get his show underway, he claimed it was the principle of the thing. Where had I heard that before? But he only paid to come this far, so what did he want? Enough money to put some real distance between him and Pirali? Immigration and Customs was par for the cross. A few miles more and we were past the last Chinese checkpoint. A no man's land for a nowhere man and we were upon and beyond the actual border. We debused. Patches of cloud swept across the roof of the world and I was sounding my barbaric yawp. "I made it! I made it!"

A cautious celebration because the only indication of Pakistan is the sign and we are just on the other side of the divide. The border post is a memorial or a marker commemorating the completion of the Karakorum Highway – 1986 – and marks the beginning of the Khunjerab Pass. Pakistani businessmen swathed in black leather jackets partially covering their traditional dress are milling about the freshly painted monument as if it were the war memorial it really is – even if the war was against nature.

The international road is about eight hundred miles long, built at a cost of four hundred lives – though it is said that a life was lost for each mile of mountain blasted away. To hear the Chinese say it, most of the casualties were Chinese. It is a fact that huge rock faces were blown to pieces by Chinese engineers along with laborers. But the three mile high pass was dubbed the "valley of blood" (or "bones" because of falls) long before China and Pakistan dreamed of their joint venture.

Hunza-inspired raids plagued travelers until early in the century, but much of the blood in this upper "valley" was spilled to relieve the altitude pain of horses jabbed in their muzzles with iron spikes. Altitude seems to have claimed many casualties. Why was the road widened on the wild side – and at the cost of so many lives (which is really neither here or there)? China and Pakistan seem to have an understanding that involves Kashmir and will be uneasy allies when it comes to India.

Xinjiang may have a business interest in the Karakorum Highway, but Beijing was looking at the larger picture.

If there was a seeker aboard this quasi-tour bus of conquerors and collectors, I did not find him or her. That distant look of the outsider, the spy on humanity who does not come in from out of the cold. Actually, it was only about 45° and with just enough passing clouds to enhance the day, but context is everything. With few people crossing this border it was obscene that a busload of us could pass this pristine way all at once.

I almost envied von Le Coq who came this way to get help for an injured British officer on the Chinese side of the border. Upon arriving at the British post in Sust, the honored archeologist ate nineteen raw eggs at one sitting – in the dead of winter – before returning to Pirali with medicine for the officer.

A trader sat next to me when the bus was ready to move.

"So far, so good. Yes?" Ms. Berlin said, standing over me. The trader gave up his seat for her.

"Don't be so glum. We look like a respectable couple. No one will look in your passport."

It was fifty miles to Sust, the de facto border. But we did not go very far before a soldier flagged down the bus. At least a dozen people knew I was without a visa and I had to consider the possibility of someone giving me away. It became a certainty by the time the soldier boarded the bus. But he slowly walked down the aisle, made an about-face and was gone. Suddenly the subdued Pakistanis, realizing that they were indeed on home ground, shook free of the subservient survival roles that had sustained them in China and began carrying on like a conquering army – or P.O.W.s returning home after years of captivity in enemy territory.

"Long live Pakistan! Long Live Pakistan!"

The chanting in Urdu grew louder and louder until I burst into song myself and was one of the boys. But my brotherhood went out the window with a carelessly tossed bottle in the Khunjerab National Park.

"Why did you do that?"

The Great Escape

"Nobody saw me do it."

The park is funded by the American Wildlife Foundation. We descended some miles before marmots, jacks-in-the-box, some standing sentinel on the colored scree, gave life to this mostly mineral kingdom. The much touted Marco Polo sheep and Himalayan ibex were as elusive as a snow leopard, but the Hunza had its source here and Tripitaka himself thought the Khunjerab was out of this world. I sensed that these gaunt mountains and gleaming glaciers were the Ithica this Odysseus was looking for. This is where the Chinese should have painted their scrolls when they wanted to reduce man to the speck that he is.

The bus broke down in what seemed the bottom of a vast well. Was this the valley of the gods or hell? Chattering salesmen had broken the spell.

"What am I doing here?" I thought out loud.

"You don't know why you travel?"

"Oh, I know why I travel, but I don't appreciate why other people travel."

There was one obvious reason for my malaise. I was literally going down, down, down to the sea. As Sidney Hillman said, "I went to Ireland to be a writer, France to be an intellectual and India to be neurotic."

You can argue that Pakistan is not India and in any case my trip was not necessary and I should have been going to Ireland instead. . . .

The Chinese ascent to the Khunjerab Pass is bucolic compared to this fabled approach to the border. Riding along the rushing river is like being flushed down Dante's vision of the universe. The devil's throat all but shut out the light miles above, and yet deeper and deeper we dropped into the ominous chasm until the very pillars of heaven closed on us. It was as if someone had dug that proverbial hole to China and ended up just short of the border. And we were making the return trip. The only word that does this gorge justice is the much abused "awesome."

Crossing the Hunza River, we passed the one-house-town of Kukshal, and a little further down the road, arrived at the Dir checkpoint. Assuaging my fear was the impracticality of sending me back to the border. But maybe they would put me on an army truck or make me wait for the next bus – if they had the audacity to look at my passport. A man my age. I had a new wife at my side and the more demented I became the more professorial my demeanor. Like the other passengers, I had only to sign a book when we debused, deferred to like an elder statesman.

And then, magically, the walls began to open. Aladdin's lamp was discovered in nearby Afghanistan, yet only the hand of God could work this miracle. Experimental potato farms were the first signs of civilized life; the river broadened and "open sesame," we had arrived in Sust. The return of the sky bode well, but this was the real border and the acid test. Immigration and Customs were fifty miles from the frontier, but these were officials with families and they could not be expected to live in space with the more Spartan Chinese.

I remained seated and pondered my fate while the legitimate tourists went through the border formalities. The Pakistanis did not like the Chinese – they would understand why I was desperate enough to enter their wonderful country without a visa. And if Immigration could not appreciate that, I was prepared to go to jail before I let them send me back. I made my move when the tourists had thinned.

"I have a problem."

"No problem." A cheerful Immigration official was greeting me. I had years over the other passengers and age meant stability, respect. Money. I double-talked, but it was all as clear as the sky above us – even if much of it still was not visible.

"You don't understand." I showed him my passport.

"No problem." The rotund man simply wrote out a pass that instructed me to report to Islamabad within three days.

Big problem, because I had no intention of reporting to the police in three days. It was mentally and physically impossible. If Immigration appeared nonchalant about my unauthorized entry into Pakistan, Hunza was almost a country unto itself and had little love for the land beyond their "Tribal Territories" (as the government referred to them). Maybe Immigra-

The Great Escape

tion was government but it didn't matter and I thought my pass was a case of passing the buck – and perhaps making a few.

The border could have been the bordello, when finding my reserve I converted my last dollar into rupees over a leisurely cup of tea. Syrupy chai. Oh, how I savored the moment, that drink that bore so little resemblance to the plain Chinese tea that I was half-convinced I had died and gone to my childhood heaven. It was official. I was out of China and the Proustian recall that came with the taste I knew as India was welcome.

"Is good?" My Immigration friend was beaming.

A nod of his head and the perennial errand boy who is on hand in Muslim countries scooted off with tray in hand to fetch me another cup of chai. My friend allowed me to sit on the Immigration veranda and tended to other business. This trip was the will of Allah, I thought, the tide of Ararat dumping me on this elevated shore when I was swimming so furiously in the opposite direction, like the resisting Jonah coughed up by the whale where he did not want to be, without a visa, but certainly with a ticket to ride.

There was a Chinese passenger on the bus. Two, perhaps. And there was an ancient invasion, a Chinese general coming to town. But this was clearly another country. I had gotten so accustomed to seeing Chinese where I had not expected them, that I was beginning to imagine that China went on forever – and it would have, had not the greatest wall in the world blocked the advance of their armies.

Crossing the Mexican border is a kind of milestone. Rubicon rather than Rio Grande. The respective frontier officials were like night and day. Copper and redneck. Yet compared to that, my arrival in Sust was on another planet.

52

A Path to Shangri-La

There is a latent explorer in almost every man whose mind is large enough to have any interests outside of himself; and it is this unused and frustrated explorer who sits beside the fire and pores, entranced and fascinated, over the Arctic diaries of Dr. Kane or the African Journals of Stanley.

Henry Van Dyke

Checking into the converted trailer next to the border post, I promised the manager that if given a discount I would put his flophouse on the map which he sold to me.

I walked along a Hunza that would not be long in flooding. It was wide at this point and much of it a riverbed that permitted me, nature's way, to skirt the town. Returning upriver near dusk, I got onto the road (it's really misleading to call it a highway).

A voice in the wilderness. "Mr. New York!" Ms. Berlin was managing to reel in a fish out of water. I would be her trophy for a few minutes, shared with some provincials – who had made the crossing with us. Being from New York brought expectations with it, perhaps an urbanity or inanity.

I carry New York around me like my appendix – an unnecessary pain in my side. I went to bed. It was tough hitting the rack sober when it was barely dark and tougher still when the barracks looked like it was going to take off. It was sandblasted overnight.

In the morning I ended up sharing a taxi with the taxi drivers, a young Hunzukut and an Italian student of Chinese foreign policy who managed to have her brain drained in Beijing. Not twenty miles down the road the Germans left the taxi in

Passu. They knew something I didn't know, but the village was too close to the border to be dilly-dallying when I was supposed to be in the capital in a couple of days.

The Hunza man was on his way to enlist in the army. He found this step distasteful, his nationalism was bound up with the Hunza, but if he wanted to get ahead this was the only road open to him.

"I must eat." His family were landowners, but his education had left him unfit for farming. Here was another minority person who wanted me to send him books. Who knows if one day I won't take him up on his invitation. and armed with books visit that lonely farmhouse above the Karakoram Highway.

Free of the tourists and with a little sugar in my system, I knew I had arrived – with a student at my side going to Karimabad.

A jeep from one of the hotels in the upper village was waiting at the side of the road for any tourist who happened to be going to Karimabad – which should have struck me like a red flag, for I found myself checking into one of those Paradise Hotels I remembered only too well in India.

It has been said that the Hunza Valley inspired James Hilton's *Lost Horizon* – and it is true that pervasive Rakaposhi hides much of the horizon. But I have to question whether the poppy fields and apricots that lend color to this spur on Borit Sar could be considered Shangri-La. That may be so compared to a land of lamas or Tibet itself, where the vegetation is sparse, but where Hilton recognized the spiritual heights he was looking for. A Lamadom seemed a more likely paradise than a bandit-infested Hunza that was a thorn in the side of the colonial British, hence the physical side of the *Lost Horizon,* written in 1933, may be found to the west of the Karakoram Mountains, while its spirituality lies to the more esoteric east.

The Northern Territories are inhabited by Kafirs – a tribe or an umbrella term for northern Pakistan's tribal people. *Kafir,* a word that crept into South African lexicon when the British held sway, is interchangeable with the "n" word. This reflected British regard for northern, though not necessarily

Hunza Pakistan, when the Briton, Hilton would not have wanted his Shangri-La populated with Kafirs. Indeed. When the hero of *Lost Horizon* tells the High Lama that Shangri-La reminds him slightly of Oxford, you don't know if it was said tongue in cheek or head in the clouds.

The Hunza reminds me, slightly, of the much smaller Atlas Mountains. The Hunzukuts could be the brothers of the North African Berbers, and descended from migrating Aryans around 1800 B.C. Much of the migration spilling out of today's Iran went east with the hardier tribes roaming the Hunza Valley. It is likely the less adventurous buried the culture they found in the tamer Indus Valley to the south and built the spacious cities that were to spread across the subcontinent.

Curiously, the first sign to hit me in this rugged Shangri-La was, "When in Rome do as the Romans do."

I asked Regazza, "What did the Romans do that was so great?"

This was a reference to Item 2 in the "Notes for Travelers" in my Karakoram Highway map: *Please observe the Moslem dress code.* Men and women, especially, were encouraged to wear something resembling a nightshirt. Item 1 reads: *Please do not photograph a) bridges; b) local women.*

Unfortunately, the Hunzukuts were doing as the Romans do. Hotels were springing up all over the place; the bazaar was beginning to resemble a Roman holiday. The day seemed near when a Hilton Hotel will make this Shangri-La official. If fundamentalism doesn't get a toehold on this precarious plateau, Karimabad will be the next Kathmandu.

Islam was slow in climbing up the valley walls, but an innate xenophobia of the isolated farmers and shepherds, former highwaymen, lends itself to a conservatism that is fundamentalist in appearance. The imbibing of "Hunza water" is an ancient custom that Islam has not been able to dry up. Islambad is trying to call the shots with a people who are still pretty much going their own way. It's no secret that the poppy seeds are being transformed into something more potent than brandy.

Was I checking into the Delux or the Paradise? It was just out of the shadow of Borit Sar whose snowy face was framed by the sunflowers that flanked my window. (Sadly this was the photo that got away.) Opening the door for me was the manager/cook/maid/maintenance man. The door was not locked; the latch had an absent lock. Something missing, go and find it. What was the manager going to do about it? He looked at me as if I had requested a bar of soap or some other unheard of amenity.

"You don't have your own lock?"

"That's right. I forgot to pack it when I left America." Don't leave home without it. I apologized for this "oversight" and the all-around-man begrudgingly set out to find a lock – and, I hoped, a key.

Suprisingly the innkeeper returned with the amenity. He didn't ask for a deposit, although I could have easily absconded with his lock and key. These were the only things I could have swiped from my bare-boned cubicle, so Spartan, if somewhat dirty, that I stared longingly at the relaxing cracks in the plaster as I would the clouds in the sky.

But I had a view that had the pull of the tides and in no time was giving in to its countergravitational force. Is it the magnetism of these great mountains that lifts man out of his lethargy, or was it the legendary apricots – also said to promote longevity. I climbed until I ran out of steam, but this was a mere shake-up cruise compared to the following day when I was determined to get as high as possible above my hovel. There were higher priced hotels, the perennial concrete boxes that stretch from the Middle East to China, but I preferred one gone to pot, and stayed put.

What is most appealing about this paradise is the absence of the most pervasive of snakes – there was simply not enough space for lawyer or lawn mower to maneuver. Or grass. The jeep was one of a handful of vehicles that had nowhere to go but down – unless the driver was crazy enough to drive over to Altit, on the same ledge that girded Borit Sar. Several villages seemed to be tumbling into the chasm that dropped away from the mountainside into the gorge far below the highway, the road paralleling the river's mad rush to Jaglot. And just as the Hunza merges with the Indus River to become something much bigger, I had to get into those mountains.

One can only marvel at the chutzpah of the British as they traversed the Hunza, as usual looking for trouble, and in the process, taming the brigand and bringing peace. Talk about being between a rock and a hard place – at this time of the year softened by summer's colors, now mostly leafy vegetable plots and poplars. April would have been bursting out all over, June springing up the mountain like yellow wildflowers, so quickly that the apricots were ripe by July. But this was not the end of the warm orange color, for the almost succulent fruit was transplanted from orchards to the flat roofs of the Hunza homes. Hardly a flat surface was spared the saffron profusion of summer's abundance until the arrival of the first rains. But the blood-red poppy would hold the highland.

Opium is for export, but the Hunza forbidden fruit is the "Hunza water" that flows none too freely when thirsty tourists are about. I was counting on this all too allusive firewater to get me through my birthday, but it would be bad public relations, not to mention a hangover, if a tourist got drunk. The Hunzukuts themselves have been drinking the "wine" since it almost made itself. The nights are cold, the tempers hot, the fermenting fruit all about them, you can't blame them for bootlegging and doing as the Romans do. But I'll be damned if I ever saw a bottle of the stuff.

What may have been harder for the British to swallow was the Hunza music. The horn was a bagpipe gone bunkers. An eerie screech with a Scottish streak droned above the persistent beat of the drums. That atonal whine that was almost Chinese, could drive a Quaker to drink – and I saw what the whine and wine could do to a strong Hunza man.

I was returning from my first day's reconnoitering, when the strains of the wild music drew me into the dry goods/music shop on a road above my hotel. Dancing to this siren song, the piercing horn of Pan, a Hunzukut was doing the wiggle of the seven veils. A hapless tourist drinking his soda tried to ignore the dancer's outstretched arms until the Hunzukut's beckoning motions were too much for the young man and he escaped into the street. Undaunted, the dancer turned his rhythmic attentions toward me, but I had been down this street before in Turpan and simply stepped outside, waiting for him to take his show on the road. Then I snapped his picture.

The more subdued Kafirs to the west play a harp that is similar to the instrument that soothed Aristotle. Muslims use "Kafir" as a derogatory term describing the highland infidels. The Hunzukuts may claim descent from Alexander's army, but the Kafirs of Chital's valleys can boast of a more musical heritage.

Another bewitching morning, the sunflowers hanging over my breakfast table, heralding the day to come. I filled my sack with dried apricots and headed for the glacier. Following the irrigation path above Baltit's baked palace, I paused at a shaded spring. From here a grand canyon jaggardly slopes up to the snows. I spied approaching women. I would lay in wait in the shadows until they were near enough to take their pictures. Surely they were coming here with their jugs, but they never reached the spring. Had they spotted me? A young Japanese student with an armful of empty bottles turned up instead.

Remaining in the shadows, I followed the chasm's cascading river until this devil's throat opened on a bit of sunlit verdure and summer. No jinni could work this magic. I was spurred on by eternal winter momentarily basking in the warm sunshine beckoning above. Gradually, the perpendicular walls widened and my claustrophobia evaporated in the alpine thaw and the aura of the most ethereal peaks on this planet.

I drank deeply from a rivulet, but sheep grazing before the receding glacier had flavored the melt-off with a bitterness that brought me down to earth. Sheep, goat turds are the black olives and raisins of the high Hunza, and you can be sure that wherever you may climb, they got there first. Human company awaited me further on. A thuggish, thirtyish woman with a German accent and a lovely colleen as frothy as a freshly poured glass of Guinness. The lass was a nurse and just what the doctor ordered.

The women were sharing goat cheese with a shepherd who was trying to induce them to spend the night in his hut. They were having no part of the horny Hunzukut and were anxious to return to Karimabad before dusk. I'll never know if Hilda had designs on the Irish girl or if she resented my own interest in this mountain flower. Though I heard about the hut and intended to spend the night there, I would have gone down the mountain with this wild Irish rose had our encounter been less thorny. We agreed to meet the following night.

Among hikers and climbers the hut had acquired a reputation as a refuge. It is plastered with mountaineer stickers from the four corners. I did not have a sleeping bag as well as a lock and I don't recall the shepherd having a blanket to spare, for what promised to be a cold night at 14,000 feet or so. Nor did striking out with the young women leave the shepherd in a very hospitable mood. Deciding to head back within the hour, I approached the glacier as a high-priest would an alter. Gothic spires rose before me as if to aspire to heaven itself. But what need had I to climb to the bell tower when I was in the navel, for this was where one prayed.

I bounded down meadow and moraine racing the sun down the mountain. I hadn't gotten very far when I was also racing the gathering fury of the fast melting snow. The channel running parallel to the path seemed barely able to contain the rapidly rising water that threatened to become my slide to Baltit, where the rushing run-off fertilized the fields below. This was an intimation of the hell and high water that was still several days away. Pakistan's worst flood in history.

I recall a British travel writer saying that he never feared being overwhelmed by events on the road – even death – but as a writer first his worst fear was that nothing would happen. And little does. Perhaps he should have gone with the flow.

53

In a Secret Land

There is a peace for the wanderer. . .in the secret lands where life has preserved the past by leaving it, or where the present itself is like the past in its remoteness. This is the peace which is known to the true traveler, which none can imagine except those who have tasted it, and which those who have tasted it once ever afterwards crave for.

W.R. Mallock

The next day I took a more horizontal trail, beginning with the road that spanned the Borit Sar's river and rounded its massive thigh high above the highway. This is the path to Passu. Bearing right at a fork in the road, I met with a sign, "NOT TO PHOTOGRAPH WOMEN OR HOUSES." Welcome to Altit – where the people don't worry about the bridge.

Beyond the women and houses is an apple orchard and some table and chairs fronting the fort. Nearby is a stall or kiosk. Forgetting that there were tourists back in Altit, I looked at the rustic cafe and pulling up a shaded chair, thought what a welcome but unlikely sight in this forbidding land. In fact, it took some time to register that I could sit here – and a lot more time before I was served by the only soul in sight. I was off to an early start and had made this side trip to see the fort and its commanding view of the void below. I had already made a stop to purchase a ditty-bag or runny sack fancied by school children that I filled with enough goodies to see me through the night if necessary. What was the saying on this misplaced bag?

Several years later, it is strange to be reading a book by another traveler who was smitten by the same remote place – though his description of the Hunza seems to be in keeping with the lost ideal of the *Lost Horizon.* The author mentions the fort and the kiosk, but missing is the gritty reality of the many people living in the scattered villages bordered by poppy fields above and beyond Altit.

Poetic license in his book extends to the legendary longevity of the inhabitants, but I don't recall anyone extraordinary, unless he/she were really an apricot-preserved one hundred. Curiously absent in the narrative is the stuffed ibex atop the fort, as prominent as an American flag planted above Iwo Jima and the symbol of the Hunza. Lack of place names lends an air of mystery to Paradise Lost, but often indicates that the traveler never finds it. The Shangri-La image could not sell if the truth were told – but beyond the bottom line considerations most travel writers are also fly fishermen who must exaggerate their catch.

Backtracking a bit through Altit, I gained altitude with the longest, mostly rock-hewn staircase (outside China) up to Sultanabad. Had the sultan lived here? It did not occur to me to put this question to the chipper uniformed school children on their way to classes.

Before entering the village I meditated on a Borit Sar framed by apple trees. A trail is often marked by the usually soothing waters emanating from the irrigating channel, which neutralized the irritating heat and focused my own energy. One of the kids thinking I was hungering after an apple, plucked one from the orchard and gave it to me. I politely received the fruit after he insisted I accept his gift. But I hadn't gone a few steps, when he called out, "One rupee!"

Arrived in Duikar high and dry. It is the last village up the mountain that is marked on my detailed map; I was counting on getting something to drink here. I had tried to get a refill in Sultanabad, but the inhabitants would only say "Duikar" and point up. However, there is no shop in Duikar and no one about the scattering of houses. Finally, spotting somebody in the field, I skirted his crops and called out, "Chai! Chai!" The most common number of my repertoire. Similar to my Cha! Cha!

The farmer led me into his house and prepared tea for me. A cedar branch hanging from the wall appeared to be a talisman. Was the evergreen one of the links with Tibet, where appreciation of its scent bordered on the spiritual? There has long been contact with Tibet; which way had the custom traveled? Or did the appreciation of this tree have its roots in the universal love of what is truly beautiful? The farmer brought me the branch to smell. Informed sources say it is the juniper that is celebrated in these parts, but I never saw their berries.

I climbed through a denuded apricot orchard to an irrigation canal, and then following the path to a gorge, hiked on to its seductive source. A waterfall was flanked by two white buildings bedecked with what looked like Tibetan prayer flags flapping from poles. A part-Tibetan Hunzukut in Karimabad, claiming to be an archeologist's guide, had pointed me in this direction, but said nothing about this sacred site. Above the white building on the opposite side of the pool were houses and the beginning of a lost hamlet.

Descending the gorge was like being dropped into a goldfish bowl. I was being observed. The young man who had spotted me hastened away. Nearer to the sacred buildings several men sat watching me intently. I felt very much the intruder. Seeing no mosque or anything resembling this site in the more accessible areas, I reckoned that a secret religion was being practiced here – an ancient rite that was beyond the pale and of necessity out of sight.

I was drawn to the pool below the white mausoleums as much out of thirst as a hungering after meaning. Approaching the hypnotic waterfall, I was taken back to the gorge above Xiahe, the Tibetan enclave in China, where the religion being practiced was more Bon than Buddhist and perhaps underground. It is true these snowy constructs looked like the tombs of Muslim holy men, but there was more buried in this enchanted place than meets the eye. All the religions that had a Ball or Baal, from Pan to the African cults with their pan American offshoots of voodoo flew the colors.

The place had all the earmarks of nature worship, for enchanting in its own right the V-shaped gorge of which I was at the bottom, opened on the most seductive view of Rakaposhi, the opposite side of the "Hunza Valley," and its near twin Diran.

Like its successors, including Judaism in its origins, Baal was basically a mountain religion. The most prominent sacred site in my mind is practically under Mount Hermon in the Golan Heights, where Christ usurped Pan and the surrender of the ego replaced the sacrifice of more sheepish things.

As I forded a stream just beyond the pool, a young man was dispatched to confront me. What did I want? I held up my empty canteen. The man filled my canteen near the base of the fall, and I resumed my crossing with the feigned nonchalance of a crook with a cat in the bag. The young man was concerned about my continuing on. I climbed up to where the older men were sitting in the shade and made a big to-do about the heat. Taking pains to avoid looking in the direction of the white buildings, I informed the men of my desire to climb up the mountain. One man spoke English quite well, but such a desire is suspect in backwaters where walking is an unnecessary evil.

"Stay out of the houses," I was warned and reluctantly allowed to pass on. Not surprisingly, when the other side of the Hunza River was considered enemy territory until the turn-of-the-century. Altit Fort had its sights trained on Nagar, but then this was no different than Bosnia or Boston where people on the other side of town are often the enemy.

Below the houses poppy fields were being tended, and a red sea extended to the precipice. Grains were also cultivated. The entire hamlet was bringing in the crops. House and yard were empty. Resuming the road to Passu, I ascended an even more ghostly landscape studded with nature's most stunning statuary. Eons of running water had shaped once jagged rocks into feminine forms. A classic case of the yining of the yang. Similar rock formations just off the Karakoram Highway are marked "sacred" but this wild lookout was their more holy source and these well-rounded boulders would also one day roll down the mountain.

I crawled into what is the holiest rock of them all and raised the term "stoned" to new heights. Was there some Sodom up here where in the absence of salt, people were turned into stone? A virtual tunnel on this shoulder of Borit had been bored out of a boulder about to spill into the vast stillness below, and it had become my window on the world. Living on the edge, my life literally hung in the balance of open-ended beauty. To the southeast mountain ranges merged, and in the setting sun seemed to run on forever. The light at the end of the tunnel. Euphoria!

The entrance of my hallowed hollow faced the Borit Sar, and beyond a chasm the path to Passu. This was probably the old road to the Kunjerab Pass, much of it carved out of the mountain that had now reclaimed it. The rock slides that had covered portions of the trail, and in places swept it away, looked recent. Nature had probably done me a favor. It was getting late and I was already around the bend, fire burning brightly in my Promethean perch. I had wanted to go that mile or so around the mountain that would reveal another side of Borit Sar, but I contented myself with having found the lost horizon – and on my birthday to boot!

Descending the mountain, I left the trail to traipse nature's Stonehenge at will, though remaining as high above on the way back as possible. I was as concerned about being waylaid as I was interested in approaching the mysterious hideaway undetected. There was no doubt about it. The whitewashed buildings were mausoleums. Looking over my shoulder and getting an all clear signal, I gingerly opened the gate to the roof. It served as a platform for a wild array of rags and flags. But all this color, this banner event, was really unnecessary. On my side melted snow and ice cascaded into the pool below, while before me an ocean of mountains caught the last rays of the sun. Before the purple mountains majesty this colorful display of devotion paled – though, admittedly, these gaily colored banderas beat plastic flowers – and like flowers, they were offerings.

Sticking to the trail, I was able to return to Karimabad before dark. I stopped by the gift shop of my friend, the guide, and apprised him of my find.

"Oh, yes, holy men are buried there," he said. But I did not recall seeing any mosques in any of the villages and neglected to ask to whom these men were holy. It is likely they were Muslim saints.

Presumably Rose was supposed to meet me in the shop. In any case the thorn was there. She was browsing for souvenirs while I had a soft drink with the Tibetan. I paid her no mind. I reminded the guide that he had promised to help me celebrate my birthday with a bottle of Hunza water. He would get me so drunk that he would have to carry me back to the hotel. Afraid of that, I was not too disappointed when the Tibetan said that a bottle of the mountain spirits was nowhere to be found.

"Maybe tomorrow. In America your birthday is tomorrow."

"I may not be here tomorrow."

"But you just got here. Three days, four days not enough time. There are many places to visit."

He was right. *The Adventure Tours* read: "Pakistan Peaks, Land of the Mountain Gods. Gypsy Trails – Journeys across Strange Lands."

Then there were the Historical Tours: "In the Steps of Alexander the Great. Marco Polo's Trail. The Far Pavilions." And last but not least, "Mortal Evidence of Man's Immortality."

The guide said he had to go on an errand, but that I should make myself comfortable; he would soon return. But I did not hang around long enough to see if he would make good his promise. I hadn't eaten in the hotel's dining room yet; I thought this was the time to have a regular meal. I had not seen Regazza since we arrived, nor, I thought, any of the other guests. Ha!

I returned to my room just in time to discover that a young Englishman was setting up base camp under my window. He said there was no room in the hotel. He was actually pitching a tent where I had my airy breakfast.

"Your tent is ruining my view. I'm staying in this room for the view."

"The mountain is very large," he haughtily replied. "My tent is not blocking your view."

Now he had gotten my goat as well. "You want to get technical," I screamed, "your putrid tent is ruining the ambience. Is my windowsill the only place in Asia you can find to park?" Realizing discretion was the better part of valor, the young punk found another place to be an outdoorsman.

The guests were already chowing down when I entered the mess hall. It was dark outside and in, a very depressing affair a little larger than my room. Hilda had been laying in wait.

"Happy birthday to you, happy birthday to you. . . ."

Her commanding German accent had, unhappily, induced the other guests to chime in. Even the shy Japanese tourist, sitting by himself, was singing. I had a second helping of dessert – which may have done the trick. I did not need Hunza water to be hung over in the morning. I would have a typical birthday, after all, and the proof was in the pudding.

54

Gilgit

New day. Yes, that's the name of the schoolboy backsack I purchased on my birthday. How could I forget it, with its dawn of creation motif picturing all of God's creatures. The stringy ditty-bag mocked me as I packed it away into my old day backpack along with everything else I owned. Common sense dictated I coast along with tea and crackers until my strength returned, but that was not my idea of a new day. If I was going to sit I may as well be on the bus to Gilgit.

Besides, Gilgit was just the place to be sick (where there were no mountains to tempt me) if I could only catch the 9 o'clock minibus coming down from Sust. I would be in the best possible shape to report late to the authorities, since they could not expect me to make the long and tedious journey to Islamabad in my condition. When I informed the guide of my continuing search for Shangri-La, he marked a valley on my map which was a day or two detour on the road to the capital – which I would avoid unless absolutely necessary. This unspoiled pavilion was close to Afghanistan and far enough away from the Silk Road to be the real McCoy.

Getting down to the road without the assistance of a jeep was unthinkable, and there weren't any available. But, even if I had to crawl down the mountain, rolling my backpack before me, like some wrong-way Sisyphus, I had enough time for tea. At least the Englishman's tent was not blocking my view, allowing me to soak up the river of ice glistening in the early morning light.

In a postcard I sent to Mona, I referred to the mountain

before me as Ulmut. Was that what the Hunzukuts called Borit Sar's glacier? If so, on another card the glacier is named Altar. Which is what it was to me up close. The real name is probably Ultar. Another postcard shows that the Pakistanis are playing the Far Pavilion angle for all it is worth, as Hunza men are seen dancing in an open field when a precipice is more like it. And these men are dancing with swords instead of invisible veils. But the most representative scene is the one beyond my window, as poplars and small houses cropping out of orchards dot the steep mountainside in their climb to the fort. Above that, obviously, there isn't space to pitch a tent.

I can not recommend the Hunza for hitchhiking. But the bus from Sust careened down the canyon to Gilgit in record time, as much to dodge bullets between warring Sunnis and Shites, as to race anything moving on the road. But oh, what a glorious morning once I was under way, under the weather notwithstanding, for there is nothing like a welcoming sun when there is a chill in the air and you are hanging out the window in a dead swoon – which made it more difficult to be descending to the baking plains.

The Pakistan Mountaineer Club is at the head of an evergreen valley that disappears with the snow-line of Rakaposhi – all 7,788 meters (25,500 feet) of it outside my window. I was a small boy eyeing his birthday cake. Never did I look up to a mountain with such longing. But the Club, little more than a shack at the side of the road, was closed and I would have been hard-pressed to find a place to recuperate in this neck of the woods. Still, had I half my normal energy, I would not have hesitated to debus and climb to her firy sesame.

An all pine and fir valley snaking up to an oh la Shangri-La – and I was lusting all the more, since much of this trip had been a tease and if the police in Gilgit compelled me to go to Islamabad the party was over. Not knowing what awaited me, I drank up the snowy mountains like a camel about to cross the vast desert.

The bus left me off at the Park Hotel and I was checked in by noon. A wonderful surprise. My room was furnished. A tasteful, rustic finish, an almost chic touch to the wood bureau and chairs. I even had a table. What riveted me most was the bed. It had a mattress. I can only speculate why the hotel is called the Park. Perhaps because you can park your car wherever you please. Or because there is a bit of green between the hotel and its restaurant. Overlooking flat mud houses that belied the cacophony outside made this insulated paradise all the more precious.

Although my return to civilization made me anxious about getting my passport stamped, I so dreaded going out that I pulled down the shade and collapsed on the bed. The chief of police was still out to lunch when I got around to seeing him. I could use a little tea myself and headed for the nearest watering hole-in-the-wall to await his return.

The mini-religious war that was underway had interrupted commerce to some extent, but Gilgit was seemingly a bustling bazaar. Huddled men sat in the dark cramped teahouse. The young waiter's unremitting stare so unnerved me that I informed the owner of this teashop that if he could not find other employment for his boy, I would take my business elsewhere.

The poor kid did not know if I were a fish or a fowl, because I resembled the bearded Pathans going about their business but without the sense of purpose that drove the besieged populace and the almost obligatory tupee that is this tribe's symbol. This Hunza hat is a version of the beret that survived into Europe's Middle Ages and would not look out of place on the Doge of Venice. The tupee (topee), which has become the word for hairpiece, is derived from the Hindu topi, and if you can top this, is worn like a rolled sock.

I passed by one, two barber shops. It was meant to be. I had not had a shave or a haircut since leaving America, and I could also use a trim before presenting myself to the police. I wanted to get a haircut in China, but I don't recall having ever seen a barbershop. Of course, it is unlikely I would see a red striped pole to mark the spot, and the only reason I knew this was a barbershop was because I noticed a fellow giving a young man a shampoo. A real dandy, I thought, and the next thing I knew, the young man's head is being shaved. Was he going into the army or a holy order?

I stepped inside. Next.

"From which country?"

"I'm afraid to tell you."

The barber was shocked. "Why?"

"I don't think Muslims like Americans."

He raised an eyebrow in disbelief.

"But I'm a good man so don't cut my throat." I asked this true believer, "Why don't you like Americans?"

The barber explained, "CIA makes trouble with Sunni and Shite. CIA kill Sunni and Sunni think it is Shite."

This sounded like our foreign policy in a nutshell. The razor-wielding fellow was claiming the CIA was setting one leader against the other, when the warring factions needed little outside encouragement to kill each other.

From the old school and still picturing a CIA of all-American Joe Colleges sticking out like Dumbo ears, I was slow to realize that the CIA had been heavily recruiting locals after the Afghan War. Those terrorists on the Agency's payroll brought to the U.S. were chickens coming home to roost. As far as the Pathans on both sides of the Pakistani border were concerned, scratch a Russian and you will find an American underneath. We thought we were using the Afghans to defeat the Russians and that we were buying their loyalty, never understanding that an Infidel is an Infidel, whether Communist or Capitalist. Or simply a nonbeliever.

Four Sunnis had been killed in front of one of the hotels several days ago. Truck loads and jeep loads of troops were driving up and down the main street of the Northern Areas. Soldiers and police, local and national, in a dozen different uniforms, armed to the teeth, were everywhere, hunting for Sunnis and Shites, both Pathans.

"Now you look like a Pathan." The barber had trimmed my beard a bit and cut off a few locks from the back of my head. I continued in the direction I had been going before I had this not-so-close shave, crossing the rickety suspension bridge over the Gilgit River to about midway. Very few vehicles interrupted the flow of pedestrian traffic. I looked down on the Gilgit. Draining the mountains on the Afghan border to the north and to the west, the river had not traveled very far, but fed by countless tributaries it is already wide. It, in turn, becomes one of the tributaries of the Indus, after merging with the Hunza a little downstream. The Indus, coming from the opposite direction, has its source in the mountain fastness of Tibet.

According to my *Traveller's Guide* the shape of Pakistan's map looks like a lion's head, with it mouth yawning into the Arabian Sea. In Tibetan legend, it goes on, the holy lake, Manasarwar, gives life to rivers out of the mouth of sacred animals and Indus is born out of Sing-i-Kabab or the Mouth of the Lion. You can see why I did not find my *Traveller's Guide to Pakistan* very helpful. But hype has been the watchword from the beginning as the name Indus has its origin in the Sanskrit word "Sindhu" meaning ocean. And it was the ocean compared to the dry homeland of the migrating Aryans. Long afterward, in 500 B.C., when Darius the Great conquered the Punjab the inscription upon his rock tomb in Persia referred to the Punjab, through which the river flows, as the land of the Seven Sindhus – named for the major rivers that form Pakistan's Nile. And so the Indus was the river of Hindus until the British mucked about, and now the Ganges is.

The Indus and Ganges have their sources in the same Himalayan fountainhead, going in opposite directions to define and form a subcontinent that is the gateway to Asia.

It was time to see the chief of police or whoever he was. Gilgit is the administrative headquarters of all the Northern Territories and for all I knew I was seeing the head-honcho for the Hunza, Chitral, Balistan and Gilgit – and he did not give a hoot. My absent visa was truly "no problem." A handgun rested on his desk. There were rifles hanging from the wall. I had not seen such a display of firepower since I was booked for "trespassing" on a public street in Palm Beach.

"Visa in Islamabad."

"But my pass says I must be there in three days. More than three days have passed and I'm too sick to go there directly."

"No problem." Gone were the days when I could pass

for a spy. It seemed I was a problem only to my own country. But then this guy really had his hands full. And what was one more rabble-rouser.

55

Undertow

My nemesis sat next to me on the bus – which put Hilda between me and the dark blue sea, and the bus driver, directly to our right.

I had not seen her since that last supper. She who had been so disdainful of doing in Rome as the Romans do was dressed up in a Pakistani outfit, wearing the traditional shalwar-qamiz. Hilda had ridiculed the Italian student for going native. Ironically, Regazza had foresworn the loose fitting clothes by the time she had arrived in Gilgit. I met her while shopping for a rug and she was ready to get her own magic carpet – an airline ticket to Islamabad and points beyond. As quickly as possible. Regazza was not particularly attractive, but that had not stopped the men from hounding her, no matter how she dressed.

But Hilda could hold anyone at bay. She was actually wearing male attire, a suit with a cut as masculine as her hair – and was very happy about her "pajamas," laughing that people did not know if she was a man or woman. Single women can expect to be hassled in Morocco, Turkey and points east. Regazza was dressed right, but ultimately clothes do not make the woman. Hilda said she had been a geography teacher in China, but as our journey progressed it was obvious that history was her obsession if not profession. She claimed she was an Austrian, but didn't know which end was up.

The other two tourists aboard the bus left us at Chilas to do some trekking, for the Gilgit plains were somewhat contained, and we were back in the big leagues in a matter of minutes and skirting the pedestal of Nanga Parbat. The mountain rises dramatically from the Indus, and then slopes up from the Karakoram Highway a good bit to the face, topping out at 8,125 meters (26,660 feet). But it's mostly downhill from here and this little-traveled leg of the Silk Road could have been the road above the Yangtze River gorges. The Yangtze gorges may be deeper and steeper, but the Karakoram Highway is higher than the Chinese river road. And drier. And rockier.

But I was looking at this river from a vastly different perspective. There were no whirlpools up here, and the rocky terrain unloosed many "LANDSLIDES." These warnings were followed by signs that encouraged the driver to relax. "Enjoy yourself, the landslide zone is behind you."

But you didn't go very far before you came across more warning signs and traveled over a stretch of road recently under debris, or half clear of falling rocks. A driver had to be crazy to throw caution to the winds even if all hell wasn't breaking loose, for there was never more than a few feet separating a vehicle from the precipice and the indigo Indus ever-wending its wild way to the sea.

When there was leeway, a loudly colored truck would scream by, but this was rare, at least at this time of day. The absence of traffic added to the presence of the ever-present river and the threatening weather. After the promising vista above Chilas we seemed to be plunging into an endless sinkhole, going down the oceanic drain – which, of course, we were, as the "ocean" was emptying into the ocean.

We had one break, perhaps at Thor. Other towns or hamlets were shown on my detailed map, but I recall seeing little more than a roadside restaurant. A man excitedly told me he was going to swim in the river, and then another passenger told me the fellow was crazy. In any case, the only way we were going to get near the river was if we didn't make one of the turns.

The early shimmer of the river gave way to darker moods and just as the Indus was a distant mirror for the changing sky, a widening of its passage was reflected in its surface. Serene when expansive, churlish when narrow, aquamarine, aqua vita, she led us on and on. . .down and down I go, round and round I go, into that spell called indigo vertigo.

Below the tributary defining Mount Falaksair, there is no indication that the Indus, too, will be a muddy river – with a little help from humanity. Here the Indus retains much of its mountain based purity and is effected by the cloud-stopping 6,000 meter Falaksair.

This is a magical but disorienting bend in the river because of the dramatic difference in climate. Not following a map at the time and barely able to keep my head above water, I was unaware that the far pavilion I was seeking was on the other side of this magic mountain. Black magic in the case of Hilda. The strain of the journey was too much for her; she was a torrent of words, white water bubbling up from her subconscious.

She had been in China for a year or two and had been apparently brainwashed. Perhaps even programmed as a kind of Manchurian candidate who vehemently defended China whenever stress activated her button. Or someone cast an aspersion on China. In passing, I had casually dropped that the Pakistani buses were better than the Chinese, perhaps pushing her button.

"That's not true. Besides the Chinese government looks after the people. America is no better. I've been to America, you know. Your Greyhound! Ha!"

"For God's sake, look at the river!" I shouted.

"You are all alike, you expect so much of China. Backwardness that you find charming and touristic in Pakistan, you condemn in China." Her short blond hair bristled. Incongruously an assault on world Jewry followed.

How could she not know that Israel and China had become fast friends with the aim of suppressing Islam, with the arms and experience supplied by Israel? Even if China publicly defended Palestine. What were the odds of Hilda being on the same bus, much less sitting next to me – or meeting her on that mountain. Was she really crazy or was this caricature provoking me?

Opposites attract. I was a magnetic field for Iron Crosses or White Huns. There is only one way to resist an undertow and that is to swim sideways. I took one of the seats vacated

Undertow

by the two hikers, but I did not have a comparable view and felt as if I had run away. The greatest sin. And my Achille's heel became my fatal attraction as I returned to my vulture's eye view.

It was not long before my presence reactivated Hilda.

"Why do you hold the Chinese to a higher standard? Can you just answer that?"

We were careening around a curve and in seconds she was at full throttle and taking me with her. Round and round we went, down and down we went, and as dark clouds gave way to night and sight no longer provided escape, I was a captive audience. My torturer, this tortured soul had evidently transferred her love for a Nazi Germany to the greatest star on the horizon, but China could only play second fiddle to the Fatherland when the going gets rough.

It had been some time since we crossed the Indus at Dassu and it would be a matter of minutes before we arrived in Besham. This town on the west bank was the last stop. The lights went on. The passengers were leaving the bus. But I remained rooted to my seat as much out of sheer exhaustion and the thought of looking for a room as I was in letting my body speak for me: the message to Hilda to get the hell out of my life! Leave me in peace. But she wasn't reading me and instead allowed the confession that she was glad that we were traveling together. Yes, there was darkness and desolation at the end of this road and no place for a woman, even Eva Braun.

Our rage was supposed to be water under the bridge. A bond. The shared experience of a couple of soldiers under fire. Who may have cracked and revealed some petty differences in opinion. What the hell. We shared the same foxhole – and now Hilda is urging me to "Come on. We must find a hotel."

I didn't budge.

"Come on, what is the matter with you? The driver said there is a cheap hotel nearby."

Wasn't it only a lovers' quarrel? The war was over for someone who thought I was a masochist or immune to venom. "We can share a room."

"Share a room?" Nothing less could have gotten a rise

out of me.

"It will be more economical." Neither one of us was *that* pressed for funds. You couldn't find more than one bed to a room in these parts. No, she wasn't finished with me yet. The bus driver was telling us we had to leave. I was too tired to resist, and so I ended up walking with Hilda to the nearest hotel. I don't know who was protecting whom.

Actually, the Silk Road was as crowded as you might expect on a sultry night in the subtropics. It was the extent of Besham. One "economical" hotel was next to the other.

The Flesh Hotel – or was that "Flush" – was a draw. But the royal Flush did not guarantee that a toilet came with it, which it did not – though you could drive your car to the foot of the stairs that led to the rooms. You had a roof over your head and your car could be conveniently parked next to a dinner table that served as a receptionist desk and was heaped with chapatti and dall. The place was more a restaurant/garage than a hotel, but I dutifully escorted Hilda to a room.

"I can't sleep here," I said.

"Why not? It will be for only one night."

I knew I could not find better accommodations, but I had accompanied Hilda to a hotel and felt that Don Quixote himself would have acknowledged that I had honored the laws of chivalry.

"I'll see you, Hilda."

"We'll go to a better hotel."

"No, I'm going to eat."

Hilda stormed out of the hotel. She was flushed. So much for Latin lovers, she must have thought. Or did Hilda think I was Jewish?

I walked to the entrance half expecting a calmer Hilda to butter up to me, but she was nowhere to be seen. Too proud.

Of course, she could have been standing in front of me. Naked light bulbs were about the size of electrification in this burg. This was just the place and occasion to get roaring drunk, but I had to content myself with taking a long walk to a new hotel outside of town that overlooked the Indus.

56

The Road to Kalam

Kesmur (Kashmir) is a province seven days distant from Pascia. Its inhabitants also have their own peculiar language. They are adept beyond all others in the art of magic, to such a degree that they can compel their idols, although dumb and deaf, to speak. They can likewise obscure the day, and perform many other miracles. They are pre-eminent among the idolatrous nations, and from them came the idols worshipped in other parts.
From this country there is communication by water with the Indian Sea.

The Travels of Marco Polo

We were going in the opposite direction of Kashmir, but this "Disputed Territory" on my map was just over the mountains to my east, and the culture of conjurers to which Marco refers transcended borders. (The Arabian Sea was then known as the Indian Sea.)

Azad Kashmir, on this side of the disputed border and just to my south, is presently a base camp for the separatist movement against India, which even considers this Pakistani controlled portion of Kashmir to be a part of India. The Indus flows the length of this wartorn state. Even in Marco's day Kashmir was partly Muslim as Islam was fast replacing Buddhism as the dominant religion; but the river has always been more of a crossroads than an obstacle. And yet, I can't fathom how Marco came to Kashmir, much less how he leaves – without the assistance of magic. Unless Pascia is Pasa or Peshawar, or Passu, which I passed through below China's border.

You can appreciate how Marco could have mistaken the

shifting border of Kashmir for the Hindu Kush or Pamir; he wasn't splitting hairs when he passed this way and did not relate his story until about another twenty-six years down the road. It is amazing that he achieves the level of accuracy that he does, when we consider that the famous Blaue Family map of Asia (1662), four centuries later, places the source of the Ganges River a couple of thousand miles to the north of its mouth, in Tashkent!

Avanti. The small bright orange card I got from the manager of the New Abasin Hotel & Restaurant reminds me that I have been to Besham. "Nice Accommodations. First Class Service. Ventilated Rooms. Flash System & Car Parking." My unanswered prayer was that Hilda would not be on the early minibus to Peshawar. Cold shoulder were not the words for her. There was hurt and a barely subdued fury in her smoldering presence, but I did not think she was finished with me yet.

Happy Valley lies due north - and beyond that about one hundred and fifty miles distant from Mount Falaksair, the eastern end of the Hindu Kush. The opposite direction of Islamabad, where I was supposed to get my visa. I intended to remain in the upper valley until the cows came home – or the rains came, and I could be reasonably sure that I had washed Hilda right out of my hair and she was safely back in Austria (or The Third Reich). I was now in Swat.

After breakfast a camera shop beckoned. I let the owner, a young Sikh, load my Canon for me. The Sikh surprised me because something was about to happen that I could not associate with this religion – a marriage of the Muslim and Hindu.

My eyes rested on a roll of green backs. I said, "Business must be very good." No one else was in this walk-in closet of a shop.

"Yes," he said, and picked up a wad of U.S. $100 bills.

I could only see cheap cameras for sale. "What else are you selling?"

"I give you a gift." The turbaned man pulled from the draw under the counter a ball of hash.

I said no thanks. A bad trip could be a one-way trip, a

dead end and I was going miles out of my way as it was. Hashish. In spirit and space, I could not be closer to India. But hash is nickel and dime stuff. Indian smugglers are bringing in acetic anhydride needed by heroin gangs in Pakistan. I did not know what was in store for me. The past was pulling me under like a Proustian cookie or Indian brownie, for the subcontinent had become my subconscious.

Opium, replacing myrr and frankenscence, as well as the silk of ancient times, was now creating Frankensteins in legendary Tashkent and Samarkand, as Central Asia developes into America's inner cities – for which the drugs are bound, via Moscow.

But it is the money and not the poppy that is the root of the evil; the poverty of the growers and the greed of the buyers; the despair of the consumers of the countless cultures corrupted by rampant materialism. Misguided and fanatical though they may be, it is this evil that the Islamic militants are resisting.

People like this friendly dealer. Who may have actually offered me opium.

I allowed myself two days to get up the valley. Kalam, the last stop, can't be much more than one hundred miles, but the van remained packed until the end of its route in Madyan, where I decided to call it a day. Marvelously maddening music had followed me up this tropical valley, and it was here, giving up the struggle to keep my head above water, that I went under for the third time.

My room had a ceiling fan and the hotel had more the air of a British bungalow in India's hill country than the standard fare – but, then again, this had been British India's hill country.

It is unlikely that the British escaped the heat of Peshawar by going up this unruly valley, which seemed more a destination of their Khyber Rifles, since it is also hot here. A mile up a side road is a trout farm below a beautiful stream. Whatever their reason, the Victorian English were truly fascinated with Swat.

57

The Sultan of Swat

*Who, or why, or which, or what,
Is the Akond of Swat?*

Edward Lear (1873)

*Now the Ahkoond of Swat is a vague sort of man
Who lives in a country far over the sea;
Pray tell me, good reader, if tell me you can....*

Eugene Field (1884)

Following the stream until too beat to go on, I waved down a car. It was the only thing on wheels I had seen in an hour. A vacationing army captain and his family had hired a taxi to drive them to a government house further upstream. It was sticky wicket for a while, but the Pakistani was an officer and a gentleman and took on an extra passenger, and as it turned out, a guest. The captain looked like King Hussein of Jordan, before melancholy – living with the constant threat of assassination — transformed him. I told him that.

"Oh, really?" The captain was amused but flattered. I joined the captain and his cousin for tea and biscuits, and when there was some skepticism about me really being an American – in Swat, no less, on this secluded road leading to a government watering hole, I impulsively pulled out my passport. And then thinking, insanely, that the warm-hearted officer would assist me in acquiring my visa, I spilled the beans.

"Please, I don't want to know this. You should go to Islamabad."

"Well, I'm sick and I thought the mountain air would

help me." Marco Polo recuperated in the Hindu Kush, when he was too bushed to go on. Running out of the north, the range also shaped Pakistan's border with Afghanistan, about fifty miles to my west.

"I am only going to Kalam for a few days."

"I didn't hear you say this. We haven't met."

"Yes, we never met." This is only a projection of the subcontinent. Food materialized on a low table. We were in the dining room of a new two-story house, also decidedly western.

"Looks good," I said.

"Would a Pakistani be served if he found himself in the same situation in America?" the officer's cousin queried.

"What do you mean?"

"My brother lives in America. Brooklyn. He says they are treated like black people." He was indignant.

"I treat black people very well. At least like everybody else." Little did I know I would end up back in New York with Pakistanis for my next door neighbors – who won't say hello.

"Help yourself," the captain said, "you are our guest."

The taxi driver was warming up to me. "America, it is beautiful country, is it?"

Brooklyn isn't so beautiful, I said, "this is beautiful." I was looking out the wide window with its vista of the narrowing valley. It was becoming crowded with new houses. I preferred my clapboard bungalow to concrete boxes.

"I want to go to America. . . .You come to my house in Swat. Very nice. Stay with us as long as you like. My uncle is a doctor, he will care for you. No problem when you go to Islamabad."

The taxi driver (owner) would not be needed for a few days and was shortly returning to town. A ride I could not pass up because I wanted nothing more than to go to bed in my bungalow.

"I will take you to Peshawar when you leave Swat. We will go the American Consulate. . . ."

"Yes, we'll be a Swat Team." Like most of the less fundamental fellows I was to meet, I was to be his ticket to ride.

"You will help me get my visa for America."

The day after I began this chapter, like any day I spend in Manhattan, was grist for the mill I've been tilting at. I found myself in the American Museum of Natural History, entranced before a life-size carving of a Kafir in front of his intricately carved doorway. It was not so much that the wooden figure on display resembled the owner of the little eatery up the valley where I was heading, as much as the fact that a middle-aged man was providing his son with some history about the Kafirs. He was, apparently, better informed than the New York Times expert in Central Asia.

When the man paused and seemed to be ready to move on to the next exhibit, I could not resist telling him how fascinated I was by what he was saying, since I had spent some time among the Kafirs.

"Please enlighten us."

As our conversation progressed and I regressed, reliving and recounting my route to within miles of the display's origin, I was reduced to babbling. I had taken this "lawyer" from Denver and his son along the Silk Road as far as Afghanistan, letting drop that I was probably being investigated by the CIA.

I had remarked that my Kafir friend resembled the carving before us, wearing a rolled hat, and that I had taken his photo. Topping that, the lawyer related that the Sultan of Swat had given his aunt a doorway, just like the one behind glass, behind the Kafir. The fact, alone, that the man was a lawyer should have been enough to alert me to his predilection to prevaricate, but in my transcended state of animation, I am bound to suspend disbelief.

"I'm looking forward to the publication of your book." The lawyer fled from the museum's Asian hall – as my own smoke detector went off, delayed as the reaction may have been.

The lawyer got his information from "A Short Walk in the Hindu Kush." The New York Times, retaining Rudyard Kipling for its Central Asian source, reported (May, 1995) that Kafirstan was a figment of Kipling's imagination. Kipling, based in Lahore, was also a newspaperman who wrote about areas he had not visited, getting no nearer than Peshawar to a Kafirstan, which he placed west of Afghanistan in his "The Man Who Would be King." This fictionalized version of Kafirstan sent the Times man down the wrong road, when in fact the real Kafirstan – Land of the Infidels – was the Islamic appellation for those animists who inhabited the Kush and had a bit of their culture transported to the American Museum of Natural History, about the time an amir in the Kabul area sent a military force to their mountain home to enlighten them. Hence, the pagan land became Nuristan or Land of Light.

In 1895, Kafirstan, as it was known to the knowledgeable powers-to-be, ceased to be. But the Nuristanis, or Kafirs as the natives of Chitral are referred to in the neighboring valley, continue to straddle a border that did not exist until the British divided and ruled. Overlooked by the amir, perhaps, Chitral holds several Kafir festivals every year.

As for the Sultan of Swat, my research leaves me with the unanswered question, who or why or which or what. Or Babe Ruth.

58

Riding that Tide to Ararat

> *Tourism to this region, which now forms Pakistan, started 4,000 years ago. The first tourist groups to arrive were the Aryans, who liked the land so much that they never left. They were followed by the Persians, the Greeks, the Bactrians, the White Huns, the Turks and the list goes on and on. Some of the distinguished tourists have been Alexander from Greece, Hsuan Tsang from China, Ibn-e-Batuta from Spain, Marco Polo from Italy and Churchill from England. Mahmood, an Afghan tourist, liked this area so much that he spent his winter vacations for seventeen consecutive years.*
>
> A Travellers' Guide to Pakistan

Commotion in the cottage opposite mine roused me from my sleep. A large family of tourists were cooking breakfast on their veranda. The sun had not yet risen, but I was grateful for the early start and caught the first minibus for Kalam. We had gone only a short distance before the passengers were being stacked on the roof – which is pretty tricky for a van. Those quaint customs that were lacking in China were reconstructing the subcontinent for me – although technically speaking, I don't know if Swat can be called the subcontinent.

The bus came to a halt. Three veiled women, shown deference, boarded and were seated. A simple gesture that brought home the importance of culture in defining a place – and a place in defining a culture, as a truly alpine scene defined high ground, I did not associate with Islam.

The weather was changing. Stalls doing an early but brisk business in blankets and jackets lined the Kalam road. Closing out sales. There were tourists up here, but most of the traffic was heading south and none too soon as Pakistanis on holiday were staying in cheek-to-jowl hotels and the white water in its turbulent rush to the sea could have been the surf at Atlantic City for all they saw. The boardwalk atmosphere continued for a bad mile before the bus came to a final stop. Well, this pavilion was not quite far enough.

I couldn't believe it. At least Kalam was not the end of the road. I continued on, praying that a lone hotel was up ahead. A carload of vacationing youths stopped for me.

"Where do you wish to go?"

"To the hotel."

"No hotel. Hotels in Kalam."

I asked the enthusiastic boys where they were going.

"To the glacier."

Just what the doctor ordered. "May I join you?" The boys were overjoyed – and more disappointed than surprised when high and behold there was indeed a hotel about ten or fifteen miles beyond Kalam.

My young friends from the lowlands warned me about staying up here. "The people in the villages are not friendly."

Three miles or so above Kalam a makeshift roadblock extorted a contribution for the right of traveling into a strictly tribal area, underscoring their point. A donation to the Fundamentalist cause, or highway robbery, but the Ushu Hotel itself was a godsend.

Sitting on an abutment jutting into the roiling Ushu River, the hotel is a Swiss chalet done up in the riotous colors of a disco truck – and not a tourist in sight.

Here the road makes a sharp turn, for the river alone can be contained by this canyon. The eye instinctively follows the flow until the chasm opens on sky and that land of light beyond Kalam. Conifers steeply rise from the opposite bank and disappear in the clouds, a promise of the pristine that had the greater pull. The only sign of civilization is the stone bridge we have crossed and the eatery/tea terrace above it. My friend whose likeness is behind museum glass was behind closed doors. Looking upstream, you can appreciate the full fury of the Ushu as it passes under the narrow span and is a mesmerizing cauldron swirling about the hotel.

I have seen few more welcoming sights – or heard more seductive sounds – but this was about the extent of my welcome. The reception desk in the Ararath Restaurant, above the rooms, was as bare as the tables. I shouted hello. A second louder hello carried my voice above the rush of Ushu and a tall young man sporting a luxurious lamb hat appeared. It is similar to the hat worn by an ex-president and founder of Pakistan, as illustrated on the rupee notes, if not more regal. The front of this high wooly crown is shaped like the bow of a sailing ship, and if I had not met the Sultan of Swat, I was now speaking to the son of a kind of akond or chief.

"I need a room."

The soft spoken man knew a little English. I was in a hurry to check in and hit the road.

"A room! A room! Kamra!" It was beginning to sink in that the patient young man was a guest.

"Friend speak English," he said.

"Where is your friend from?"

"Uganda." Is this a province I haven't heard about?

"Where is Uganda?" I asked.

"Africa." I had stayed with Indians when I was in East Africa, but I hadn't recalled that Muslims or Pakistanis had emigrated there. In any case, I visualized a black African, not making the obvious connection.

The young man's name was Fazel. As we were speaking, his Pathan roommate appeared. He was a not so swarthy swashbuckler who could be more smoke than fire. He is wearing the standard topee.

"Hello. How are you!" A cheery greeting.

"Hi," I said. "You're from Uganda." It was as much an implication as a question.

"How did you know?"

I told him I had spent some time in Uganda myself. He was delighted.

"You are from Uganda. Join us, come, come!"

"I need a room."

He wouldn't hear of it. "My friend knows everybody in

the District. We can sleep anywhere. Where are you going?"

We were going to the lake, at least that was our destination. It was as if my husky Ugandan friend had been expecting me – or that perhaps I had an appointment with him. The middle-aged man is identifying himself as Doctor Ali Khan.

I can well imagine how Marco felt, a man younger than myself, returning home to ridiculing friends and family. "Marco Millione," they called him, referring to his many incredible stories. Or newly acquired wealth? Of smuggled gems? Polo had more adventures than I, but mine are more psychic than physical, and the hard-driving merchant could not have had the same need to communicate. That's why I keep scraps of paper like the receipt for one cup of tea I got at the Ararath (the "h" is optional") Restaurant. Ararat is the Hebrew version of the Persian word for mountains – and here I've been carrying on about riding that tide to Ararat, where "all men are Noah's sons" (as Richard Wilbur so poetically put it).

By the time we had hiked up to the next village, I had determined that the good doctor was not necessarily of the medical kind. Ali told me he was actually a druggist, permitted to sign his name "doctor" – good enough for my purpose. In fact, we made a stop at a herbal shop where Ali chatted with the fellow "druggist." Across the way, we had tea in the cramped house of Fazel's friend. I had gotten away from concrete, and beyond the herbal shop, I don't recall any other stores on this road to nowhere.

Kohistan, where we were, is really no more a part of Chitral than it is of Swat, and as such is practically the Hindu Kush which, according to that other tourist Ibn Battutah who came this way in the fourteenth century, means "Hindu Killer." But in what language? The reasoning behind this name is that so many Indian slaves perished in the almost impassable snows, but the nearest I come to Kush in the Indic language is Kushti, which means "sacred thread." But who named the mountain range?

Whatever the word means, it sounds Semitic in origin, and just as Noah begat the father of Kush, there would seem to be a link with the Israelites here. Of course, if you believe in

Noah's Ark then it is plausible that just as there were two Caucasus Mountains, there could have been two Kushs (or perhaps it wasn't in Ethiopia after all), and that somewhere up here is the "Mount Ararat" of the Ark of Noah, confused with the Ark of the Covenant – which some scholars place in Ethiopia.

Is this Hindu Kush the final mooring place of the Biblical boat that survived the great flood? The Muslims place the Ararat of the deluge nearer to the Euphrates River in southern Turkey than the biblical location; the same passengers, perhaps, but closer to home, as the Hebrews are "the people who crossed the Euphrates." But Central Asia is as good a guess as any.

To Alexander the Hindu Kush was just another Caucasus or "Alpine Barrier" that may have simply become the Indicus Caucasus. The Hindu word for pleasant is "khush," which is close in meaning and sound to the word for "sacred thread." Well within the Northwest Territory and peaking out 25,236 feet above sea level, the splendid Tirich Mir is sacred, with or without a Noah's Ark.

Could Noah's Ark be a metaphor for that ark that housed the word? A refuge from the rising tide of contradictory currents that promised to inundate humanity. Beyond this long shot there is a biblical connection in the Kafirs religious ceremonies. On display in the Museum of Natural History in New York is a silver chalice, which could also contain the seeds of Zoroaster or Zarathustra, with its good and evil duality. The Kafir's good god Imra is counterpoised to a prince of darkness, Yush – which with its connotation of death, our Arabian traveler could have confused with Kush. Maybe Ibn was right, after all. And maybe the mountains were just known to have caused the death of many Hindus – if in fact that is true.

If there is any poetry in all this, then the Pathans or Kafirs who populated the southern slopes of the Hindu Kush, are descendents of a lost tribe of Israel. They could have walked, they could have sailed, for the prevailing winds would have taken Noah's Ark to the higher Hindu Kush or beyond. . . .but I've become one of Cowper's

> *"Philologists who chase*
> *A panting syllable through time and space;*
> *Start it at home and hunt it in the dark*
> *To Gaul, to Greece and into Noah's Ark."*

Though I never heard it said when I was in the land of the Pathans, I have recently learned what might amount to confirmation of my intuition.

Pathan legend holds descent from King Saul through his son Afghana. In time another descendent of a lost tribe of Israel, Qais, was chosen by Mohammed to spread Islam among his people, settling in what we now call Afghanistan.

Today, descent from Alexander strikes a more romantic note in the western mind.

59

Alexander's Ragtime Band

> *In the province of Balashan (Badakhshan), the people are Mahometans and have their own peculiar language. It is an extensive kingdom....and is governed by princes, in hereditary succession, who are descended from Alexander by the daughter of Darius, king of the Persians. All these have borne the title in the Saracenic tongue of Zulkarnen, which is the equivalent of Alexander....*
>
> *The horses bred here are of a superior quality and have great speed. Their hoofs are so hard that they do not require shoeing....They say that not long ago there was still found in this province horses of the strain of Alexander's celebrated Bucephalus, which were all foaled with a particular mark on the forehead....*
>
> *In this kingdom there are many narrow passes and natural strong points which leave the inhabitants with little fear of any foreign power trying to invade them....*
>
> Marco Polo

"Are you sure this thing will be safe here?" I left my bag with the herbalist. We were ready to resume our trek, and I could not carry my backpack any further. Ali reassured me, "Fazel's father is the chief of the entire area. Nobody would dare touch your bag."

I had not seen a doctor walk in fifty years, but Ali's camera was worth more than my whole kit and kaboodle. Though I recalled what had happened to me in China, I was sure that he would not be part of any disappearing act.

Ali said he was making a movie, a travelogue of sorts. I expressed surprise that he would leave his practice in Uganda to film Swat.

"Incidental. I'm buying land from Fazel's father. The check is being held up at the bank."

I trusted the improbable pair – under even less probable circumstances because it was par for the course. It was about noon when tourists began rolling by in a cloud of dust turning a halcyon day into hell. Luckily, it was time for my friends to pray. Facing the river, Fazel's arched back was to Falaksair. The mountain was the primary source of Ushu, one of those trout streams that entranced the young Marco when he took to the high ground to cure his illness.

Fazel may have been bowing to Mecca, submitting to Allah, but as the rapids carried me along, distancing me in light-years from the nearby road, I felt as if his offering of self encompassed all of nature. That he was giving himself to Ushu as well as Allah. But Fazel was more focused on actual prayer than union with what Allah had created – and in this neck of the piney woods it was out-of-this-world.

Even the Pope approves of Muslim ritual and has said they truly know how to pray. Standing off to the side some feet away, I took Fazel's photo. The most striking thing about Alexander's descendent is his hat, at that moment looking like the headdress of an American Indian, without the feathers. A furry top hat, rimless with the back part sloping away. Its prominent front definitely projected a high station that was borne out by Fazel's bearing. Take the wooly knots out of his hat, replace sheep's hair with Hunza rubies and the other goodies studding these hills and you would have a Papal crown. And everywhere that Fazel went the lamb hat was sure to go. It defined him.

Superfically. Many customs in the area go to the core of a people, differed from valley to valley. A custom still common in Chitral resembled the potlash of the Inuit or Eskimos of northwestern Canada. Like the Kafirs, the people of coastal Canada celebrate success by giving things away. Prestige is bound up with the size of the feast. Generosity is almost equated with courage. The expansiveness of the true warrior.

Fazel resembled an Armenian more than the fairest American Indian, while Ali Khan brings to mind the Old Man of the Mountain, with a few cosmetic touches.

The Old Man of the Mountain was a self-styled prophet (aren't we all?) who had his enemies murdered by drugging his disciples, offering them paradise on earth, if they did his bidding. The young men got hooked on hashish, and in killing the Old Man's enemies, became assassins or the hashish eaters. I am not making any connections.

Alexander, to the best of my knowledge, passed this way a little to our south, via Lowari Pass, having come from the Buddhist center to-be of Gandhara in the spring of 326 B.C. The Bodhi tree would not take root in the Kush until several centuries later when the Kushan. . .Eureka! The shortening of Kushan to Kush may deride my tide to Ararat, but supplies us with the semantics if not the Semitics of this elusive syllable.

The Kushan were a branch of the Yeuh Chih, who were run out of Gansu provence into Xinjiang by a local ruler, and in crossing the Tien Shan or Heavenly Mountains, ended up beyond Lake Balkhash, near the Russian steppes.

This tribe, very much resembling the American Indians, beginning their forced migration near the start of the Silk Road, remain settled for a while among the Indo-Scyths, before establishing their empire in the Hindu Kush. The Kushans extended their rule and Buddhism as far east as the Upper Ganges. As this was basically the land of the Indus, it would be logical that this region would be named the Hindu Kush. But this is poetry as well as logic. The religion penetrated well into Afghanistan, though, with the collapse of the empire, the Shiva cult succeeded Buddhism. The Metropolitan Museum of Art has a phallic icon in ivory (from Swat) that is emblematic of shiva and the envy of an elephant.

This did not deter the intrepid Tripitaka who passed this way when Hinduism was vying with Buddhism – and every other cult under the sun – for spiritual supremacy. The seventh century monk taking the northern route of the Silk Road, had gone as far west as Tashkent, before heading south for Samarkand and Bactria. Referring to the Hindu Kush, the tripper had written about a Pholosina for his Chinese readers. But the first and maybe greatest Chinese pilgrim coming this way was Fa Xian, who had taken the southerly route to study under the Indian masters, in Gandhara in the middle of the fourth century. He has nothing noteworthy to say about the Hindu Kush.

Perhaps that is the way it should be. But Aristotle referred to the Hindu Kush as the Great Asiatic Parnassus, and from the ancient Greeks on down, one horde or another has tried to rule both sides of this great divide. In the wake of the Kushans came the White Huns, the Samanids of Bukhara, the Mongols, Timur and Timurids and a host of other tourists that put these mountains on the map.

This is not reflected in the Metropolitan Museum of Art, where their map shows the land west of Kashmir to be "Swat Valley" and Gandhara to be only in Pakistan. The Hindu Kush is out of the picture entirely, so that while one museum on one side of Central Park is stuck in a time warp, the age of dinosaurs and diamonds, as most of the Victorian displays on Asia in the Museum of Natural History have not been updated and can fit in a hall reserved for a baby dinosaur, the museum on the east side of the Park could have a better sense of place.

Here I've gone off on another wild Kush chase, when Americans don't even know or care how America came by its name. And just when Alexander was getting into the swing of things, cutting a swath across Swat in his headlong rush to the Indus and his Waterloo not long after. Alexander penetrated deep into Kashmir, with every intention of subjugating the subcontinent; take on the white man's burden. But a subtropical rain brought his weary soldiers to their ragged knees and did-in Alexander's beloved horse, Bucephalus, whose memory lived on in the city named after him (the horse).

I had always thought that Alexander had turned back thinking that this dark continent was not worth the candle, but his soldiers had simply had enough and refused to go on. Alexander's tour de force had turned into a mutiny. Going on a less grueling excursion, the tourist from Macedonia took his group on an Indus cruise, and homeward bound had regained command.

But without his beloved horse, Alexander's passions became even more unbridled, and hindsight reveals not so much a great general as a prototype for the gringo sowing his oats in Mexico. Alexander's boundless cruelty became an inspiration for every barbarian from Attila to Hitler. Less racist historians would have referred to an Attila the Great and an Alexander the Greek.

Alexander was the first celebrity "A" type, clean shaven, a spitting image of Mick Jagger. In short, Alexander could get no satisfaction. Granted, he had a bigger and bloodier stage to act out his fantasies, make his own kind of music, and going whole hog by the time he had returned to Persia. Alexander's marriage and that of his officers and soldiers to Persian women were meant to spawn the first master race. By this time, Alexander had declared himself a god, demanding due respect.

I am playing fast and loose when I say that Fazel is a descendent of Alexander. But with more than ten thousand men taking native brides, with generous dowries, the conquering army made a big splash in Asia's Olympic gene pool. Who knows? (Even without his lion's mane or curly locks, the sensuous debaucher from Macedonia bore a marked resemblance to the rock star. Alexander, of course, was your first Rolling Stone.)

> *Come on along, come on along*
> *to Alexander's ragtime band.*
> *Come on along, come on along*
> *it's the greatest in the land. . . .*

60

A Kafir in Nuristan

A man with a Kalashnikov strapped to his back stopped the chief's son. I asked the doctor, "What's the problem?"

"I don't know," answered Ali. "I don't speak their language. I only speak Urdu and English."

The man with the automatic weapon asked Fazel how much he was charging to be our guide. I was ready to take his photo when he made it clear he would shoot me before I shot him.

"You must be very careful here," Ali cautioned me. "Even I am considered a foreigner, and I was born not very far from Kalam."

"It's hard to believe you were with the muhjahidin," I remarked.

"Oh, yes, I shouldered a gun. The whole business," the doctor defended himself, as he looked like he could not walk another step. "We all went."

It was only after I had returned to the States that I suspected that if Doctor Ali had anything to do with the Afghan rebels, then maybe his connection with Uganda was not so innocent. Hadn't Uganda provided a home for terrorists, as we now refer to independence movements?

I had marveled at the Afghan's success in driving the Russians out of Kabul, until I learned that Rambo had become a "freedom fighter." The Americans and Pathans were obviously the good guys, and because of Hollywood the rest is history.

"These people aren't very friendly, are they?"

"They are conservative." The doctor was examining

me. "And for God's sake, Tony, you must dress properly."

"Jesus, what would happen if I wore my shorts?"

We took our leave of the armed man. The glacier was a sorry sight as glaciers go, but the inside of iceboxes was the nearest that these lowlanders got to winter, and they frolicked about the long-frozen snow as if it were the fountain of youth. Two men were hacking away at the dirty ice, a keepsake they could resurrect in their refrigerators. The road itself had been cleared of compacted snow early in the summer, so that the motorist had only to reach out his window to become a part of this winter wonderland. The glacier had become a parking lot. Or in the spirit of progress, a drive-in glacier.

Our sights were set on the lake. But this was the height of surreality. Vacationers, some from as far away as Lahore, in western dress, running a fundamentalist gauntlet to cavort in this melting mess, when all about them hardened men subsisting on grains and grazing livestock, had just fought a Holy War to prevent the encroachment of this sort of nonsense. We didn't walk very far, before Ali, giving in, waved down a northbound jeep.

We were bogged down in the first stream we came to. The doctor and Fazel, the son of a chief, remained by the jeep, but the cooling ride had so charged my batteries that I trucked on, shedding my fatigue like a snake slipping out of old skin. Open sesame. The idea alone that a glacial lake awaited me was uplifting, but man can't live on ideas alone and I had eaten little else all day. A mile into my solo flight – I reluctantly sat down. The jeep never materialized.

Any other time I would have been thankful for having the opportunity to approach the lake under the best possible circumstances, but given my situation, I could have been pushing my luck. I returned to the jeep. Foiled again, when the prize was worth the pain and failure doubled it.

Our ride couldn't be repaired. We hopped onto another jeep returning from a little fishing expedition, apparently going all the way to Peshawar. An American had hired the chauffeured vehicle (if it didn't belong to an Agency) and paused to wash his pathetic fish in the stream.

"You don't have fish in America, Tony?"

It did seem like a long way to go to bag a couple of guppies. The lanky man, apparently, was demonstrating that he was indeed a sportsman and didn't have other fish to fry – although he could have been both a fisherman and a spy. What were the chances of running into this guy? Perhaps, our ambassador to Pakistan. There wasn't a peep out of me. I identified more with Ali's ragtime band.

My bag was as I left it. I had to strain to make out what the proprietor of this little shop was saying to me.

"I would like to go to America. You will write a letter for me?"

I ended up in the hotel after all. Ali and Fazel had allowed me to fend for myself. They were in a hurry to return to the Ushu. I didn't say no to this aging druggist, but did try to discourage him about his dream. There would have been no harm in writing a letter, but I was dizzy from the irony of all this – me sponsoring the muhjahidin. I expected a young hustler to get in step with the rest of the world and try to finagle his way to the promised land, but that this old man steeped in his ways on this remote mountainside – after knocking America – also wanted to climb aboard the bandwagon, was a bit much. I don't dismiss he has gotten here without my help.

I joined Fazel and Ali for a meal in the small restaurant above the bridge. Falaksair was already cloaked in clouds, but the river roared its approval and I knew I had found my far pavilion. The last tourist had long returned to Kalam. There were only the three of us and a few locals sipping tea at the next table. As the sky darkened and the temperature dropped the conversation came around to religion.

"What is your religion?"

"You could say I'm a Muslim."

Ali was flabbergasted. "No!"

"Well, I submit to God. Whether I like it or not."

"That's not enough," Ali advised me.

"You must uphold the five pillars of Islam. Say there is one God. Pray five times daily. Give alms. Observe Ramadan, and, if possible, make a pilgrimage to Mecca." In Arabic the essence of submission, or Islam, is Sharia or following the path. Fazel looked on intrigued, as Ali went on in this barely understood language. "Say there is only one God, follow the five laws and you really will be a Muslim, Tony."

I told Ali I thought I could do more good without affiliations of any kind.

Fazel said something to Ali in Urdu. "He says that if you become a Muslim, you can live here. He will give you land."

I believed Fazel. If the chief's son would have said he could make me king, I would have been skeptical. I had demonstrated a love for the mountains, and said I would like to return here with Mona. I had something else going for me. My beard, which had caused me so many problems in Argentina, was regarded in the opposite light in Pakistan. At least in the Northwest Territories where it was seen as a symbol of support for fundamentalism. And of course the mad are God's messengers.

Maybe I would have been a feather in the cap of the chief's son. Giving away land reflected the magnanimity associated with prestige, but a proselyte was worth his weight in Korans. Unlike the Christian missionary who takes land, the Muslim was giving it away. Here is your real Salvation Army, for better or worse.

It is curious how the most religious people in Central Asia, the tribes inhabiting the opposite sides of the Karakoram Mountains, were the most lawless, the least holy, until they received their respective word. Was it time alone that tempered the Tibetan's savagery, only in need of a guiding hand, or the temperament of the race (Mongol) with its bottomless capacity for submission, unmatched by the people west of this heavenly range? And maybe there is something about a religion with roots in the desert that is unforgiving.

I told Ali to tell Fazel that ritual didn't work very well with me. Don't the holy men of every religion come around to going off into the wilderness with a begging bowl? Were you going to hold a fakir to the same standards as the less evolved? All roads lead to Mecca. By my fifth cup of tea I might as well have been drinking beer. Finally, I said, "I don't want to give the appearance of being an apologist for the Muslims. Not when you can sentence a writer to death."

Ali pretended he did not hear me. Do we have the whole story on Rushdie? His crime was not that he mocked a religion but that he deliberately provoked a pious but simple segment of society, discrediting an entire group. If the more fundamental Islamists really want to punish Rushdie, they should take away his computer.

I'll give you a death sentence. Just write a beautiful line about the inherent evil of capitalism. And see how you're allowed to wither on the vine. The true revolutionary was considered insane under communism – and is driven insane under capitalism. The two sides of the same materialistic coin. Any struggle against this sad state of affairs is a Holy War in my book.

In any other book that would have been Ali speaking. He gave me no indication that he had a problem with the good life. Nor did Ali do any Israel bashing. I still don't know what to make of Ali except that he seemed to have too many fingers in the pie.

I interrupted their conversation. "All I'm saying, Doctor, is that if I made such a drastic move, I would give the impression of bias."

"Bosh. I'm telling Fazel you'll think about his offer."
"It's not an offer I can't refuse?"
"I don't understand."
"I really have a problem with prayer."
"There is no substitute for prayer, Tony."

And there isn't. Ali was not talking about Hail Marys, or any other kind of recitation or pleading on bended knee. No, the Muslim went all the way, in the most abject position, an expression of total submission. There may be those who just go through the moves, as in any religion, but the true expression of their faith is so humbling that the true believers can't be bought or sold. And therein lies their greatest threat to the fabric of a weakened society held together by the dictates of fashion. (The fascism of fashion.)

But compared to me, Ali is probably an all-American.

Fazel, on the other hand, had not been contaminated by the outside world, beyond his fleeting contact with summer tourists – which could only reinforce his faith. I will never forget him at prayer, yet I will always think of that glacial lake I never saw when I think of him – and vice versa. For the poetry here is not so much in the impression he left upon me, but in a postcard I bought in Mexico. I pick up the thread I followed through *Tramping to Jerusalem,* for beneath the photo of a beautiful lake nestled against the face of a mountain – this rock of faith above the tree line – is this caption:

> *I searched for God, and I couldn't find Him (Her)*
> *searched for my soul, and couldn't find It*
> *searched for my brother and found the three.*

The saying, written in Spanish, is attributed to Dostoevski. I don't know if I have illusions about the nature of my quest, or brotherhood, but there is that allegorical vein, not always visible, that runs through my life that seems to speak to more than aimless wandering. The wind may blow my censored ship this way and that, but the tidal currents carry the day.

The brother in the other. The brotherhood that can only exist when we move beyond the tribe, and are in the same boat spiritually – where all men are Noah's sons.

My search for Noah's ark in Turkey, long after I had purchased that Mexican postcard, was more a literary than a literal scouring after that phantom vessel. I spent only half a day on Mount Ararat; it took me that long to determine the ark is nothing but a syllable. My search for the ark became a search for a refuge, some place or someone who had resisted the inundating tide of ignorance. Shangri-La.

61

A Long Walk in the Hindu Kush

Traveling is like a trip to the opera. Writing about it is like going home and with the assistance of subtitles, watching the performance on television. At the opera you are living from moment to moment, caught up in the spectacle you don't quite understand. This journal has become the longer journey with those enlightening footnotes absent when I am on the run.

Fazel's offer was not really so surprising as this was not the first time that I was befriended by the son of a chief among a people better known for their hostility than their hospitality, though obviously this connection was beyond me at the time. I had been the guest of a chief in Sarawak, Borneo, taking away from the experience a ceremonial blanket that amounted to a conversion of sorts.

Am I unraveling or weaving my own ceremonial blanket, for Sarawak was the land of the White Rajahs, the inspiration for Lord Jim. The uninitiated reader may think I was fancying myself as The Man Who Would Be King, when I brought up Fazel's offer. Yet if you play on a large enough stage, open as the opera, letting it all hang out, you will run into a lot of characters. In every imaginable setting.

The eagle's nest of an eatery had no inside tables, and late evening was becoming a bit uncomfortable. The owner, Abdul, is a real character and has told Ali that he is a great climber. Ali and Fazel will be returning to Kalam in the morning, so Ali has instructed me to go nowhere without Abdul – who talks softly but carries a big stick. The restaurateur keeps the automatic weapon in his kitchen, which is basically an open fire. The hawk-eyed Abdul sleeps on the bunk against the wall.

Ali told me to drop by his room before I went to breakfast. He had agreed to write a doctor's note for me. I knocked on the door.

"Come in. Good morning, Tony."

Fazel and the doctor were sitting up in bed. I had forgotten that they would be sharing the same room – the custom in much of the world – which meant the same bed. The old freedom-fighter looked like a barrel of laughs wearing his hat, while the rest of him was under cover. He enjoyed my astonishment.

The doctor had not written the note. No problem. He would remain in Kalam for at least a few days and promised the letter would be ready for me when I came by. I left my friends to their own devices and went over to the Eagle's Nest for breakfast. The really nameless terrace is reached by rickety stairs that discouraged all but the most thirsty and famished. The tree branch that passed as a railing did not inspire confidence.

The sun was rising above the partially veiled Falaksair. This glorious mountain on this shining morning, the Ushu lifting me higher and higher, appeared to be ushering in a paramount day. I had arrived. I had a problem with guns, but if the world wasn't my oyster, I would settle for my soft-boiled egg, and could think of no better way to start the day than to have breakfast up here. My usual fare was dall or pulau. Lentils or a rice dish. I was raring to go, but Abdul, the restaurateur, would not accompany me. He was going to Kalam. I would have the mountain to myself.

Abdul was low enough down the mountain to have no qualms about being photographed. He needed no coaxing to remove his big stick from the stone wall of his homey kitchen. Armed to the teeth, he posed in front of his restaurant. Standing there woodenly, with his flinty glint, triangular head and Clark Gable ears, Abdul looked a lot like a bearded Norman Mailer after a strict diet. Crowned with his Pathan beret, dressed to kill. This photograph of my restaurateur friend outside this shack, flags flapping above the roughly shingled roof, is what is required to bring up-to-date that window on Kafirstan in the

Victorian castle on Central Park West, the museum.

Solo, I set out for the heights. Except for the tourists who drove up to the glacier on jeeps, the only other things on wheels up here were the Daliesque trucks used to transport logs down to the valley. The lumberjacks were boys accompanying their handworked harvest atop the trucks, standing as comfortably as sailors at the bow of a bark or passengers on a lark. The depictions in the mobile murals could range from Mecca to occult symbols and parrots, generally lost in a lavish display of flowers – similar to the amuck trucks of South America. A hallucinatory sight rumbling down a mountain bearing down at you.

Above the logged area I was signaled by two teenagers who made it clear that I was to proceed no further. Cupping their hands, making circles or rings with their fingers, they were indicating that they wanted to see my camera. By shrugs and gestures – the stuff of a jester – I made them understand I did not have a camera. Not the zoom lens they were familiar with, since my rudimentary Canon was in a small cloth case hanging from my belt. The ragamuffins kept pointing to my Hunza pack, thinking that the more sophisticated camera they suspected me of carrying was concealed.

Tiring of charades, I pressed on. I was bigger than these sons of bitches and if they got tough, would go into my Kung Fool stance. I hadn't gone another fifty feet into this mountain greenery, now devoid of much of its scenery, when a rock went zipping by my head. All the while the boys had kept their distance like frightened animals of the forest, snarling wolves. I responded to this show of fangs by letting out a war cry, and using my pack as a shield, advanced. As these primitives took stock of me, I made a big display of fumbling around in my bag as if I were reaching for the obligatory weapon of the white hunter. A boom lens. They retreated.

I thought that this back road climbing above the hotel that Abdul had pointed to would take me up to the shoulder of Falaksair. It was not exactly the least challenging way up there. Another rock fell at my feet as I passed below a scattering of huts. Now there were three of the bastards intent on stopping me in my tracks. They knew by now that I was unarmed. I started yelling again. I half-remembered the Kurdish youths who interrupted my ascent of Mount Ararat with a shower of stones. They were more plentiful on that hardscrabble slope.

A young man stepped outside his hut. Sizing up the situation, he shouted to the half-pint xenophobes to back off.

"Asslam-o-Alaikum," I called to my rescuer. "Chai, chai."

"Waalaikum-Asslam." He motioned for me to join him and made some tea. This was more like it.

"Khush Amdeed. Welcome." Kush!

The man spoke some English. I remarked how beautiful the area was, but expressed chagrin at the sight of all the freshly felled trees near his home. He complained about loggers who had been up there recently, thinning out the forest. Before long he would be living on a barren hillside.

To avoid suspicion, I informed my benefactor that I was on my way to Kalam. This was the high road alright, but all paths led to the valley and I was now headed in that direction. Whatever questions the man may have had about this unlikely saunter seemed to be answered by my manner – mad as a hatter.

I came upon a large cluster of huts in a clearing. Except for a couple of women I imagined I had seen, the hamlet seemed deserted. Fearing the welcoming committee was not done with me, I hastened my step. This primitive community was at the edge of what would be a fantastic ski slope in the Rockies, but right now only a swarm of sheep had the run of it. Climbing to higher ground, I could see that a man had been swallowed up by his flock. I felt human eyes on me and had to resist the urge to become a downhill racer and get the hell out of here. The weather was also closing in on me; this meant that it was unlikely I would have another shot at the mountains, and beauty, perhaps magnetism, overcoming fear, I climbed even higher.

I was rewarded with a sunburst and a strawberry patch that seemed to go on forever. Once again strawberries saved the day, and I was following my mouth as well as my nose – and none too soon as I had left an egg and chapati at the Eagle's

Nest and was running on empty. Serendipity followed those who took the least traveled way, who flew on a wing and prayer and let the devil... go to hell. But this time I was going up and not down as I did in Tibetan China, and enjoying the eagle's view denied me in that strawberry field.

My movable feast up the mountain must have been disarming to anyone uncomfortable about my presence up here. But there was a method to my madness beyond hunger – and the primacy of the pristine. Going up seemed the surest way to get down. Uncertain that I could manage the sharp incline and whatever else might be involved in a demoralizing descent directly below, I intued that I could maneuver the shoulders of this mountain like a monkey his master's. Heading north again and coming under the face of Falaksair, I intended to descend upon the village above the hotel and walk back to the Ushu along the road I had taken with Fazel and the doctor.

At the rate I was going, I could spend the night here. The swathe of strawberries, practically stretching to the snow, was contained by a stand of birch twisted into the most incredible shapes. Like myself, the stunted trees were unraveling high above the valley, papyrus-like bark prominent as Spanish moss, written in the wind. Heedless of any eyes that might be upon me, I unsheathed my camera and shot the enchanting dwarves.

I had my fill of the psychedelic berries. Visibility was excellent to the northwest. Possibly, I was looking upon Trichmir itself, the loftiest heights of the Hindu Kush. Below me, the Ushu was a ribbon far beyond the hotel, the thread that held together the patchwork of farms that partially blanketed the valley. Nice, but I had not come here for this and was obviously off course and getting nowhere fast. The carrot and stick had kept me going for the last hour, but with the dramatic appearance of storm clouds sailing up the valley, the muleteer's lash alone drove me on.

High altitude does strange things to man and decidious trees alike. I was soon making my way through an extraordinary grove just below the snow line. I left the cover of the enchanted forest to traverse a ravine. I heard shouting. Up ahead sheep were pasturing in a bleak rain-lashed landscape. Drinking tea, two shepherds were huddled together under a pastic lean-to. Evidently these young men commanded the pass through which I had to make my exit.

"Where are your friends?" This was not a reassuring welcome.

"They are coming," I replied.

"You must drink tea." The head honcho was bidding me to join them.

"No, thank you." I cheerily waved, and was about as nonchalant as a stroller in the park – at midnight. Once out of their sight, I ran like a deer who has just sniffed some gun powder. Even if the shepherds weaponry was no more sophisticated than a stone. More shouts. Maybe they were aimed at sheep instead of deer. I was taking no chances as the shepherds had apparently made a precipitous departure, and the loud shouts indicated they were gaining ground. Caution the better part of my dissipated valor, I made a wide sweep through an evergreen forest, trotting a good mile away from any route sheep were likely to employ in their descent to the village.

There was no sign of the wooly animals when I emerged from the forest somewhat sheepish myself. This was the first time today that I was happy to see a home. Anything resembling a home. Some of the huts were little more than clods pasted to the side of the mountain and could have been shepherds' refuges. I had left the Stone Age behind, yet it felt like I was running a gauntlet in the upper reaches of the village, where fields gradually gave way to houses. Hostility was tempered by curiosity.

But the indelible picture of the villagers I had taken with me is their reverent manner upon leaving the mosque. These men saw beyond me. Fortunately.

62

No Room in the Ark

Pride in ancestry is property, but generosity is piety.

Muhammad

My spirits dropped with the barometer. The air became oppressive and I could not climb high enough to cool off. Rain clouds continued to fill the upper valleys and playing about the summits, signaled the end of summer.

I was the only guest in the hotel, and Abdul, asking what I had paid, said I could sleep in his restaurant for half the price. It would not have been the first time I slept in a restaurant, but reckoned if I wasn't wrecked first, that I would be out of the country within a week and that a few rupees were not going to make or break me. In fact, the more economical quarters would break me.

It was sheer will that took me up to the shoulders of Falaksair. I had never fully recovered from my yellow plague, and when the rains would not let up, I contentedly stayed put in my pavilion. From my partially protected terrace, I reveled in the rain as if it were manna from heaven. In the morning I set out for Kalam. Abdul must have left earlier.

A half-mile or so below the restaurant is a schoolhouse. Oblivious to the rain, children were playing in the yard. A child let me have a rock for the road. Another parting shot from a small boy followed. A suitable sendoff for an infidel. The schoolmaster prevented a still smaller boy from pelting me, and chewed out the entire class. I don't know how far I walked before I got a lift.

I was only pelted with rain, but the combination of mud

and concrete was unappealing. And I was that much closer to sea level. I may as well have been for all the effort, or lack of it in this resort, to blend in with the alpine scene. If I had any complaints, I had come to the right place.

The doctor and Fazel were happy to see me. Ali had not written the note, and it was only with some prodding and in return for a note of my own, that he addressed a letter to whom it may concern, about the reason for my delay in reporting to the proper authorities. The doctor/pharmacist, was staying at the hotel of his friend who claimed to embody the Chamber of Commerce. Ali appeared to be promoting something, too, and aware of my expertise in selling iceboxes to Eskimos, encouraged me to put Kalam on the map.

I regret I did not photocopy the doctor's note. It was a classic. I was under Ali's care, taking an array of medicines for what read like a deadly disease, and there was no way for a healthy man to make the journey from Sust to Islamabad in three days, as required, much less a sick man. In those two or three handwritten pages there was no clue as to how I ended up in Kalam.

"Haven't you overdone it?"

"No. I know these people. A short letter would mean nothing to them."

Ali and the owner of the hotel had big plans for me. I was to write the script for the movie they were making, and was supposed to accompany them in their tour of the surrounding valleys. For a while it appeared as if I was to be the privileged prisoner of the Great Khan himself, but I convinced Ali that I really had to be moving on.

"Anyway, isn't this a bad time to be out shooting a movie?"

"Why?"

"The rain." Was I allegedly so sick that I was unaware that all hell was about to break loose – as it usually does in early September? Or was my doctor/pharmacist suffering from an overdose of the herbal remedy he was taking for a sore throat.

"Oh, it will stop tomorrow."

Maybe Ali truly believed that apres moi le deluge, but

the torrential rains did not wait for the metaphysician to leave town. A few days later a Reuter news item, buried somewhere in those back pages of the *New York Times* reserved for in back of beyond, read, "More than 1,000 people are missing after heavy rains this week in the part of Kashmir region controlled by Pakistan. . . ." Nobody was keeping count in Swat. I never did hear from Ali and Fazel.

The perpetual downpour caused landslides and floods in villages throughout northern Pakistan. "Residents blamed widespread deforestation," continued the article, and this definitely contributed to the deluge. Another article in the *Pakistan Observer* preferred to place the blame for much of the flooding on India. This is not as paranoid as it seems – and there is one flood that is definitely not an act of God.

India is flooding Pakistan with chemicals used to process heroin. In the states of Punjab, Jammu and Kashmir, camels make return trips to India loaded with automatic weapons, gold and silver – and all that surplus heroin, manufactured mostly in Afghanistan. Pakistan had become the hub of a new Golden Triangle as pressure from the west on Thailand, Burma (or whatever they are now calling it) and Laos has shifted the killing fields – now under water, many Pakistanis thought, because of India's damming of their rivers upstream and improper flood control.

Having no luck hitching, I allowed myself to be packed into a minibus headed in the direction of Peshawar – the hub of the hub and the gateway to the Khyber Pass. My final descent out of the mountains and into the static air of impending doom and gloom left me defenseless against the cascading flow of the Qawwali – wailing counterpoint to the white water that followed us down the valley. The devotional drums of the traditional music transported me to the lowlands faster than I was prepared.

"From where are you?" A young man in stylish western clothes was sizing me up.

"The U.S.," I said. It wasn't going to stop raining.

"America! George Bush! What do you have against the Muslims!?! You attack us in Iraq and do nothing in Bosnia!"

"Listen! Do I look like George Bush? I haven't even been to Vietnam." Thinking back on Ahmed's ridiculous outburst, I sensed the dandy was afraid the Islamists in the bus would shave his mustache and he was really putting on a show. He may also have been sending me on a guilt trip. He and his friend Kooky had come from Lahore to vacation in Kalam.

Ahmed's chubby, lighter-skinned friend has perked up. "America. I've always wanted to go to America."

"You and your uncle."

"Yes, my uncle, too."

Kooky was in his early twenties and was decidedly more interested in Michael Jackson than George Bush. But even he was bound by the national obligato of condemnation of America – kept at low-key, to be sure. Soon, the pudgy young man was playing up to my appreciation of nature, pretending to give a hoot about the passing scenery.

"Look how pretty!" And so it went until we arrived in Mingora – which happened to be the town where the taxi driver – the hopeful émigré lived.

My new friends intended to catch a regular bus from Mingora to Lahore, but many of the roads had been washed-out and we found outselves in the same boat. In need of a place to sleep. By the time we arrived at a restaurant to take stock, Ahmed had changed his tune. An old man gave me a quizzical look from under his topee. I asked Ahmed where the old warrior got his hat. They exchanged a few words in Urdu.

"Do you like it?"

"Sure." The engaging ancient was smiling – or laughing at me.

"He wants you to have it."

"But...." The graybeard was pushing his topee on me.

"Take it," Ahmed said. "It's old. He has another one upstairs."

"Does he want to go to America?"

"No. It's the custom. You admired it; he gives it to you."

I can't say there were no strings attached to Ahmed's generosity.

No Room in the Ark

"Why are you bothering with your visa? You're an American, you will be leaving the country. Their only concern is that you have an airline ticket." I didn't buy that.

Ahmed was more proper than dapper. Neat as a pin, while Kooky was something of a pinhead. A bowling pin, and Ahmed knew just how to roll over him. I seem to recall his saying he was a low level bureaucrat, and if he was uncomfortable with me, it wasn't so much that I was an American but that I was un-American. The topee was on my head. And none too soon as I left the restaurant every inch the Pathan (but for my large boots), with the Kooky tourist at my side. The older Ahmed had instructed his unlikely companion to accompany me to a travel agency.

Ahmed looked after our belongings, in all likelihood realizing he had sent us on a wild-goose chase, since capturing one would be my only hope of being airborne. I gave no thought to what he might have up his starched sleeve. When Kooky and I returned to the restaurant, it was time for my young friend to hold down the fort while Ahmed and I sloshed about in and out of traffic, taking the starch out of him, as we inquired about accommodations.

"You and Kooky were gone almost an hour. And he couldn't get any information?" There was less suspicion than insinuation in his remark. Kooky was incompetent. I was now in capable hands. Incidentally, "Tony, I want you to help me go to America."

"Look, man, you and the taxi driver down the street and everybody else I meet. I'm the last American you want to ask for help. I don't know if they are going to let *me* in the country. I've already threatened to renounce my citizenship.

"If you want to go to the consulate in Peshawar, fine, fine, but...."

On second thought, that's all I needed was to show up in an American Consulate in Pakistan with my track record, but there was no need to renege (if there is indeed a consulate in Peshawar).

"No, no. All that is required of you is that you write me a letter when you return to America." Ahmed didn't get into the particulars. And Kooky? Every man for himself.

"You and Kooky are welcome to visit with me and my wife for a week or so, but I can't sponsor anybody." I'm not rich, I added.

"I have money. No problem." And Ahmed and Kooky tried to demonstrate that by footing the bill. We returned to the restaurant in a dismal drizzle in the dark but decibel shattering street, shadowing a lone cow that had apparently missed the ark. It was, after all, a rain of Biblical proportions.

Underscoring the "Sinking Ship" hysteria that gripped so many Pakistanis, besides the "unemployed," was an article that appeared a couple of days later (September 11, 1992) in the *Pakistan Observer* that headlined "Thousands Evacuated. " In a twist of irony a boat is shown assisting the evacuation. The "Opinion" piece in question, written around the drawing of a boxing glove ("Our Punch") clenching a pen, appears above two columns of "Sayings of the Holy Prophet." It reads:

> In the old days sailors used to be very upset when they noticed the rats were abandoning their ship....A sure sign that the ship would sink on its next voyage. The state is frequently spoken of as a ship, and one can suppose that the young unemployed youth are the rats who leave the ship when they think that the future of Pakistan is bleak.
>
> One such Pakistani youth made three unsuccessful attempts to seek asylum in Germany on one plea or another, but he was deported and had to return to Pakistan....The fourth time he claimed refugee status because he said he was gay....The plea was accepted by the Germans and he is now happily settled in Germany, enjoying his newly gained freedom from moral restraints....

63

Peshawar to the Khyber Pass

He was handsome....with a taste for wandering through unexplored portions of the earth, and he arrived in India from nowhere in particular. At least no living man could ascertain whether it was by way of Balkh, Budukhstan, Chitral, Beloochistan, Nepaul or anywhere else. The Indian government, being in an unusual affable mood, gave orders that he was to be civilly treated, and shown everything that was to be seen; so he drifted, talking bad English and worse French, from one city to another, until he foregathered with her Majesty's White Hussars in the city of Peshawur, which stands at the mouth of that narrow swordcut in the hills that men call the Khyber Pass....

"The Man Who Was"
Rudyard Kipling

I awakened to people brushing their teeth outside my room. They had slept on cots outside my door. I did not have a refreshing sleep and was glad the comedy team had joined my act – though now it seemed like they meant business and I was their bargaining chip. Swat Express Travels was of no help, and we were on the first southbound mini or Mickey Mouse bus.

I had not seriously considered going to Peshawar. I had my fill of low adventure, but there we were in the middle of nowhere, or rather, Nowshehra, on the south bank of the cresting Kabul River. I thought I would be able to get my ticket in Peshawar. The reputedly exotic city was only twenty miles out of my way. I still had hopes I could avoid the capital. And what soldier of fortune could resist the lure of the fabled Khyber Pass – even if he was suffering from battle fatigue. I would die with my boots on.

To be sure, the Khyber Pass was in the back of my foggy

mind only; getting to Peshawar seemed impossible, let alone going on to Afghanistan, but that's where the road west led, when we poured into a three-wheeled motorcycle cab, and roared off at a good twenty miles per hour in a driving shower of manna and monoxide, with a maniac at the helm.

I had passed up the Pass in those halcyon sixties and early seventies, when Kabul was one of the stops on the hippy high road, which led through that swordcut in the hills, slashing its way into Kashmir. There, a fork in the silt road took the seekers who survived the Ganges up to Nepal or alternately going through Southeast Asia to trail's end in Singapore, where they paused long enough to wash-up before boarding a ferry for Indonesia and some of that magic mushroom soup. Out of season myself, I managed Nepal and what was open to me before waiting for my ship in Singapore. The Indonesian Consulate had closed the door in my face (lack of funds) and I ended up taking a slow boat to Sarawak, when headhunters were still practicing their craft.

Looking through the prison or prism of my time warp, I now considered the Khyber Pass passé, with little interest in the present intrigues that wracked Afghanistan and its eastern border. Nor did I know the borderlands were off-limits to foreigners until it was too late. . . .And so for the benefit of the CIA, Mossad, etc., concerned about my whereabouts or what I'm about, it wasn't even a lark or an ark that took me into no man's land, no foreign order from beyond our border but the Fates themselves. Somebody has to keep you informed.

Peshawar was a disappointment for reasons beyond the aftermath of the Afghan war that left this provincial capital with the predictable problems. The refugees had been relocated to nearby camps, but the malaise of Asia and the rest of the world remained. The taxis, alone, with a nerve jangling decibel range left me limp; my bed came with wet sheets. . . .and the usual complaints underscored when water was under foot and it was time to go home. A vast subcontinent was very much a part of my past and I wanted the book closed on it – it was time to go to Mona.

Evening was a taste of the Arabian nights – large plates

of brass and copper, surrogate suns in the darkness of the old city, a touch of brightness, which I believe is the title of my old Indian friend's book about the Bombay brothels. I had a very different guide now, on a markedly different tour, a less sanguine market where one enjoys the dish, without handling the merchandise.

Kooky and I were sauntering about the ancient bazaar and souk – if that's the Urdu word for it. "Souk" is market in Arabic, which has greatly flavored and favored a lingua franca – Urdu – that includes Turkish and tribal languages also, mostly northern in origin. But when India gained its independence and lost its western and eastern regions to a newly formed Pakistan divided by hundreds of miles and vast differences in culture and race, the then West Pakistan tried to foist Urdu on what was to become Bangladesh.

Mountain customs spilled into Peshawar. I admired the handsome blankets I had seen in upper Swat where they were used as cloaks.

"You like, Mr. Tony? I buy for you. Good souvenir."

And a practical one, but I demurred. Kooky saw me as his ticket to America, and he was trying desperately to make his down payment in whatever coin was available; conning me about his wealthy family on the one hand; but with the other, vowing his willingness to wash dishes in America, if that's what it took to make it. And yet he had obviously dined on more than rice and chapati and had not overly exerted himself to come by it. I can not recall what he did to earn a living. By the end of the day I was coming to the realization that I would not be flying from Peshawar.

"My uncle is a nuclear physicist in Karachi. You will stay with him when you go to Karachi, Mr. Tony." It was truly amazing what the magic word, the *open sesame*, America, could do for your image in the third or fourth world. If ever a frog was turned into a prince, it was in these murky waters.

"Please. Don't call me mister. Tell me something. Why do you want to go to America if you have so much money? America is no longer the Promised Land." But he had already bought the Brooklyn Bridge. And little he wanteds was for sale in Pakistan.

"I have a cousin in Brooklyn, He says it is pretty."

"He's lying to you. He is ashamed to tell you that he is still washing dishes." Or driving a taxi.

"No, Mister Tony."

Most of the Afghan rugs in old Peshawar were sold out of an office building, four or five stories high. We end up in a tiny room on the third floor where several refugees from the war were having their dinner in the familiar embrace of their wares. There was something striking about these merchants, so soft sell that I imagined these men to be Sufi. The mystics of the Muslims, seekers beyond the divisions of religions: "Lamps are different, but the Light is the same."

A touch of brightness, indeed. We don't come full circle, but rather wind down spirally – spiritually if the Gods favor us. The elusive brother becomes brotherhood, wherever there is light. What was a 500 watt bulb compared to this Aladdin's Lamp?

We were invited to dig into the merchants' meal of scrambled eggs. There was an amazing grace about these men, a dignity enhanced by their robes and trim beards. Like men reading sacred texts they never removed their hats. I was really sightseeing, but when we finished eating, I bought a small mat that showed a camel with what looked like a banner planted in one of its humps. Why the flag? I asked. It was actually a sail, for isn't the camel a " ship of the desert?" Once the camel was the ship of state. Indispensible.

Nearer to our hotel, in the new section of Peshawar, the desert ship had been replaced by the warship. Tanks and all the refinements of modern warfare had been woven into the very – the literal – fabric of Afghan life. The Arabesque flowers that had once graced Afghan rugs had been replaced by Kalashnikov rifles; the magic of these carpets had been perverted by the nightmare the weavers had not left behind them. What ghoulish shopper would purchase their handiwork of rocket launchers and strewn bodies? And yet these refugees had to work out the horror of the war and earn a living.

The rug had been pulled from under me. Designs that

once held you entranced and were an invitation to meditation were supplanted by atrocities. These late twentieth century tapestries depicting Afghan life and death amounted to an allegorical call to arms that sounded across the land long after the last departing Russian and Rambo. Without an obvious common enemy giving a semblance of cohesion to Afghanistan, sectarianism racks a country that even the British could not subdue; as early as 1919 recognizing it as a sovereign and independent nation (which doesn't mean that Britain stopped playing the Great Game).

A visit to the carpet shops was like a trip to the museum, yet there is no more grotesque perversion of harmony than in these carpets – outside modern museums. What had amounted to a welcome mat had been defiled – reduced – to the obsessive style of today's artists whose twisted personalities screamed out from their splattered canvas and mutilated sculpture. An important difference between the Afghan's handiwork and the nihilistic play of the modern artist is that the nightmares of the refugee is history and serves a purpose.

Ahmed was waiting for us in the restaurant of the hotel. "My God! I thought something happened to you. I called the police."

This wasn't hard to do. Uniformed men were crawling all over Peshawar. Ahmed was chewing out Kooky. I said it was all my fault.

"No, it is not," Ahmed responded. "He said he'd only be gone an hour or two. Kooky should know better. This isn't America, where you can just walk the streets as you like." Ahmed was on a roll, with no regard for reality. "I'm going to the Khyber Pass tomorrow, Tony. Do you care to come along?"

That would bring me that much closer to the nightmare. And if I ever had a calling for war, it faded before I left the military. But here was this proper fellow wanting to take to the hills, not by a long shot a swashbuckler, and my own sense or obligation to witness, prompting me to consider a Khyber Pass that had not emerged from the mist of time and the prevailing weather. No matter my sorry condition, Ahmed had made me an offer I could not refuse. I could not look the war horse in the mouth, succumbing to the rumble of the "Drums," and the spirit of my very own Sabu. The gates of hell were too near to avoid. My only fear was that the tourists may have done what the British and other terrorists could not.

Kooky was still snoring away when we left the hotel. In the light rain we boarded the wrong bus, a wretched rusty wagon that impelled us to secure more amenable means of riding when we embarked on the second bus. This could only mean, despite our lower status, climbing up the ladder on the back of the bus, and holding on for dear life topside. Securing the best perch on this howl, we crawled along the floorboards on the roof of the bus to the bow. A protective railing caked in rust just barely boxed us in.

Inside and outside the bus, you had to be extremely careful of what you held on to. Jagged edges were everywhere. No passenger should have been allowed to board this tin can without proof of a tetanus shot. Falling off the roof of the bus could be risky business, also, but this amounted to nit-picking after considering the fates of my shipmates.

I am a man of many hats and the one that seemed to fit most comfortably was the one I was wearing.

"You resemble a Pathan, Tony." In fact, I was more at home up here than Ahmed. My topee and my clothes had a ragged enough edge to them for me to pass for a returning Afghan refugee. My harried expression could only raise an eyebrow as these men took things in stride, but I was soon passing inspection. A large sign warned: "Foreigners Are Not Permitted to Proceed Beyond this Point."

"Hey, that's me! I have to get off this damn thing."

"No problem, Tony. Foreigners don't ride on the tops of buses." A uniformed man scanned the roof of the bus. From his ground position he did not even give me a second look. A hatless blond man drew no attention either.

"Isn't he a foreigner?" Ahmed spoke to the man in Urdu. His no-nonsense air alone indicated he was indigenous – at least since the time of Alexander.

We passed through an independent enclave that was probably the Afghan sponsored Pushtunistan (Pathanistan).

Peshawar to the Khyber Pass

This was home to many of the refugees or tourists as my Pakistani guidebook might refer to these latter-day guests in this buffer zone between Afghanistan and Pakistan. The tiny principality mostly subsisted on the manufacture of heroin and the huge black market in contraband. The availability of weaponry, apparently, was not considered the most troubling problem here. What really made Pashtunistan beyond the pale was the sale of liquor. And if it seemed that I was evolving into the man who would be king, mixing my Kipling, I would have given my kingdom for a beer.

A few miles beyond the camps and mud-walls that appeared to go on forever, forts held the high ground. We had come under the jurisdiction of the Khyber Rifles, who stood dressed to kill outside their post. They could have been the doormen for the Taj Mahal Hotel. Wearing their dress uniforms, topped with red turbans, the soldiers appeared to be as nappy, if not happy, as they were in the days of the British Raj. A future tourist attraction on parade – though I don't doubt their rifles were loaded. The elite fighting unit was disbanded at the end of the Third Afghan War in 1919, but this British legacy had been resuscitated.

The Khyber Pass, obviously, was not listed in my little tour book, but this was the High Adventure, Low Gear, Trail of Alexander, Mogul Moments, Forgotten Forts Remembered Again, rolled up into one madcap ride. Was my questionable guide trying to kidnap me, gone around the bend, himself, or simply trying to make points with this little Cook's Tour. This Low Gear, High Anxiety trip was definitely out of character for Ahmed, but he saw America at the end of this rainbow and was emboldened by my own background, just as I liked the idea that my Sancho Panza was an Urdu-speaking civil servant.

I passed inspection, with barely an upward glance in my direction. I was getting seasick, but giving little thought to the chaos likely to be awaiting us, dreading the ride back. What I disliked most about a return trip was the ride over old ground at the end of the day and a second night in my concrete block in Peshawar's cacophonous center. So disturbed was I at the thought of returning to my wet sheets, I regretted leaving my bag behind and passing up this opportunity of traveling through terra incognita, incognito. Kabul seemed preferable to Karachi.

Carefully placed stones on the side of the hill read: "WELCOME TO KHYBER RIFLES." The welcome probably dated from before the last Afghan War. Of more recent vintage was the cigarette ad that bid you "Welcome to Afghanistan." Or was that a joint. I thought the forgotten brand would be burned into my mind. Ironically, like a prop, a nearby camel resembled a giraffe rubber-necking in the upper branches of a thorny tree. A one-hump camel or dromedary. Further on in Herat, ancient travelers traded in their Bactrians for these Arabian camels. In this no man's land there are many mixed breeds. The sun came out as we entered a Khyber Pass known for temperatures pushing 120°. (But this is not Afghanistan.)

Kipling's swordcut is a defile that narrows to two hundred yards, ample room for the army of Darius the Great and the invaders who followed in his wake. But a tight squeeze for today's legions of the damned encamped at the side of the road in the shadow of limestone cliffs towering as high as one thousand feet. With more than five and a half million refugees scattered between Pakistan and Iran, you could stumble upon them anywhere. In the Khyber Pass most of the refugees could be found to the east of Fort Ali Masjid and the head of the Khyber stream. Two streams form the bed of the defile and are home to a people whose existence is as unpredictable as the source of the water. Running for more than thirty miles, much of the Pass isn't nearly as dramatic as it is near Landi Kotal Fort, close to the border. The air is so heavy with despair and displacement that even at this high point, it was tragic.

"I have never done anything like this." Ahmed was ecstatic. I was fascinated by his transformation. From Kafka to Ali Khan. I wrongly credited myself with Ahmed's metamorphosis; the talisman who imbued him with his new found dementia or daring, that sense... absence of fear that occurs when the free spirit is near – "America is big" and the luck of the Irish would rub off on him; what the hell was the Khyber Pass after going up, down and around China; my good fortune would not fail him on his holiday. No, it is more accurate to say, perhaps, that removed from the familiar, the spirit was able to move him – and the rest was an object in motion.

Turigan was the last stop. A restaurant and a bite to eat. The waiter worked with the Americans during the war. He said he loved the Americans. He survived by living in a time-warp.

"Why doesn't America do anything for these people?" Ahmed asked.

"Would it be politically expedient?" I replied.

Border-bound we were packed into a pickup truck. A young man wearing a hat like mine struck up a conversation with the tourist, Ahmed. "He doesn't believe you are an American."

"Neither do I." The man was returning home to Kabul. He lost his family in the war and had been living in Peshawar. He pointed to my camera. Ahmed said, "He says don't take anybody's picture without their permission. They will pull the film out of your camera. Or worse."

This Afghan seemed friendly enough. "He would like you to be his guest in Kabul. You can stay as long as you like."

What could this refugee be returning to? But again, I was cursing myself for leaving my bag behind. I would only have stayed in Kabul long enough to get my bearings. I could have ended up on the Trans-Siberian railroad after all. If I got out of Afghanistan alive.

64

A Short Walk in Afghanistan

> "Oho, art thou lickspittle of the English? Go in tomorrow across the border to pay service...."
> The Blind Mullah hated Khoda Dad Khan with Afghan hatred; both being rivals for the headship of the tribe; but the latter was feared for bodily as the other for spiritual gifts....
> This is the worst of all ill-considered handling of a very large country. What looks so feasible in Calcutta, so right in Bombay, so unassailable in Madras, is misunderstood by the North and entirely changes its complexion on the banks of the Indus.
>
> The Head of the District
> Rudyard Kipling

We were left off a few hundred yards from the Afghanistan border. A park provided an almost shielded overlook of the border post and a contingent of Khyber Rifles. Stealthily, I took their photo, thinking that this joy ride had gone far enough. But Ahmed was still on his roll.

"Shouldn't we go to the border?"

I would live up to my reputation. We were beyond the Khyber Pass and the range of a proposed tour – official tour – but I hesitatingly gave the marching orders. If we were questioned, Ahmed would be my new doctor. A psychiatrist. With little effort, I could be the imbecile who did not know any better, should we be questioned.

Beyond the guards, the Khyber Rifles, at the side of the road is a sign in English: YOU ARE ABOUT TO ENTER AFGHANISTAN. The normally reserved Ahmed, oblivious of the Khyber Rifles, stood beside the sign. "Please take my picture, Tony."

A Khyber Rifle approached me. The guard said something in Urdu. In response, I drooled.

"He wants you take a group photo."

Sure enough. Two rows of Khyber Rifles had materialized. I had emptied the building. Ahmed standing at the center, the soldiers were at parade rest. Not fifty feet away the refugees streamed by, the refuse of war piled on carts, a swarm of the disposed and the possessed. In traffic that went both ways, an army of ragged stragglers freely crossed the border. A man who blended into the crowd may have been making what would have to be a very spotty spot check. A floating population that shared this frontier engulfed the two sinking ships of state.

It was my turn. Decked out in my beige beret, Chinese Army canteen slung over my shoulder, looking like I had one Singapore Sling too many, I stood there beaming, the American military advisor to the Khyber Rifles proudly showing off his charges. Ahmed snapped away. Had I my wits about me, I would have borrowed a "rifle" and posed properly. Of the nine men who lined up, only a couple or so were in possession of their automatic weapons – though the whisk booms planted in their headgear appeared fierce enough. Unlike my troops, I lacked the red drooping sash (and, as it turns out, my canteen. Momentarily).

Pushing our luck a little, we climbed the steep knob behind the Khyber post. Ahmed was questioned, but we gained permission to take this high ground and take stock. We were just beyond the mouth of this devil's throat. The Khyber Pass is so much a part of the Kiplingesque, the high point of British adventurism, that I could not make the association with ancient Buddhism. But there remain traces of this more spiritual time far below the forbidding palisades and the forts that command the Pass. Kafir Knot, the citadel of the Kafirs, is here, shards from Asoka's kingdom and the Greco-Bactrian states, but I could only hear Hollywood's echo of the Khyber. (Recently, I came upon one of Mona's old Kipling books.)

The fractured and bleeding presence was so much with me that I could not imagine a life before the Khyber Rifles and the first British incursion in 1837. Afghanistan, being one of

Britain's larger losses in the Great Game and its attempt to girdle Asia, you must wonder if her surviving hostility against the Afghans might stem from sour grapes. An Englishman, a respectable travel writer, commenting on the Afghan War, said that it could not happen to a more deserving people.

Ahmed had managed to get permission to cross the border. Did he bribe somebody? What or who was Ahmed, really?

"Come on, Tony."

I was heading for the other side, when a guard called something out. Ahmed interpreted. "He wants to know who you are."

"Don Quixote."

"From what country?"

"Tell him I'm the American ambassador to Afghanistan."

"I don't think you have one."

I was looking at the signs just beyond the border. One sign in English announced the relief work being done by Canada.

"I'm the Canadian ambassador." I think this poor fellow had already absconded. Most of the signs were discouraging. One sign described the mines you could encounter on the road to Kabul. The signs in English probably dated from 1989, when peace looked at hand, but I saw no signs of cars and people who could read English.

This was no place to be sleepwalking. I could not quite believe that I was part of the pedestrian traffic. To be sure I have blindly walked into miserable situations before, but Afghanistan was almost another Vietnam. In some way it had been a part of me for years, yet despite my cavalier approach, I was ill-prepared to come face to face with it. Sancho Panza had become my Virgil, as we descended into this futuristic limbo. The drama of Khyber had been replaced by a bleak grayness where the survivors of the flood mingled with the survivors of war and all is a bloody metaphor. There was no room in the ark – and on every level life was imitating art.

The mines, the endless oppression caused by displacement, reminded me of Israel. Not a few hundred yards beyond Pakistan's border on the south side of the road, stood Afghanistan's abandoned border post. Faded signs welcomed hippies. I was twenty years too late. That image of the era, the error of my ways, seized me with a melancholic nostalgia. A half-mile into Afghanistan, a bridge spanned a dry riverbed. It was guarded by a heavily armed militia of sorts. Blade runners. Rambo. Had I walked into a class B movie? These poor souls who knew nothing but war were still playing at being soldiers, I thought. But a clearer look back seems to indicate that these young men were guerrillas securing the road to Kabul. It was less than four hours away.

    A quarter of a mile up the riverbed was another refugee encampment. How long could this wide wadi remain their home before the sandy bottom was under water. Trees seemed out of place here. Stalls and rickety sheds marked our way. The only permanent structure was a huge truck container surrounded by plastic fuel jugs. A sign in front of this supply depot was partially blocked by an old man with a vacant stare. He would be a safe enough subject for my camera.

    A rough looking man pointing to my camera approached me. Certain that this gorilla wanted to take my camera away from me, I wondered if I should stand my ground. Considering how far my diplomatic immunity would carry me here, I called out to the browsing Ahmed.

    "What the hell does this guy want? I only took a picture of the sign. Tell him how good Canada has been to Afghanistan."

    "He wants you to take a picture of his friends."

    The sign read "Security Guard." Fifty yards off the road, flush up against a cliff was a guerrilla camp. Street soldiers without a war, but this was only a brief intermission in the fratricidal strife. Ten year veterans, and not one of them out of their twenties. The camera happy man had led Ahmed and me back to his comrades. Armed with their Chinese rocket launchers and automatic weapons, they posed for posterity. Did they think I was with the New York Times? They practically demanded that I photograph them. You did not know if these guys would break your camera because you took their picture, or because you did not. Only vanity would vanquish these people.

Ahmed asked the guerrillas if they would launch a rocket for him. A man stirring a big pot of stew put aside his ladle and fired the launcher. Excited by this sense or nonsense that he was part of their adventure, Ahmed asked if he could have a shot at it. Voila, the Milquetoast became Rambo as Rimbaud who had undergone his own transformation years ago, placed his hands over his ringing ears. Not that they weren't ringing to begin with, but these decibels left me debilitated for a few long moments.

"Try it, Tony. You'll like it."

I disliked Ahmed for this macho or martial display. The man was in his thirties, there was no excuse for it. Though I guess such a transformation is predictable in the humorless martinet. If he was so enamored of destructive toys that go boom, boom, why didn't he go to Bosnia with the muhjahidin and put his life where his mouth was. So this was what was behind Ahmed's uncharacteristic spirit, the cheap thrill of being near the action, that rush that has nothing to do with wanderlust but everything to do with pornography, a basic emptiness filled with loud noises and forbidden pleasures. Oh, Ahmed was so thoroughly American. I would have no part of his coming to this country.

I could see Indus Guides extending the range of their tours into Afghanistan. For ten dollars a tourist could fire a rocket launcher, and for a little extra, lunch with the muhjahidin. For now these war games were restricted to the most enterprising travelers, and I must say that Ahmed remained immaculate through it all. I looked like a casualty myself, but as long as Ahmed identified me as an American, my rough edges went unnoticed. I was a big shot. Today all but the most marginalized third and fourth worlders are aware that a Westerner can't be judged by his wardrobe. But Ahmed had more than his shirt going for him. In a part of the world where people know their place, his boldness spoke of privilege.

The first major town on the road back to Peshawar was an island of opulence – be it behind the counter – in a sea of misery. We must have passed by it on the way to Afghanistan, this duty-free oasis that remained a mirage to all but the monied.

Ahmed was fondling odd photographic equipment, conned by a persuasive salesman, when I realized the antique camera he was about to buy was Russian. I discouraged him from buying the thing.

"Why shouldn't I purchase a Russian camera?"

"Would you want an American samovar?" Who but gunrunners and drug dealers and manufacturers would come to this God forsaken place. Indeed, they lived behind the mudwalls of the traditional villages at the mouth of the Khyber Pass. Most of the stores were closed because it was the eve of a holy day, and Ahmed was the only shopper about.

Again, we rode in the air-conditioned class of the bus. This relic had transported wheat to Afghanistan, and what remained was the chaff swirling about in the heat. I got the stuff in my eyes and ears and had a taste of unbaked bread, but it was a small price to pay for otherwise fresh air, until we were back in Peshawar.

Going around a huge traffic circle and pie-shaped park and refreshment stand, I remarked about this refuge for couples. All of them men.

"It must be difficult being a young man in Pakistan."

"Yes, this is the reason I must go to America," Ahmed pleaded, not beating around the bush. "You cannot meet women as you do in the West."

"Seek political asylum," I advised.

"You mock me. You must help me."

"Listen," I shouted above the roar of the three-wheelers. "If the Chinese can get asylum on the grounds that they can only have one child, then you should get asylum because you're not getting the opportunity to have *any* children."

65

A Sinking Ship

...*Our leaders, political, social and religious have made such a society that quite a large number of young persons would sell their souls to the devil to escape this society and take refuge in Europe. This is a matter that merits serious attention. It is a disgrace to our country and society that whenever America or any European country invites applications for immigrants, millions of people, young and old, rush to the visa office to obtain their passports to their earthly paradise. People beg, borrow or steal lakhs of rupees needed to obtain forged visas to America. Hundreds are deported back to Pakistan, but that does not deter others from persisting in their attempts to settle in another country.*

More from *Pakistan Observer*

For every line of self-criticism, Pakistan's newspapers churned out paragraphs about Indian disintegration and their blame for much of what ailed Pakistan. Sagging morale was boosted by the prospect of Enemy #1 coming apart. You think you have had it bad – look what's happening on the eastern side of the border. And much of what I had read about India in 1992 sounded convincing. Recently, the Public Broadcasting System (PBS) televised propaganda about India's booming middle class of one hundred some odd million people – playing down that other caste-ridden eight hundred million or so who have absolutely no hope of boarding the Titanic (which may be their salvation). The conflict in Kashmir was just the tip of the iceberg.

India was the place for American businessmen to get around pollution laws and fair labor practices.

Had I known that Kabul had been bombed recently, I

would have been less troubled about returning to Peshawar. At the rate I was going I could easily have become a part of that flood of refugees with sacks on their backs on the road to Kabul – without a scorecard.

I really had not made up my mind about Kooky and Ahmed. My old lifeguard instinct, the fool rushing in, was in conflict with my own precarious situation and my lack of any real feeling for them. Ahmed was a stuffed shirt and Kooky could not keep his tucked in. I'll say this for Ahmed, he made no attempt to hide his contempt for me. His plea was becoming a command, when in my heart of hearts, I remained Kipling's *The Man Who Was*. And, granted, the Khyber Rifles were not Her Majesty's White Hussars, but few beyond Kipling's character could have enjoyed my Carte Blanche.

After eating we toured the street market in the rear of the hotel. Ahmed bought a wild array of nuts to take back to his family. When we returned to the room he shared with Kooky, we were greeted by Kooky's "uncle." Kooky had mentioned that his uncle would be able to provide me with the rupees needed to buy an airline ticket for the states. The idea was to give me the black market rate.

The problem was that I would not be able to buy my ticket here – or anywhere, unless I had a valid receipt for the exchange of my travelers checks. This I only half-suspected. Nor did I know where this transaction was supposed to take place. Maybe they just wanted to see the color of my money, but I told them I had better change my travelers checks at the bank. That's all I needed was to get stuck with hundreds of dollars worth of worthless rupees – and no ticket. I told Kooky's uncle I would go to the bank.

"But the bank is closed tomorrow and you don't have a visa."

All of a sudden the lack of a visa meant something. What was the hurry? I went along with the game anyway. The following morning Kooky, his uncle and myself scooted down to Dean's Hotel on a three-wheeler. The long low-slung bungalow was a holdover from the British heyday, and was to Peshawar what Raffles was to Singapore. Even if I was the only tourist there – and trying to change travelers checks at that, and had the backpack that Kipling left behind. It was a tranquil isle in a sea of traffic, and I made the most of its spacious green grounds. To think I passed up this refuge because I feared the price of a room here might place an airline ticket out of my reach.

I could not cash my checks. There were no two ways about it – I was going to Islamabad. Finally. My bus was right across the road from Dean's sanctuary. Waiting in the garden for the departure of my bus became one of the more pleasurable moments of my entire trip. Basking in the golden silence of an early sun, with barely a hint of the heat to come, I just wanted Kooky and his uncle to float away. But it was I who was cast adrift. Through it all, I was still clinging to my bag.

Not a rifle shot away, was the commanding fort that inspired Kipling. If Dean's wasn't here then, at least a reasonable facsimile was, and I can see the old jingoist hotfooting it to the bar after, perhaps, a phantom tribesman took a potshot at him. You can still get a drink here for an unreasonable price.

We had checked out the railway station yesterday evening, and there would be about a half-day delay due to flooding. The bus trip to Rawalpindi was only a few hours, but thinking of my more enjoyable train rides, I pined to be a passenger, reluctant to pass up an opportunity to stay off a bus even if it meant a very long wait. What was a little hell and high water compared to a bus ride? I would find out.

Kooky saw me off at the bus station, giving me a bag of apples as a going-away present. He looked so harried trying to please me. Not only was I yelling at myself, but my outbursts had become public. At least I was more fun to be with for Kooky than the tyrannical Ahmed. Whatever Kooky's motives and schemes, he finally got to me as he called out to the departing bus.

"Don't forget to write, Tony!"

Oct. 5, 1992

Dear Kooky, Asslam-o-Alaikum!
    Thanks again for the kindness you have shown me. I trust that you and Ahmed returned to Lahore safely,

A Sinking Ship

and were spared the worst effects of the flood.

Riding through the flood area revealed just how terrible it was; nor was the train ride itself a pleasant experience, and arriving in Karachi, I was very sorry you hadn't given me the address of your nuclear scientist uncle.

I stayed in Rawalpindi only long enough to get my visa in Islamabad, a real run-around, my "genius" (as you would say) not withstanding. The Ministry of Interior was not impressed with my status.

Obtaining an airline ticket (the necessary discount) involved some trickery beyond my diminishing patience. On the other hand, had I changed money with your Peshawar uncle as you urged, I would still be in Pakistan. Is not "genius" respected in your country!?! No problem. Inshaallah we will meet again. *Tony.*

God help me. Taking care of damage control, Ahmed answered.

March 14, 1993

Dear Friend Tony,

We, I mean Kooky and Ahmed were too much pleased to find your letter. But we were surprised that we got your letter after five months. We could not understand the reason. Why did this letter reach late to us....We get any letter from American within fortnight. We are quite well and spared ourselves from the worst effects of the flood. We are trying our best to come to America. Insha-Alla very soon we both will be in America and again we will have a good company and you will be our comrade in America's visit. We both remember the good time we spent in Swat and Peshawar with you. I am sending of you the photographs of Peshawar and Afghanistan. President Bush has gone and Clinton is in power. What do you think about him? Is he a good person? Is there possibility for us and you to see a war free world during his presidency? OR he is crazy just like Bush?

Pay our compliments to your wife, your friends and those you like the most.

Yours Sincerely,
Ahmed and Kooky

66

Rolling Down to Rawalpindi - for Eid Milad

> *The only persons who did not share the general regard for the White Hussars were a few thousand gentlemen of Jewish extraction who lived across the border, and answered to the name of Pathan....*
>
> The Man Who Was
> *Rudyard Kipling*

> *We were slaves during the British Raj and that was very bad. But there is no harm in recalling that law and order was better in those days....*
>
> News Post Sept. 1, 1992
> The International News

The Pathans called the White Hussars "children of the devil." It is my feeling that today's government may be seen as coming from the same stock. Pakistan's coziness with Iran may be related to Iran's support of the non-Pathans in the western part of Afghanistan. Showing favoritism to Iran-backed factions, which cements the centuries-old bond that it has with its spiritual mentor. While the Pathans were one of the less manageable minorities on a borderless deck awash with loose cannons. (Kooky and Ahmed were not Pathans.)

If ever a country was caught between the devils and the deep blue sea, it is Pakistan. Here it is, partly tongue in cheek, pining for the good old days of that other Big Brother: "*America was always so helpful and considerate. They gave us their Korean tanks; they chose our dictators for us; and for our peace and quiet, disposed of the two most noisy among them. It is they who gave us the title front line state, and even took Bashir, the*

Rolling Down to Rawalpindi – for Eid Milad

camel driver, on a grand tour of USA."

In fact the tongue was dripping with venom. More from The International News: *"And though we were bushwhacked by George, and he ran away with the balance of the money owed us for playing the frontline idiots. . . ."*

Peshawar was still on the front line. The same newspaper ran an article about unexploded bombs, scrap meant to be fodder for the steel mills that went off, when they were unloaded at the mills. These explosive imports were part of the Afghan War surplus.

"Hello, Tony."

I was looking out the window at the bucolic bus station. I was slow to turn around. The CIA, a voice from the past catching up with me – an old China hand tapping me on the shoulder – who could it be?

"Tony, a rupee." The young beggar had heard Kooky. Admittedly, his knowing my name gave him an edge over his colleagues. I tossed the kid an apple.

The bus station was uncharacteristically empty. I was one of a handful of passengers who would attempt to cross the Indus on this tin can. With the sun here to stay and this strange peace in the loading area, I was loathe to leave, longing for the tiled mosque in the old quarter. I wanted to feel this peace in optimum circumstances, and for ten minutes be like a normal tourist – though there's nothing peaceful in that.

The bus seemed to be racing the rising river. It made a quick stop at a restaurant near the Indus. The swollen fleuve was like a large lake that had spilled over its banks. It may have already crested at this juncture, where the Kabul is swallowed up by the Indus – though it would be some days before the high water inundated the south. I stood behind a large tree as the swollen river lapped at my feet. We then embarked again, seemingly sailing across the river and into the sea of humanity in Rawalpindi.

It was Friday, Muhammad's birthday, with no chance of acquiring my visa until at least Saturday. With Islamabad being the showcase of Pakistan, a cardboard capital, I would have to be accommodated by the stepsister of the twin cities. No problem. I had the address of a Planeteer hotel in Rawalpindi, and compelled to indulge in a luxury, was soon taxiing toward the city where the real work was done.

Rawalpindi is on the wrong side of the tracks, and in due course we were crossing them. A strangely quiet ride took us past the small mosque and the ancient railway station, which tugged at me the way trains always did before I slept on one Chinese train too many. The old quarter exuded the calm of a backwater – perhaps enhanced by the fact that the railway workers were on a hunger strike. At least they were on August 28th when the *Frontier Post* showed a photograph of the forlorn strikers, looking all the more pathetic sitting on the ground, in some cases barefoot.

The striking workers looked like prisoners of war. Above their photo was an article about Pakistan's Chief Justice, on tour in the U.S., delivering a speech at the New York Bar Association. He was dispelling the impression that Pakistan was a fundamentalist country. Anything but that. The Pakistani newspapers were rife with articles about the smuggling of children into the Emirate States, Qatar, Amman, Sharjah, Dubai, Bahrain, Kuwait, and last but not least, Saudi Arabia, for whom Americans went to war. There is evidence that the camel children are sold to a drug mafia and that their "organs are of further use," besides being forced to race frightened camels for the amusement of the idle rich. Protesting workers everywhere were getting the business end of the police baton. . . .Discontent mounted throughout the nineties.

Anyway, the federal minister for religious affairs said that Pakistan was moving toward a "true welfare Islamic state," but American lawyers would have none of that.

One flight up the stairs of a paradise hotel is the receptionist desk and the restaurant – and a quiet cup of tea. In a few moments I would have a ringside seat for the procession of celebrants who had brought half the city to the broiling side street up the road.

It was good seeing people celebrating and not just surviving; so gratifying to see the colorful bunting and the band, that a pied piper was able to draw me away from my table and into the costumed throng. This was Eid Milad, the Muslim Christmas, and the procession was not unlike those Italian affairs on New York's lower East Side – except the New York Italians were honoring San Gennaro, while Muslims from every walk of life were emulating as much as celebrating their Prophet. From Karachi to the Khyber Pass.

A touch of Catholicism in the huge heart hanging from a man's neck. And a man in Arab headdress leading the holy parade is probably playing at being The Prophet. Muhammad's birth is so near in time and place to that of Jesus (six or seven hundred years in that era was just so much sand) that it occurred to me, not for the first time, that beyond trotting out the manger scene for its ho, ho, ho authenticity, the celebration of Christmas as we know it, is more a pagan ritual than an expression of Christianity. We are more comfortable with Santa Claus than its Semitic roots. (Although the real Saint Nick was born in Turkey.)

38. And I have followed the religion of my fathers Abraham and Isaac and Jacob. It never was for us to attribute aught as partner to Allah.
The Holy Koran

The flood was in the back of my mind. There was no sign that the "King River," flowing 1,700 miles before reaching the sea, was inundating much of the country.

67

Islamabad —
Vis-a-Vis a Visa

Only the British conquered the Subcontinent from the South and faced tough resistance when they reached the North. Finally, when they left, after two hundred years of rule, they abandoned a world only they could have created. Army garrisons, forts and outposts, railway tracks, dark bungalows, grand messes, deserted air fields, beautiful churches and quiet graveyards.

Travel Tips

My present room was heaven compared to my purgatory in Peshawar. A sweaty night, but with little traffic in the back streets below, a relatively quiet one. Like a jungle floor, there was a delightful decay about my accommodations. I went up to the roof before going to bed and looked out on an almost rural Rawalpindi lit up like a Christmas tree. Most of its million inhabitants seemed to congregate on the main road.

I returned to the roof in the early morning, took my wash off the line and then slowly made my way to the road. I stopped at enough travel agencies to intue that a flight out of here would be no picnic. Getting to Islamabad was a draining ride or two of cacophony and color and carbon monoxide. I had little else for breakfast.

Islamabad, after Kampala, is probably the most improbable capital in the world. Not on most maps, it appears to be one of Italo Calvino's Invisible Cities. Most of the vehicles crawling in the direction of Islamabad were diverted before actually coming to this Camelot. They would remain in the real world.

This broad unfinished Washington was constructed by Greek architects in 1961. A subliminal tribute to Alexander who had a habit of building his own invisible cities in Pakistan and passed through nearby Taxila, before his infamous Indus cruise.

The nomadic conquerors from the north, the Ghaznis, Ghoris, Khiljis, Tughluks, Lodhis and Suris may not have left much of an architectural imprint, but Babur was a builder and after his defeat of the last of the Afghan kings in 1526, ushered in the Moghul's golden age. They left behind masterpieces in stone and marble, including the Taj Mahal. The Moghuls built Lahore Fort and altered the symmetry of Pakistan with the Shalamar Gardens – where President Rafsanjani of Iran received the key to the city (and the hearts of the fundamentalists).

A Grand Mosque holds the high ground against the cooler Margalla Hills, one reason for transferring the capital from Karachi to the edge of the world. One excavation site had become an inhabited (human) jungle and is an interesting juxtaposition to a skyline limited to the Foreign Ministry and the Ministry of Interior.

One of the larger travel agencies had directed me to the immigration office, where I foolishly went. The chauffeur for a Connecticut-based aid group poetically came to my assistance.

I had firsthand experience with the kind of aid Connecticut gives fascist governments, when an Argentine soldier in one of South America's less welcoming railway stations let me have the non-business end of his made-in-Connecticut automatic weapon in the stomach, but this perhaps unsuspecting Pakistani was a godsend, driving me halfway to the Ministry of Interior on the other side of town, leaving with me the name of a high-ranking official.

There I was across the road from an interminable field and afraid the official would be out to lunch by the time I got to the Ministry. Luckily, I was able to flag down a passing taxi and made it to the bureaucratic Acropolis in a matter of minutes. I presented myself to the front desk in the lobby and gave the guard the slip of paper with the official's name. A quick phone call, and relieved of my camera, I proceeded to the elevator and up to the fifth or sixth floor.

Getting a taste of the red tape in an outer office and the

prospect of unraveling the Gordion knot, I produced my doctor's note from my friend Ali Khan and began babbling like the sick man that he described. I was dealt with promptly, superseding other characters with connections and shown into the office of the official. I was with the man as long as it took him to read Ali's outrageous letter – apparently on the mark, because I was dispatched as if I had the plague. And I mean dispatched, because it was necessary to have some forms photocopied, and I was being sent to a shopping mall to have this done.

"I'm sick! Why can't I have the copies made here?"

"We don't have a copy machine here."

Bullshit, I thought. I stepped outside, went into a government printing office at street level, but it looked hopeless. I had to have the forms back within the hour, or I was required to return in the morning. Panic. I practically commandeered the limo of a diplomat ready to drive off in the direction of the mall. They are, after all, a diplomatic breed and what better way to dispose of a madman than to take him to the mall.

Actually, the diplomat spoke to me as if I were an old friend. But I only recall that he had spent time in Washington and like a diplomat agreed with everything I said.

I had just enough time to get my copies and a fruit drink and I was back on the road, fit to be bound and gagged. I don't know how I returned to the Ministry, but I got back just under the wire. In a few minutes time the official had completed the necessary paperwork for me to be eligible for a visa. But where was it?

"You must go to the passport office."

Predictably that was on the other side of the town. It closed at one o'clock. More hysteria. I had a half-hour, and after my rollercoaster ride through Asia, the thought of returning here was unthinkable.

It's a matter of life and death. I work my manic magic and in a matter of seconds I have a lift to a bus stop. Wrong one! Fifty yard dash and I plow aboard. Ten minute ride, asking directions. The passport office is near the carpet shops. A mad dash down the street and I breathlessly arrive at the nondescript walk-up squeezed between two carpet shops. A hookey street. This can't be it. It's it! It's it, the rug-man is telling me.

I ran up the stairs in a frenzy. Cool it! Cool it! Your life will be in some flunky's hands. Five minutes to closing time and I enter an outer office. A fellow is reeking of condescension. A gofer whose accent indicates a stay in the States.

"We are closed. You must return tomorrow."

The shit hit the fan. "What are you talking about!?! My watch is working!" But he didn't want to. "We have five more minutes. . . ." The more I talk the louder and more rapid my speech – if that's the word, as I brought down the wrath of God from my crescendoing screech. I was apoplectic, apocalyptic. The man is persuaded that perhaps something can be done today, after all. I was led to a stately office – entirely out of place in this dumpy building.

Apparently, the large distinguished-looking gentleman at the desk is having a little tete-a-tete with a family of future Americans. I give them a dose of the real America. The world must stop for us. With just enough condescension the eminent gentleman signs one of the papers I've given him. The gofer has returned to his hole and I am to go back to him. Visa, with a green stamped gratis, has filled much of the last unmarked page in my passport.

It's official. Dox Quixote had arrived. There was no reprimand or raised eyebrow – none that I noticed – about entering this spy besotted country without a visa. But then they had my number, the letter. China's loss had been their gain.

I had five days to leave the country.

68

Check Mate

And ye will be paid on the day of resurrection only that which ye have fairly earned.

3:185 Al-Quran or The Koran

Returning to the street, I was still an object in motion. Karachi was only about a thousand miles or so away, but who could measure the light or dark years involved in such a journey. Even the number of days required to get there. I was not thinking about the length of the stay I was allowed, but the need to move on – the compulsion – and know where I stood. If there was a travel agency here, it did not occur to me to check it out. And had I gone anywhere in Islamabad, it would have been to the mosque -- but this gleaming beacon was on the outskirts of town. I had to weigh a visit to the sacred sanctuary against the fact that the bus to Rawalpindi stopped across the street.

I suspect this was the Murree Road, which took the top brass up to Islamabad's Camp David -- a hill station to the north that was in all likelihood abandoned by the British when they vacationed there. Iran's President got the key to Lahore -- though it was probably in Islamabad that he received the first Persian translation of a Koran to appear in Pakistan.

Heading for the railway station in Rawalpindi, I had little hope that the trains would be in operation, realizing that even if they were running, they had better be buoyant. On the plus side travelers would be discouraged from riding on a train in the literal wake of a flood washing down to the sea. But I envisioned the airy rides I had enjoyed in rural India.

Check Mate

News reports had been tracking the progress of the high water, but this was complicated by the many mouths the Indus had to feed. A number of rivers merged with Pakistan's Nile, damned rivers that had not been regulated properly and had contributed considerably to the devastation. This had caused yet another scandal.

If I could not sail to China, I wanted to sail away from Pakistan. There was always the romance of the sea, and I wanted desperately to wind down and get the wind back into my own sails. Karachi was my port of call in 1967, when I was homeward bound.

The trains were still running. I was unaware of the hunger strike, if it was not already over. Things moved along at their usual unhurried pace as I rested under a shed of little-used rickshaws and pony carts. I had no problem buying a ticket for the following morning, at an unsolicited foreigner's discount – which foreigners did not need, even if they did not have the price of a drink, which cost about the same as a rail ticket to Karachi.

And this was first-class, but an air-conditioned class was also available. If this meant that the windows opened or there was a fan in the coach, or even a cooling system, I don't know. The first-class discount could not have lured too many foreigners aboard the train, nor did I see anyone in the second, really third-class, remotely resembling anyone from the west or anywhere beyond the borders of the subcontinent. Air-class cost a pretty rupee.

With some effort I found the building where I was to buy my ticket and get my reservation. This bungalow was across the way from the station and is an interesting antiquity that was nearly empty. While waiting for the transaction, I noticed a worker drinking tea. It wasn't long before I was served and making myself at home on a couch. A taste of Sahib lacking across town, where I had made an earlier attempt to leave Rawalpindi.

Sky Lord Travels would not change my travelers checks. Nor could I cash my checks in the bank.

My tour of the travel agencies was more than spinning

my wheels. When I'm in places I would rather not be, I tend to gravitate to them the way old sailors eventually find themselves by the dock in the bay. Travel agencies have a magic about them, often offering you an air-conditioned world and an escape from noisy and hot, dusty or flooded streets.

The deal was that I had to prove to the bank that I was cashing my checks for immediate purchase of my airline ticket. Most banks would not change my checks anyway. The most fascinating travel agency was underground. A kind of concrete bunker or candlelit bomb shelter. I'll assume the agency had a power failure, but then I did not see any tickets being sold and there was something clandestine about the place. It appeared to cater to Pathans.

Pathan is actually another word for Afghan, the eastern part of Afghanistan that once had the power and voted against the admission of Pakistan into the United Nations. In 1949 the relations between the two countries were so strained that Pakistan flew over the border and bombed the Pathans. Later that year, Afridi tribes, fearless Pathans, announced the establishment of the new state of Pushtoonistan (Pakhtunistan), adopting a flag of a rising sun behind a red mountain. This was probably the flag that flew over my Eagle's Nest north of Kalam – where the owner posed with his war surplus.

Diplomatic relations between Pakistan and Afghanistan were broken off in 1955 and resumed two years later. But the continuing strife between the Pakistanis and the Pathans culminated with Pakistan again bombing the Pathans in 1961. The Russian menace, the Afghan War, apparently, brought the bordering countries together, as well as those other kettles of fish in Kashmir and the Kutch to the south, perhaps persuading Pakistan that it had too many irons in the fire.

The Indo-Pakistan war of 1965 was related to both regions. Pakistan's forcibly holding on to an unwilling East Pakistan (Bangladesh) resulted in another war between India and Pakistan in 1971. The war lasted less than two weeks with Pakistan accepting an unconditional surrender, and losing its quasi-colony as well – albeit fellow Muslims. The war over Kashmir is one of those endless conflicts that take me back to

Sudan and Israel, and some places I have not visited.

Further complicating Pakistan's politics, was the official conversion, in 1997, of the North West Frontier to "Pukhtoonkhwa" (Support Pukhtoon) – indicating that the Pusto-speaking Taliban, controlling much of Afghanistan, by 1998, were now carrying a lot of weight within Pakistan. Beyond the Pathan community. But the politics change as often as the spellings.

Many Islamists accuse the Taliban (Religious Students) of being puppets of the Pakistan military and security forces, who in turn have been accused of having a hand in the drug trade. Curiously, these young muhjahidin are supported by Saudia Arabia. Saudi insurance.

69

Karachi Choo Choo

Railway termini....are our gates to the glorious and unknown. Through them we pass out into adventure and sunshine.

E. M. Forster

The early morning was cool enough to enjoy my walk to the railway station. Outside my hotel was a stall the Lonely Planet had put on the map. A newspaper stand that made life more bearable for the denizens upstairs.

I wanted to bring home more than yesterday's newspaper and the few odds and ends I picked up here and there, but I had a train to catch. The station was insulated by the railway village that served it since the days when the trains were run by the English and passengers were the likes of E.M. Forster.

Breakfast was available in the small restaurant across the wide way. Fumes from the kitchen drove me out into the road. In the rear of this teahouse is a dak – the nearest thing to my preferred dock. In Kipling's day this building was responsible for the Indian Post. Nice place to write a card.

Time to see about train's estimated time of arrival. At least a couple of more hours to wait. That's alright. I had four days. I stepped outside. No imprint of anything motorized remains with me. Delightful. A whiff of manure in the air. The part of the station itself that attends to passengers was little more than waiting rooms and the first-class restaurant that is the railway's Holy of Holies. A place to prepare for the straight and narrow.

Which track? No information on that yet. With the

heat getting to me, I went into the high ceiling restaurant. The sun streaming through its elevated windows is burned into my circuitry like the cathedrals of Europe. The half-light of the halfway house. Is all this worth the candle? For what they are worth, my memories is life regained – you've lived as much as you have remembered.

A perusal of the Sunday International News hits me with this front page headline: *Death Toll in Floods Rises to 1,707.* You know it is double that. Next to this, in much smaller print, the headline reads: *13 Die in a Road Accident.* It's not related. I'll have another more substantial bite to eat before the long haul. Oh, yes, waiter, could you please fill my canteen with boiled water?

"Yes, Master."

My waiter is an elderly one-eyed man who could never break this nasty habit. My order is some mush that includes an egg. An hour passes. I'm in no hurry, but this is ridiculous. Finally, the waiter returns with my order. I don't recognize the egg and question the waiter. He points to an uneatable object on my plate.

"This is a fresh egg?" I ask.

"Yes, Master, fresh,"

"I've never seen an egg like this."

"All eggs like this," the one-eyed waiter replies. He sees something I don't see, but I can't bring myself to complain.

I walk across the overpass and board the train for Peshawar. Wrong train, but right track. I manage to get off the train before it chugs out of the station. I find and board the train to Karachi, which is a half-day late, but this was par for India without the floods, and Spain under Franco. I'm shown my compartment and my ragged body is transformed by rage.

"Where are the windows? I need light!"

"Sir, the windows are here." The conductor leaves.

I looked through the iron bars behind two small half-windows. Innovations to keep out the sun and sons of guns, and, perhaps, to prevent passengers from escaping. My compartment was at the end of the coach, so that its entrance was a few feet from the gangway. And did not open on the aisle but the door to the coach. Master, indeed!

Smoke was coming out of my ears and the strangest sounds from my mouth. My cellmates were bewildered, concerned about my behavior. Particularly the gentleman who sat on the rack below my own. The racks were attached to the wall where you usually find the often half-glass doors to your compartment – which means you normally have light and air coming from both sides of the coach.

"You have a problem, Sir?" The man beneath me had spoken.

I had dumped my pack on the rack that would be my bed. My own carriage was about to go off its track. I stepped back in the dim light and just glared at the poor fellow. He had become like those fish so accustomed to living in dark caves that they lose their vision. The great Persian poet, Sadi, may have seen it differently:

> *Oh, thou, full man! Barley-bread pleases thee not;*
> *She is my sweetheart who appears ugly to thee!*
> *To the houris of paradise purgatory seems hell;*
> *Ask the denizens of hell; purgatory is paradise!*

"Damn!"

"What is it, Sir?"

"Just look at this place!" Of course, I was the fish – and I was out of water. Flipping out in my effort to return to the sea. And my concerned cabinmate, going to live with his son in Karachi, perhaps displaced by the flood, had as much appreciation of my plight as the fisherman does for his catch making all those jerky movements at his feet. I was stewing in my juices, on my way to early dehydration. Degradation. Where were my powers of meditation when I needed them most? Gone with the last gram of Vitamin B.

Filled with myself or not, my stomach was shrinking to the size of my brain. Like those naked fakirs on the banks of the Ganges, I can live on little more than love, but there must be a decent interlude between insane situations and disappointment if you are to roll with the punches. Another writer might take this opportunity to look back with longing to China's much maligned trains. China, itself. If I were capable of any comparisons at the time, it was only with India. China had become another trip – planet – as journeys I had made years ago through the subcontinent had surfaced.

I have a vivid memory of trying to enter a partially open toilet, and seeing a man lying on the floor who had kept the door closed with his legs. Half naked, he was actually holed up there, practically in the hole himself, in, I assume, an effort to elude the ticket collector or conductor. I really can't determine when or where I disturbed this abject fellow. Was it on this packet of miseries they called a train?

I was leaving the compartment.

"Sir, where are you going?" The train was rolling out of the station. I replied to the concerned man that I could not remain in the compartment.

"But this is your compartment. You shouldn't leave here."

"Why? Am I quarantined?"

"It's not safe to be walking about."

I informed my friend that it might not be safe if I stayed in the compartment. Another cabinmate told me to take my bag with me if I left. There were three or five other passengers in the compartment besides myself, as many as the remaining racks. I must have been the ugliest American on the planet, but these somber men were as accommodating as could be expected. I decided to sit by the half-window in the half-light and allowed the grating sound of my own wheels turning to give way to the calming mantra played on the tracks by the train.

Traveling east, we were moving into the darkness that would come to India early. Yes, we were heading in the wrong direction, but only the tracks are straight and narrow – the way has never been direct. Scrub and hardscrabble had succumbed to the still swollen Jhelum, one of the streams paying tribute to the voracious Indus. The retreating Jhelum had probably wreaked the most havoc on the already war-torn Kashmir, and took more than four hundred lives on the island of the same name. At this point I have little recollection of the human tragedy outside my window beyond the day-to-day struggle to survive. Desert and flood, desert and flood and the calamity of a country in extremis.

The Chenab was the next large river that we crossed, and in our passage towards India, rolling over the Punjab. Another river to cross and then with dusk, we were upon the Ravi. From this river, Lahore seemed to stretch to the very gates of India – and the name still conjures up one of the more sparkling jewels in India's British crown; when they became the successors of the Mughal emperors.

Thanks to Akbar much of the consolidation and organization of India was fait accomplis. Until the independence of the subcontinent, the British monarch used as his Indian title that of the Mughal emperors, Kaisar-I-Hind. And so, when we marvel at how the British were able to give form to that miasma that has brought many a white man to his knees, we must look to that noble descendent of Timur and perhaps Genghis himself, Akbar. One source claims that the Mughals were Mongols. Mughal sounded more respectable. As if the Shalamar Gardens, the Taj Mahal, tiled mosques and exquisite paintings of fiery red embossed with gold didn't give these steppe children entry to a place of higher calling.

Their extravagant taste is a carryover from the days of the great Khans, when silk textiles were woven with large quantities of gold thread (lampas). Marco Polo knew these glimmering fabrics as "cloth of gold," often used as currency on the trade routes.

Lahore, depending on what you read, was once the capital of Pakistan – and Karachi was not. Whatever, with a population of about 5,000,000, Lahore was the capital of the Punjab and is to Islamabad what New York is to Washington, D.C. – in almost every respect, including travel time. Which means that despite its perhaps precarious location squeezed in between Afghanistan (or, rather, the Pathans) and Kashmir, it is near the action. Possibly wishing to reflect its Islamic drift – as opposed to the more catholic stance of the Mughals – Lahore has been renamed Faisalabad. As far as most maps are concerned, that's another one of those invisible cities. The sign in the railway station indicated that I had arrived in Lahore.

I could not believe it. I had friends in Lahore, but unaware of the route of the Karachi Choo Choo, I was totally unprepared for a visit I had written off in Peshawar, not even bothering to get a phone number. Despite my apparent inability to know when to say when, I knew that as much as I wanted to break this journey, the thought of taking on Lahore singlehandedly at this moment was unappealing. A false move and I could disappear around the proverbial bend.

Were it just a little earlier, had I been able to consider Lahore's considerable treasures, I would have made my escape from the train gang with the devil in pursuit. But like the stoic gentlemen in my cell, I had already, with Muslim resignation of another age, accepted what appeared to be the inevitable. (I would have been dealing with Ahmed and Kooky on their own turf, but this would be something of a homecoming compared to my present imprisonment.)

In the morning I would do Lahore my way. And if it were possible in this shrinking world to find a travel agency with a map of it, and I was capable of taking a hard look at it, I would have realized that New Delhi was much nearer than Karachi. But I really was an object or abject in motion and going with a flow which happened to be moving inexorably to Karachi. And here, in Lahore, was Kipling calling out across the city and the years: When your Demon is in charge, do not try to think consciously. Drift, wait and obey.

It is possible that the gates of India would have been closed to me, but the disturbing thing to the once agile traveler, or unraveler, is that I did not even see the dime, much less have the ability to turn on it. India may have been the last place in the world I wanted to visit, but that was before I was ready to pack it in with Pakistan, and because I could not pull myself out of the quicksand of the past. Even now the idea of India makes me stammer, but had I a magic carpet, a time machine, I would have made that break in the journey and gone on to India and the next station of the cross. Which could have been Fatehpur, the introduction to this book.

I want to see how India stacks up against Pakistan's projection of it, so at odds with America's promotion of this nuclear power that has learned to love the bomb and may not have Islam's best interest at heart. The atom – there is your Shiva and the worship of this creative destroyer has surpassed the love of Vishnu. The subcontinent created Shiva and ultimately will leave the world quaking with his atomic ejaculation. The coming of the Lord, indeed.

Continuing on to India would have closed a circle, maybe tied a noose, and Lahore, even behind glass, was projecting what I could expect on the other side of the Sutlej River. Just beyond the city the river divides the Punjab into its respective parts, with the Indian portion, the more populated, stretching all the way to Tibet. For all I know, I had a glimpse of the great mosque or the Lahore Fort, but what really stays with me is that hodgepodge of Punjabis that filled the streets and portended a perilous disembarkation.

Part of the Mughal legacy is a priceless collection of Korans, scriptures laced with lapis azuli. One shows a Mughal-like Alexander descending to the bottom of the sea. The subcontinent? There is that Persian link here, but also the propensity of the world to appropriate the wayward general.

Akbar was really a Turkoman and not the refined Mongol who comes by way of Persia. Actually, the Mughals also descended from Turkic forebears. With so many rivers on this ancient crossroads, it has to be one of the more simmering pots and its spilling over on to the train.

I retreated to my upper bunk.

> *I fled from men to mountain and desert,*
> *Wishing to attend upon no one but God;*
> *Imagine what my state at present is,*
> *When I must be satisfied in a stable of wretches.*
>
> Sadi

70

In the Wake of the Indus Flood

You cannot travel on the path before you have become the path itself.
                                                                Buddha

...Asia is not going to be civilized after the methods of the West. There is too much Asia and she is too old. You cannot reform a lady of many lovers, and Asia has been insatiable in her flirtations aforetime. She will never attend Sunday school, or learn to vote save with swords....
                                                                Rudyard Kipling

Alexander's mutinous tour group did not persuade this raging alcoholic to turn back until they were at the banks of the Beas River, the then Hyphalis, which runs through the Lahore District.

What's become of Kipling's newspaper office in Lahore? How interesting to be British and visit the haunts of your grandfathers. Akin to being a German with relatives who had been in the war – except the British make no apologies for the mess they have made of the world. Indeed, some Englishmen have been so bent out of shape by the white man's burden, that even today they can talk about the Great Game as just another chess match – and complain about the Oriental treachery that did them in. Why do we let them off the hook so easily? Because we have always played the same game? Are we so impressed with the plagiarizing Shakespeare and the Big Stick? Or is it the guiding hand of the Monarchy that keeps us in line? Made for television comedy.

Dark came early; I don't recall if our compartment had a door or not. If we did it was usually open. The light directly overhead remained on the entire night, but it was dim enough not to disturb me. Strangely, I'm left with a warm feeling about it – like a stationary moon, the one constant in our Stygian rumble through the night.

Alexander did not fare well when he passed this way. Sniping tribes harassed the retreating spoilers through much of Pakistan. Our own descent to the sea followed the courses of the Ravi and Sutlej Rivers, passing Harappa around nine or ten. The city was contemporary with Mesopotamia. We had long left Lahore's industrial zone, the mills and cotton fields that fed them. Unseen amber tracts of grain followed the train, and then around midnight, rocking around the clock, we pulled into Multan.

My bag swollen with papers and rags had become my pillow. I had removed my shirt, but the night air had caught up to us and I left my grainy perch to slip into something. We were now traveling southwest, yet India's frontier retreated little. And then we were heading toward India again, crossing the Sutlej River, and still rocking through the night, following the course of the Indus, when the Sutlej and the Punjab were no more.

In darkness, we passed in time and place the beginning of the Indus civilization that endures to this day in India. Excavations at Harappa revealed a city belonging to the Chalcolithic culture, lofty citadels like the Sumerian ziggurats of the Euphrates and Tigris valleys. This Indi-Sumerian period takes us back to about 3000 B.C.

Ancient Sumerian texts refer to an eastern land called "Meluhha," source of pearls, inlaid furniture, ivory, hardwood and jewelry. So fabled was the Indus valley that it was thought to be Prester John's magic kingdom, centuries later when the Nestorians journey east. Flat-bottomed boats depicted on ancient seals are similar to boats in use today. The wildlife revealed in the seals, elephants, rhinos...has mostly vanished – or never was. The unicorn had a special place in society.

Beyond the bars of my window, on the banks of the Ravi River, this ancient civilization went on for a thousand miles, deep into the Indus valley, culminating in the priestly Kingdom of Mohenjo-Daro, south of Sukkur. Discovered here was a dancing figure thought to be Shiva, in style and spirit emblematic of India – contrasting with a famous marble sculpture of a bearded shaman or priest reflecting the mask-like quality of the Mesopotamian busts, also unearthed here. The hard corners of the Euphrates valley seemed to be evolving into the fluid culture that spread to India itself. India's stratified society also appears to have its origin here. In Mohenjo-Daro, people knew their place.

Pre-dating Buddhism is a seal that bears a seated cross-legged figure; another shows a Bodhi tree, also symbolic of Buddha. As in Babylonia, the cult of waters thrived here, and now the remaining buildings of well-burned brick may well have been under water.

By mid-morning, we were at that juncture before Sukkur, where the eastern tributaries, that great basin for the Himalayas, had been swallowed up by the still gorged Indus. Had we gained on the crest? We followed in the wake of the flooded river, funereal cars hellbent on reaching Karachi.

I try to account for each mile in the spirit of the archeologist searching for that one shard that brings it all together; or, like the paleontologist seeking the fossil that can give form to a life. Yes, we travelers are the architects and the archaeologists of the soul.

Unless we understand the underlying factors or currents that push us this way and that, the voyage remains meaningless. This question did not arise early on when there were places I wanted to be, but once I came out of the mountains and walked in the valley of death, I needed to see a fossil beneath the folly.

James Joyce's *Last Words* may provide perspective: "A man of genius makes no mistakes. His errors are volitional and are the portals of discovery."

And on we rolled to Karachi.

It is amazing that something so central to the human condition as travel can be considered beyond the pale. But then our ivory towers have been constructed by sticks in the mud, and so we have respectable publishers – so-called New Left – who have never published a book on travel, when migrations, individual and collective, are the essence of history, literature and life itself. All the great thinkers and tinkers have been travelers. . . .

For all the one and two week getaways, the rhythm and booze cruise, we are so sedentary, fixed in our ways, that the mention of Odysseus, or rather Ulysses, takes us to Dublin. Eternity reduced to a day – and while we may see the universe in a grain of sand, it is not quite the same as being a beach bum, or seeing the sea.

Each uncovered mile or memory is yet another milestone or calcified bone revealed, that much sand or dust brushed off the Rosetta Stone that points to True North – or a paving stone on the Appian Way of the soul.

By mid-morning I was traveling between the compartment and the kitchen. There was no real dining area, and I was considered an interloper. This must have been second class, the car housing the kitchen. We prisoners in first class had our food brought to us. My cabinmates were looking after my bag, but I wasn't very careful about my own pockets. I was sitting near the kitchen, basking in the sun, when the train went into a tunnel. The land was flat – had we gone under the river? Just before we plunged into darkness, a young man sat next to me, and presto! When I returned to my first class dungeon, I discovered that whatever I had in my pocket was missing.

It may have been my ticket or my Pakistani guidebook that was swiped, it was not that important. I returned to the kitchen area and informed the soldier or guard posted there what had happened. Eventually the missing item was recovered, but not without raising a little hell. I was told to remain in my cabin.

But as the train gained on the flood, I felt more and more like an intruder at a funeral – like standing vigil at the side of dead villages. Never did I feel more the outsider. Perhaps that was because I was rolling by, barely touched by the calamity. Yet privy to the most personal distress – people stripped of everything, but for a few rags all traces of their existence washed away.

In the Wake of the Indus Flood

Somewhere down the line we had slowed to a snail's pace. Not knowing where we were lent itself to this sense of being in limbo. Human flotsam washed over the train. Were they passengers? Who would turn them away? Was this a funeral car or a lifeboat? Is there redemption in reliving this journey – baring belated witness? Did I feel guilty because I would soon be above all this – the river its cargo of sorrow.

My *American Voyageur* comes to mind. But for the ending, it is a non-fiction book, as I wind up the voyage being confined to my cabin and escaping through my porthole, jumping into the sea. In the continuing spirit of life imitating art, up to a point, I was now being ordered to stay put. Just getting from one car to the other was fraught with danger, and while I was not about to jump ship, I did abscond from my compartment and looked out the now open window on the other side of the car.

My left hand rested on the sill. This heavy porthole had a metal frame, and I was careful not to touch this jagged escape hatch. A view of the sky was escape enough. Peace. But I was under a Damocles Sword, and like a guillotine, the window dropped.

"Damn!" My curses trailing off, I returned to my cabin. My mates look on in amazement.

"Sir!" My somber friend was appalled at my language.

"This damn train! Look at my hand for Christ sake!" In the semi-darkness of our tomb nobody had noticed the gash running an inch or so below my white knuckles. A trickle of blood topped my swelling hand. There it was, fated; inflated, red, white and blue. I was once again flying the colors. The concerned man grimaced. He was apprehensive, genuinely disquieted by my wound and my outrageous reaction to the accident.

But I could have been just another victim of the flood outside the window. My friend's involvement ended with the suggestion that I should do something about my hand. I sat there dumbdounded, in pain. Yes, now we were in the same boat.

71

Arrival in Karachi

East of Suez, some hold, the direct control of Providence ceases; Man being there handed over to the power of the Gods and Devils of Asia....
Mark of the Beast
Rudyard Kipling

The confluence of my streams of consciousness with the actual course of my journey may appear fantastic, because while much of my writing is spontaneous combustion, it is shaped by the cognition of past events. So what may seem like clever fabrications meant to jibe with my exploratory jazz is really the other way around and the way to unravel. But again the real poetry or doggerel is in the dogged journey – the dog days. Bow wow!

Accidents don't always give much warning, but the window was one waiting to happen. If the Boy Scout's motto is to be prepared, the free spirit will let the chips fall...I had some bandaids tucked away somewhere.

"Please get some ice!" I shouted.

"Where?" Had hell frozen over? What was I asking of the poor man? A vendor had been making the rounds with a bucket of soft drinks and I had noticed ice. "Go to the kitchen!" I commanded, and I proceeded to lick my wounds as my shipmate went in search of the icy salve. A few minutes later the concerned man returned to our compartment without ice. He said that his way to the kitchen was blocked. My real fear was tetanus, but didn't see there was much I could do about that, beyond keeping my hand covered and staying out of harm's way. Within an hour the iceman cometh.

"Ice! I need ice!" I even bought a soda. A young wretch outside our compartment mimicked me. "Ice! I need ice!"

I wrapped the unsterile salve in my cleanest shirt and applied it to my hand – and my head and my face. Nearly emptying the bucket of its ice, I was soaking wet. A river fed by too many tribulations and a flooding consciousness that would no longer be contained by its banks.

All that talk about hell – it was just that. This was the River Styx. Like the Indus itself we snaked our way through the sandy Sind. We had remained in Purgatory – and still I had the good fortune to be able to take a bath.

Hyderabad was the next stop. I had been to Hyderabad in India. Sand castles rising from the beach. More dislocated people. My hand and head throbbed. The cursed heat. Soon I was getting more ice. By late afternoon I was venturing forth into a less crowded corridor.

I peeked into the compartment behind ours. It was empty but for a young man. What unheard of luxury, I thought. I sat opposite the polished fellow, looking out the window. Could it be I was walking around free? Who does this guy know? He's a medical student, believe it or not. Didn't he hear my symptoms earlier?

By morning I was as fragmented as a fruitcake, and the choo choo itself became a metaphor for my train of thought. On the western bank of the Indus, we were able to skirt the delta, and chugging westward over undistinguished desert, head directly for the Arabian Sea and crazy Karachi.

I can't help thinking about that other great river that defines the subcontinent – long ago I compared the Ganges to the subconscious. The Ganges, with all its problems, did not leave me with Pakistan's despair. Pakistan's flood didn't help matters, but it seemed more a reflection than a cause of the resignation. India is so steeped in the ancient ways that it is hardly effected by current events.

A much larger India further distances the Hindus from corruption and the sense that the center is not holding– because the center is an individual matter. A lot of India's magic lies with an unfathomable world that the Ganges personified. Beyond its high mountains, I saw no such distancing or transcendence in Pakistan. Except for the mosque. Westernized people especially, were everywhere touched by an air of hopelessness and helplessness beyond Mammon's succor.

We would soon be in Karachi. I had to act fast. Scheme. I had no plans. Nothing new in this, except that I was hanging by a thread. When I had the world on a string. I'm being very friendly with the medical student. Shouldn't I be in the hospital, I'm asking the obliging student. Would he happen to have an uncle in Karachi who is a nuclear physicist? Has he ever thought of going to America? But what was this strange alchemy that had brought so many doctors into my orbit?

No, my new cabinmate would not be going to America any time soon. And he was in no position to do more than board a bus with me when we left the station. His friend, however, happened to be a travel agent. My hand has moved to the back of my head, and the aspiring physician is not overly concerned with an infection. Enough beer had remained in my blood to immunize me against tetanus, but my injury develops into what one doctor called a trigger finger.

The travel agency is not very far from the Officers' Club. If these were naval officers, it was as close as we got to the sea.

The Club was across the way from the less tranquil traffic island that boasted of a first-class hotel. World-class. It was there the student took me to await the arrival of his friend whose agency was around the corner. Maybe it was closed, but here in the glittering lobby of the hotel it was hoped I would check into, the agent began reeling in the big fish. I spent the night in the Gulf Hotel. Two nights in what is a strictly Islamic establishment that seems to cater to that part of the Persian Gulf not rolling in petro dollars.

72

American Express

And when nothing goes according to plan
Or one has no plan to go to
The chain of uncommon events
That breaks our link with "reality"
Takes on cosmic tailoring
Comic in retrospect
But tight fitting at the time
And forever uncomfortable

From Under the Southern Cross
Tony Cammarata 1976

A ship out of here was out of the question. Shipping in Karachi had fallen on hard times. The mainstay of the seaport – had only been developed in recent centuries by Hindu merchants. Arab invaders introduced Islam but it was really some years before Islamic architecture flowered into the remaining fragments scattered about the city.

As humble as my hotel was, I was not inclined to move. There was something very fundamental about the no-nonsense Gulf that I found very appealing. Not a slave holder in the bunch. I did not know what I was getting into, but I was welcomed and the Gulf was peaceful. No uninvited guests. That such a place could hold me was a measure of how far I had traveled.

After wasting most of my time trying to pin down the travel agent to a non-existent discount, I was off to the bank with just enough money to cover the cost of the ticket and another night or two at the hotel. Again, none of the banks would cash my checks.

I interrupted my rounds of the banks to visit another travel agency, where I was informed that Air Lanka was the only airline that provided a discount, unavailable at the first agency. The agent is furious when I tell him that I am going elsewhere to do business. I have used his toilet, I drank his tea, and he feels he has made an investment in me. I have become so befuddled, apparently helpless, that he is totally unprepared for my decision.

The agent has hopped into a cab with me, trying to discourage me from going to another agency, which happens to be across the avenue from American Express. Wanting to avoid any complications, I got out of the taxi a good five blocks of hellish traffic before my destination. But now it comes back to me. The agent thinks I've gone completely bananas as we are nowhere near a travel agency. He's trying to reason with me, finally giving up after hounding me for a block and returns to the tailing taxi. What fate awaited me if I didn't act? I can see the headlines: **American Tourist Kidnapped by Travel Agent.** It's not so much that time has eroded my memory but that it was buried by the shear unpleasantness of it. There is nothing more crushing than absurdity.

American Express is practically a landmark in a low-rise city. It's all of seven or eight floors, and is "Our Man in Havana." You can't miss this monument to the fast lane; the money and the military are never far away. I even saw three westerners leave the place. It was not a travel agency they were with. I went into Travel International (Private) Ltd. and got what I believe was my voucher for the airline ticket. With this voucher I was directed to the American Express across the street.

Waiting on line to complete the transaction I was laid low by Shiva's revenge. At least I will have a decent place to do what does not come so naturally. I think. I'm directed here and there and lo and behold, I must contend with yet another hole. American Express indeed! The long and short of it is I came away from Travel International (Private) Ltd. without my airline ticket. That would be acquired at the airline office itself.

Finally, a fugitive from the law of averages, I arrive at Sri Lanka's airline office. I must surrender my passport! Is there another crime I've committed? I have no money, no ticket, and now no passport – now that I have my visa. I have my receipt for the cost of the ticket. And I would be remiss to my fellow travelers if I did not say that the fare to New York, via Sri Lanka, was 21,870 rupees. I have not been informed that the stopover is three days and three nights. Or it hasn't registered. I have other concerns.

"What do you need my passport for? Can't you see that it is valid?"

What the quasi-official sees is a hysterical man who bares little resemblance to a passport photo that is more wrinkled – sat on, slept on, rained on more than is possible in a lifetime – than the sunburst around my eyes. Smile lines, indeed! Air Lanka also notices my irregular entry into Pakistan, and is aware of my visaless stay.

In any case, every passport must pass muster with the U.S. Consulate. I turn over my ticket to freedom, feeling like Marco when he thought it was time to abscond from Kublai Khan. But Marco was a pet as well as an asset. I imagine Pakistan wanted me on the loose as much as it wanted the General Secretary of PPP, who was pictured being carted off to jail in the September 13th issue of the International News. (He had protested for the release of another opposition member. The demonstrators were marching towards Islambad's Parliament building.)

Islamabad is a safe haven compared to Karachi. With at least an hour's wait before the U.S. Consulate is finished with my passport, I cross the street and walk into a hotel, not out of place in Palm Beach. The city is bustling with soldiers and assassinations, but there remain these oases which I no longer relate to. Years of scrounging around erase that month of intermittent luxury I shared with Mona in China, before she took a cue from Marco.

In 1967, I spent an hour or two here when my Gulf-bound ship called at Karachi. My only vivid memory of that walk up from the dock is of a camel-drawn cart. It was the first one I had seen on that around-the-world trip. I thought that my chance of seeing a dromedary was equal to that of one passing through the eye of a needle, thinking that they had gone with the monoxide laden wind.

If I fly to Sri Lanka, I'll come close to retracing my steps – backwards. After embarking from Manila, a mermaid whispered "sail on, sail on, to Ceylon." A dream, climbing old Kandy mountain, and in an enchanted temple seeing Buddha's tooth. I was not ready for Buddha's tree, though. I had wonderful friends in Ceylon, including a doctor who was a saint and his beautiful wife. God! But the doctor had died, and sensing all that remained of the island I loved is the Bank of Ceylon (everything else has been changed to Sri Lanka), I did not look forward to returning. And for awhile I did not think I would go anywhere, because when my passport was eventually returned to me, it was strongly suggested that I get a new passport photo.

I had my ticket, and, predictably, I am scheduled to leave at midnight. One minute to. I have spent the whole day playing this foggy game, but recall very clearly heading for my dock in the bay, intending to leave Karachi, if not by sea, at least with something to wash away the nightmare of the afternoon.

I had been dragging my bag all around town, arriving at the port looking like a sailor who just missed his ship. I had to take two buses to get to the port of Keamari. Within a few minutes of my arrival my ship was coming in. It was piloted by "Captain Charli."

It's a small charter boat – No. 11-D. Charli hands me his card. It reads "USA-Pan Am," covering all the bases. "Fishing to any way," reads the bottom of the card. On the other side the old skipper is advertising, "For going to see tortoise on beach. . . .moonlight sea turtle egg." Is Captain Charli the brainstorm of some long gone Pan Am pilot? Is he a creation of John Steinbeck?

I had fallen into a tourist trap. This is less a tease than torture, for it is not tortoises I want to see, but ships. Karachi is only shipping six percent of the national cargo, so here is Captain Charli and his crew trying to hook tourists. And who might they be? Personnel from airlines who have not gone under? And where are the fish, for that matter?

Back from the pier is a small upstairs restaurant, the kind of ramshackle refuge where I have been known to enjoy a jugful when it was available. But I am drinking enough tea to float a battleship, and it is easy to drift off to those faraway times and places.

73

Departure. . . .

*...and never the twain shall meet
Till Earth and Sky stand presently at
God's great Judgement Seat....*
The Ballad of East and West
Rudyard Kipling

This is the edge of the port. Not a trace of what was. Beyond Captain Charli's armada is a bit of beach that beckoned. The sandy point is occupied by soldiers, but I don't care. It provides a sea view. I saluted someone and held up my canteen.

Just beyond this military post is the shore road. I decided to seek out a taxi driver in no great hurry. It's only late afternoon and I would like a Cook's Tour on my way to the airport. Some hidden dollars have turned up.

One guy wants a fortune, two or three drivers don't have all day; but as I walk towards the lighthouse, I encounter a worn man in his late thirties who is looking out over the breakwater to some distant shore. He's waiting for me.

Hamid is an ex-seaman, one of three thousand who have lost their jobs in recent years, and he still feels the lure of the sea. That's his taxi at the side of the road. He's in no hurry. You want to see the beach, no problem; anything, boss. We are kindred spirits, sharks who have chased their prey up the beach and are no longer in the swim of things. The beach area, the built-up part, is more like the American gulf than the Arabian Sea, as the Emirates call the Gulf that we know as Persian and which we have made our own. Oil refineries were across the road from where Hamid picked me up. But this American Gulf

Departure....

of Mexico is condo land, and we are soon heading for Karachi's old section.

I see my camel and mosques and sights that are timeless. Graffiti is all over the place. I have paid the beautiful Urdu script no mind because there are other things on it, but now I have an agreeable translator. Obsessions and national traits have changed little since Marco Polo flirted with the subcontinent. The handwriting on the wall reveals an almost overwhelming interest in the occult. Pseudo doctors advertise talism (from whence our talisman), kadas or houses of magic where stone-hearted lovers are melted like wax and become like slaves, and the cursed are cured through the incantation of powerful words. Is this Urdu or voodoo?

Much of the writing on the wall is political and reflects a split in the Pakistani psyche that widened with the Gulf War. As war fever gripped the people, walls were chalked with pro and anti-Saddam slogans. The pro-Kashmir, pro-Palestinian and anti-Zionism scribblings have been on the wall a lot longer.

Hamid's concern was not Israel but Kashmir – that vale of tears, that sight unseen had moved so many poseurs to poetry. For years this land between the Indus and the Himalayas had been synonymous with an accessible Shangri-La, until Pakistan and India both wanted this mostly Muslim land for its own. Hamid had shared its anguish in one of Pakistan's incursions and believed the worst war was yet to come.

My taxi driver wasn't quite of this world. He seemed steeped in that profound sorrow that grips so much of the subcontinent.

We were leaving the old quarter. And I hear the muezzin calling the faithful to a prayer. The endless note is a hauntingly, beautiful cry. An expression of continuity and community, a drone that becomes a melodic longing for union with Allah. Like Islamic music itself, this call to prayer exalts the divine while being an expression of it.

That drone that can be as colorless as a dromedary is the unadorned song of the desert. But when we get beyond our fixation with frills, the music opens unseen doors. Tarab. The

Koran forbids all but uplifting music, yet why would anybody in his or her right mind want to listen to something that is otherwise? Or create anything that is not an expression of their divinity.

The sight of that dromedary, the desert ship, being my long ago link with Karachi, struck me the way dolphins do after several days at sea, when this normally omnipresent porpoise keeping its distance is finally seen. What is a ship on the ocean without this playful pointsman to show the way? Nor would the desert be the same without its ship.

My own captain seems to be going around in circles, when it turns out that Hamid wants to take me to a carpet shop, which is a warehouse, factory and showroom. I assure Hamid that I don't have the price of a rug – nor do I want to take home anything I can't stuff into my grab-bag, especially since I'll be spending a few days in Sri Lanka first. No problem, no extra charge. I trust Hamid – and I'll be doing him a favor as he gets a commission whether or not I bite. What the hell, I have plenty of time, and what is a visit to Pakistan without seeing Persian miniatures or maxima. And I wanted to neutralize that war-torn theme or thread I carried away from Peshawar.

I don't know whether I'm going or coming when we pull into the driveway of Salima Marble Works. Not to worry. This is also Salima Bokhara Carpet. We are in the suburbs, but Salima is a virtual museum, and I am engulfed by the fluid mosaic of these magic carpets. Frozen music that melts with focusing and carries me away. I saw the world in the warp and weft of the carpet.

Not a museum, it is what it is and that is what I like about it, this treasure-trove of carpets, rolled and unraveled scattered all over the place. I'm entranced by floral designs that grew out of pre-Islamic Iran, in the infinity of flowers, continuity in a bud growing out of a leaf and like the music itself seemingly going on forever. But then, you would expect these designer denizens of the desert, creators of miniatures, to see the universe in a grain of sand. And like the music of the Mughal court, adorned with the rugs of Persia (Bokhara is near Samarkand), many cultural strands have gone into the weave.

Departure....

Geometric patterns grew out of the Roman and Byzantine traditions, but the buds flowered into prayer rugs that became holy vehicles to meditation, magic carpets to the mosque within, and the enduring poetry of the snowflake. The pedigreed Afghan Persian that I ended up purchasing may well be a captivating piece of crap. But I doubt it, and I thank Hamid for taking me for a ride.

It's getting dark and I would be more comfortable if I were at the airport and getting some of the formalities out of the way. It is a long way to the airport, but the traffic doesn't thin. Hamid is cursing the government, the worsening deterioration in living standards....and I find myself slipping into his shoes, because I seem to be on my way to Kennedy Airport.

My taxi driver is more American than I. He's been to at least Canada, and he looks like he has traveled much further than that. Hamid has been on heroin for years, and he is lighting up. Try it, you'll like it, Hamid is suggesting. This cannot be. I didn't even know you could smoke heroin, but my captain is getting unmoored and that is not tobacco he is smoking. Or hash. At another time, perhaps, I'd be concerned about the police. Maybe I would be paranoid about being set up, but this was par for the course.

Here I am having my first honest conversation since arriving in Asia and the man is a dope addict! Is this what it takes? Hamid says yes, this is what it takes or he would not be able to hack it. He is supporting his family on peanuts. And just look around you. No, the stuff doesn't get in the way or interfere with his work. He is just tired. But he has to kill the pain. I like the guy; I'm genuinely concerned.

"Man, can't you stop?"

Hamid looks at me and says, "I don't want to."

It is a dark, dreary rush hour. A murky stream of congested, coughing traffic. This is your Asian Styx, and I seem stuck in it. But why would all these vehicles, and half-lit buses with their open doors and cargo of hapless passengers still be heading toward the airport? Hamid has tuned me out. What more is there to say? "Hey, man, are we going the right way?"

It has been the longest day, the longest ride, but the

sign in English indicated that the sparkling, spanking new airport was near. This cathedral-like terminal with its high ceilings and beautiful tapestry hanging above the check-in counter. I could not believe I was arriving – on a wing and a prayer, perhaps, but arriving.

There is this sinking feeling that I am abandoning ship, leaving my friend to his own vices. Yes, a friend. Not only had he not hustled me, but he offered to split his commission from my purchase. And thanks to Hamid I returned home with more than yesterday's newspaper, though I can not rule out that he would have liked me to return to the States with something a lot lighter than a carpet. No, Hamid was taking medication. And not once had he hinted that he wanted to go to America, much less indicate that I should be his ticket to ride.

The guy was committing suicide. What parting advice could I give him?

"You know, you're a great guide, you speak English well. You could conduct a tour. You ought to get into something like that. Westerners relate to you." But I had not considered that tourists seemed more interested in seeing tortoises than in joy riding around a collapsing Karachi.

"In New York? You can help me?"

Hamid was deadpan – a dead man.

> ....*but madness is the golden rule*
> *burn out, born again*
> *golden fool, golden fuel,*
> *the phoenix's rising*
> *is in the consuming.*
>   Under the Southern Cross
>   Tony Cammarata 1976

73

Serendip

Departing from the island of Angaman and steering a course something to the southward of west, for a thousand miles, the island of Zeilan presents itself....It is governed by a king whose name is Sendernaz. The people worship idols and are independent of every other state. Both men and women go nearly nude, only wrapping a cloth around the middle part of their bodies. Their food is milk, rice and flesh, and they drink the wine drawn from trees....There is the best dyewood here that can be met anywhere.

The island produces more beautiful and valuable rubies than are found in any part of the world and likewise sapphires, topazes, amethyst, garnets and many precious stones. The king is reported to possess the grandest ruby that ever was seen, a span in length, the thickness of a man's arm, brilliant beyond description....It has the appearance of a glowing fire....The Great Khan, Kublai, sent ambassadors to this monarch with the request that he should let him have this ruby....The king's answer was he would not sell it for all the treasure of the universe.

Furthermore, I must not omit certain matters that I heard when I visited the island on my homeward voyage. In....Zeilan there is a very high mountain....the ascent to the top is impractical excepting by means of iron chains. Some persons attain the summit where the tomb of Adam, our first parent, is reported to be found. Such is the account given by the Saracens. But the idolaters assert it contains the body of Sagamoni. (Buddha)

Marco Polo

Arriving by air in Sri Lanka is sacrilegious. Unless you are a bird. Going through Customs and Immigration in the pre-dawn darkness was purgatory. Leaving Sri Lanka a couple of days later at 2:30 A.M. was also an unholy experience, but maybe hilarious in the telling of it, when you have refused to pay a departure tax. I felt the Sri Lankans had added insult to injury by shanghaiing you to this unhappy isle at an ungodly hour, only to be done with you at an equally devilish time in order to squeeze the last dollar out of you. Remaining in Sri Lanka more than one day, apparently had canceled my transit status.

    My most enduring memories are darkness. I arrived in Asia, in the dark; I left in the dark; I remain in the dark. Am I confusing my arrival in Sri Lanka with my arrival in Hong Kong three months earlier? If I continued in the same projectory around Asia I had unwittingly taken, I would have indeed gone full circle, if not completely around the bend. I would have returned to Hong Kong – in all likelihood in the darkness.

    I was tempted to fly to Hong Kong in 1967, when friends offered me a small fortune to smuggle some precious stones to the Crown Colony. Outside of the cities, Ceylon had changed little since Marco Polo's time. He neglected to mention the ancient habit of betal-chewing, which leaves the chewer with an orange mouth. But one observation Marco did make indicates the terrible transformation that old Zeilan has undergone in the last twenty years: "The people of this island are no soldiers but on the contrary are abject and timid creatures. When they need soldiers, they bring in Mahometans from other countries."

    Who knows at what time I left a nearly empty Karachi airport to fly about 1,500 miles in the opposite direction of London, my ultimate transit stop. In London, I believe, I transferred to another plane. It could have been worse. I'm lucky I did not end up in Australia. The flight was particularly disorienting since transit stops never involved leaving the airport, had rarely amounted to more than a few hours of uncomplicated waiting. A double bummer for a man who came to Ceylon by sea and left by sea a quarter of a century earlier.

    I still have my historic, geographic passport with my visa stamped in Colombo harbor. A year later, my visa for Sudan would be stamped over my visa for Ceylon. That passport is the color and length of a greenback and, with its extra pages, notations and exotic postage, more precious than the king of Zeilan's bloody ruby. Incidentally, the Great Khan never got his covetous hands on the king's heirloom.

It was already steaming when I left the Colombo airport. I had a voucher for the Goldi Sands Hotel, and a van for the beachside resort was waiting for me outside.

I shared the van with a young British couple who had just arrived from London. Probably on my plane. The lad looked like a refugee from an English soccer game. I cried foul, but the honeymooners were in their own world and the Goldi Sands was only about fifteen minutes north of the airport in Negombo. I would not be seeing Colombo harbor – which was probably just as well – but in the strangest twist of serendip I was returning to the town where my doctor friend had lived.

For the moment I could only think of going to bed, but I took a sentimental look out my window to the inviting catamarans, outrigger canoes little-changed since my last visit to Ceylon, before I hit the sack. That I could resist going to the beach and watch the returning fishing boats sailing up to the shore with their fresh catch, was a sign of just how far gone I was. But I am not a napper no matter how long I go without sleep, and I was down for lunch – down and out – before very long.

I had only today and tomorrow to see what time and circumstance had wrought. Sadly it was time enough. Sailboats still beached on my once pristine shore, but with the hotels and tourists came everything from a quasi-resident snake charmer to unseen Tamil Tigers (though the Tigers were mostly in the north). The scene was a bit like Acupulco, partitioned and protected and reeking of greased tourists who could have been in Mexico for all they cared. It was not much further than Sri Lanka for them, and a hell of a distance to go for a tan. For one week. The beach seemed divided between the English and the German speaking tourists who thought nothing of a little civil war when it came to fun and rum in the sun. Make mine Three Coins Lager.

The dry spell was over, the outriggers still charmed like clouds crossing the sky, but there was among the fishermen and the once colorfully dressed women awaiting them, a coldness that was unnerving. Mostly men wore the saris or wraparound and there were motors. Of course, the tourists were enough to bring about an unpleasant change, but there was an undercurrent, almost an undertow, that seemed to be dragging the people down that went beyond the pull of progress; as if some dark force had been stirred up by the war that contaminated the most pacific people.

My Buddhist friend had been one of the kindest men I had ever met. Truly a saint – and to think he was a doctor! Was his death political? I had forgotten his name, but to be his friend was to be treated like royalty. I literally got the red carpet treatment when visiting friends one night. The red rug about a hundred feet long reached the road.

The violence between the Tamil minority and the ruling Sinhalese had been brewing for years, but by the nineties almost everyone had been touched by the terrorism, as Sinhalese turned against each other. I had not known that a monk had been involved in an assassination back in the fifties. I will never forget my friend telling me that he was Sinhalese and the word meant "lion race." My reaction to this information could have mirrored Marco's, had he been so informed; Zeilan (Ceylon) evolved from what had become a misnomer, as the name meant the "land of the lions." But Sri means Holy – Holy Land in Sanskrit; Serendip was coined by Moorish traders from Arabia.

In ancient times the west knew this spice scented isle off the tip of India as Serendip, perhaps associated with silk, as one school has the name evolving from Seres or silk, but by the seventeenth century it spelled out serendipity or a faculty for happening upon fortunate discoveries.

Sri Lanka. The sound alone of that name seemed to portend great change, as radical Tamil Hindus, no longer intimidated by the lions, called themselves Tigers. The lion race had also come from India, conquering the more primitive Vedda hunters, before Buddhism, brought here with a branch of the Bodhi tree, took root, and the lion lay with the lamb.

Are the universal upheavals taking place a form of postcolonialism or post-traumatic stress? The stress of no longer knowing your place – or wanting your place in the sun, next to the tourist, or passengers as they were called at the turn-of-the-century. European domination arrived with the Portuguese, followed by Dutch and English rule and the colonial penchant for creating dark-skinned clones. Christianity was superimposed on the Buddhist and Hindu cultures, later revived; but walking up the shore road, I felt as if I had returned to a Bermuda gone to pot.

    I wanted to go for a swim, but I was so unfocused I did not dare remove my clothes and chance the loss of my ticket. Nor was the ocean inviting, as badly as I needed to go in the water. This was my element, but human excrement had yet to be washed out to sea. No one would have dared soil the Goldi Sands, but that was not for me either, and I was below the cluster of fishermen huts. The only running water for them and their families was the ocean. I was too tired to go anywhere, but too listless to lie on the beach without going into the water. My romantic Indian Ocean. I felt like a disembodied spirit, so removed from what had so captured my imagination.

75

Sunset

> They said that once the sand
> gets between your toes
> you can't leave the beach
> and God knows did I understand
> the pull of that tide
> but I wasn't there for the sun or sea
> especially
> but the sky and all of God's creation
> under it
> the only real show in town
> and I was moving on when
> people got in my hair.
>
> When I Was a Lifeguard
Tony Cammarata

Like wine the old haunt improves with time. In your mind. You can feel you are going home again when home did not exist. Which is one reason you can't go home again. But then so much of the world has been my home because in loving it, it was mine. And out of this love grows the feeling that the best things in life are free.

Using my dinner voucher, I sat at the edge of the dining area before going to bed. As close to the sea, as far away as possible from the pink-skinned unfortunates who could never know the way it was. Or appreciate it. Fittingly a band played the limbo and other Caribbean strains that only increased my separateness.

I awoke in the morning without a clue to how I would

spend my day. I wanted to be out of here by midnight to make certain that I did not miss my plane. Maybe I should try to track down my friend, try to uncover some sign of his having passed this way, if he had indeed died. It wasn't as if I were searching for a needle in a haystack. How many prominent doctors would have practiced medicine through at least the seventies? Surely there remained family or friends who could redeem my little detour to "Fantasy Island." And allow me to connect with something more fixed than an outrigger canoe – though that seemed appropriate. But I wanted this unplanned journey to my past to approximate a pilgrimage.

Nor did I have the time or even inclination, really energy, to go off to someplace as dear to me as Kandy. This would require a long train ride. All I needed was another flood. My head ached at the thought of such an undertaking at this crucial 11th hour. The spreading terrorist activity did not bode well for me.

Kandy, where Marco's Saracens claimed could be found the tomb of Adam. But it is Buddha's tooth that is resting in the Temple of the Tooth. The Temple became a pilgrimage site that Muslims claimed for their own, maintaining, according to Marco, that the holy relics actually belonged to Adam. Including, I presume, the rib from which Eve was shaped. If Muslims at that time, about 1293, really venerated what they thought were the remains of Adam, it is possible that the father of Buddhism, already dead about 1,800 years since the beginning of time, had earned the sort of homage they could only associate with Adam.

I recall the Perahera, a torchlit procession to the Temple of the Tooth, but what is burned into my mind is the torturous bus ride, high above the sea of palms that gave way to rice paddies and tea plantations and pinnacles better serviced by iron chains – and maybe trains.

The Bodhi tree was even further away, to the north in Anuradhapura, where Thomas Merton fell in love with those meditating giants of stone that breathed new life into the questioning Christian – before his message of a more catholic faith ended with his questionable death in Thailand (where he strongly opposed the Vietnam War). The widely respected monk had dared to imagine and maintain that there was another way. My own memory of Anuradhapura is that the Bodhi tree provided me with shade and a respite from foraging monkeys, stupas and sari-clad women bathing in the water tanks. The voyeur had yet to become a voyageur.

And now like a zombie, I was making inquiries in the shops off the shore road. Yes, a doctor, I would repeat, he had a wife and two children. I stopped at one shop and bought a Coke; memorable because I had not bought a cola in years. A form of civil disobedience. The shops opened on the road, and I turned around at the approach of a motorcycle. A beautiful child crossing the road was heading towards me. He was no higher than the handlebar of the motorcycle, now inches from his head. I had just enough time to open my mouth – and turn my face as I heard the inevitable thud.

The boy had not uttered a sound. No one in the shop was aware of the accident, and I said nothing as witnesses reacted in a muffled horror. As pedestrians scurried about, I picked up my coke, and without even turning, I continued in the direction I had been going – away from the tragedy.

I was filled with shame, but I had had my quota of misery and simply could not look at the possibly mangled body of the child – much less do anything for him. Ah, yes, the decent thing would have been to try to do something. I would have reacted differently at another time. I also feel that if you can't comfort someone, your presence at the scene of an accident or crime is nothing more than ghoulish.

It was the end of my search for a living or even dead link to Sri Lanka. Oh, to return to a place you loved, only to learn that it had died with the person who had come to symbolize it. Not a trace of my saintly friend. Nothing remained for me on this far shore – beyond the outriggers that took me away from it.

For years I have noticed dead birds at the side of the road, deaths related, probably, to insecticides; weakened birds hit by cars. I was always a little more careful as I hiked along, thinking there but for the grace of God go I. You live by the road, you die by the road. In my more exhausted states, realizing how lucky I have been to have survived, I sensed that the birds were like sacrifices – that it was either them or me. There must be something to the sacrificial nature of enduring cultures that is reflected in the cosmic scheme of things.

That child's death (I assume) became symbolic of what every country has given up so that a selfish few can live in the fast lane – for the "good" life and the endless cycle of greed and oil spills that it takes to sustain it. The death of nature, the sacrifice of purity to satisfy the perversity of power. The sacred and the profane. In the end we have sacrificed this lonely planet.

But the word is rape. Murder. We can only sacrifice for something higher, and with the blessings of the Universal – and there is no proxy involved. No virgins or flowers, but something that was more precious to Abraham than his son. His ego. It is the only thing that impedes transcendence, and the way of the Tao. The true power of experiencing bliss without conquest: *"I am different. I am nourished by the great Mother."* No lean and hungry look here.

The happy hour came early. Or is it a holy hour when one beer makes you one with the world. I was in the Sevana Restaurant, unable to forget the accident. Motorcycles. A suitable symbol for the destructive noise that provides the illusion of power. I had seen no ox carts today. I wondered if the bejeweled elephants still paraded through Kandy. Every day had been the Year of the Monkey, but leopards and bears and bamboo forests were fast giving way to the tea plantations of the English. Is it worth a bloody cup of tea?

One thing seemed unchanged. Or seemed to be thriving. I saw a Komodo-like dragon, huge reptile, very similar to a baby dinosaur, rummaging in the garbage across the way from the Goldi Sands. In the motorcycle and the giant reptile I saw Alpha and Omega, as we close the circle, the beginning and the ending living side by side. And how typical, if apocryphal, that Marco Polo reported that Adam's tomb was in Ceylon. This tragic metaphor for good fortune also spoke of beginnings – and the giving in to temptation. We can liken Sri Lanka to the Fall.

A microcosm of the corruption of what had been good in this world for all its faults.

Across the road from the Sevana Restaurant is the Seashells Hotel. How perfect for a shell of a man, an old beach bum with itchy feet. But I was more like a limpet than Barnacle Bill the sailor. My luck had run out with the tide. And contrary to what I used to tell the stoned lifeguards, I was not getting high on low tide – when the departing waters revealed the bounty of the sea. I was obsessed with the small boy and the loss of innocence. Yes, we must offer up our egos, but maybe the Pied Piper in the Sky requires more sanguine payment, bound up with the law of karma. The boy's number was up, and the land of lions had its sacrificial lamb.

I went out to a jetty of tables bringing me nearer to the ocean. Let the master hypnotist Poseidon take me out to sea. Time to flip another coin (Three Coins are illustrated on the label of my lager), look to the equatorial sun sinking below the Indian Ocean. And the swaying coconut palm became my Bodhi tree, my mast, and three ochre-colored sheets to the wind, I sailed on, sailed on to Ceylon and the way it was.

> *They say that clear wine is a saint,*
> *Thick wine follows the way of the sage.*
> *I have drunk deep of saint and sage;*
> *What need then to study the spirits and fairies?*
> *With three cups I penetrate the Great Tao.*
> *Take a whole jugful – I and the world are one.*
> *Such things as I have dreamed in wine*
> *Shall never be told to the sober.*
>
> Li Po